THE EDUCATIONAL LEADERSHIP CHALLENGE:
REDEFINING LEADERSHIP FOR THE 21ST CENTURY

THE EDUCATIONAL LEADERSHIP CHALLENGE: REDEFINING LEADERSHIP FOR THE 21ST CENTURY

*One Hundred-first Yearbook of the
National Society for the Study of Education*

PART I

Edited by
JOSEPH MURPHY

20 NSSE 02

Distributed by THE UNIVERSITY OF CHICAGO PRESS • CHICAGO, ILLINOIS

National Society for the Study of Education

The National Society for the Study of Education was founded in 1901 as successor to the National Herbart Society. It publishes a two-volume Yearbook, each volume dealing with a separate topic of concern to educators. The Society's Yearbook series, now in its one hundred-first year, presents articles by scholars and practitioners noted for their significant work in critical areas of education.

The Society welcomes as members all individuals who wish to receive its publications. Current membership includes educators in the United States, Canada, and elsewhere throughout the world—professors, researchers, administrators, and graduate students in colleges and universities and teachers, administrators, supervisors, and curriculum specialists in elementary and secondary schools.

Members of the Society elect a Board of Directors. The Board's responsibilities include reviewing proposals for Yearbooks, authorizing the preparation of Yearbooks based on accepted proposals, and appointing an editor or editors to oversee the preparation of manuscripts.

Current dues (for 2002) are a modest $35 ($30 for retired members and for students in their first year of membership). Members whose dues are paid for the current calendar year receive the Society's Yearbook, are eligible for election to the Board of Directors, and are entitled to a 33 percent discount when purchasing past Yearbooks from the Society's distributor, the University of Chicago Press.

Each year the Society arranges for meetings to be held in conjunction with the annual conferences of one or more of the national educational organizations. All members are urged to attend these meetings, at which the current Yearbook is presented and critiqued. Members are encouraged to submit proposals for future Yearbooks.

The Educational Leadership Challenge: Redefining Leadership for the 21st Century is Part I of the 101st Yearbook. Part II, published simultaneously, is titled *Educating At-Risk Students.*

For further information, write to the Secretary, NSSE, College of Education m/c 147, University of Illinois at Chicago, 1040 W. Harrison St., Chicago, Illinois 60607-7133.

ISSN: 0077-5762

Published 2002 by the
NATIONAL SOCIETY FOR THE STUDY OF EDUCATION

1040 W. Harrison St., Chicago, Illinois 60607-7133

First Printing
Printed in the United States of America

To L. C., the Diplomate

About the Editor

Joseph Murphy is the William Ray Flesher Professor of Education at The Ohio State University and the President of the Ohio Principals Leadership Academy. He is also the Chair of the Interstate School Leaders Licensure Consortium. His work is in the area of school improvement, with an interest in leadership and policy. He has authored or co-authored twelve books in these areas and edited another eleven. His most recent book (with Catherine Shiffman) is titled *Understanding and Assessing the Charter School Movement* (Teachers College Press, 2002).

Editor's Preface

School administration as an area of practice and a field of study came into its own during the 20th century, particularly in the post-World War II era. Historical analysis helps us to see that the profession grew from two powerful taproots: insights from the corporate world, especially the area of management, and knowledge from the university, particularly the behavioral sciences. A cursory glance at the content of educational administration preparation programs will confirm the domination of these two perspectives.

We also know that as the profession developed it established defined ways of thinking about and engaging in leadership activities. These include emphases on: (1) the processes of school administration (e.g. decision making, problem solving), (2) the roles, tasks, and functions of school leadership, (3) the theoretical infrastructure undergirding the profession, and (4) methods of learning about school administration.

The central thesis of this volume is that the ways of thinking about school administration that we relied on for most of our history provide an inadequate platform for educational leadership in the 21st century. Because of powerful political, social, and economic shifts in the environment in which schools are nested, as well as significant changes in the educational industry itself—in the ways we understand learning, organize and manage school organizations, and relate to clients—new foundations for the profession need to be built. Indeed, a fair amount of work over the last twenty years of ferment in educational administration can be classified as either direct or indirect efforts to reground the profession.

This volume attends to the development of a framework for the next era of school administration. The essence of this development is chronicled in Chapter 4, which constructs a framework that pushes corporate ideology and behavioral sciences from school administration's center stage. The blueprint provided there focuses less on the activities of school leaders and more on the valued ends of school organizations. Specifically, it is argued that the profession needs to underscore school improvement, democratic community, and social justice. It is here that the raw material for reculturing the profession is to be found.

Most of the volume is devoted to analyzing what school administration might look like if we rebuild the profession around our most profound understandings of learning, justice, and community. But before we undertake that assignment, the authors in Chapters 1-3 lay out some of the changing forces that have pushed school administration out of its historical orbit. With those three chapters and Chapter 4 as a backdrop, new perspectives on school leadership are assembled, beginning with analyses of the three key concepts in the conceptual blueprint—school improvement, democratic community, and social justice. In Chapters 8-11, authors offer portraits of value-anchored leadership for the key actors in the schooling enterprise—teachers, parents, principals, and superintendents. Finally, the last two chapters turn to the issue of recasting the education of leaders who will populate a profession built on valued ends rather than on the perspectives that supported school administration for most of the 20th century.

JOSEPH MURPHY
Alexandria, Ohio
December 2001

Table of Contents

PAGE

THE NATIONAL SOCIETY FOR THE STUDY OF EDUCATION iv

DEDICATION. v

BOARD OF DIRECTORS OF THE SOCIETY, 2000-2001; CONTRIBUTORS TO THE
  YEARBOOK vii

ABOUT THE EDITOR IX

EDITOR'S PREFACE xi

CHAPTER

Section One
Building the Foundation for Understanding and Action

1. UNDERSTANDING THE EVOLVING CONCEPT OF LEADERSHIP
   IN EDUCATION: ROLES, EXPECTATIONS, AND DILEMMAS,
   Ellen Goldring and *William Greenfield* 1

Section Two
Understanding the Challenges of School and District Leadership at the Dawn of a New Century

2. THE CONTEXTUAL TERRAIN FACING EDUCATIONAL LEADERS,
   Catherine A. Lugg, Katrina Bulkley, William A. Firestone,
   and *C. William Garner* 20

3. UNPACKING THE CHALLENGES OF LEADERSHIP AT THE SCHOOL
   AND DISTRICT LEVEL, *Kenneth Leithwood* and *Nona Prestine* 42

Section Three
Reculturing the Profession

4. RECULTURING THE PROFESSION OF EDUCATIONAL LEADERSHIP:
   NEW BLUEPRINTS, *Joseph Murphy* 65

5. SCHOOL IMPROVEMENT PROCESSES AND PRACTICES: PROFESSIONAL
   LEARNING FOR BUILDING INSTRUCTIONAL CAPACITY,
   James P. Spillane and *Karen Seashore Louis* 83

6. LEADERSHIP FOR DEMOCRATIC COMMUNITY IN SCHOOLS,
   Gail C. Furman and *Robert J. Starratt* 105

7. LEADERSHIP FOR SOCIAL JUSTICE, *Colleen L. Larson* and
   Khaula Murtadha 134

Section Four
Reshaping Leadership in Action

8. BUILDING LEADERSHIP INTO THE ROLES OF TEACHERS,
   Mark A. Smylie, Sharon Conley, and *Helen Marks* 162
9. RESHAPING THE ROLE OF THE SCHOOL PRINCIPAL, *Gary M. Crow,*
   Charles S. Hausman, and *Jay Paredes Scribner* 189
10. SHIFTS IN THE DISCOURSE DEFINING THE SUPERINTENDENCY:
    HISTORICAL AND CURRENT FOUNDATIONS OF THE POSITION,
    C. Cryss Brunner, Margaret Grogan, and *Lars Björk* 211
11. REPOSITIONING LAY LEADERSHIP: POLICYMAKING AND DEMOCRATIC
    DELIBERATION, *Sharon F. Rallis, Mark R. Shibles,* and
    Austin Swanson 239

Section Five
Recasting the Development of School Leaders

12. PREPARING SCHOOL LEADERS FOR SCHOOL IMPROVEMENT, SOCIAL
    JUSTICE, AND COMMUNITY, *Diana Pounder, Ulrich Reitzug,*
    and *Michelle Young* 261
13. RETHINKING THE PROFESSIONAL DEVELOPMENT OF SCHOOL LEADERS,
    Frances K. Kochan, Paul Bredeson, and *Carolyn Riehl* 289

NAME INDEX 307
SUBJECT INDEX 309
PUBLICATIONS OF THE SOCIETY 312

Section One
BUILDING THE FOUNDATION FOR UNDERSTANDING AND ACTION

CHAPTER 1

Understanding the Evolving Concept of Leadership in Education: Roles, Expectations, and Dilemmas

ELLEN GOLDRING AND WILLIAM GREENFIELD

Leadership in education is an ambiguous and complex concept, and the diffuse and highly fragmented nature of theory and research on school and school district administration and leadership reflects this conceptual fuzziness. Divergent perspectives within the academy, among policy makers and constituents at the local, state, and federal levels, and among school and district administrators add to a growing swirl of competing and often conflicting role images and expectations.

Contemporary images of the principalship and the superintendency increasingly evoke calls for "special" kinds of leadership: that it be constructivist, transformational, facilitative, instructional, developmental, distributed, or moral, for example. Images of the school administrator have been shaped over the past 100 years by various ideas, each in their time serving to orient and focus practice and offering practitioners and researchers alike a framework for making sense of the work of school administration: the early ideological grounding in philosophy and religion that was prevalent in the 1800s; the highly prescriptive managerial perspective, concerned with efficiency and focused on functional administrative tasks, that characterized the 1900-1945 period; and the behavioral sciences perspective that dominated much of the field during the 1946-1985 period (Murphy, 1999).

Ellen Goldring is Professor of Educational Leadership at Peabody College, Vanderbilt University, in Nashville, Tennessee. William D. Greenfield, Jr. is Professor and Chair of the Department of Educational Policy Foundations and Administrative Studies in the Graduate School of Education, Portland State University.

The behavioral sciences image influenced preparation curricula and the study of practice to some degree, but has lost much of its original luster with challenges over the past two decades to modernist views of organizations and leadership. While the "managerial efficiency" conception of the work of school administration also has been tempered somewhat since its emergence during the early 1900s, images of the school as a rational-technical "system of production" remain firmly embedded in the psyche of policy makers and pervade most educational reforms promulgated since the early 1980s. Indeed, this image is alive and well with current and intensifying "quality-control" pressures to measure and assess student, teacher, and school performances, and the concurrent expectation that administrators and teachers will "adjust" instructional strategies to yield more effective learning outcomes for children (Bush, 2001). Few contest the desirability of achieving such aims, but the qualities of schools and the work of teaching and of school and district leadership embedded in many reform initiatives are much more complex and difficult to achieve than one might infer from the rhetoric of the reform. The uncertainty, turbulence, messiness, and unpredictability of the milieu of schooling, and the essentially "people-changing" goals of schools, make teaching and the work of school administration and schooling reform a daunting challenge.

Schools and school districts, as socio-political and highly normative systems, are nested within larger social, cultural, economic, and political environments containing other dynamic institutions. The characteristics of these systems, and the interactions of schools and districts with other institutions within these systems, represent markedly different circumstances from those faced by administrators in other contexts.

Buffeted during the past 20 years by successive waves of educational reform, educational administration is more aware today than at any time in the field's history of the complexities and challenges of public education, and of the importance of effective educational leadership to the enduring good health of that institution (Murphy & Louis, 1999). What does this mean? This chapter explores three arenas we believe provide a partial answer to this important question:

1. Special conditions of the work itself that make administering and leading public schools difficult and certainly different from such work in other contexts;

2. Central forces in the school's environment that shape the specific challenges of educational leadership and administration in public education; and

3. Critical and recurring dilemmas inherent in administering and leading schools and school districts.

Special Conditions Within Public Schools

Four key conditions distinguish the day-to-day work in educational administration from administrative work in other contexts and suggest a unique milieu and special challenges for the school and district leader:

1. The *moral dimensions* of educational leadership and administration;
2. The *stewardship of the public's trust* in the institution of public education;
3. The *complexity of the core schooling activities* of teaching and learning; and
4. The highly *normative and people-intensive character* of the school workplace.

MORAL DIMENSIONS OF THE SCHOOL LEADER'S ROLE

As Dewey (1922) implored over 75 years ago, public educators have a special responsibility to be *deliberately* moral in their conduct. After all, the children attending public schools are impressionable and vulnerable; they have no choice in what or how they are taught; and for all practical purposes most children cannot choose to go to school elsewhere. Much of the work of school administration involves making value judgments about the right thing to do in the face of more than one desirable choice. At other times the challenge may be choosing the least harmful from among several undesirable alternatives.

Resources of time, money, materials, and staff effort are limited, and choices need to be made. These dilemmas come in many forms. Examples include decisions about students' needs (Shall we purchase a reading program to help the lowest performing second graders improve their reading and comprehension ability, or should we invest in a program to increase student engagement among the sixth graders?); teachers' professional development (Shall we send our 10th grade English teachers to a workshop on introducing a multicultural perspective into the curriculum, or should we invest in staff development that will facilitate whole-school reform and improved faculty collaboration and teamwork?); curriculum improvement (Shall we enrich the curriculum by adding more choices for gifted students, should we increase the number of math courses required of every student, or should we improve the quality and depth of the existing math and science curriculum?); and instructional strategies (Shall we invest in developing authentic instruction and a thematic curriculum throughout the school, or would it be better to offer supports such as tutoring or child care to individual students?). School administration done well entails deliberate and thoughtful wrestling with the moral dilemmas inherent in choosing a course of action and genuinely working toward what is best for all children in the school or district. This is the central responsibility of the school or district leader. Despite the field's historical reluctance to recognize the centrality of the management of value dilemmas to the work of the profession, attention to the importance of the moral dimension of school administration is growing (for example, Begley, 1999; Greenfield, 1999; Starratt, 1991).

STEWARDSHIP OF PUBLIC EDUCATION

At the center of the stewardship role is the expectation to guide and develop the public's understanding of and support for what public schools need to be doing, the goals they should be achieving, and the critical role of *public* education in developing a more socially just and democratic society. There are political as well as moral dimensions to the stewardship of public education. Enactment of this important but neglected aspect of the school administrator's role would have school leaders address four key challenges.

First, undermine the anti-intellectual sentiment, so prevalent in our country, that academic learning is useful only for a few and not needed by all. The public needs to understand that a child's failure to develop skills in reading, writing, mathematics, and science will severely limit his or her ability to enter and to succeed in the changing workplace. Today there are fewer jobs for unskilled workers, and those that are available usually do not pay a livable wage.

Second, encourage communities to influence elected officials and local business leaders to adopt policies and implement practices to improve those life circumstances of children that interfere with their ability to succeed in school. Needed changes include a livable wage for working parents, affordable housing, day care for infants and young children, and health care. While school administrators can influence these matters only indirectly, such improvements would help provide the social foundation children need in order to succeed in school. This foundation is largely present for the middle-class child. It is absent for large numbers of poor children (Graham, 1993).

Third, help communities understand that schools face the new and difficult challenge of ensuring that *all* children (including poor children and children of color) achieve academically, and that to accomplish this goal will require important changes in how schooling occurs. This is a relatively new goal in the history of public education, and its achievement will require changes in the curriculum, in teaching practices, and in the school leadership strategies of principals and superintendents.

Finally, cultivate support for the development of intercultural competence among children as an explicit and important goal of public education. That is, build the capacity of public schools to ensure that children representing different races, ethnicities, social classes, languages, physical abilities, and religions are inter-culturally competent and prepared to live, learn, and work in a multicultural society.

A key function of the stewardship role is to help community members, especially those who do not have school-age children, understand how the goals and activities of schooling today are different from those of the past, why they are so critical, and how broad and active support of its schools by a community actually can help public schools be more effective, both in their immediate benefits to children and in their longer term benefits to communities and to the nation as a whole.

COMPLEXITY OF THE CORE ACTIVITIES OF SCHOOLING

While consideration of the complexity of teaching and learning has been at the periphery of educational administration for most of the century, the past 20 years have seen increasing attention to studying the complexity of the relationship between teaching and learning, and the leadership, administration, and organization of schools. Contributing to the complexity are changing views of the learner, the teacher, and the curriculum, changes associated with students' staying in school longer, a greater diversity of students in attendance, and increased expectations for the academic achievement of *all* students served by the school (Little, 1999; Rowan, 1995).

The effects of leadership and administration on teaching and learning are indirect and difficult to assess (Hallinger & Heck, 1996), although there is recurrent and compelling evidence that effective leadership by principals and superintendents can improve both teaching and learning (Hoachlander, Alt, & Beltranena, 2001). Complicating the matter further, the technology of teaching itself is not fully understood or developed, and children arrive at the schoolhouse door with a tremendous diversity characterizing their readiness and their motivation to learn.

Results of several studies illustrate a few of the many factors associated with the relationships between teaching and learning. While increased time-on-task seems an obvious strategy to improve student achievement, Yair (2000) suggests student engagement with instruction is critical, that engagement rates can be influenced by instructional practices, and that students of color and white students respond differently to different engagement strategies. While academic learning climate is important, Goddard, Sweetland, & Hoy (2000) suggest that students' earlier learning and the cognitive schemata they bring to the learning task also are important. Sweetland and Hoy (2000) find teacher empowerment in classroom and instructional decisions have an independent and positive impact on student achievement in middle schools.

Outcomes in student learning may be affected by many different variables, and there remains a great deal of uncertainty about what works. Even within a single school or grade-level, there often are broad differences among teachers in their grasp of recent developments in learning theory and/or grounding in the subject area being taught. In addition, the academic climates and cultures of schools and classrooms are highly varied, both within and across districts. Further complicating matters, state legislatures and local school boards expect schools to accomplish more than ever before in terms of the cognitive development of *all* the children in attendance.

THE HIGHLY NORMATIVE AND PEOPLE-INTENSIVE CHARACTER OF SCHOOLS

Schools are highly normative organizations, and educational leadership and administration are extremely people-intensive activities. The goals of schools are cultural and developmental, and getting things done in a school requires heavy reliance on face-to-face interaction with teachers and others; people themselves are the medium and the focus of a school's efforts. More than most other institutions, virtually all of the daily work that occurs in public schools involves people working with and through people to influence people—students, parents, teachers, school principals, and superintendents, working with and through others, ultimately and most importantly to enhance the cognitive, social, emotional, and physical development of children.

The normative complexity of schools makes this "people work" more critical and more complicated than it is in other communities of practice. Teachers' practices, both in their classrooms and in interactions with students, parents, and other teachers, are shaped by work-group norms (Lortie, 1975). These norms reflect shared understandings, beliefs, values, and attitudes about teaching and learning, and about children, parents, and the broader goals, purposes, and activities of schooling generally. Reform of school practices requires changing the school work-group's norms. Norms are changed or reinforced in large part through an interpersonal medium—this is what is meant by the phrase "talk *is* the work" of school administration (Gronn, 1983).

Changing teachers' beliefs about good practice is a normative challenge and is dependent on the construction of shared meaning through social interaction. This is why effective school leaders rely so extensively on face-to-face interaction with teachers. Listening genuinely to teachers' ideas, concerns, and feelings is critical. Gaining the trust of teachers is essential if one hopes to have an authentic discussion of schooling practices: what is working, what needs to be improved, and how best to accomplish those goals. Teachers' practices are driven largely by their beliefs about what works. Simply providing teachers with research evidence about more effective practice (as in the rational-technical approach to change reflected in so many school reform initiatives) often is not sufficient. For school practices to change in a real and lasting way, teachers themselves must believe in the efficacy of those practices.

Changing the cultures of schools and districts is thus central to efforts to introduce and sustain changes in schooling practices (Little & McLaughlin, 1993). Resistance to change in schools is essentially a cultural challenge, and face-to-face talk among teachers and between teachers and administrators is critical in reducing resistance and building support for change. Talking (and listening) are key behaviors associated with managing the emotional and cognitive dissonance among teachers and among community members that occurs with efforts to change schooling practices. The school principal is the key agent in stimulating, shaping, and reinforcing shared meaning within a school, and face-to-face talk that cultivates and is responsive to reinforcing or redefining the shared sentiments and values of teachers is the primary medium by which the work of leading and administering occurs in effective schools.

Central Forces Shaping Educational Leadership

Educational leadership is further complicated by the dynamic social, economic, and policy contexts in which schools are situated. Central forces shaping this milieu include critical changes in school demographics, hybrid school governance structures, accountability frameworks, and the professionalization of teaching.

CHANGING SCHOOL DEMOGRAPHICS

Enrollment in public schools more than tripled during the 20th century. The student population will continue to rise through 2005 and then will remain at 47 million for at least 5 years (Snyder, 2001). Higher enrollment is generally associated with more diverse student bodies, overcrowding, and diverse and pressing student needs.

Greater ethnic, racial, and linguistic diversity increasingly characterizes many communities and their schools. The mix of K-12 public school enrollees is: 62.9% White, 17.1% Black, 15% Hispanic, 3.9% Asian or Pacific Islander, and 1.1% American Indian or Alaskan Native (Snyder, 2001). Ethnicity is closely linked to poverty and the holding power of schools. For instance, 36.4% of Black and 33.6% of Latino families with children lived in poverty in 1998 compared to only 14.4% of White families. Minority students, with the exception of Asian/Pacific Islander students, are much more likely to drop out of school than White, non-Hispanic students.

The structures of families with children of school age continue to change dramatically. From 1970 to 1998, there was a 500% increase in the number of families headed by men who had no spouse present and with children under 18. Similarly, there was a 260% increase in the number of families headed by women with no spouse present. The significance of single-parent households is illustrated by the extremely high poverty status of single-mother households with children under 18 as compared to the poverty status of other families.

Student participation in special education services has increased. To date, 13.0% of the student population has been diagnosed with special needs. Approximately 50% of students who receive special education services now receive them in regular classrooms (Snyder, 2001). It is becoming more and more difficult for parents to be available for their children and the schools. The economic barriers and cycles of poverty that many families face contribute to unstable and unpredictable relationships among children, parents and schools (Coleman, 1987; Smrekar & Goldring, 1999).

HYBRID SCHOOL GOVERNANCE

Schools are facing hybrid governance structures characterized simultaneously by local and centralized control (Cohen-Vogel and Goldring, unpublished manuscript). Site-based decision making, teacher empowerment, and parent responsiveness are centerpieces of a bottom-up perspective. Local school councils composed of educators, parents, and community members set policies, evaluate principals and discuss curriculum. Teachers are adding to their portfolio out-of-classroom responsibilities, such as serving on collaborative problem-solving teams, acting as mentors for new teachers, and designing school-based curricula.

Concurrently, educational leaders face strong centralized controls. Because of the system of financing public education in the United States, including special entitlements such as Title I, schools are completely dependent for resources on central governments. Textbook acquisitions, curricula adoption, and personnel policies create systems where schools are "nodes in an administrative neural network" (Guthrie, 2001, p. 361). In many urban districts, for example, power and leadership are consolidated at the system level (Wong, 2000). From Chicago to Oakland, big city mayors are appointing powerful chief executive officers with far-reaching authority to hold school personnel accountable, reduce waste and inefficiencies, and focus the total school system on teaching and learning. Termed "integrated governance," this system-wide perspective provides coordinated linkages among the multiple layers of governance to support schools and reduce competing authorities (Wong, Dreeben, Lynn, & Sunderman, 1997, p. 1).

Local school reform and responsiveness "is occurring within a continued framework of central policies and priorities" (Crowson, 1992, p. 2). These hybrid governance expectations from local, state, and system-wide actors often leave school leaders with competing pressures. Leaders are challenged with balancing the demands and expectations of various governance structures.

HOLDING SCHOOLS ACCOUNTABLE

Recent trends such as state assessments and school report cards have added complexity to the role of school leaders. *Education Week*'s "Quality Counts 2001" report shows that 45 states now issue school report cards, while 27 states also rate schools and/or identify low-performing schools. Many states rank schools solely on the basis of student test scores on standardized assessments. Others include in their evaluations data on topics such as school attendance, holding power, and patterns of course taking (Adams & Kirst, 1999).

Constituencies external to schools increasingly drive accountability frameworks. The business community pressures the public educational system to graduate students who are able to "work smarter" in today's "information society" (Consortium on Productivity in Schools, 1995). Achieve, an independent, bipartisan, non-profit organization formed in 1996 by corporate CEOs, is a constant driving force behind the accountability movement, stressing high academic standards and accountability for performance (Achieve, 2001).

Governors and state legislatures play key roles in designing, implementing, and assessing accountability plans. School report cards, monetary incentives, and threats of state takeover all increase the state's influence on local school sites. Under President George W. Bush's education plan, titled *No Child Left Behind*, the federal government will require increased accountability and effectiveness from Title I funded programs. Critics suggest that these external accountability mechanisms reduce local discretion, autonomy and creativity; narrow curriculum; and constrain teaching pedagogy (Toenjes, Dworkin, Gary, Jon, & Antwanett, 2000).

Although uniformly implemented and externally imposed accountability systems are gaining more attention, school-based accountability frameworks rooted in school workplace norms and local decisions also are used to set school-level goals, assessments, and consequences. Internal accountability frameworks are touted by some as a more effective means of changing classroom practices because "teachers' motivation originates inside the schools, where their collaboration can affect teaching directly" (Adams & Kirst, 1999, p. 485). Whether driven internally or externally, accountability will continue to have an impact on educational leadership.

The challenges for educational leaders are twofold. First, educational leaders must play a key role in articulating and setting standards and measures of accountability and aligning local expectations with external frameworks. Second, leaders will need to engage teachers in meaningful, collaborative discourse on standards and measures, while providing professional development opportunities and other supports to help them meet established goals (Newmann, King, & Rigdon, 1997).

DEVELOPING TEACHER PROFESSIONALISM

Teacher quality and professionalism have been recurrent themes of school reform and improvement efforts (Sykes, 1991). Specific reforms are geared toward increasing entry requirements and strengthening professional standards (Elmore, 1990). Accrediting bodies emphasize the professional commitments of teachers, including development of expert knowledge and a strong ethic of service to clients (National Board for Professional Teaching Standards, n.d.).

An emerging view of teaching, referred to as the "new professionalism," conceptualizes teaching as part of a communal endeavor, moving ". . . away from the teachers' traditional professional authority and autonomy towards new forms of relationships with colleagues, with students and with parents. These relationships are becoming closer as well as more intense and collaborative" (Hargreaves, 1994, p. 424). New teachers are mentored instead of supervised, teams of teachers replace hierarchies, in-service education gives way to continuous professional development, and partnerships, rather than liaisons, are central to the new professionalism in teaching.

Teachers are members of various professional communities, ranging from in-school groups, such as departments and grade levels, to out-of-school groups, such as associations, professional networks and subject matter associations (Little & McLaughlin, 1993). McLaughlin and Talbert (1993) found that "teachers' responses to today's students and notions of good teaching practice are heavily mediated by the character of the professional communities in which they work" (p. 8).

Although many forces point toward professionalization, other reform measures contribute to a heightening sense of deprofessionalization associated with standardization of teaching. As teachers feel pressures to focus on what is measured, to teach to the test, and to rely on scripted lessons "that work," there is less room for professional discretion in the classroom (Sykes & Millman, 1995). Despite union leaders who are trying to champion educational reform and a move to "professional unions," "innovative forms of cooperation between labor and management have unfolded in relatively few districts," with reliance in most districts on the prevailing industrial model that attempts to control working conditions and protect jobs (Sykes, 1999, p. 241).

Taken together, these key forces—demographic trends, hybrid forms of governance, pressures for accountability, and teacher professionalism—shape the context of leadership for our nation's schools. Leaders cannot ignore or resist these forces; they are too strong and too profound.

Recurring Dilemmas of Educational Leadership

The social, political, educational, and organizational contexts in which school leaders work are continually changing, and are not necessarily changing in harmony. In fact, they are typically asynchronous (Dimmock, 1996; Holmes, 1965). For example, principals often face mandated programs that do not meet the needs of their changing student bodies. Teachers sometimes are bound by union contracts out of synch with the norms and values of their particular school, while superintendents are expected to respond to federal mandates even though resources are not available. Zero-tolerance policies may require expelling a student even though it may not be in the best interest of the child. Contexts are continually changing, and leadership, by definition, revolves around managing the emerging dilemmas. Dilemmas are highly intertwined and linked with the forces affecting schools (Berlak & Berlak, 1981).

Although dilemmas are not resolvable, they are managed in the context of the leadership role.[1] They are the durable value conflicts that leaders face again and again (Ogawa, Crowson, & Goldring, 1999). Dilemmas are neither problems to be solved nor short-term issues to be addressed. Dilemmas reveal deeper "contradictory stances" that present a paradox of competing positions, either of which might be embraced. Dilemmas occur when "constraints and uncertainty make it impossible for any prized value to triumph" (Cuban, 1992, p. 6). Leadership requires a continuous struggle over competing values and unattractive options. To lead, however, is to confront dilemmas, not let them "fester and multiply" (Cuban, 1996, 2001; Glatter, 1996).

There are numerous recurring dilemmas that educational leaders face. They all involve competing values, such as the professional value of autonomy to decide what transpires in one's classroom and the organizational value of cooperation and coordination that requires teachers to work together (Cuban, 2001; Leithwood and Steinbach, 1995). Dilemmas associated with leading and managing, the system and the environment, and participatory decision making and individual authority are discussed next as examples of the unique role challenges faced by educational leaders.

LEADING AND MANAGING: PURPOSING AND IMPLEMENTING

One recurring dilemma is the concurrent expectation to *lead the school* toward the improvement of instruction and to *manage the school* so that there is enough stability and certainty for the organization to function efficiently. To lead and to manage effectively are enduring role expectations of school principals and superintendents. These expectations are not new, but the dilemma is becoming increasingly difficult to manage as the public's expectations rise, as school-specific student achievement results are reported in local newspapers, as school administrators and teachers are evaluated in light of student performance, and as schools are expected to engage a broader civic and social audience (Goldring & Hausman, 2001). The dilemma is somewhat easier to manage in wealthier and larger districts and schools, in contrast to poorer and smaller districts, due to the availability of resources to employ needed support staff to assist, primarily, with managerial demands.

Managing and improving instruction are central to the principalship and to the superintendency, and there is growing pressure to manage threats to the stability of the system more effectively. Communities once thought to be safe havens from the violence and crime stereotypically associated with more urban environments no longer hold that promise. Communities are becoming more heterogeneous and complex; there are more children whose families are living below the poverty line; and there are growing numbers of children of color and of children whose native language is not English. Each of these conditions complicates the challenges of improving and managing teaching and learning, and together they add unfathomable complexity to administering schools and districts.

CULTIVATING THE SYSTEM *AND* WATCHING THE ENVIRONMENT

Another recurring dilemma is the necessity to manage and develop *internal* operations while concurrently monitoring the environment and anticipating and responding to *external* exigencies. Historically, school principals have focused internally, striving to maintain smooth day-to-day school operations, while superintendents have focused externally, influencing and managing the district's environment, responding to board members, and cultivating a positive district image.

These expectations are continuing, but there are also new foci. Superintendents increasingly focus internally, accounting for how individual schools are performing, and attention to the district's environment has broadened to include state and federal legislative agendas. Principals now devote more attention to the school's immediate community, as well as to the broader environment, including the state department of education, the legislature, and partnerships with businesses and foundations.

Reformers claim that schools should be the focal point of entire communities, so that they can meet the divergent needs of students, especially those most at risk of failure (Bronfenbrenner, 1979; McLaughlin, 1994; Wong et al., 1997). Initiatives such as community development and full service schools reflect broad-based efforts to address the deepening distress in many urban communities (*Empowerment*, 1995; Timpane & Reich, 1997). With pressure for closer links between schools and their communities, school leaders face the dilemma of how to balance internal and external efforts.

Under high-stakes testing and statewide accountability systems, educational leaders are confronted with ongoing pressures to show good results quickly and regularly. However, leaders also must simultaneously "bridge the connection between the conditions of education and the total conditions of children" (Kirst, McLaughlin, & Bassell, 1989). The additive nature of the educational leadership role is a concern. Principals and superintendents already lack sufficient time to perform all of the responsibilities expected of them.

Emergent expectations of the principalship include the management and anticipation of political and cultural dimensions of the school's environment, while emergent expectations of the superintendency include more careful attention to the performances of individual schools. Support no longer is a given, and fostering a credible image in the public's eye is a key and recurring challenge for all school administrators, particularly superintendents.

PARTICIPATORY DECISION MAKING AND INDIVIDUAL AUTHORITY

A third recurring dilemma for school administrators is the need to balance participatory leadership with the simultaneous imperative to assume the responsibility to make and implement difficult decisions that may not be endorsed by the collective. Leadership often involves taking a stand, however unpopular with others. Participatory leadership, also referred to as shared, collaborative, distributed, or group leadership, focuses on decision processes that involve others.

In education, participatory leadership rests on the idea that active participation by teachers, parents or community members in school decisions will lead to enhanced school effectiveness (Leithwood & Duke, 1999). It is believed that those closest to teaching and learning, namely teachers, and those with the most knowledge about the children, namely parents, should be involved in decisions because they hold expertise that is crucial to enhancing education. It also is believed that when teachers and parents are involved in decision making, they will be more committed and motivated to implement and support change, and a sense of ownership for the school can develop (Murphy & Beck, 1995; Hess, 1991).

Obviously there are many different ways to involve others, and the most appropriate orientation depends on many mediating variables. Leadership that is inclusive calls for different skills and abilities than does a more directive and less invitational approach. While each orientation has its advantages and disadvantages, principals and superintendents often face circumstances that require immediate action. But acting without consultation may be interpreted as a failure to lead properly.

Much has been written about the virtues of collaboration. However, collaboration and participatory decision making create a very real dilemma for school administrators as they are pressed to lead schools and school systems with the "accountability buck" stopping at the principals' and superintendents' doors. Formal authority is vested in the educational leader, by virtue of his/her position. The responsibility inherent in these positions requires making tough choices that may not be satisfactory to parents, teachers, or others. How many times have school superintendents been terminated as they enrage constituents, all the while claiming to make the hard choices needed to enhance learning for all children? School leaders are caught in the dilemma of encouraging participation and fostering a consensus model while they rely on individual authority to influence important decisions and outcomes.

Conclusion

The context of educational systems is complex, dynamic, and fluid, suggesting numerous scenarios that could influence the ways in which leaders enact their roles and manage dilemmas. In this sense, there is a real interaction among the roles, forces and dilemmas confronting educational leaders. One possible scenario is that school systems continue to be relatively bureaucratic and centralized. Many of the recent policy reforms, such as state curriculum frameworks, content standards, and accountability testing, assume that schools are "nodes in an administrative neural network" and are "operational recipient[s] of these good policies" (Guthrie, 2001, pp. 362-363). In this case, educational leaders may have incentives and inducements to follow a more managerial, administrative role. Leaders may want to focus actions and decisions on compliance and stability.

A second scenario is that schools and school systems will become increasingly autonomous, functioning in a less centralized, quasi-market context. Recent trends of both public and private school choice options, such as charters, magnets, and vouchers, illustrate this scenario. In Arizona, for example, a proposed law would allow principals to be operationally and financially independent of their districts (Stricherz, 2001). In this case, leaders may have incentives and inducements to build partnerships with multiple constituencies, responding to and engaging with both external and internal audiences and partners to define, implement, and monitor a school's resources and programs (Hill, Pierce, & Guthrie, 1997).

A third scenario, a communitarian view, places schools in a larger context of social action and community, decrying the dichotomy between markets and bureaucracy (Etzioni, 1998). In this case, school leaders are located more prominently in the center of discourse, educating the broader public about the importance of, and the need to support, the critical connections between schooling and the "good society." Social justice may be the overarching reference point for leadership in this case.

While some children live in an environment that provides them with adequate and effective opportunities to learn what society believes they need to know and be able to do, many children must rely on the school's curriculum and good teaching for such learning. Adequate curriculum and pedagogy are critical to our ability to serve the learning needs of all children. If not acquired in schools, such learning is not likely to happen, particularly for poor children, children of color, and second-language learners (Graham, 1993).

School and district administrators face a difficult fusion of roles, contexts, and leadership challenges. Regardless of which scenario(s) the future holds for schooling, the public needs to be reminded why public education is in the public's interest. School principals and superintendents are the natural stewards of public education, and it is in their interest to foster strong community support for public education. Such leadership requires that school administrators understand and be committed to curricular, instructional, and organizational strategies that make it possible for all children to succeed academically. And, just as important as knowing what to do, school administrators must have the will and the courage to act on that knowledge.

NOTE

1. There are many different approaches to understanding the dilemmas, and there is a growing body of literature addressing the concept. Winter (1982), for example, describes three types of dilemmas. The first type, ambiguity, emerges when leaders face dilemmas ". . . of inevitable and deep-seated complexities of a situation" (Dimmock, 1996, p. 142). In the second type of dilemma, judgments, situations present complexities but they are not quite as ambiguous, and thus they lead to some type of action. Problems, the third type of dilemma, lend themselves to some type of response or action, but as action is taken in one domain, other aspects of the same situation become problematic. Cuban (1996), in contrast, distinguishes among broad types of dilemmas in three areas—the purpose of education, strategies for change, and the outcomes of schooling. Others tend to focus on the ethical dilemmas of educational leadership, and dilemmas of specific roles, such as implementing school restructuring (Dimmock, 1996; Campbell, 1996).

REFERENCES

Achieve, Inc. Mission statement. Retrieved May 15, 2001, from http://www.achieve.org

Adams, J., & Kirst, M. (1999). New demands and concepts for educational accountability: Striving for results in an era of excellence. In J. Murphy and K. S. Louis (Eds.), *Handbook of research on educational administration* (pp. 463-490). San Francisco: Jossey-Bass.

Bush, G. W. (2001). No child left behind. Retrieved May 15, 2001 from http://www.ed.gov/inits/proposal

Begley, P. T. (1999). *Values and educational leadership*. Albany, NY: SUNY Press.

Berlak, H., & Berlak, C. (1981). *Dilemmas of schooling*. London: Methuen.

Blumberg, A. (1985). *The school superintendent: Living with conflict*. New York: Teachers College Press.

Bronfenbrenner, U. (1979). *The ecology of human development*. Cambridge, MA: Harvard University Press.

Campbell, E. (1996). Suspended morality and the denial of ethics: How value relativism muddles the distinction between right and wrong in administrative decisions. In S. L. Jacobson, E. S. Hickcox, & R. B. Stevenson (Eds.), *School administration—Persistent dilemmas in preparation and practice* (pp. 63-74). Westport, CT: Praeger.

Cohen-Vogel, L., & Goldring, E. *School choice in the public market: Magnet programs and patterns of influence*. Unpublished manuscript, Department of Leadership and Organizations, Peabody College, Vanderbilt University.

Coleman, J. (1987). Families and schools. *Educational Researcher, 16*(6), 32-38.

Consortium on Productivity in Schools (1995). *Using what we have to get the schools we need: A productivity focus for American education*. New York: Institute on Education and the Economy, Teachers College, Columbia University.

Crowson, R. (1992). *School-community relations under reform*. Berkeley, CA: McCutchan.

Cuban, L. (1992). Managing dilemmas while building professional communities. *Educational Researcher, 21*, 4-11.

Cuban, L. (1996). Reforming the practice of educational administration through managing dilemmas. In S. L. Jacobson, E. S. Hickcox, & R. B. Stevenson (Eds.), *School administration—Persistent dilemmas in preparation and practice* (pp. 3-17). Westport, CT: Praeger.

Cuban, L. (2001). *How can I fix it*. New York: Teachers College Press.

Dewey, J. (1922). *Human nature and conduct*. New York: Random House.

Dimmock, C. (1996). Dilemmas for school leaders in restructuring. In K. Leithwood, J. Chapman, D. Corson, P. Hallinger, & A. Hart (Eds.), *International handbook of educational leadership and administration* (pp. 135-170). London: Kluwer Academic Publishers.

Elmore, R. (1990). Introduction: Changing the structure of public schools. In R. Elmore and Associates (Eds.), *Restructuring schools* (pp. 1-28). San Francisco: Jossey-Bass.

Empowerment, a new covenant with America's communities: President Clinton's national urban policy report. (1995). Washington, DC: U.S. Dept. of Housing and Urban Development, Office of Policy Development and Research.

Etzioni, A. (1998). *The essential communitarian reader*. New York: Rowman & Littlefield.

Glatter, R. (1996). Managing dilemmas in education: The tightrope walk of strategic choice in autonomous institutions. In S. L. Jacobson, E. S. Hickcox, & R. B. Stevenson (Eds.), *School administration—Persistent dilemmas in preparation and practice* (pp. 18-29). Westport, CT: Praeger.

Goddard, R. D., Sweetland, S. R., & Hoy, W. K. (2000). Academic emphasis of urban elementary schools and student achievement in reading and mathematics: A multilevel analysis. *Educational Administration Quarterly, 36*(5), 683-702.

Goldring, E., & Hausman, C. (2001). Civic capacity and school principals: The missing link in community development. In R. Crowson & B. Boyd (Eds.), *Community development and school reform*. Greenwich, CT: JAI Press.

Graham, P. A. (1993). What America has expected of its schools over the past century. *American Journal of Education, 101*, 83-98.

Greenfield, W. D. (1999, April). Moral leadership: Fact or fancy. Paper presented at the annual meeting of the American Educational Research Association, Montreal, Canada.

Gronn, P. C. (1983). Talk as the work: The accomplishment of educational administration. *Administrative Science Quarterly, 28*, 1-21.

Guthrie, J. (2001). Contracted solutions to urban education problems. In M. Wang & H. Walberg (Eds.), *School choice or best systems: What improves education?* (pp. 357-374). New York: Erlbaum.

Hallinger, P., & Heck, R. (1996). Reassessing the principal's role in school effectiveness: A review of empirical research, 1980-1995. *Educational Administration Quarterly, 32*(1), 5-44.

Hargreaves, D. (1994). The new professionalism: The synthesis of professional and institutional development. *Teaching and Teacher Education, 10*, 423-438.

Hess, G. A. (1991). *School restructuring Chicago style.* Newbury Park, CA: Corwin Press.

Hill, P., Pierce, L., & Guthrie, J. (1997). *Reinventing public education.* Chicago: University of Chicago Press.

Holmes, B. (1965). *Problems in education: A comparative approach.* London: Routledge & Kegan.

Hoachlander, G., Alt, M., & Beltranena, R. (2001). Leading school improvement: What research says. Atlanta, GA: Southern Regional Education Board.

Kirst, M. W., McLaughlin, M., & Bassell, D. (1989). Rethinking children's policy: Implications for educational administration. Palo Alto, CA: Stanford University, Center for Educational Research at Stanford, College of Education.

Leithwood, K., & Duke, D. (1999). A century's quest to understand school leadership. In J. Murphy and K. S. Louis (Eds.), *Handbook of research on educational administration* (pp. 45-72). San Francisco: Jossey-Bass.

Leithwood, K., & Steinbach, R. (1995). *Expert problem solving.* Albany, NY: SUNY Press.

Little, J. W. (1999). Organizing schools for teacher learning. In L. Darling-Hammond & G. Sykes (Eds.), *Teaching as the learning profession: Handbook of policy and practice.* San Francisco: Jossey-Bass.

Little, J. W., & McLaughlin, M. W. (Eds.). (1993). *Teachers' work.* New York: Teachers College Press.

Lortie, D. C. (1975). *Schoolteacher: A sociological study.* Chicago: University of Chicago Press.

McLaughlin, M. W. (1994). *Urban sanctuaries: Neighborhood organizations in the lives and futures of inner-city youth.* San Francisco: Jossey-Bass.

McLaughlin, M. W., & Talbert, J. E. (1993). Contexts that matter for teaching and learning. Palo Alto, CA: Stanford University, Center for Research on the Context of Secondary School Teaching.

Murphy, J. (1999, April). The quest for a center: Notes on the state of the profession of educational leadership. Paper presented at the annual meeting of the American Educational Research Association, Montreal, Canada.

Murphy, J., & Beck, L. (1995). *School based management as school reform.* Thousand Oaks, CA: Corwin Press.

Murphy, J., & Louis, K. S. (1999). *Handbook of research on educational administration.* San Francisco: Jossey-Bass.

National Board for Professional Teaching Standards (n.d.). What teachers should know and be able to do. Washington, DC: Author.

Newmann, F. M., King, M. B., & Rigdon, M. (1997). Accountability and school performance: Implications from restructuring schools. *Harvard Educational Review, 67*, 41-74.

Ogawa, R., Crowson, R., & Goldring, E. (1999). Enduring dilemmas of school organization. In J. Murphy and K. S. Louis (Eds.), *Handbook of research on educational administration* (pp. 277-295). San Francisco: Jossey-Bass.

Rowan, B. (1995). Learning, teaching, and educational administration: Toward a research agenda. *Educational Administration Quarterly, 31*(3), 344-354.

Smrekar, C., & Goldring, E. (1999). *School choice in urban America: Magnet schools and the pursuit of equity.* New York: Teachers College Press.

Snyder, T. D., & Hoffman, C. M. (2001). *Digest of Education Statistics, 2000.* (NCES No. 2001-034). Washington, DC: National Center for Education Statistics.

Starratt, R. J. (1991). Building an ethical school: A theory for practice in educational leadership. *Educational Administration Quarterly, 27*(2), 185-202.

Stricherz, M. (2001, January 17). Law giving principals new powers under fire in Arizona. *Education Week,* p. 22.

Sweetland, S. R., & Hoy, W. K. (2000). School characteristics and educational outcomes: Toward an organizational model of student achievement in middle schools. *Educational Administration Quarterly, 36*(5), 703-729.

Sykes, G. (1991). Fostering teacher professionalism in schools. In R. Elmore & Associates (Eds.), *Restructuring schools* (pp. 59-96). San Francisco: Jossey-Bass.

Sykes, G. (1999). The "new professionalism" in education: An appraisal. In J. Murphy & K. S. Louis (Eds.), *Handbook of research on educational administration* (pp. 227-250). San Francisco: Jossey-Bass.

Sykes, G., & Millman, J. (1995). Assessing teacher performance. In S. Bacharach & B. Mundell (Eds.), *Images of Schools* (pp. 239-282). Thousand Oaks, CA: Corwin.

Timpane, M., & Reich, B. (1997). Revitalizing the ecosystem for youth. *Phi Delta Kappan, 78*(6), 464-470.

Toenjes, L. A., Dworkin, A., Gary, L., Jon, H., & Antwanett, N. (2000). The lone star gamble: High stakes testing, accountability and student achievement in Texas and Houston. Unpublished manuscript, The Sociology of Education Research Group (SERG), Department of Sociology, The University of Houston.

Winter, R. (1982). Dilemma analysis: A contribution to methodology for action research. *Cambridge Journal of Education, 12*(3), pp. 166-173.

Wong, K. (2000). *Mayoral control as a reform strategy to raise performance in urban schools.* Manuscript.

Wong, K., Dreeben, R., Lynn, L., Jr., & Sunderman, G. (1997). Integrated governance as a reform strategy in the Chicago Public Schools. Chicago: University of Chicago, Department of Education.

Yair, G. (2000). Not just about time: Instructional practices and productive time in school. *Educational Administration Quarterly, 36*(4), 485-512.

Section 2
UNDERSTANDING THE CHALLENGES OF SCHOOL AND DISTRICT LEADERSHIP AT THE DAWN OF A NEW CENTURY

CHAPTER 2

The Contextual Terrain Facing Educational Leaders

CATHERINE A. LUGG, KATRINA BULKLEY,
WILLIAM A. FIRESTONE AND C. WILLIAM GARNER

It is a truism that the context of a given locale and era shapes leaders (Burns, 1984; Johnson, 1996), and contemporary educational leaders function in complex and highly variable local contexts. To be effective, leaders need to be sensitive to the contexts and dynamics outside the schoolhouse walls as well as to those they see on a daily basis. Some local educational leaders face staffing shortages, while others face a problematic school board. Some may be coping with severe budgetary constraints, while more fortunate leaders have enjoyed years of fiscal stability. Any given feature can interact with other aspects of the educational landscape. For example, a school leader may need to scale a craggy and formidable mountain of state accountability measures, while beneath this mountain might lie the shifting fault lines of a volatile, and perhaps volcanic, national economy.

Nevertheless, for all of this contextual dynamism, there are some emerging patterns and features that contemporary educational leaders

Catherine A. Lugg is Assistant Professor of Education in the Educational Administration and Educational Policy Programs at the Graduate School of Education, Rutgers University. Katrina Bulkley is Assistant Professor of Educational Policy at the Rutgers University Graduate School of Education. William A. Firestone is Professor of Educational Leadership and Policy, Chair of the Department of Educational Theory, and Director of the Center for Educational Policy Analysis at the Graduate School of Education at Rutgers University. C. William Garner is Associate Professor of Education Administration in the Graduate School of Education at Rutgers University.

need to recognize in charting their own course. This chapter seeks to map the contextual terrain facing contemporary educational leaders, noting six key interrelated features of the ever-shifting landscape: the political, the economic, the financial, the accountability, the demographic, and the staffing terrain.

The Political Terrain

The political terrain faced by educational leaders is marked by contests at the local, state or national levels over resources, as well as over the scope and direction of public education. As a contested public good, public education involves multiple and shifting stakeholders and constituencies, from parent groups to business and industry groups, teachers unions, administrator groups, and individual political actors and beyond. Each is vying to determine "who gets what, when, and how" in public education. For example, the determination of a supplemental funding bill can greatly influence the condition of a local school district, depending on who "gets it," what time of the fiscal year it arrives, and whether it's a direct or indirect transfer of funds.

Public education has remained prominent on the national political radar screen since the 1983 publication of *A Nation at Risk* (National Commission on Excellence in Education). This report, while having little positive effect on federal education policy (Berliner & Biddle, 1995; Lugg, 1996), successfully nationalized the discussion surrounding the health of public education. For better or worse, it linked the vitality of the military and national economy to the performance of the educational system. The political focus regarding public education shifted in the direction of "quality" (student achievement) and away from issues concerning equity and access (Lugg).

The report also illustrated the political appeal of connecting education to other sectors of American society, most particularly the economy (Lugg, 1996). At the time of the report's release, the U.S. was in the midst of one of the worst recessions since the Great Depression (Schaller, 1992), and there was great anxiety regarding our economic competitiveness with other nations. Comparisons were drawn between Japanese industrial performance and that of the U.S., with the U.S. looking increasingly weak. These economic comparisons quickly led to various educational comparisons, and many people concluded that the U.S. public educational system was underperforming as well (Berliner & Biddle, 1995; Murphy, 1991).

Although there was little change at the national level regarding educational reform—despite some talk of moving more power to local schools—states began to take an aggressive stance in revitalizing public schools. Most important, there was increased centralization of educational policy making at the state level, as governors and state legislators sought more influence in education. As one educational researcher observed in 1995, "During the past decade, the American states have engaged in a massive use of policy in seeking to reform their public schools" (Mazzoni, 1995, p. 53). Consequently, the size and scope of state involvement greatly expanded, including increasing intrusion into the "technical core" of schooling, around issues such as what should be taught, how it should be taught, and how it should be assessed.

A key change resulting from the increased state presence has been a shift in policy focus. Before the 1980s, state educational policy tended to focus on inputs and process issues rather than on outputs and student academic achievement. However, with the rise of global economic and educational comparisons, states have refocused their policy concerns to emphasize standards, accountability and the improvement of student academic performance, particularly as measured by standardized assessments. Presently, 49 out of 50 states have statewide assessment systems in place, and in almost half of the states the stakes attached to these results have been gradually "ratcheted up" (Cizek, 2001).

In addition, with the re-authorization of ESEA, by 2005 each state will have to implement a system of statewide assessment in the areas of reading and mathematics for all grades 3 through 8. While the federal government is mute on what kinds of assessment programs should be implemented, this centralizing trend will continue at the state level, since states have the power to determine what assessments are to be employed.

Paradoxically, alongside increased centralization other reforms have been designed to decentralize publicly funded education. Some of these have involved a push towards increased control at the school site (e.g., through site-based management and charter schools). The tension between centralization and decentralization has led some to call for a new role for school districts—one in which they are viewed more as service "providers" than as school operators. School leaders in this new environment are expected to respond to increasing state demands while assuming new roles within their buildings (budget managers) and providing increased "instructional leadership" (Fullan, 1991). It appears that the increasing quantity of state policy is requiring local leaders to make more policy themselves (Fuhrman & Elmore, 1990).

Other reforms have sought to devolve some educational authority by placing it in the hands of parents. Open enrollment policies, which allow students more access to public schools within and outside their districts, have been popular. In addition, growing political support has emerged for nontraditional publicly funded methods of educational delivery that go outside the traditional district structure, such as home schooling, charter schools, and school vouchers (in limited areas). Touted as a means of promoting greater educational choice and competitiveness, these alternatives have become increasingly common since the 1980s. Yet, they remain largely on the periphery of the larger system of educational provision. The vast majority of U.S. students still attend the traditional public school.

These state and national political pressures have changed the day-to-day activities of local educational leaders since the 1980s. Principals and superintendents publicly acknowledge the importance of bolstering student academic achievement, and most work mightily to ensure better outcomes on state-level assessments. With the federal government now mandating statewide testing, these political pressures on local administrators will only increase.

Politics is not, however, all state and national. Local educational leaders also face a host of challenges that are entirely local (Deal & Peterson, 1999; Merz & Furman, 1997), from bond referenda to ideologically divisive school boards and contentious labor relations. These local political features can at times complicate and confound state-driven educational reforms (Fullan, 1991). Nevertheless, the most dramatic change in the political landscape is the increased role of the states and the federal government. Consequently, the most pressing political issues to which educational leaders must attend are:

- What are the major national and state political trends that may affect my school?
- How might these trends interact with reform efforts already in place (either through local, state or national action)?
- At what point should I become engaged in political or policy-related activities to influence or respond to changing ideas around reform?

(See Fowler, 2000, for a further discussion of these issues).

The Economic Terrain

As noted above, one of the political appeals in *A Nation at Risk* by the National Commission on Excellence in Education was the connection between education and economics. Although this connection is logical and seems innocuous, it fills the economic terrain with strange and challenging features for school administrators. This is because education must deal with two sets of economic associations. Consequently, economics and education have a relationship that is symbiotic and also synergistic, meaning that the combined effect of their interaction may be greater than the sum of the two effects taken independently (Garner, in press).

The first set of associations between education and economics revolves around the basic meaning of economics, which is the acquisition and use of scarce resources to satisfy unlimited wants for goods and services. One entity that uses resources and has a great number of wants for goods and services is a school district. But education is itself a limited resource and a desired good or service. Consequently, education may be both an economic user and a provider. A school district needs money (a scarce resource) from tax revenues to satisfy its unlimited wants for curricular offerings. At the same time, society needs educational services (a limited resource) to prepare people to satisfy the unlimited wants of businesses and industries. And people need education to prepare them and their children for jobs that will pay them the money needed to satisfy their unlimited wants.

Because a quality education program depends on the money (a resource) available to a school district, the amount of wealth in the community has an economic impact on the school district. However, the wealth in a community also depends on the quality of the products of the educational system. Thus, a strong local economy and strong education are symbiotic and synergistic.

The second set of associations begins with the suggestion of the relationship between education and economics that can be traced back to 1776 and the work of Adam Smith (1976). Smith recognized the value of human ability—especially ability acquired through education and training—to a business and to society. Later research by Schultz (1963), Denison (1962), Benson (1978), and others provided evidence of the relationship between education and economic growth. The focus of the argument used by Schultz and others is referred to as human capital theory. It proposes a direct relationship between the investment of time and resources in education and production and individual earnings.

A conventional measure of the production of goods and services in the U.S. is the Gross Domestic Product (GDP). A similar measure of production used by each state is called the Gross State Product (GSP).

Production measures could also be monitored for the geographical regions within each state; however, they typically are unavailable. Researchers have shown that educational investment is related to production as represented by the measures of the GDP and GSP.

With respect to individual returns, the following table is based on the U.S. Census Bureau report for 1998 on the relationship of education to earnings.

TABLE 1

1998 MEDIAN EARNINGS:
FULL-TIME, YEAR-ROUND WORKERS BY LEVEL OF EDUCATION AND GENDER

| | MEDIAN EARNINGS | |
EDUCATION	FEMALES	MALES
Less than 9th grade	$14,132	$18,553
9th to 12th (no diploma)	15,847	23,438
High school graduate (includes GED)	21,963	30,868
Some college, no degree	26,024	35,949
Associate degree	28,337	38,483
Bachelor's degree	35,408	49,982
Master's degree	42,002	60,168
Professional degree	55,460	90,653
Doctoral degree	52,167	69,188
For all levels of education	26,711	36,679

Another measure of the relationship between education and personal earnings is the internal rate of return. In this research the lifetime earnings of people at different levels of education are related to the cost of that education up to and including the level of education being measured. The higher the earnings and the lower the cost, the better the return on investment. Researchers over the past 40 years, such as Becker (1964), Psacharopoulos (1981, 1985), and Woodhall (1987), have demonstrated that elementary education and then secondary education provide the best return. Because of the return measures, some researchers argue that there is a serious underinvestment at the early childhood/elementary level. This consideration is especially important to underdeveloped regions where policy makers have to decide how to allocate their scarce public resources.

The challenge for educational leaders is to determine which educational services will ensure a positive return for the community's investors (taxpayers) and graduates. There are larger economic forces at play with which local leaders must contend. Toffler and Toffler (1995) see civilization as a movement through three waves. They propose that civilization is now moving from a second wave, which is the industrial age, into a third wave, which is based on "mind-work rather than muscle-work" (p. 79). Mind-work depends on knowledge. Today, more economically successful people engage in mind-work. As a result geographical areas where mind-work people live have a strong local economy that offers a greater return to investors. If there is no local demand for mind-work workers, then high school graduates capable of mind-work (and of securing a higher paying job) can be expected to leave the area. The potential for negative synergy is strong.

Reich (1992) also points to the quality of knowledge needed by people in reference to their financial potential. He proposes that civilization is moving from high-volume (mass production of goods and services) to high-value businesses (goods and services tailored to meet the particular needs of people and businesses). Within the high-value enterprises, he suggests that there are major job categories ranging from routine production jobs up to symbolic-analytic jobs. The symbolic-analytic category requires more education, and correspondingly, workers in these jobs earn more money. To support his claim, Reich presents data demonstrating the widening income gap between the workers in the lower and higher job categories. The challenge for educational leaders is to prepare their students either to enter the symbolic-analytic jobs or to continue their education for such positions. The challenge for a community is to be attractive to industries offering these positions so that capable graduates will remain.

The economic terrain presents educational leaders with a set of circumstances in which there is no single model to follow when determining which educational programs and services should be offered. This is because the economic terrain varies from community to community. If regional production returns weaken and the economic environment deteriorates, a dramatic parallel may develop in education. An extended decline in such a relationship explains why some areas in the United States—especially certain urban and rural areas—have a standard of living (and educational system) comparable to that of a less developed country (Garner, in press).

To navigate their economic terrain successfully, school leaders must take a proactive role. The Interstate School Leaders Licensure Consortium (ISLLC) standards (1996) are explicit in their expectations for school leaders in the context of a changing economy, the shift to a postindustrial society and a global marketplace, and a greater reliance on technology. They propose that school leaders:

• Have high visibility in the community,

- Develop relationships with community leaders,
- Establish partnerships with business and higher education institutions,
- Reach out to religious, political and service agencies,
- Secure available community resources for their school, and
- Ensure the appropriate and wise use of public resources.

In addition, the ISSLC expects school administrators to respond to and influence "the larger political, social, economic, legal, and cultural context" and to actively participate "in the political and policy-making context in the service of education" (p. 20). When school leaders establish and maintain these connections, they must ensure that all policy makers understand the symbiotic and synergistic relationship between education and the local economy.

The Financial Terrain

Two important shifts in the financial terrain—one largely consolidated 20 years ago, and one still under way—have combined to move the accountability of school leaders from the local elected school board to more distant entities (the state and federal government). The first shift is in the growth in state funding for public education. In the 19th century, education was locally funded. However, the state share increased gradually after World War I through the 1980s. Since then, the proportions have been fairly consistent, with state and local governments each contributing 42 percent and the balance coming from the federal government (National Center for Educational Statistics, 2000). Typically, federal funding comes through targeted programs where funds must be directed to specific uses or categories of children—e.g., low achievers or disabled children. Conditions accompanying this funding constrain local leaders regarding how these and other funds are spent. State funding usually comes on a per capita basis, but some of it may come through targeted programs as well. In any case, as states have paid a greater percentage of operating costs, they have come to expect local entities to be more accountable for how these funds are spent.

The second important shift concerns how state funds are distributed among school districts. Often, state aid has been used to compensate for the differences in funding available to local school districts. In the 1970s advocates for poor children began suing state governments to increase the equity in spending across districts within a given state.

The frequency of these suits increased in the 1990s, as did the variety of grounds on which they were brought (Picus, 2001). Litigants moved from demanding equity (either in per pupil funding or for taxpayers) to demanding educational "adequacy." This term is difficult to define, but it redirects attention from financial inputs to high minimum student outcomes. Schools are to ensure that students learn what they are expected to learn (Clune, 1994). This definition has at least two implications. First, it requires states to define what an adequate education is—hence, the emphasis on outcomes, which, we will see, fits with some current approaches to accountability. Second, if all children are expected to receive an adequate education, an emphasis on "adequacy" provides an argument for expecting different levels of expenditures for students with different needs. This, in turn, permits higher expenditures to educate disabled, low-income, or other children from groups that historically achieve at lower levels (Ladd & Hansen, 1999).

While these have been the major trends, the financial situation varies considerably among schools, districts and states. Variation among schools is difficult to document, but variation among states and districts is quite clear. For example, Utah spends relatively little on education: $4049 per pupil in 1999. New York spends about twice as much: $8174 per pupil. However, funding is distributed more equitably among districts in Utah than in New York. One standard deviation from the state average per pupil expenditure is $482 in Utah. It is $1643 in New York, more than three times greater. Thus, while more money is spent on education in New York, there is greater inequity (Editorial Projects in Education, 2001). Even allowing for differences in cost of living, the challenge leaders face in securing funding for their schools varies widely within and across states.

As the financial terrain shifts, educational leaders must address two questions. The first is "How do I increase the resources for my school?" To some extent, this may require accommodation to state accountability systems. Leaders are finding that even when strong rewards and punishments are not linked to state test scores, the public's confidence—and its willingness to pay for services—is linked to strong performance. In addition, leaders may be forced to turn to nongovernmental sources, including the community (in the form of volunteers or local foundations), businesses and welfare agencies of various sorts, for additional funds, volunteers' time, or other services and materials.

The second question is "How do I mobilize resources to increase effectiveness?" This is not a matter of obtaining more funding but of using what is available more effectively. While there is no clear consensus on how to accomplish this, at least four notable possibilities can be pursued by school and district leaders (Ladd & Hansen, 1999).

- Reallocate personnel to reduce class size (Krueger & Whitmore, 2001). This seems to be especially effective in lower grades.
- Prepare low achieving children through preschool programs (Barnett, 1995).
- Focus investments on professional development (Cohen & Hill, 1998). While the evidence in this area is not as strong, increasing the pedagogical and content knowledge of existing teachers seems to contribute to student learning. The costs of professional development are not well understood, and typical approaches may not be the most effective (Miles, Bouchard, Winner, Cohen & Guiney, 1999).
- Redesign teacher pay. The greatest part of school budgets goes into personnel, but those allocations are currently not designed to motivate improvement. The single salary schedule now in use typically rewards length of service and further course work, but it provides little incentive for improving teaching performance. Merit pay strategies have been tried and usually produce poor results. Other options that are now being considered include collective merit pay—i.e., rewarding the entire school staff, incentives for knowledge and skill development, and paying teachers for assuming additional assignments (Firestone, 1994).

The Accountability Terrain

As noted above, accountability to entities beyond the local school board has become increasingly important for local school leaders, as has accountability for the outcome—rather than the process—of education (Adams & Kirst, 1999). The idea of accountability implies that someone external to the school or district is holding people "to account." Educational leaders have always dealt with bureaucratic accountability: the accountability of a subordinate to a superior, as in the teacher to the principal and the principal to the superintendent (Adams & Kirst). There is also long experience with political accountability to the locally elected school board.

Recently, two new forms of accountability have received greater attention. One is market accountability. Here the markets hold providers of services accountable. Public schools have always competed with private and parochial schools (Perkinson, 1991). Since magnet schools were developed as a response to desegregation pressures, they too have provided some choice within the public system. The rise of charter schools and vouchers and the expansion of home schooling have widened the range of choice. To date, the effects of these new market forces is unclear (see Rofes, 1998). The greatest change is found in the few places where large numbers of students have new options through vouchers, charters, and other forms of public choice (e.g., Milwaukee and parts of Arizona). If school leaders looked to other countries where choice is more firmly established, however, they might find themselves spending much more time marketing their schools to the public and recruiting students than they have in the past (e.g., Gewirtz, Ball, & Bowe, 1995). It is not clear that comparable expansion of choice is likely in the U.S. However, such expansion has the potential to force a reallocation of American school leaders' time from internal to external functions, especially in the areas of marketing and fundraising.

More important has been the introduction of political accountability for both schools and districts to meet state expectations. This is a direct result of the growth of state influence in education. A state's accountability system includes four elements: an entity to be held accountable (e.g., a school, a teacher, or a student); performances for which the entity is held accountable; standards that the entity is to meet; and rewards, penalties, and interventions (Ladd, 1996). The accountability question arose, in part, because states began providing more support for education and felt some need to ensure that those funds were well spent.

As accountability has become more prominent, the focus has shifted from accountability for inputs or processes to accountability for outcomes. This is reflected in a growing interest in student outcomes and the spread of state standards and testing. In 1982, 36 states tested students; 49 do so now, and in more subjects than ever before (Cizek, 2001; Odden & Dougherty, 1982). The current Bush administration is requiring the states to test students even more often.

The pressure on school leaders to respond to accountability demands has increased in most states. The nature of that pressure depends on several aspects of state policy, including:

- The range of content included in the state accountability system. Some states focus only on language arts and mathematics, while others test in more areas.
- The cognitive level and nature of the assessments. Some assessments are geared more to basic skills, while others assess "higher

order thinking." A parallel, but not identical, distinction exists between states that use multiple choice tests and those that use various kinds of items requiring students to construct responses. The latter are usually more intellectually challenging.

- The rewards and punishments linked to assessments. At a minimum, almost every state publishes test scores by school, but some states increase the stakes by requiring students to pass tests to graduate or to be promoted, by providing rewards to high performing schools, and by threatening to take over low performing schools.

These accountability systems present both challenges and opportunities to school leaders. At a minimum, leaders need to attend to test scores in a way that was not necessary when the only tests were locally administered and the results were not publicized. A school's record in helping children pass tests is now a matter of public record. School leaders have at least two choices in responding. They can look for expedient means to raise test scores—regardless of their larger consequences. This leads to teaching to the test and, in extreme cases, to cheating. Clearly, the preferable response is for the school leader to be more focused on the school's educational enterprise, to seek ways to help teachers become more effective educators, and to help children become stronger learners.

The advantage of a state accountability system is that it can help not only the leader but also the entire staff to improve student achievement. Leaders can capitalize on these external measures to focus a school staff's efforts. When the state accountability system and leaders' own goals align, the former becomes a useful tool for energizing staff. For instance, in research currently being conducted by two of the authors, a district math coordinator who had been trying to reform her district's math curriculum in a direction congruent with the standards of the National Council of Teachers of Mathematics (NCTM) told us that with a new state test, "we found out we could no longer teach to the test. We had to actually teach stuff . . . It was real stuff. We had to teach the kids to think, to problem solve. . . ."

Even where leaders find the state accountability system a useful tool for reform, a number of important questions remain. These include, at a minimum:

- How do I mobilize the time, funds, knowledge and staff leadership resources needed to help improve instruction?
- How do I ensure that responses to state testing improve instruction for all children rather than become a motivation for

ignoring some students (e.g., especially high or low achievers) and pushing unsuccessful children out of the school?

- What do I do to ensure that "untested" content areas are not ignored?
- How do I work with my staff to maintain a humane environment where children learn to enjoy learning and do more than just prepare for tests?

To return to the political terrain, one problem with state accountability systems is that they change frequently. California has experienced major battles over its standards and assessments, and these battles have led to dramatic changes. Arizona and Kentucky are other states that have seen extensive changes (Whitford & Jones, 2000). Other states have undergone less dramatic changes. These changes may result from disputes among educational experts, parental objections, or changes in state administrations. The challenge for school leaders is to maintain a focus on improving student learning when the measures, incentives, and the very definitions of appropriate learning sometimes undergo substantial change.

The Demographic Terrain

In addition to these policy issues, important demographic trends are shaping the experience of educational leaders, and this influence is likely only to grow. Currently, public education is undergoing an expansion in student numbers. Student enrollment is expected to grow from 51.5 million students currently to 55.2 million by 2020. This increase in the school-age population is coupled with a dramatic rise in the aging population, thanks to the onset of retirement by the baby boomers. These demographic shifts prompted Harold Hodgkinson to ask, "When the kids are out of the house, will the baby boom retain its commitment to education?" (quoted in Olson, 2000, p. 32). This growth will not be evenly distributed, but rather focused in particular areas, especially large metropolitan areas.

American society is also increasingly diverse. The number of non-Hispanic Whites is falling as a percentage of school-age children. In 1972, 79% of the student population was White non-Hispanic. By 1999, that number had shrunk to 64%, with the percentage of Hispanic children rising from 6 to 15 percent (Jamieson, Curry & Martinez, 2001). Current projections are that by 2025 Hispanics will represent roughly 25% of all school children (Olson, 2000). In California, one of the states most influenced by these changes, Sonia Hernandez of the California Department of Education commented, "From an educational standpoint, the state in general . . . has really not prepared for this influx of new students . . . not just in sheer numbers, but also in the special needs they bring to the classroom" (quoted in Olson, 2000, p. 34).

An increasingly contentious political environment has accompanied this increase in diversity. For example, Proposition 187, adopted in California in the late 1990s, attempted to restrict access to public schooling for children of illegal immigrants. In Arizona, a recently adopted referendum may severely limit the use of bilingual education. In addition, court decisions and referenda have inhibited (or attempted to inhibit) the use of affirmative action in admissions decisions, which has reduced minority enrollment in some selective postsecondary public schools.

Immigration is also shaping the demographic picture. According to current estimates, 820,000 legal and illegal migrants come to the U.S. every year (Fowler, 2000, p. 212). This means that the U.S. is experiencing its largest immigration wave since the turn of the 20th century. In 1999, 20% of school-age children had at least one "foreign-born" parent (Jamieson et al., 2001). Many of these immigrants and their children have limited proficiency in English, placing greater strain on public school systems and fueling the political debates over bilingual education.

Over the last decade, the child-poverty rate has actually decreased (Olson, 2000). However, there has been substantial growth in the number of children growing up in families that are among the "working poor" (23% of children under 18 in 1998) (Annie E. Casey Foundation, 2001). Some neighborhoods, predominantly in urban areas, have an increasing concentration of what is called "extreme poverty," where the family income is less than 50 percent of the federal poverty line. Finally, the poverty rate for young children is much higher than for any other age group. This has implications for a broad range of issues including malnutrition, child care and brain development. According to one source, "Although many factors put children at risk, nothing predicts bad outcomes for a kid more powerfully than growing up poor" (Annie E. Casey Foundation).

Changes in the economic picture also have important implications for public education. In particular, the continuing shift in the workforce from manufacturing to information and technology places demands on schools to provide a workforce appropriate to these growing sectors (Fowler, 2000). At times, the demographic shifts in the population

and workforce put pressures on school leaders to accommodate conflicting demands. The continued political focus on education is likely to
be tied to these population and economic shifts.

These new challenges will be faced by an increasing number of states
and localities over the next twenty years. Local and state leaders will
need to respond by adapting programs and policies. Leaders must ask:

- What changes do I need to put in place to respond to a changing
  student population, ranging from creating or expanding specialized programs for students with particular needs (e.g., bilingual
  education) to building capacity for different kinds of instruction
  that support students with diverse backgrounds and needs?

- How do I promote instruction that both serves students with an
  increasing variety of needs and focuses student learning in areas
  appropriate for the new economy?

- How can I increase supplemental programs such as breakfast
  and after-school offerings if I have more children in poverty?

- How can I better promote my school/district/state public education program to garner public support from an increasingly
  aging population?

The Staffing Terrain

The final contextual terrain facing educational leaders is staffing.
This area can be divided into two large issues: 1) coping with labor
shortages, and 2) recruiting and maintaining a qualified and diverse
professional staff. After decades of having a reliable stream of teachers
and principals, many school districts are facing shortages (Educational
Research Service, 1998; Hussar, 1999). The National Center for Education Statistics projects that the U.S. will need anywhere from 1.7
million to 2.7 million public school teachers by the 2008-09 school
year (Hussar). In 1998, the National Association of Secondary School
Principals (NASSP) and the National Association of Elementary
School Principals (NAESP) commissioned a national survey of public
school superintendents that indicated shortages of qualified building
principal candidates across school types. Forty-seven percent of the
surveyed superintendents reported shortages at the elementary level,
55% reported shortages at the junior high/middle school level, and
55% reported shortages at the senior high level (Educational Research
Service). These principal shortages were consistent across location
and type of school district—suburban, urban and rural (ERS).

The current and projected shortages are largely due to retirements, a growing student population, career changing, and large teacher and administrator turnover in some areas (ERS, 1998; Hussar, 1999). Many experienced teachers and principals are retiring or leaving the profession, and this trend is projected to accelerate (ERS; Hussar). Rising student enrollments in general and a growing need for teachers in specialty areas such as special education, bilingual education and science education may further exacerbate these shortages. Staff turnover also has implications for teacher and administrator quality, since loss of experienced staff members generally translates into a reduction in the quality of instruction. This can be particularly acute in distressed urban areas, where highly qualified administrators and teachers seek better working and salary conditions in suburban school districts (Anyon, 1997).

Yet, in the areas of compensation and work environment, many aspiring teachers and principals, regardless of racial and/or ethnic background or work location, are concerned that they are sorely undercompensated for the increasing demands placed on them (ERS, 1998; Kantrowitz & Wingert, 2000; Tirozzi & Ferrandino, 2000). Historically, teachers have been underpaid (Blount, 1998; Perkinson, 1991; Rousmaniere, 1997; Tyack & Hansot 1982). While teacher compensation has improved in the last 20 years, it has failed to keep pace with compensation of similarly educated professionals (see Kantrowitz & Wingert, pp. 40-41). Historically, principal compensation has been generally better than teacher compensation (Blount), but it is still cited as a top reason for not entering the profession (ERS; Tirozzi & Ferrandino).

The other staffing issue facing educational leaders is increasing the racial and ethnic diversity of qualified professional personnel. Currently, both the teacher and principal corps are overwhelmingly White (ERS, 1998). Only 13% of teachers come from minority groups, and 40% of all U.S. schools have no minority teachers (Eubanks & Weaver, 1999). Similarly, the percentage of minority principals working in public schools remains low, with only 16% of all principals coming from a minority group (ERS). The professional population contrasts with a student population that is roughly 30% minority (Eubanks & Weaver). These are national figures. In some areas of the country the disparity between percentages of minority professional personnel and minority students is far greater (Eubanks & Weaver). This lack of minority teachers and administrators is highly problematic, given the written and unwritten cultural codes of proper school conduct that are expected of children (Delpit, 1995). Cultural clashes can and do occur, with students generally on the losing end. A more diverse teaching and administrative staff could make both staff and students more sensitive to different ways of thinking, understanding and acting (Delpit).

To address teacher shortages while expanding the diversity and quality of the professional staff, some school districts and states have greatly intensified their recruiting and retention efforts. Houston offers signing bonuses for teachers in hard-to-fill areas. The city of San Francisco has begun to offer subsidized housing to aspiring teachers. Some school districts, such as those in New York and Chicago, have recruited teachers from overseas, while other districts have expanded the use of "emergency certification," or hiring teachers without the proper pedagogical and professional experience (Kantrowitz & Wingert, 2000). In certain areas, the available pool of substitutes from which to recruit teachers has been drained (McGinn, 2000). Some districts and states have also expanded professional development offerings, including tuition reimbursement for those professionals who seek additional education.

To expand the pool of principal candidates, some districts have started to groom candidates from within (ERS, 1998; Tirozzi & Ferrandino, 2000). The "tap on the shoulder" by a watchful superintendent or building principal can give teachers who are undecided about entering educational leadership the needed push to seek administrative licensure (ERS; Lashway & Anderson, 1996). This seems especially critical to recruiting minority candidates (ERS). Some states and localities have also scaled back or eliminated many of the hurdles to administrative licensure, enabling those with business or political but little educational experience to become educational leaders. However, other states have stiffened licensure requirements, in the hope of ultimately improving teacher quality and building stronger student academic performance. Educational leaders need to keep in mind the following questions when hiring and retaining staff:

- Are the faculty and administrative staff highly qualified?
- Does our staff reflect the diversity of our community and nation?
- If members of the faculty and staff were hired under "emergency certification," have they acquired the proper academic credentials and professional licensure?
- Are we grooming possible candidates from within?

Given the ongoing and projected shortages of qualified teachers and principals, coupled with the need to build a more diverse professional staff, the staffing issues facing educational leaders are complex. Grow-ing enrollments and shifting licensure requirements further compound these shortages. A critical danger facing educational leaders in coping with these shortages is a bifurcated staff, where some teachers and prin-cipals are highly qualified, while others are hastily recruited through the back door of "emergency certification" and never acquire the proper professional education and credentials. Such dilemmas are typical of historical periods of shortages (Anyon, 1997; Tyack, 1974).

Navigating the Contextual Terrain in the 21st Century

Today's educational leaders are working in situations marked by great complexity. In this chapter, we have mapped the key features of the present day landscape surrounding educational leaders (politics, economics, finance, accountability, demographics and staffing). These areas have their individual complexities, but they are also interrelated and tend to overlap.

Three prominent and interconnected features seem to dominate the contemporary educational landscape. First, the shifting of the national economy away from "muscle-work" towards "mind-work" and the concurrent demand for a highly educated labor force have generated political demands for greater educational productivity. For better or worse, Americans view the health of the economy as depen-dent on the academic productivity of the public educational system. With the nation now sensitized to the slightest change in the econ-omy, it is reasonable to assume that economic concerns will continue to be crucial in shaping public education policies and practices.

Second, this economic shift has caused states to play a much larger role in both funding public education and regulating it (Mazzoni, 1995). Since the 1980s, when the national economy began its transi-tion to mind-work, states have greatly expanded their regulatory role by establishing requirements for curricula, tightening graduation and promotion requirements, mandating continuing professional develop-ment for educators, and generally increasing the requirements for entry-level professionals. States have also experimented with various deregulation schemes (for example, charter schools), but these have tended to move the regulatory authority from the local to the state level—a centralizing outcome in the name of decentralization.

Finally, with the states playing a greater policy role, the regulatory authority has been expanded to include various accountability measures to ensure instructional compliance and competence in local school districts. "Accountability" has come to mean state-established academic standards that all children are expected to meet, and these standards are typically assessed by state-mandated tests. And recently, educational accountability via statewide testing has been granted federal status, thanks to ESEA's reauthorization. Given the political concern regarding the economy and the expanding fiscal and regulatory roles of states, the demand for greater educational "accountability" through the mechanism of state testing will expand.

Educational leaders will need to pay particular attention to these three dynamics—the economy, state level policy, and accountability through testing—if they hope to successfully navigate the current educational terrain. While there are certainly other features that need attention, depending on local contexts, it appears that these three are the most pressing for *all* educational leaders. It is hoped that this chapter has provided a compass.

References

Adams, J. E., & Kirst, M. W. (1999). New demands and concepts for educational accountability: Striving for results in an era of excellence. In J. Murphy & K. S. Louis (Eds.), *Handbook of research on educational administration* (2nd ed., pp. 463-490). San Francisco: Jossey-Bass.

American Educational Research Association. (2000). *AERA position statement concerning high-stakes testing in pre-K-12 education*. Washington, DC: Author.

Annie E. Casey Foundation. (2001). *Kids count*. Retrieved from www.aecf.org

Anyon, J. (1997). *Ghetto schools: A political economy of urban educational reform*. New York: Teachers College Press.

Barnett, W. S. (1995). Long-term effects of early childhood programs on cognitive and school outcomes. *The Future of Children, 5*(3), 25-50.

Becker, G. S. (1964). Human capital: A theoretical and empirical analysis, with special reference to education. New York: National Bureau of Economic Research.

Benson, C. S. (1978). *The economics of public education* (3rd ed.). Boston: Houghton Mifflin.

Berliner, D. C., & Biddle, B. J. (1995). *The manufactured crisis: Myths, fraud and the attack on America's public schools*. Reading, MA: Addison Wesley.

Blount, J. M. (1998). *Destined to rule the schools: Women and the superintendency, 1873-1995*. Albany, NY: SUNY Press.

Callahan, R. E. (1962). *Education and the cult of efficiency*. Chicago: University of Chicago Press.

Cizek, G. J. (2001). Conjectures on the rise and fall of standard setting: An introduction to context and practice. In G. J. Cizek (Ed.), *Setting performance standards* (pp. 3-17). Mahwah, NJ: Lawrence Erlbaum Associates.

Clune, W. H. (1994). The shift from equity to adequacy in school finance. *Educational Policy, 8*(4), 376-394.

Cohen, D. K., & Hill, H. C. (1998). Instructional policy and classroom performance: The mathematics reform in California. *Teachers College Record, 102*(2), 294-343.

Deal, T. E., & Peterson, K. D. (1999). *Shaping school culture: The heart of leadership*. San Francisco: Jossey-Bass.

Delpit, L. (1995). *Other people's children: Cultural conflict in the classroom*. New York: The New Press.

Denison, E. F. (1962). *The sources of economic growth in the United States*. New York: Committee on Economic Development.

Editorial Projects in Education. (2001). *A better balance: Standards, tests, and the tools to succeed: Quality Counts 2001*. Bethesda, MD: Editorial Projects in Education.

Educational Research Service. (1998). *Is there a shortage of qualified candidates for openings in the principalship? An exploratory study*. Retrieved March 18, 2001 from: http://www.naesp.org/misc/shortage.htm

Elmore, R. F. (1993). The role of local school districts in instructional improvement. In S. H. Fuhrman (Ed.), *Designing coherent educational policy: Improving the system* (pp. 96-124). San Francisco: Jossey-Bass.

Eubanks, S. C., & Weaver, R. (1999). Excellence through diversity: Connecting the teacher quality and teacher diversity agendas. *The Journal of Negro Education, 68*(3), 451-459.

Firestone, W. A. (1994). Redesigning teacher salary systems for educational reform. *American Educational Research Journal, 31*(3), 549-574.

Fowler, F. C. (2000). *Policy studies for educational leaders*. Columbus, OH: Merrill.

Fuhrman, S. H., Elmore, R. F. (1990). Understanding local control in the wake of state educational reform. *Educational Evaluation and Policy Analysis, 12*(1), 82-96.

Fullan, M. (1991). *The meaning of educational change*. New York: Teachers College Press.

Garner, C. W. (In press). *Education finance for school leaders: Strategic planning and administration*. Englewood Cliffs, NJ: Prentice Hall.

Hussar, W. J. (1999). *Predicting the need for newly hired teachers in the United States to 2008-09*. National Center for Educational Statistics. Washington, DC: US Government Printing. Retrieved March 18, 2001 from: http//nces.ed.gov/pubsearch/pubsinfo.asp?pubid=1999026

Interstate School Leaders Licensure Consortium. (1996). *Standards for school leaders.* Washington, DC: Council of Chief State School Officers.

Jamieson, A., Curry, A., & Martinez, G. (2001). School enrollment in the United States—Social and economic characteristics of students. *U.S. Census Bureau: Current population reports.*

Jerald, C., & Olson, L. (2000). *Quality Counts 2000: Who should teach.* Bethesda, MD: Education Week.

Johnson, S. M. (1996). *Leading to change: The challenge of the new superintendency.* San Francisco: Jossey-Bass.

Kantrowitz, B., & Wingert, P. (2000, October 2). Teachers wanted. *Newsweek, 136*(14), 36-42.

Krueger, A. B., & Whitmore, D. M. (2001). The effect of attending a small class in the early grades on college-test taking and middle school test results: Evidence from Project Star. *The Economic Journal, 111*(468), 1-28.

Ladd, H. F., & Hansen, J. S. (Eds.). (1999). *Making money matter: Financing America's schools.* Washington, DC: National Academy Press.

Ladd, H. F. (1996). *Holding schools accountable.* Washington, DC: Brookings Institute.

Lashway, L., & Anderson, M. (1996). Developing school leaders. In S. C. Smith & P. K. Piele (Eds), *School leadership: Handbook for excellence* (3rd ed., pp. 72-100). ERIC: University of Oregon.

Lugg, C. A. (1996). *For God and country: Conservatism and American school policy.* New York: Peter Lang.

Mazzoni, T. L. (1995). State policy-making and school reform: Influences and influentials. In J. D. Scribner & D. H. Layton (Eds.), *The study of educational politics* (pp. 53-75). Bristol, PA: The Falmer Press.

McGinn, D. (2000). There's just no substitute. *Newsweek, 136*(14), 42.

McNeil, L. M. (2000). *Contradictions of school reform: Educational costs of standardized testing.* New York: Routledge.

Merz, C., & Furman, G. (1997). *Community and schools: Promise and paradox.* New York: Teachers College Press.

Miles, K., Bouchard, F., Winner, K., Cohen, M. A., & Guiney, E. (1999). *Professional development spending in the Boston public schools.* Boston: Boston Plan for Excellence.

Murphy, J. (1991). *Restructuring schools: Capturing and assessing the phenomena.* New York: Teachers College Press.

National Alliance of Business. (2000). *Improving performance: Competition in American public education.* Washington, DC: National Alliance of Business.

National Center for Education Statistics. (2000). *Digest of Educational Statistics, 2000.* Washington, DC: Author.

National Commission on Excellence in Education. (1983). *A nation at risk: The imperative for educational reform.* Washington, DC: U.S. Department of Education.

National Council of Teachers of Mathematics. (2000). *Principles and standards for school mathematics.* Reston, VA: National Council of Teachers of Mathematics.

Odden, A., & Dougherty, V. (1982). *State programs of school improvement: A 50-state survey.* Denver, CO: Education Commission of the States.

Olson, L. (2000, October 27). Children of change. *Education Week.*

Perkinson, H. J. (1991). *The imperfect panacea: American faith in education, 1865-1990.* New York: McGraw-Hill, Inc.

Picus, L. O. (2001, December). Defining adequacy: What does it mean for school board members? *American School Board Journal, 188*(12), 28-30.

Psacharopoulos, G. (1981). Returns to education: An updated international comparison. *Comparative Education 17*, 321-341.

Psacharopoulos, G. (1985). Returns to education: A further international update and implications. *The Journal of Human Resources 20*, 583-604.

Reich, R. B. (1992). *The work of nations.* New York: Vintage Books.

Rofes, E. (1998). *How are school districts responding to charter school laws and charter schools?* Berkeley, CA: Policy Analysis for California Education.

Rousmaniere, K. (1997). *City teachers: Teachers and school reform in historical perspective.* New York: Teachers College Press.

Schaller, M. (1992). *Reckoning with Reagan: America and its president in the 1980s.* New York: Oxford University Press.

Schultz, T. W. (1963). *The economic value of education.* New York: Columbia University Press.

Smith, A. (1976). *An inquiry into the nature and cause of the wealth of nations.* Chicago: University of Chicago Press.

Smith, S. C., & Piele, P. K. (Eds.). (1996). *School leadership: Handbook for excellence* (3rd ed.). ERIC: University of Oregon.

Tirozzi, G. N., & Ferrandino, V. L. (2000, October 18). Principals' perspective: The shortage of principals continues. *Education Week.* Retrieved June 5, 2001 from: http://www.nassp.org/news/views/prin_short1000.htm

Toffler, A., & Toffler, H. (1995). *Creating a new civilization.* Atlanta, GA: Turner Publishing.

Tyack, D. (1974). *The one best system: A history of American urban education.* Cambridge, MA: Harvard University Press.

Tyack, D., & Cuban, L. (1995). *Tinkering toward utopia.* Cambridge, MA: Harvard University Press.

Tyack, D., & Hansot, E. (1982). *Managers of virtue: Public school leadership in America, 1820-1980.* New York: Basic Books.

Whitford, B. L., & Jones, K. (2000). Kentucky lesson: How high stakes school accountability undermines a performance-based curriculum vision. In B. L. Whitford & K. Jones (Eds.), *Accountability, assessment, and teacher commitment: Lessons from Kentucky's reform efforts* (pp. 9-24). Albany, NY: SUNY Press.

Woodhall, M. (1987). Human capital concepts. In G. Psacharopoulos (Ed.), *Economics of education: Research and students* (pp. 21-24). Oxford, UK: Pergamon Press.

CHAPTER 3

Unpacking the Challenges of Leadership at the School and District Level

KENNETH LEITHWOOD AND NONA PRESTINE

Reflecting the prevailing sentiment of the public at large, governments in many parts of the world show little patience for the usual pace of educational change. One of the primary reasons for this impatience is the largely uncontested link, in the minds of many policymakers, between a globally competitive national economy and the quality of a nation's schools. As one major consequence of this impatience, governments routinely eschew small-scale trials, pilot studies, and research and evaluation of their preferred policy initiatives, choosing instead to move immediately to large-scale implementation (Hanushek & Meyer, 1996). Large-scale school reform has been underway in many locations—for example, the U.K.; Victoria, Australia; Chicago; New Zealand; and many U.S. states—for the past 15 years, after a considerable period of dormancy triggered by failed initiatives during the 1960s (Fullan, 1999).

While these reform efforts are not identical in all respects, they often share a remarkable number of features, most prominently a central concern for holding schools more accountable. As a consequence, a much greater emphasis on accountability is a critical part of the context in which school and district leaders now work. Furthermore, although initiated at the national or state level, successful implementation of such accountability-oriented reforms depends significantly on the practices of such leaders. For this reason, it is surprising that there has been so little research explicitly examining the nature of effective school and district leadership practices in this accountability context.

This chapter consists of two main sections. The first section reviews what we know about the challenges facing leaders in highly accountable contexts and the nature of productive responses on their

Kenneth Leithwood is the Associate Dean of Research at the Ontario Institute for Studies in Education at the University of Toronto. Nona A. Prestine is a Professor in the Department of Educational Policy Studies at Pennsylvania State University.

part. This review encompasses both theoretical and empirical literatures, and most of it is specifically focused on school-level leadership.
While little evidence has been reported about district-level leadership
in accountability-oriented contexts, such leadership appears to be central to success. The second main section of the chapter reports a case
study of an exemplary district's efforts to make the most of large-scale
reform initiated in the state of Illinois. This case adds considerably to
our knowledge about effective district leadership in the context of
large-scale, accountability-oriented reforms.

Educational Leadership and Accountability

The framework used for summarizing the challenges faced by leaders, and the nature of effective responses, is a four-fold classification of
approaches to accountability developed as part of a recent seven-coun-
try study (Leithwood, Edge, & Jantzi, 1999; Leithwood & Earl, 2000).
Each of these approaches—market, decentralization, managerial, and
professional—is rooted in different and sometimes incompatible sets of
assumptions about what is wrong with schools, what they ought to be
like, and how to bring about change. Specific accountability strategies
associated with each of the four approaches call on substantially different school leadership capacities for their successful implementation.
Each approach, furthermore, is often associated with negative and
unintended outcomes; a major leadership challenge is to mitigate such
unwanted effects.

MARKET APPROACHES

Sometimes referred to as the exit option, this approach to accountability increases the competition for students faced by schools by
implementing greater choice: opening boundaries within and across
school systems, privatizing schools, and creating charter schools, magnet schools, academies and other specialized educational facilities.
Competition also is increased by altering the basis for school funding
so that money follows students (e.g., vouchers, tuition tax credits), and
by publicly ranking schools based on aggregated student achievement
scores. These tools are often used in combination.

Advocates of this approach to educational accountability (e.g.,
Chubb & Moe, 1990) hold a set of assumptions about how such competition is likely to result in greater student achievement. First, increased
competition allows parents and students to select schools with which
they are more satisfied and which better meet their educational needs.

Second, parents who are more satisfied with their child's school provide greater support to that school and to their child's learning. Third, students are likely to be more engaged when their own learning styles are matched to a particular school. Fourth, when teachers have chosen their work settings and have been active in designing their own schools' programs, they will be more committed to implementing those programs effectively. Finally, all of these outcomes will combine to increase student achievement, attendance, and educational attainment (Elmore, 1990; Raywid, 1992).

Market approaches to accountability assume an ideal set of responses from school leaders (e.g., Kerchner, 1988), as suggested by the label "salesperson" or "entrepreneur." Of course, having a good "product" to sell is the first order of business. These leaders market their schools effectively, develop good customer/client relations, and monitor "customer" (student and parent) satisfaction. To prosper in such contexts, school leaders continuously redesign their organizations in response to fast-changing market conditions. They collect data about competitors' services and prices and find niches for their schools. They have exceptional levels of clarity about their missions because these missions are viewed as a central criterion in parent and student choices.

Evidence about how school leaders actually respond to increased market competition, while still relatively modest, suggests a more complicated reality. First, choice arrangements vary considerably in the autonomy awarded principals: as an explanation for the few differences found in the practices of U.S. principals of magnet and nonmagnet schools, Hausman (2000) pointed to the wide array of district policies regulating all principals in the district. Second, evidence demonstrates that some school choice settings actually put very little pressure on leaders and schools to compete. This is the case when a school is oversubscribed (Hausman), or when it serves parents and students who, for economic and other reasons, feel unable to travel to a school outside their own neighborhood (Lauder & Hughes, 1999).

Finally, school leaders facing the same competitive conditions may respond quite differently for reasons associated with their individual abilities, values, beliefs, and motivations. Grace (1995) interpreted his evidence as three quite different responses by individual school leaders. One group of leaders welcomed the more managerial role they believed was implied in policy changes. A second group was preoccupied with the loss of a professional orientation to schools, and concerned about managerialist values encroaching on their work. The third group actively opposed those features of market approaches to school reform that they believed were unlikely to lead to school improvement. Other evidence suggests that competition has unpredictable effects on the propensity of principals to engage in instructional leadership: some find little time for such leadership, while others increase their attention to it (Hausman, 2000).

DECENTRALIZATION APPROACHES

When decentralization of decision making is used for purposes of increasing accountability (the voice option), one of its central aims often is to increase the voice of those who are not heard, or at least not sufficiently listened to, in the context of typical school governance structures. When this is the goal, a *community control* form of site-based management (e.g., Wohlstetter & Mohrman, 1993) typically is the instrument used for its achievement. The basic assumption giving rise to this form of site-based management is that the curriculum of the school ought to directly reflect the values and preferences of parents and the local community (Ornstein, 1983). School professionals, it is claimed, typically are not as responsive to such local values and preferences as they ought to be. Their responsiveness is greatly increased, however, when the power to make decisions about curriculum, budget, and personnel is in the hands of the parent/community constituents of the school. School councils in which parent/community constituents are a majority of the membership are the primary vehicles for exercising such power.

In countries such as New Zealand and Australia, where school reform has been substantially influenced by the philosophy of "new managerialism" (Peters, 1992), creating more efficient and cost-effective school administrative structures is a second central goal for decentralization. Typically, this goal is pursued through the implementation of an *administrative control* form of site-based management that increases school-site administrators' accountability to the central district or board office for the efficient expenditure of resources. These efficiencies are to be realized by giving local school administrators authority over such key decision areas as budget, physical plant, personnel, and curriculum. Advocates of this form of site-based management reason that such authority, in combination with the incentive to make the best use of resources, ought to get more of the resources of the school into the direct service of students. To assist in accomplishing that objective, the principal may consult informally with teachers, parents, students or community representatives. Site councils are typically established to advise the principal, with membership at the discretion of the principal.

Decentralization approaches to accountability assume a role for school leaders as teachers to those with newly found voices, usually parents and/or teachers. This approach to accountability assumes that the school leader's role is to "empower" these people and to actively encourage the sharing of power formerly exercised by the principal. School leaders, it is assumed, will act as members of teams rather than sole decision makers, teaching others how to make defensible decisions and clarifying their decision responsibilities. School leaders will also embrace the belief that through participation in decision making, teachers and parents will be more committed to the results of such decision making, and the decisions themselves will be better. The school leader becomes the keeper of the process, not the outcome of the process.

Evidence of the effects on school leaders of decentralization or school-based management in its various forms is quite extensive (e.g., Bullock & Thomas, 1997). These data indicate that assumptions about the role of school leaders in decentralized settings sometimes describe what actually happens in practice, but this is not the whole story. Decentralization is associated, as well, with a radically increased emphasis on budgetary considerations and less attention to providing leadership about curriculum and instruction. Decentralization greatly increases the time demands on school leaders (and the need for more attention to time management), intensifies their role and, under competitive conditions, may isolate them from other administrative colleagues outside their own organization (Finkelstein & Grubb, 2000).

When parent-dominated school councils are part of decentralization, principals often provide leadership in respect to both internal and external processes associated with councils. Internally, principals often find themselves setting the agenda, providing information to other council members, assisting council decision making, and developing a close working relationship with the council chair. Externally, principals often act as strong, active supporters of their school councils, communicating with all stakeholders about council activities and promoting the value of councils for the work of school staffs (Parker & Leithwood, 2000).

MANAGEMENT APPROACHES

Managerial approaches to accountability include systematic efforts to create more goal-oriented, efficient, and effective schools by introducing more rational procedures. The main assumption underlying this approach is that there is nothing fundamentally wrong with current school structures, but the effectiveness and efficiency of schools will be improved as they become more strategic in their choices of goals, and more plan-oriented and data-driven about the means used to accomplish those goals. This approach encompasses a variety of procedures for "strategic planning," especially at the district level, school development planning (Giles, 1997), and monitoring progress (e.g., the accountability reviews managed by New Zealand's Education Review Office), as well as multiple procedures for school improvement planning (see the states of Illinois, Florida, and Missouri, for example).

Management approaches to accountability assume that effective school leadership conforms to what is sometimes labeled "strategic management." Those exercising this form of leadership are skilled in collecting data and interpreting it systematically. They develop, with their staffs, clear manageable goals and priorities for school improvement. Progress in accomplishing such goals is carefully monitored and plans are refined accordingly. Because district resources and cooperation often are needed to accomplish school priorities, school leaders find it productive to develop especially good working relations with their district colleagues.

Evidence reviewed by Southworth (1998) suggests that these assumptions about effective leadership for school improvement have considerable real-world validity but that they are only part of the picture. In two projects carried out by the Cambridge University Institute of Education, successful school improvement appeared to depend on establishing and sustaining a culture of inquiry and reflection, a commitment to collaborative planning and to staff development, high levels of stakeholder involvement, and effective coordination strategies. Establishing these conditions depended on school leadership that emphasized the use of systematic evidence, was focused on student learning, and encouraged careful monitoring of both teaching and student progress. "Strategic management" in these projects also entailed developing school improvement plans from the results of inquiry and reflection, and carefully monitoring and evaluating the implementation of those plans.

PROFESSIONAL APPROACHES

There are two substantially different accountability strategies that have a professional orientation. One of these approaches manifests itself most obviously in the implementation of professional control models of site-based management (SBM). The other approach encompasses the "standards movement" as it applies to the practices of teachers, administrators, and occasionally others. What these strategies have in common is a belief in the central contribution of professional practice in the schools to the outcomes of schooling. They differ most obviously in the practices they choose for their direct focus. In the case of professional control site-based management, the focus is on school-level decision making, whereas teachers' classroom instructional and curricular practices are the focus of the standards movement.

Professional control site-based management (Murphy & Beck, 1995) increases the power of teachers in school decision making while also holding teachers more directly accountable for the school's effects on student achievement. The goal of this form of site-based management is to make better use of teachers' knowledge in such key decision areas as budget, curriculum, and, occasionally, personnel. Basic to this form of site-based management is the assumption that professionals closest to the student have the most relevant knowledge for making such decisions (Hess, 1991), and that full participation in the decision-making process will increase their commitment to implementing whatever decisions are made. Participatory democracy, allowing employees greater decision-making power, is also presumed to lead to greater efficiency, greater effectiveness, and better outcomes (Clune & Witte, 1988). Site councils associated with this form of SBM typically have decision-making power, and while many groups are often represented, teachers have the largest proportion of members.

A standards approach to accountability in the traditional professions emphasizes heavy control of entry to the profession by government, with responsibility for subsequent monitoring of accountability turned over to members of the profession itself (e.g., colleges of physicians, lawyers' bar associations, colleges of teachers). Such an approach requires clear standards of professional knowledge, skill, and performance, something the professional standards movement in education set out to define beginning in the U.S. in the early 1980s. Different products of the standards movement are available now as the basis for the licensure of entry-level teachers (e.g., INTASC's Model Standards for Beginning Teacher Licensing, Assessment, and Development) and school administrators (e.g., the State of Connecticut Department of Education standards for administrators), as well as for recognizing advanced levels of teaching (e.g., The National Policy Board for Teaching Standards) and school administrator performance (e.g., the ISLC Standards; Education Queensland's "Standards Framework for Leaders").

Professional approaches to accountability assume that leaders have an increased need to stay abreast of best professional practices and to assist staff in the identification of professional standards for their work. In professional approaches to accountability school leaders need to both set expectations and create conditions for professional growth. It seems likely as well that these leaders will find it productive to monitor progress of staff toward the achievement of professional standards, buffer staff from external distractions, and help parents to understand and appreciate such standards. It has also been suggested that school leaders will need to mobilize resources to meet not just higher but more sophisticated standards. They will need to be vigilant about such unintended side effects of standards as the narrowing of curricula. In schools identified as low-achieving, maintaining teacher morale and helping ensure equitable treatment of students also seem to present a challenge for school leaders with this form of accountability (ERIC Clearinghouse, 1999). But there is a dearth of systematic evidence about the extent to which these implications for school leaders come close to describing reality.

"BUNDLED" APPROACHES

So far, we have synthesized the results of empirical and theoretical research about the leadership practices demanded by four different approaches to increasing the accountability of schools. These practices are required for the effective implementation of accountability policies; they are also capable of ameliorating the sometimes unintended or negative consequences of those policies.

These different approaches to increasing accountability in schools make quite different assumptions about the status of schools and what is required to improve them. Each approach places unique demands on school leaders that require at least partly distinctive responses to be "effective." However, most reform initiatives bundle together into a single package elements of all, or most, of the four approaches to accountability (see Adams & Kirst, 1999), in the process creating significant dilemmas for both school leaders (Wildy & Louden, 2000) and district leaders.

The extent to which externally initiated reforms actually result in school improvement depends a great deal on the ability of potential implementers to make sense of the reforms, to find them meaningful. So, in the face of policy eclecticism, and the resulting sense of confusion and uncertainty, school and district leaders with their staffs, parents, and other stakeholders need to locate and adopt elements of external initiatives that align with their schools' directions and make sense in light of schools' goals and priorities (Forsyth & Tallerico, 1998).

Regardless of the particular nature of the eclectic mix of policies and assumptions faced by a district or school, effective leadership will always, for example, buffer staffs from their tendency to feel they must respond comprehensively to demands for policy implementation from governments. In addition, it will provide individualized support to staff (Bay, Reys, & Reys, 1999; Gantner, Newsom, & Dunlap, 2000), challenging them to think critically and creatively about their practices (Tacheny, 1999), building a collaborative culture, developing structures that allow for collaboration to occur (Gantner et al., 2000), and fostering parents' and community involvement in the education of their children (Bauch & Goldring, 1995; Detert, Kopal, Mauriel, & Jenni, 2000).

A Case Study of Effective District Leadership

In this section of the chapter, we describe how school and especially district leaders are effectively responding to standards-based reform in Illinois. Setting student standards and measuring their achievement has been part of many state government reform initiatives for some time now, and one that is often incorporated into each of the four approaches to accountability discussed above. But while there have been numerous studies of standards-based reform initiatives, little attention has been paid to the role of district leaders in the implementation of these initiatives. In previous efforts to change schools, those who treated administrators as either inconsequential or as obstacles to go around usually have had to rethink their strategies to take these individuals into account (e.g., Sizer, 1996).

While standards-based policies aim at significant changes in the classroom, the core technology of teaching and learning is embedded or nested (Knapp, 1997) within multiple contexts, including (but not limited to) the school, district, community, and state. Any state-level policy initiative directed toward teaching and learning must "reach through" these multiple contexts, and both district and school leaders are important resources for this task. Collectively, administrators act as gatekeepers for reform policies, and their translation and interpretation, support or neglect of these policies makes a crucial difference in implementation efforts (e.g., Elmore, 1995; Massell & Goertz, 1999). This is clearly illustrated by administrators' substantial control over the various capacity-building mechanisms available in school organizations to assist in implementation efforts; their considerable impact on staff commitment and engagement with reform initiatives; and their role in establishing the legitimacy of the change initiative, to cite three examples.

The role of administrative leaders may be most critical at the early stages of reform implementation (McLaughlin, 1991). Both the pressures and supports needed to overcome the sheer inertia of the system as new policy is introduced may be leveraged most effectively by those in administrative positions. This early implementation stage appears to be an especially significant time because the provision of extra resources, or reallocation of existing ones, is necessary, and the visible commitment and support of leaders is critical (McLaughlin, 1987). However, these supports, pressures, and resources are by no means guaranteed through the mandating of state policy (Firestone, 1989). Administrative leaders who do not endorse a given policy initiative have become adept at symbolic responses and superficial compliance.

The case described here was carried out in one Illinois school district during its third year of successful implementation of the state learning standards. Several questions were posed: how did this district respond to the state learning standards? why did it respond in this way? what was the role of district administrative leaders in this process? what does the implementation of state-driven learning standards and accountability measures require at the district level?

BACKGROUND

In 1997, the Illinois State Board of Education (ISBE) established state learning standards and benchmarks to be implemented in all schools. The standards framework, building upon and expanding the previously published State Goals for Learning (1985), covered seven learning areas: English/Language Arts, Mathematics, Science, Social Studies, Physical Development and Health, Fine Arts, and Foreign Languages. For each learning area, the new document listed a number of goals (five for English/Language Arts, five for Mathematics, three for Science, and five for Social Studies, followed by learning standards, ranging from two to six, for each). Finally, progress indicators ("benchmarks") for gauging students' achievement of each standard were established for each of the standards for early elementary school, late elementary school, middle/junior high school, early high school, and late high school. All administrators, teachers, and school board members throughout the state received copies of these standards.

Publication of the Illinois Learning Standards also prompted re-placement of the state assessment test with the Illinois Standards Achievement Test (ISAT) in Spring, 1999, a test administered at grade levels 3, 5, 8, and 11. There were several significant differences between the old and new tests. First, the new test was touted by the State Board as a direct measure of the new state learning standards and benchmarks. Second, individual student achievement scores would now be available (they had not been formerly), as would school-level measures of achievement. Third, ISAT was designed as a "raise-the-bar" test that would be significantly more challenging and rigorous than the previous test; technical evaluations (Rau, 2000) as well as informal teacher and administrator assessments of the ISAT appear to validate this claim.

Scoring well on the ISAT at all levels requires critical reasoning, higher-order thinking, and multi-stage problem solving skills as well as expanded and accelerated content. As Rau (2000) noted, "High scores on ISAT will require a fundamentally different and better kind of teaching, coherent and focused curricula and textbooks, and more engaged, disciplined and persistent students" (p. 16).

While ISAT is not a high stakes test for students, since perfor-mance on it is not directly linked to promotion or graduation deci-sions, it is clearly high stakes for schools and districts. As with the pre-vious test, results for schools and districts are published in local newspapers and reported in the "School Report Cards" mandated by the State Board of Education. Also, the state is in the process of devel-oping a new school designation system that will rank and label schools based on their ISAT results: Exceeds, High Meets, Meets, Below Stan-dards, Academic Warning, and Academic Watch (ISBE, 2000). These designations are to be determined by the percentage of students who meet or exceed state standards (cut scores established by the state) for the five areas tested by the ISAT (reading, mathematics, writing, sci-ence, and social studies). Those schools doing well or showing signifi-cant improvement can earn relative freedom from state oversight and receive public recognition and even monetary rewards. Those doing poorly face an array of remedial actions and sanctions, including state audits, state board of education coaching, state-set performance tar-gets, case managers, or even state intervention in the management of the school (ISBE, 1999; Rau, 2000).

DISTRICT CONTEXT

Fairview School District (pseudonym) is an elementary (K-8) school district in Illinois encompassing ten schools: 6 elementary (K-3), 2 intermediate (4-6), and 2 junior high (7-8). The district employs 15 administrators and 262 teaching staff who have an average of 17.3 years of experience. Student enrollment in the district is just over 4000, 38% of whom are listed as low income.

The district has five formal goals, each accompanied by a vision statement, a values statement, and an action strategy for accomplishing the goal. An annual school improvement plan, aligned with the district's goals, is developed for each building in the district by grade-level teams. These school improvement plans guide the overall instructional efforts and professional development initiatives in each of the buildings. From 1995 to 1998 the district scored just above average on the state tests. Results of ISAT testing in 1999, however, placed the district either below or right at state averages.

FAIRVIEW'S RESPONSE TO THE STATE STANDARDS: THE BEGINNINGS

Faced with the publication of the new state standards, benchmarks, and test (ISAT), the district decided to take a proactive stance. As the Assistant Superintendent explained, "I don't think that the standards are the end-all, be-all. I don't think they are 'the' answer. But they certainly are a reality right now. We had the choice of either ignoring the whole situation and running the risk that it would tear the organization apart and diminish what we do, or finding some way to use them to reach the goals of the district. And we decided upon the latter." Another district administrator added, "The fact of the matter is, we can't change the learning standards and benchmarks or the ISAT. They are not going away. So then you have to ask yourself, 'Do I agree with these?' and if I do, let's make it happen. If I don't, then I am going to have to find a way to render unto Caesar and to do what I think is right, in addition to complying with the state. But I didn't think the standards were bad. They are a fairly reasonable description of all kinds of knowledge and skills that you would expect kids to have and be able to do."

Having decided early that it needed to integrate the standards and benchmarks into the curriculum, the district next faced the issue of how to proceed. While the standards and benchmarks are fairly clear statements of what students should know and be able to do, they say little about what teachers might do to help students meet the standards. Solving this problem while assuring some kind of teacher ownership of the curriculum quickly became the challenge for district leaders.

The district first convened a group of teachers from all grade levels who "crosswalked" the then-current district curriculum (i.e., specified its relationship) to the state standards and the benchmarks. But this was only a first step, one that had to be followed by something that would, as one involved teacher said, "be good and useful to classroom teachers; something that would point to a process that could be used in classrooms. It would have to be something that would say to everyone, 'Hey, wake up and smell the coffee—things have changed.'"

The district chose to limit initial attention to language arts and mathematics. This still represented a major undertaking, since the language arts area alone consisted of five goals, 11 standards, and a total of 112 benchmarks across all school levels. Under the guidance of the Assistant Superintendent, the district team first translated or deconstructed the standards from the benchmark levels provided by the state (early elementary, late elementary, and middle/junior high school) to objectives for individual grade levels. As one of the teachers on the district team explained, "We did not want the standards and benchmarks to be seen as only the problem of the 'assessment grades,' where the ISAT is administered. Nobody would want to teach third grade, because that's where ISAT is given and they would bear the whole brunt of the results. We knew that all grade levels had to become responsible and contribute to the effort. So we literally took the standards and benchmarks and kind of developed our own standards and benchmarks for each grade level."

DEVELOPMENT OF STANDARDS, ASSESSMENT, AND INSTRUCTION: THE SAI MODEL

This preliminary work resulted in the Standards, Assessment and Instruction model (SAI). A district-wide initiative, SAI was intended to assist the district, schools, and teachers in using the Illinois Learning Standards for assessing student learning and improving instruction. The model was based in large part on the constructivist learning tenets and instructional practices advocated in *Understanding by Design* (Wiggins & McTighe, 1998). The purpose of each of the three strands of SAI was to align and seamlessly integrate the standards and benchmarks issued by the state with the district's grade-level goals, the district's goals with the schools' improvement plans, the schools' improvement plans with teachers' classroom objectives, and teachers' objectives with the student learning outcomes.

SAI is built on three core values consistent with the district's primary goal of increasing student performance through the school improvement process: (1) Everyone—students, parents, teachers, administrators, custodians—knows what students are supposed to know and be able to do; (2) Everyone takes responsibility for student learning, with a primary focus on teaching students to become responsible for their own learning; and (3) Everyone uses data in making instructional decisions. To provide at least some additional understanding of SAI, we will briefly describe its component parts—standards, assessment, and instruction.

STANDARDS

This component of SAI identifies the desired results of student learning and is based on the Illinois Learning Standards. As we noted above, SAI seeks to align the state's standards and benchmarks with the district's grade-level goals; the district's grade-level objectives with the schools' improvement plans; and each school's improvement plan with individual student learning.

An example helps illustrate the Standards strand of SAI. State Goal 6 in mathematics states: "Demonstrate and apply a knowledge and sense of numbers, including numeration and operations (addition, subtraction, multiplication, division), patterns, ratios and proportions." State Learning Standard 6.A narrows this to: "Demonstrate knowledge and use of numbers and their representations in a broad range of theoretical and practical settings." State Benchmark 6.A.3 for the Middle School level (8th grade) narrows this even further: "Represent fractions, decimals, percentages, exponents and scientific notation in equivalent forms."

Using this Middle/Junior High School Benchmark, the district curriculum team at Fairview then created objectives for each grade level that led directly toward the designated benchmark year. The final step was to convert the State Benchmark into language that students and parents could understand (e.g., "Use numerals up to 10 digits and 4 decimal places, and write place values as powers of 10. Compare and convert common fractions, decimals, and percents"). Each State Goal, Standard, and Benchmark has corresponding learner objectives at each grade level.

These learning expectations are communicated not only to teachers and students but also to parents through a unique feature of SAI, the "I Can Do It" sheets. These sheets contain all the objectives (in language arts and mathematics) for learners at their grade level and are given to each student as a checklist. Through these sheets as well as classroom posters, the district aims to communicate to the students the explicit expectations derived from the state standards and benchmarks. As the Assistant Superintendent noted, "We believe that clear objectives translate into clear expectations and this means that students don't have to guess about what the expectations are, about what they will be accountable for." A building principal who was also on the district curriculum team added, "If you went into any classroom in this building, all the standards and benchmarks and learner expectations are on a chart on the wall."

ASSESSMENT

With objectives identified, the next step for the district was to determine what type of evidence to collect in order to assess whether or not the student had actually met a given objective. Three main categories of evidence were selected (not including ISAT results): SAI tests, student portfolios, and the "I Can Do It" sheets.

The SAI assessments, modeled after ISAT, are given three times a year (fall, winter, and spring) at the beginning of each of these cycles. They were created by a district curriculum committee of classroom teachers and administrators. The tests include multiple choice items and also incorporate problem solving activities and essay writing. Fall and winter tests are used to inform teachers, parents, and students about which standards and learning objectives the student has already mastered and which still need work. Building level results are provided to principals, classroom level results to teachers, and individual results to students. Data collected from these assessments are used at both the school and classroom levels to assist with the planning of instruction and professional development for the rest of the cycle. The final cycle of SAI testing, in the spring, is summative, and results are used in assigning student grades as well as planning for the following year's instruction.

Student portfolios provide another important means of assessment. In each classroom there are two or three large blue tubs filled with hanging files. The tubs are used for storing samples of student work collected over each cycle. While classroom teachers are free to contribute to these portfolios of student work, student ownership is emphasized. For the most part, students themselves decide what work represents their best efforts and provides clear evidence that they have mastered learner-specific objectives. These "exhibits" then become another measure of progress toward meeting specific learner objectives.

Tied directly to both the SAI assessments and the student portfolios are the "I Can Do It" reports. At the end of each cycle, students go through their portfolios and identify their best work. After examining their work samples from the portfolios, their formative test scores, and any other daily classroom assignments and assessments, students mark on the "I Can Do It" sheet whether they feel they have successfully mastered the objectives listed for the cycle.

After each of the first two formative SAI tests and subsequent evaluations of the students' mastery of grade-level objectives, teachers come together at the building level to analyze data from all sources and evaluate their instructional plans. Grade-level teams then meet and develop plans, network for best practices, and identify areas of weakness. This promotes development of instructional plans that lead to informed and data-driven changes and/or modifications in classroom instruction as well as the identification of professional development needs. At the end of the year the summative SAI test is given. The results of this assessment, as well as the results of ISAT, are then used to inform instruction for the next school year.

INSTRUCTION

The final component of the SAI model, instruction, is the strand that guides decisions about classroom teaching and learning practices. The guiding logic is that by looking at what students should know (the standards/learner objectives) and comparing that with what they do know (through assessment), all teachers in the district should be able to modify their instruction to improve student learning.

This strand calls for teachers to review current data on student knowledge and begin planning instructional units using research that identifies best instructional practices. As part of this effort, district-level curriculum teams composed of teachers and administrators were convened to identify instructional best practices in the focus areas of language arts and mathematics. The overall tenets that were considered to be instructional "best practices" and that guided each team's efforts included such concepts as engaged learning, constructivism, discovery learning, and problem solving.

Building-level SAI teams then convened for an intensive two-day professional development session with the district-level team to become knowledgeable about and skilled in these instructional approaches. The building-level teams then became the primary carriers of this information to teachers in each of the individual schools. Overall responsibilities of these teams are wide-ranging and include translating SAI into the school's culture by helping staff to be mindful of the state standards, developing staff competency and comfort with a variety of student assessments, assisting teachers in using data to make instructional decisions, and providing guidance in instructional practices.

This strand of SAI has received the least direct district attention. As the Superintendent noted, "The end goal is having kids master in their classrooms those things we want them to know and be able to do. You can treat instruction as a black box if you want to, and we do in this district. We say [to teachers], 'This is your job. You are a professional. I don't care in what order you teach things. I don't care whether you use our materials or not. I don't care. That's your job. That's a professional decision.' But we do pay attention to what comes out of that black box." The Assistant Superintendent added, "When you look at successful teachers, they don't have common instructional practices. The independent variable is teachers' understanding of and internalization of [his/her] instructional philosophy and orientation. Once they have that, they can form a confident relationship with students, and learning is just something that happens in such a relationship. You have to allow for innovativeness as well as providing structures and supports, and that's what we're trying to do here."

THE ROLE OF DISTRICT LEADERSHIP IN STANDARDS-BASED REFORM

This district's response to the state learning standards and benchmarks presents an interesting amalgamation of data-driven accountability and constructivist pedagogy. Considerable importance was assigned to aligning district and school curriculum with the state learning standards and benchmarks and using data to make instructional decisions. But there also was a strong emphasis on developing authentic pedagogy that placed a high premium on intellectually demanding tasks requiring higher order thinking and problem solving skills (Newmann & Associates, 1997). Multiple and frequent measures of student performance were used to demonstrate students' mastery of learning objectives. Instruction was left largely to the discretion of individual teachers but was supported by research-based best practices, coordinated professional development opportunities, and frequent collegial networking for ideas and suggestions.

It seems evident from this case that district leadership was much involved and played a significant role in shaping and defining Fairview's response to the state standards and benchmarks and the accompanying accountability measure, the ISAT. There also appear to have been at least three critical points at which such involvement was most effective.

CATCHING THEIR ATTENTION

A critical part of the district's implementation effort was to promote awareness of the standards and benchmarks and the district's response to them. As the Assistant Superintendent noted, "A big part of this whole endeavor was that we first had to overcome inertia and catch everyone's attention. Because teachers and kids were paying attention to something. It just was not the standards."

District administration started from the idea that what gets measured is what gets valued and instituted the SAI formative and summative assessments. As one district administrator commented, "So far I would tell you that from the amount of response I've gotten from the process, that's absolutely true. The SAI formative assessments have certainly caught the attention of especially teachers but also parents and kids and principals. Some of it has been negative but I expected that . . . But our overall intent worked—we do now have everyone's attention."

CAPACITY BUILDING

While SAI assessment gained people's attention, productive change required addressing the dilemmas and conflicts it created. The remaining components of the SAI model served this purpose. What was measured did become what many people paid attention to, but as a building principal noted, "Okay, as a teacher you get this data back [from the SAI assessment] and what do you do with it? We had to have an answer to 'So what?' or 'What do I do now?' Otherwise the whole thing would have ground to a halt right there and we would have one more test score that didn't tell us a thing, that didn't change a thing." From the district's perspective, it was imperative to have in place the kinds of supports and resources that would address these questions and concerns and move the process forward. A strong, in-house, systemically aligned professional development program was developed to accomplish this.

SAI professional development responsibilities were a shared responsibility in Fairview, consistent with the pedagogical aims of SAI. As the Assistant Superintendent noted, "To me, it's like Russian nesting dolls. What the assistant superintendent has to do with principals is identical in every conceptual way with what the principal has to do with teachers, which is identical in every conceptual way with what the teachers have to do with the kids. All the elements are the same. You have to get their attention. You have to show them information that gives them a chance to get better. And you have to give them the tools to use that will help them get better."

The tools to improve were provided primarily by the district and building SAI teams. Building SAI teams were given a two-day training session by the district SAI team at the beginning of the school year (other one-day sessions were also scheduled for each of the three cycles).

The district team, composed of classroom teachers and administrators, first completed a two-week training in *Understanding by Design* (1998) given by Wiggins and McTighe. This group assumed overall responsibility for the SAI-related professional development planning. One of the district SAI team members noted, "Our approach (with the building SAI teams) was sort of like 'train the trainer' but it was more of a 'train the facilitator.' We see the building SAI teams as our counterpart in every building. The kinds of activities and information we give to the building SAI teams we expect they will then use and distribute in their buildings." The district team supplied all the training activities that the building teams subsequently used in providing professional development for their own faculties.

An important feature of this training was an evaluation component. Every activity the building teams went through was evaluated and analyzed in terms of how it might be used in their individual schools. Thus, even with professional development, the SAI commitment to continuous evaluation and assessment for improvement was evident. As a last step, each building team completed a one-year plan for how they would support SAI in their building.

PUSHING STANDARDS-BASED REFORM (SBR) BEYOND THE CENTRAL OFFICE

District administrators believed that they had to clearly understand the connection between state standards/benchmarks and the teaching/learning processes in classrooms. This understanding was necessary before they could be of much assistance in designing, coordinating, and promoting effective standards-based reform. As the Assistant Superintendent pointed out, "[SBR] has to start at the district level but traditionally the state goes after district levels from a compliance standpoint. And that never makes an impact in the classrooms."

As this case illustrated, implementing learning standards effectively is likely to be a good deal more expensive and time-consuming than initially anticipated. School districts often make compromises that approximate "real" implementation or that serve as a proxy for it. For example, by "crosswalking" their curriculums with state standards, school districts produce a proxy for the standards that may satisfy the compliance demands of the state. But it is unlikely that this proxy will result in any real change in schools and classrooms.

Fairview, on the other hand, used state-imposed standards to leverage its own goal of providing continuous improvement in student learning. The Assistant Superintendent aptly summarized the understanding behind the development of the SAI model when he noted,

"The only way to make standards work is you have to make them work in classrooms. So you have to build a whole system based on classrooms and what you want to see happen there—not on compliance with the state. The concept is planning backwards. Anybody worth his salt plans backwards. You look at what is your ultimate goal, and you get there by figuring out what you need to do and your checkpoints along the way. The problem is that school districts tend to be focused on the end goal of compliance with the state, which is a purely bureaucratic, paper-shuffling activity. You have to get people to understand that this is not the end goal. The end goal is not having the crosswalk. The end goal is having kids master, in their classrooms, those things that we want them to know and be able to do. When you have that in place, then your school-level data will fall into place, and your compliance with the state will come into place. If you don't do these things, then all you're going to be testing with ISAT is SES [socio-economic status] and nothing else."

Conclusion

The two main sections of this chapter have explored, in different ways, the demands on and opportunities for educational leadership in the context of large-scale, accountability-driven reforms. Such a context, now ubiquitous for the work of school and district leaders, gives rise to challenges for which many administrative leaders are not well prepared. In the first section of this chapter, concerned primarily with school-level leadership, we portrayed this context from four quite different perspectives—the market, decentralization, professional, and managerial approaches to accountability. Although based on very different assumptions about such fundamental matters as the purposes and means of reform, each of these approaches assumes that the work of school leaders is fundamental to their success. But each holds a different view of what such leadership entails.

Market approaches to reform view school leaders as salespeople for their organization and entrepreneurial in disposition, creating market niches, ensuring excellent customer service, and helping their organizations respond quickly to the changing demands of the educational marketplace. Decentralization approaches place school leaders in the role of team builders, ensuring that school decisions reflect the preferences of an extended and more empowered group of stakeholders. Advocates of professional approaches to accountability and reform require school leaders to be knowledgeable about best professional practices and to ensure effective use of staff expertise in the functioning of the school. Finally, managerial orientations press leaders toward more rational processes for determining and pursuing priorities. The decisions of these leaders are to be "data-driven."

Although these four approaches to reform are conceptually distinct, actual reform initiatives are usually an eclectic bundle of tools or strategies drawn from several or all of them. The potential confusion created by such eclecticism places its own sets of demands on school leaders, such as buffering staff from counterproductive policies and building school improvement initiatives that create a space for external reforms while giving primacy to the needs of the school's own students and parents.

The second section of the chapter began to address the gap in our knowledge about effective district leadership responses to large-scale, accountability-oriented reform. Rooted in the state of Illinois' standards-based reform, this section described the strategies used by one district's administrative leaders to ensure that the state's reform had substantial positive consequences for teaching and learning across the district. These strategies were aimed at drawing teachers' and administrators' attention to the state's reform, building the district's capacity to further develop the reform into an instrument powerful enough to have a positive influence on instruction, and then implementing the now fully developed reform in classroom and schools. District administrators were quick to assess the strengths and weaknesses of the state reform initiative and to integrate the initiative into their own improvement efforts. This entailed creating temporary structures in the district for further development work involving many school-level people, and ensuring that the work undertaken by people within those structures was widely communicated to school personnel in the district. Implementation in schools was fostered by a significant professional development initiative on the district's part.

Evidence in the first section of the chapter points to a school leader's role that many would judge to be untenable. Evidence found in the second section, however, suggests what is possible to do at the district level to address this problem. Together, this evidence creates a strong case for the importance of district leadership and the value of retaining strong district structures.

REFERENCES

Adams, J. E., & Kirst, M. (1999). New demands and concepts for educational accountability: Striving for results in an era of excellence. In J. Murphy & K. S. Louis (Eds.), *Handbook of research on educational administration (2nd ed.)*. San Francisco: Jossey-Bass.

Bauch, P., & Goldring, E. (1995). Parent involvement and school responsiveness: Facilitating the home-school connection in schools of choice. *Educational Evaluation and Policy Analysis, 17*(1), 1-21.

Bay, J. M., Reys, B. J., & Reys, R. E. (1999). The top 10 elements that must be in place to implement standards-based mathematics curricula. *Phi Delta Kappan, 80*(7), 503-506.

Bullock, A., & Thomas, H. (1997). *Schools at the centre? A study of decentralization*. London: Routledge.

Chubb, J., & Moe, T. (1990). *Politics, markets, and America's schools*. Washington, DC: The Brookings Institution.

Clune, W. H., & Witte, P. (1988). *School-based management: Institutional variation, implementation, and issues for further research*. New Brunswick, NJ: Eagleton Institute of Politics, Center for Policy Research in Education.

Detert, J. R., Kopel, M., Mauriel, J., & Jenni, R. (2000). Quality management in U.S. high schools: Evidence from the field. *Journal of School Leadership, 10*, 158-187.

Elmore, R. (1990). Choice as an instrument of public policy: Evidence from education and health care. In W. H. Clune & J. Witte (Eds.), *Choice and control in American education, volume 1: The theory of choice and control in education*. New York: Falmer Press.

Elmore, R. F. (1995). Structural reform and educational practice. *Educational Researcher, 24*(9), 23-26.

Elmore, R., & Fuhrman, S. H. (Eds.). (1994). *The governance of curriculum: 1994 yearbook of the Association for Supervision and Curriculum Development*. Alexandria, VA: ASCD.

ERIC Clearinghouse on Educational Management (1999). Accountability. *Research Roundup, 16*(1).

Finkelstein, N., & Grubb, N. (2000). Making sense of education and training markets: Lessons from England. *American Educational Research Journal, 37*(3), 601-632.

Firestone, W. A. (1989). Using reform: Conceptualizing district initiative. *Educational Evaluation and Policy Analysis, 11*(2), 151-164.

Forsyth, P., & Tallerico, M. (1998). Accountability and city school leadership. *Education and Urban Society, 30*(4), 546-555.

Fullan, M. (1999). *Change forces: The sequel*. London: Falmer Press.

Gantner, M., Newsom, J., & Dunlap, K. (2000, April). *Reconceptualizing the role of the principal: Giving voice to the silence*. Paper presented at the annual meeting of the American Educational Research Association, New Orleans, LA.

Giles, C. (1997). *School development planning: A practical guide to the strategic management process*. Plymouth, UK: Northcote House Publishers.

Grace, G. (1995). *School leadership: Beyond education management*. London: Falmer Press.

Hanushek, E., & Meyer, R. (1996). Comments on chapters two, three, and four. In H. Ladd (Ed.), *Holding schools accountable: Performance-based reform in education*. Washington, DC: The Brookings Institution.

Hausman, C. S. (2000). Principal role in magnet schools: Transformed or entrenched? *Journal of Educational Administration, 38*(1), 25-46.

Hess, G. A., Jr. (1991). *School restructuring Chicago style*. Newbury Park, CA: Corwin Press.

Illinois State Board of Education. (1999). *Performance-based accountability: System overview*. November 17. Springfield, IL.

Illinois State Board of Education. (2000). *Performance-based school designation system: Progress report and 1999-2001 interim warning/watch list recommendations*. January 19. Springfield, IL.

Kerchner, C. T. (1988). Bureaucratic entrepreneurship: The implications of choice for school administration. *Educational Administration Quarterly, 24*(4), 381-392.

Knapp, M. S. (1997). Between systemic reforms and the mathematics and science classroom: The dynamics of innovation, implementation, and professional learning. *Review of Educational Research, 67*(2), 227-266.

Lauder, H., & Hughes, D. (1999). *Trading in futures.* Buckingham, UK: Open University Press.

Leithwood, K., & Earl, L. (2000). Educational accountability effects: An international perspective. *Peabody Journal of Education, 75*(4).

Leithwood, K., Edge, K., & Jantzi, D. (1999). *Educational accountability: The state of the art.* Gutersloh, Germany: Bertelsmann Foundation Publishers.

Massell, D., & Goertz, M. (1999, April). *Local strategies for building capacity: The district role in supporting instructional reform.* Paper presented at the Annual Meeting of the American Educational Research Association, Montreal, Canada.

McLaughlin, M. W. (1987). Learning from experience: Lessons from policy implementation. *Educational Evaluation and Policy Analysis, 9*(2), 171-78.

McLaughlin, M. W. (1991). The Rand change agent study: Ten years later. In A. R. Odden (Ed.), *Education Policy Implementation* (pp. 143-156). Albany, NY: SUNY Press.

Murphy, J., & Beck, L. (1995). *School-based management as school reform.* Thousand Oaks, CA: Corwin Press.

Newmann, F. M., King, M., & Rigdon, M. (1997). Accountability and school performance: Implications for restructuring schools. *Harvard Educational Review, 67*(1), 41-74.

Ornstein, A. C. (1983). Administrative decentralization and community policy: Review and outlook. *Urban Review, 15*(1), 3-10.

Parker, K., & Leithwood, K. (2000). The influence of school councils on school and classroom practices. *Peabody Journal of Education, 75*(4), 37-65.

Peters, M. (1992). Performance indicators in New Zealand higher education: Accountability or control? *Journal of Education Policy, 7*(3), 267-283.

Rau, W. C. (2000). *Brass knuckles in velvet gloves: Illinois' school designation system as a case study in centralized state educational planning.* Unpublished paper. Bloomington, IL: Illinois State University.

Raywid, M. (1992). Choice orientations, discussions, and prospects. *Educational Policy, 6*(2), 105-122.

Rosenholtz, S. J. (1991). *Teachers' workplace: The social organization of schools.* New York: Teachers College Press.

Sizer, T. R. (1984). *Horace's compromise: The dilemma of the American high school.* Boston, MA: Houghton Mifflin.

Sizer, T. R. (1996). *Horace's hope: What works for the American high school.* Boston, MA: Houghton Mifflin.

Southworth, G. (1998). *Leading improving primary schools.* London: Falmer Press.

Spillane, J. (1994). How districts mediate between state policy and teachers' practice. In R. F. Elmore & S. H. Fuhrman (Eds.), *The Governance of Curriculum* (pp. 167-185). Alexandria, VA: ASCD.

Spillane, J. P., & Jennings, N. E. (1997). Aligned instructional policy and ambitious pedagogy: Exploring instructional reform from the classroom perspective. *Teachers College Record, 98*(3), 449-481.

Tacheny, S. (1999). If we build it, will they come? *Educational Leadership, 56*(6), 62-65.

Wiggins, G. P., & McTighe, J. (1998). *Understanding by design.* Alexandria, VA: ASCD.

Wildy, H., & Louden, W. (2000). School restructuring and the dilemma of principals' work. *Educational Management and Administration, 28*(2), 173-184.

Wohlstetter, P., & Mohrman, S. A. (1993). *School-based management: Strategies for success.* New Brunswick, NJ: Rutgers University.

Section Three
RECULTURING THE PROFESSION

CHAPTER 4

Reculturing the Profession of Educational Leadership: New Blueprints

JOSEPH MURPHY

Over the years, a number of colleagues have provided reviews of the profession in which they have taken stock of the field of school administration with the aim of helping us explore our development, locate the profession in the larger world of education ideas and practice, and offer insights about alternative futures (see Boyan, 1981; Boyd & Crowson, 1981; Campbell, Fleming, Newell, & Bennion, 1987; Erickson, 1977, 1979; Griffiths, 1988; March, 1978). During the last dozen years, some of my own work has attended to this stock-taking and directing function. Indeed, it is that work that provides the architecture for the current volume in general and the section on "reculturing the profession" in particular (Murphy, 1999). While elsewhere I have spent considerable space unpacking the historical foundations of school administration (Murphy, 1992), the spotlight in this volume is on informing the development of the next era of the profession.

The thesis of the chapter can be summarized in the following way:

(1) For some time now, the profession has been marked by considerable ferment as it has struggled to locate itself in a post-behavioral science era. During this era of turmoil, the historical foundations of the profession have been thrown into question, especially the legitimacy of the knowledge base supporting school administration and the appropriateness of programs for preparing school leaders.

Joseph Murphy is the William Ray Flesher Professor of Education at The Ohio State University and the President of the Ohio Principals Leadership Academy.

(2) A broad cut through the work of scholars in the field during this period provides some insights about new scaffolding on which to rebuild the profession. To be sure, the period has been marked by dysfunctional accommodations and limited vision about alternative futures. Nonetheless, a careful reading of the work of colleagues across the intellectual spectrum offers up a framework for rethinking school administration. Specifically, we see a powerful combination of three key concepts that provide new anchors for the profession—school improvement, democratic community, and social justice.

(3) Each of these anchors individually, and all three collectively, offer great promise for repositioning the profession of school administration. Together, they channel the work of colleagues into collective action around a coherent framework for school administration. The entire volume is predicated on this proposition. Part 3 of the book is given over to an exploration of each of these three new groundings, while parts 4 and 5 examine what such a reculturing will mean for research, policy, and practice in educational leadership.

This chapter[1] is devoted to two issues. First, I make the case for the new foundation for the profession as noted above. I begin by reviewing the methods traditionally used to define the profession and its work. I suggest that these methods will not prove successful in reculturing school leadership and argue for an alternative method to locate an appropriate portal to the future. In so doing, I retrace the steps that led to a new perspective, one that is based on the powerful unifying concepts of social justice, democratic community, and school improvement.

Second, using this alternative way of framing the profession, I present one framework for recasting the concept of leadership. In the process, I define school leadership in terms of three metaphors: moral steward, educator, and community builder.

Reculturing: The Bankruptcy of Traditional Ways of Doing Business

THE TRADITIONS

I will begin by laying out the traditional ways of thinking about school administration as a profession in general and the design of preparation and development of school leaders in particular. While there are a variety of possible approaches, let me present a roadmap that encompasses the four most well traveled pathways: Primacy of mental discipline (processes); primacy of the administrator (roles, functions, tasks); primacy of content (knowledge); and primacy of method.

A focus on mental discipline posits that particular content is less important than the development of processes or metacognitive skills. With deep roots in the dominant 17th and 18th centuries' understanding of learning, a mental discipline perspective views content as a vehicle for the development of important faculties such as observation, judgment, and perception. In this category one might include work on: (1) processes—such as the early work of Griffiths (1958) on administration as decision making or the more recent research of Leithwood (Leithwood & Stager, 1989) on administration as problem solving; (2) thinking/reflection—such as the scholarship of Ann Hart (1993), Chuck Kerchner (1993), and Karen Osterman and Robert Kottkamp (1993); and, at least for our purposes here, (3) ethics and values—such as the writings of Jerry Starratt (1991) and Lynn Beck (1994). In the practice wing of the professional edifice, one need look no further than the quite popular assessment centers of the National Association of Secondary School Principals and the National Association of Elementary School Principals to see the vitality of the mental discipline approach that grounds the profession.

Highlighting the role of the administrator privileges issues related to the activities of school leaders. A review of the literature reveals that the key constructs here are: (1) *roles*—as portrayed in the work of Arthur Blumberg (Blumberg & Blumberg, 1985), Larry Cuban (1976), Susan Moore Johnson (1996), and Richard Wallace (1996) on the superintendency; Hartzell, Williams, and Nelson (1995) and Catherine Marshall (1992) on the assistant principalship; and Terry Deal and Kent Peterson (1990), Ellen Goldring and Sharon Rallis (1993), Phil Hallinger and Charlie Hausman (1994), Ann Hart and Paul Bredeson (1996), Karen Seashore Louis (Louis & Murphy, 1994), Nona Prestine (1994), Tom Sergiovanni (1991) and a host of others on the principalship; (2) *functions*—described in work by Martha McCarthy, Nina Cambron-McCabe, and S. B. Thomason (1998) on law; David Monk and Marge Plecki (1999) on finance; and Phil Young (Young, Place, Rinehart, Jury, & Baits, 1997) and William Castetter (1986) in the personnel area; and (3) *tasks*—as described in the writings of John Daresh (1989) and Tom Sergiovanni and Jerry Starratt (1988) on supervising employees.

Spotlighting content places knowledge at the center of the administrative stage. Historically, this approach has two epistemological axes—discipline-based (or technical) knowledge and practice-based

knowledge—axes that are regularly portrayed as being under considerable tension. Reform efforts in the current ferment tend to spotlight
this knowledge sector of our four-part framework. Work devoted to
the technical or academic domain is of three types: (1) struggles over
the meaning and viability of knowledge-based foundations for the profession; (2) attempts to widen the traditional knowledge domains that
define school administration, e.g., the infusion of ethics and values,
cultural and gender-based perspectives, and critical viewpoints into the
profession; and (3) analyses and initiatives either to recast the knowledge base of the field for the future (e.g., the recent NPBEA and
UCEA curriculum development work) or to establish a new discipline-
based ground for the profession (e.g., policy analysis). In the practice
domain, one main thrust has been the relegitimization of the craft
aspects of the profession, including the recognition of ideas, such as
"stories," that came under heavy critique during the scientific era. A
second thrust has been the work of scholars like Paula Silver (1986,
1987) and Ed Bridges and Phil Hallinger (1992, 1993) to codify and
make more systematic practices that have traditionally been available in
only an ad hoc form.

Finally, the field of school administration can be conceptualized in
terms of methods. Like the other three areas, methods can be viewed as
a basis for redefining school administration. As with mental discipline,
methods pull processes into the foreground while often, but not always,
pushing other issues into the background. One line of work in this area
has focused on efforts to strengthen methods in educational administration research. In addition, much of the work in school administration in this domain has been in the service of developing a more robust
portfolio of designs—in both the research and application domains. On
the issue of a more robust portfolio of research strategies, the work of
qualitative methodologists such as Yvonna Lincoln (Lincoln & Guba,
1985) and of scholars employing non-traditional approaches (see Griffiths, 1991) is noteworthy. In the application domain, the scholarship of
Bridges and Hallinger (1992, 1993) on problem-based learning is
becoming increasingly woven into the profession, as are a renewed
emphasis on case studies and an array of strategies such as journal writing, novels, films, reflective essays, and autobiographies.

AN INADEQUATE GUIDE

The central dilemma that we face is that none of these four ways of
thinking about the profession is likely to provide the appropriate conceptual scaffolding for reculturing the profession. Let me demonstrate

this by examining how the most popular line of work on redefining school administration—the development of a more robust body of scholarship—is unlikely to carry us to the next phase of development. Similar cases could be made against any of the other three elements of the framework as well.

A single breakout point. The central problem is that our fascination with building the academic infrastructure of school administration has produced some serious distortions in what is primarily an applied field. It is difficult to see how renewed vigor in this area will do much to extract us from these difficulties. As a matter of fact, a case can be made that such efforts simply exacerbate existing problems and deepen the fissures that mark the profession. To begin with, since academic knowledge is largely the purview of professors, the focus on technical knowledge places the university in the center of the field—a sort of pre-Copernican worldview of the profession. This perspective creates serious reference misalignment, strongly suggesting that the primary reference group for academics is other professors.

There are other reasons to believe that a primary focus on content, especially technical knowledge, is as likely to reinforce problems as it is to lay the foundations for reculturing school administration. If one believes that the best predictor of future behavior is past behavior, then a content-based attack on the problems of ferment and fragmentation will probably solidify the orientation of professors to the various academic disciplines rather than to the field of school administration, with its problems and challenges. The quest for deeper and more robust knowledge becomes little more than academic trophy hunting. Under this scenario, new content, no matter how appealing the topics, is no more likely to improve the profession than did the content being replaced. I believe that there is ample evidence of this dynamic already in the "more appropriate" knowledge areas being mined today (e.g., ethics, social context, critical theory, and so forth).

Keeping the spotlight focused on academic knowledge also leads to, or at least reinforces, the belief that better theories will be the savior of administrative practice. That is, if we can just develop better theories, the educational world would be a better place, educational administration programs would be stronger, and graduates would be more effective leaders. The problem is that the development of better, or more refined, or more elegant theories in and of itself will have almost no impact on the practice of school administration. Such work has not had much impact in the past, it is not having much influence now, and it is unlikely to be more efficacious in the future. Worse, this work often reinforces the centrality of the university, makes knowledge an end rather than a means for improvement, privileges knowledge over values, and, quite frankly, diverts energy from other, much more needed work.

All of this has led us to spend considerable time talking about constructing what might charitably be labeled as a "bridge to nowhere." That is, having made academic knowledge the coin of the realm, and having seen its inability to penetrate the world of schooling, we have been forced to develop strategies to try to transport knowledge from the academic to the practice community. The focus is on the development of knowledge in one place and its transfer to another. I think that if we have learned anything over the last 30 years, it is that this bridge metaphor is largely inappropriate. When you examine this issue in a clear light, you really do not see much interest in actually doing the work necessary to build this bridge. People on both sides of the river seem to be fairly content where they are. What's more, if through some magic the bridge were ever constructed, I do not think it would end up carrying much traffic.

A related case can also be developed against making practice-based knowledge the gold standard for reculturing the profession. The central problem here is that the practice of educational leadership has very little to do with either education or leadership. Thus weaving together threads from practice to form a post-theory tapestry of school administration is a very questionable idea. A number of analysts have concluded that schools are organized and managed as if we had no knowledge of either student learning or the needs of professional adults. Others have discovered that the schools are administered in such ways that educational goals are undermined and learning is hindered, especially for lower ability students. Still others have built a fairly strong case over the last 70 years that the profession has drawn energy almost exclusively from the taproot of management and the ideology of corporate America. The message—perhaps to state the obvious—is that this practice knowledge is not exactly the raw material from which to build a future for the profession.

I do not mean to dismiss knowledge as unimportant. Scientific inquiry, scholarly insights, and craft knowledge will offer useful substance in the process of reculturing school administration. In fact, we will not be able to create a future without these critical components. However, if we expect a concerted effort primarily on this front to provide sufficient material to construct a new profession, we will likely be disappointed. Worse, over-reliance on the cultivation of knowledge, either in academia or in practice, is likely to exacerbate deeply rooted problems in the profession. And what is true for a focus specifically on content holds also, I argue, for methods, processes, and administrator roles and functions.

A collective attack. If none of the four traditional ways we have thought about the profession looks promising as a vehicle to help us recast our understanding of school administration, will not continued progress on all fronts guide us in our efforts? It is possible to envision a productive tension among the four ideas that, in turn, fosters creative dialogue and action. But the history of the field does not allow us to be too sanguine about this collective strategy. There is little reason to expect any common platform to result from this approach. It seems more likely that continued fragmentation and an absence of synergy will thwart the progress of the profession.

The more recent evidence on this strategy—which Donmoyer (1999) calls the "big tent" philosophy (p. 30), and which Campbell and his colleagues (1987) characterize as "paradigm enlargement" (p. 209)—is not encouraging either. After 15 years of following this approach, the arena of school administration today looks a good deal like Weick's (1976) famous tilted soccer field or, perhaps even more aptly, like typical American high schools of the last half of the 20th century, which Powell, Farrar, and Cohen (1985) have labeled "shopping malls." We have responded to the challenges of purpose and development largely by ignoring them, or at least failing to grapple with them thoughtfully. We have done exactly what high schools have done; we have created a plethora of specialty shops for everyone who wants to move into the big tent. And like the players and fans in Weick's soccer game, we have allowed everyone to establish his or her own rules and his or her own definitions of success. Everyone has his or her own booth in the tent and goes about his or her business with very few tethers to anything like a core, and little concern for coherence. Largely unencumbered by mutually forged benchmarks and standards, everyone carries on with considerable thoughtfulness—or at least politeness—and with very little real conflict. Autonomy and civility rule. School administration as a profession stagnates.

Doing nothing. If traditional frameworks offer insufficient force—either on a strategy-by-strategy or on a collective basis—to reculture the profession, then where do we turn? Before moving on to what I believe is a way out of this impasse, let me review a third possibility that is seen increasingly in the literature. This third option is to dismiss the notion that common scaffolding for the profession is a worthwhile idea. Certainly the discussion of a core for reculturing school adminis-tration will cause consternation if not alarm among some colleagues. The very concept of a core carries the potential to privilege certain ideas while marginalizing others. Let me acknowledge at the outset that this is a quite legitimate concern and one that we had to struggle to address in developing the Interstate School Leaders Licensure Con-sortium's *Standards for School Leaders*. Yet the concern is not sufficient, at least from where I sit, to merit delaying action. I believe that this third avenue of response—rejection of the possibility of an alternative framework—is likely to lead to, in the words of Evers and Lakomski (1996a), "skepticism and enfeebling relativism" (p. 342).

Recognizing that all knowledge and action are political does not mean that all knowledge and action are equal. I believe that Willower (1998) provides the high ground here when he reminds us that "some constructions of reality are better than others" (p. 450). I would go further and suggest that in the world of ideas, diversity is not in and of itself a virtue. More important, I would encourage us to be skeptical of the viewpoint that a common framework for redefining the profession will only advantage some ideas and marginalize others. Centers can empower as well as constrain.

A NEW PERSPECTIVE

So far, I have argued that doing nothing—giving up or resisting the search for a directing future for the profession—is not a wise idea, nor is it necessary to protect the interests of scholars with diverse view-points. I have also suggested that a concerted effort to move to a new era for school administration by focusing on any given element of extant framework we use to define ourselves, e.g., the production of new theoretical knowledge, will not likely serve us well either. Finally, I maintained that an eclectic or big tent strategy in this era of ferment is as likely to be riddled with problems as to be marked with benefits. What is left? One answer lies in Herbert Kliebard's work (1995). Building on the ideas of Dewey, Kliebard introduces a patched-together concept called a "principle of correspondence" (p. 57). This is his way of describing Dewey's efforts to recast problems not in terms of selecting among alternatives but in terms of "the critical problem of finding a principle" (p. 57) to provide correspondence among valued dimensions of a profession. For me, this approach provides a way of recasting a dilemma that by definition is not solvable into a problem that is, or at least may be, successfully attacked. In effect, it provides a new way of defining the profession—a "synthesizing paradigm" (Boyan, 1981, p. 10) that focuses on defining aims rather than stirring the academic caldron or parsing out administrative activities.

How can we frame a principle of correspondence to meet our needs? While there is a good deal of open space here, it probably is desirable to hold any principle of correspondence to the following seven standards:

- It should acknowledge and respect the diversity of work afoot in educational administration yet exercise sufficient force—or what Boyan (1981) refers to as "intellectual magnetism" (p. 12)—to pull much of that work in certain directions.
- It should be informed by, and help organize ideas from, the current ferment.
- It should promote the development of a body of ideas and concepts that define school administration as an applied field.
- It should provide hope for reconciling the enduring dualisms described by Campbell and his colleagues (1987) that have bedeviled the profession for so long (e.g., knowledge vs. values, academic knowledge vs. practice knowledge) and should, to quote Evers and Lakomski (1996a), provide a "powerful touchstone for adjudicating rival approaches to administrative research" (p. 343).
- It should provide a forum where mere civility among shop merchants in the big tent gives way to productive dialogue and exchange.
- It should be clear about the outcomes it will use to forge a redefined profession of school administration; in other words, it should provide the means for linking the profession to valued outcomes.
- It should establish a framework to ensure that the "standard for what is taught lies not with bodies of subject matter" (Kliebard, 1995, p. 72) but with valued ends.

Where might we find such a principle of correspondence? A number of thoughtful colleagues have provided frameworks that offer the potential to meet Kliebard's (1995) criterion of "reconstructing the questions as to present new [alternatives]" (p. 49) and that fit at least some of the standards outlined above. My purpose here is not to develop a comprehensive listing, nor is it to evaluate each of the examples. My limited objective is simply to show how some colleagues in the profession have helped us exit the current turmoil by employing strategies that fit into the broad category of "principle of correspondence."

A number of such efforts stand out. At least four with a knowledge-base flavor deserve mention. To begin with, there is Griffiths' (1995, 1997) recent work on what he refers to as "theoretical pluralism" (1997, p. 371), but theoretical pluralism that is intrinsically yoked to problems of practice. There is also the scholarship of Willower (1996) on naturalistic philosophy or naturalistic pragmatism. A related line of work, which might be best labeled "pragmatism," has been developed by Hoy (1996). The scholarship of Evers and Lakomski (1996b) on "developing a systematic new science of administration" (p. 379)— what they describe as "naturalistic coherentism" (p. 385)—is a fourth example of a principle of correspondence at work. The most important example with a practice focus is the work of Bridges and Hallinger (1992, 1995) on problem-based learning. Ideas bridging both the academic and practice camps have been provided by Donmoyer (1999), who introduces the concept of "utilitarianism" as a potential way to redefine debate and action in the profession and by Murphy (1992), who discusses a "dialectic" (p. 67) strategy.

Thus, a number of colleagues have begun doing some of the heavy lifting to help us conceptualize new ways to think about reculturing school administration. Individually and collectively, they offer bundles of ideas—such as a problem-solving focus and emphasis on the concrete—highlighting the sense of possibilities that offer real promise to the profession.

At the same time, each of the approaches I have just mentioned falls short when measured against our standards for a principle of correspondence. With the possible exception of the last two (Donmoyer, 1999 and Murphy, 1992), each approach remains too closely associated with one or the other of the traditional ways in which we have framed the profession, in nearly every case with a focus on knowledge production. We can, however, build on these and other breakout ideas to move a little closer to our goal.

The question at hand is this: When we layer knowledge about the well-known shortcomings of the profession onto understandings developing in the current ferment, and then apply the notion of a principle of correspondence with its imbedded standards, what emerges? Three powerful synthetic paradigms become visible: social justice, school improvement, and democratic community. Each of these offers the potential to capture many of the benefits revealed by the standards and in the process reculture school administration. Collectively, they offer a robust model to overhaul the profession.

The next three chapters unpack each of these synthetic models. In each case, the authors explore what the particular framework might mean for the profession of school administration. Authors of later chapters investigate what anchoring school administration in concepts such as social justice, democratic community, and school improvement implies for school leadership as an applied discipline. Before we proceed to these analyses, however, it is helpful to examine the changing definition of "leadership" in a profession built on the foundations of social justice, school improvement, and democratic community.

New Foundations: New Understandings of Leadership

In this section, I use three metaphors to sketch a portrait of leadership for the recultured profession—moral steward, educator, and community builder. In so doing, I acknowledge a debt to Sergiovanni (1991), who reminds us that "changing our metaphors is an important prerequisite for developing a new theory of management and a new leadership practice" (p. 69).

MORAL STEWARD

The metaphor of the administrator as moral steward takes on many forms. However, at its core is one fundamental belief: that "the new science of administration will be a science with values and of values" (Greenfield, 1988, p. 155). Moral leadership acknowledges that "values and value judgments are the central elements in the selection, extension, and day-to-day realization of educational purpose" (Harlow, 1962, p. 67).

As moral stewards, school leaders will be much more heavily invested in "purpose-defining" (Harlow, 1962, p. 61) activities and in "reflective analysis and . . . active intervention" (Bates, 1984, p. 268) than simply in managing existing arrangements. This means that people who want to affect society as school leaders must be directed by a powerful portfolio of beliefs and values anchored in issues such as justice, community, and schools that function for all children and youth. They must maintain a critical capacity and foster a sense of possibilities, and "bring to their enterprise a certain passion that affects others deeply" (Sergiovanni, 1991, p. 334). They must view their task more as a mission than a job; "they must develop strong commitments to important things and model them persuasively" (Moorman, 1990, p. 101); "the task of the leader is to create a moral order that bonds both leader and followers to a set of shared values and beliefs" (Sergiovanni, 1989b, p. 34). Therefore, moral leadership means that tomorrow's school administrators must use their personal platform to "engage participants in the organization and the community in reinterpreting and placing new priorities on guiding values for education" (Moorman, p. 98) and in rebuilding "structures so that they celebrate the intended educational purposes of the school community" (Bates, p. 268).

At a quite practical level, leadership as moral stewardship means seeing the moral and ethical implications of the thousand daily decisions made by each school administrator (Beck & Murphy, 1998). In its most comprehensive and concrete form it means building an ethical school (Starratt, 1991) while meeting the "moral imperative to provide real learning opportunities to the whole of the student population" (Osin & Lesgold, 1996, p. 621).

EDUCATOR

The educational roots of the profession of school administration atrophied over the course of the 20th century as the field gravitated toward conceptions of leadership based on scientific images of business management and social science research. In the recultured profession proffered in this volume, there is an explicit acknowledgment of the "pathology of such an approach to educational administration" (Bates, 1984, p. 26). Stated more positively, there is a recognition that "the deep significance of the task of the school administrator is to be found in the pedagogic ground of its vocation" (Evans, 1991, p. 17), that a key to reculturing is changing the profession's compass from management to education. The educator metaphor legitimates Bill Greenfield's (1995) proposition that "although numerous sources might be cultivated, norms rooted in the ethos and culture of teaching as a profession provide the most effective basis for leadership in a school" (p. 75). It infuses what Evans (1998) nicely describes as the "pedagogic motive" (p. 41) into the lifeblood of school leadership. It repositions leading from management to learning (Institute for Educational Leadership, 2000). It requires, as Rowan (1995) has observed, that leaders be "pioneers in the development and management of new forms of instructional practice in schools, and [that] they . . . [develop] a thorough understanding of the rapidly evolving body of research on learning and teaching that motivate[s] these new practices" (p. 116). Because the challenge for educational leaders will be "to refocus the structure [of schooling] on some new conception of teaching and learning" (Elmore, 1990, p. 63), they will need to be more broadly educated in general and much more knowledgeable about the core technology of education in particular. "Instructional and curricular leadership must be at the forefront of leadership skills" (Hallinger, 1990, p. 77). In a rather dramatic shift from earlier times, school and district administrators will be asked to exercise intellectual leadership not as head teachers, but as head learners.

COMMUNITY BUILDER

The job of the administrator as community builder unfolds in three distinct but related dimensions (Murphy, Beck, Crawford, Hodges & McGoughy, 2001). The first venue is with parents and members of the school environment. Here the role of the administrator is to nurture the development of open systems where access and voice are honored. On a second level, the struggle is to foster the evolution of "communities of learning" (Zeichner & Tabachnich, 1991, p. 9) among professional staff. Finally, an unrelenting focus on the creation of personalized learning environments for youngsters is a central aspect of the community building function of school leaders.

The job of a community builder requires a multitude of new ways of doing business (Beck & Foster, 1999). Leaders need to adopt strategies and styles that are in harmony with the central tenets of the "heterarchical" school organizations they seek to create; they must learn to lead not from the apex of the organizational pyramid but from a web of interpersonal relationships—with people rather than through them. Their base of influence must be professional expertise and moral imperative rather than line authority. They must learn to lead by empowering rather than by controlling others. "Such concepts as purposing, working to build a shared covenant" (Sergiovanni, 1989, p. 33), and establishing meaning—rather than directing, controlling, and supervising— are at the core of this type of leadership. Empowering leadership, in turn, is "based on dialogue and cooperative, democratic leadership principles" (Bolin, 1989, p. 86). Enabling leadership also has a softer, less heroic hue. It is more ethereal and less direct: "Symbolic and cultural leadership are key leadership forces" (Sergiovanni, 1989, p. 33). There is as much heart as head in this style of leading. It is grounded more in modeling and clarifying values and beliefs than in telling people what to do. Its goals include "ministering" (Sergiovanni, 1991, p. 335) to the needs of organizational members, rather than gaining authority over them, and creating "new structures that enable the emergence of leadership on a broad basis" (Sykes & Elmore, 1989, p. 79). This is more reflective and self-critical leadership than bureaucratic management.

As community builders, school administrators must encourage "others to be leaders in their own right" (Sergiovanni, 1991, p. 335). Administrators need to stretch leadership across organizational actors and roles (Spillane, Diamond, & Jita, 2000) to ensure that leadership is deeply distributed (Elmore, 1999). They also need to demonstrate the ethic of care to all members of the larger school community (Beck, 1994).

Conclusion

In this chapter, we assembled the raw material to be used in rebuilding the profession of school administration. We selected the foundations that we did because we concluded that the traditional ways of defining the profession were inadequate to the task of reculturing. We also believe that the work of many colleagues across the full spectrum of the profession exposes the presence of a powerful synthesizing paradigm that can carry us into the future, one that fuses the three powerful constructs of school improvement, social justice, and democratic community. In concluding, we described three metaphors that correspond to these concepts and that create an alternative platform for thinking about school leadership.

NOTE

1. This chapter is built from two earlier investigations on this topic (Murphy, 1992, 1999).

REFERENCES

Bates, R. J. (1984). Toward a critical practice of educational administration. In T. J. Sergiovanni & J. E. Corbally (Eds.), *Leadership and organizational culture: New perspectives on administrative theory and practice* (pp. 260-274). Urbana: University of Illinois Press.

Beck, L. G. (1994). *Reclaiming educational administration as a caring profession.* New York: Teachers College Press.

Beck, L. G., & Foster, W. (1999). Administration and community: Considering challenges, exploring possibilities. In J. Murphy & K. S. Louis (Eds.), *Handbook of research on educational administration* (2nd ed., pp. 337-358). San Francisco: Jossey-Bass.

Blumberg, A., & Blumberg, P. (1992). *The school superintendent: Living with conflict.* New York: Columbia University, Teachers College.

Bolin, F. S. (1989, Fall). Empowering leadership. *Teachers College Record, 91*(1), 81-96.

Boyan, N. J. (1981, February). Follow the leader: Commentary on research in educational administration. *Educational Research, 10*(2), 6-13, 21.

Boyd, W. L., & Crowson, R. L. (1981). The changing conception and practice of public school administration. In D. C. Berliner (Ed.), *Review of research in education* (Vol. 9, pp. 311-373). Washington, DC: American Educational Research Association.

Bridges, E. M., & Hallinger, P. (1992). *Problem-based learning for administrators.* Eugene, OR: University of Oregon, ERIC Clearinghouse on Educational Management.

Bridges, E. M., & Hallinger, P. (1993). Problem-based learning in medical and managerial education. In P. Hallinger, K. Leithwood, & J. Murphy (Eds.), *Cognitive perspectives on educational leadership* (pp. 253-267). New York: Teachers College Press.

Bridges, E. M., & Hallinger, P. (1995). *Implementing problem-based learning in leadership development.* Eugene, OR: University of Oregon, ERIC Clearinghouse on Educational Management.

Campbell, R. F., Fleming, T., Newell, L. J., & Bennion, J. W. (1987). *A history of thought and practice in educational administration.* New York: Teachers College Press.

Castetter, W. B. (1986). *The personnel function in educational administration* (4th ed.). New York: Macmillan.

Cuban, L. (1976). *Urban school chiefs under fire.* Chicago: University of Chicago Press.

Daresh, J. C. (1989). *Supervision as a proactive process.* New York: Longman.

Deal, T. E., & Peterson, K. D. (1990). *The principal's role in shaping school culture.* Washington, DC: U.S. Department of Education, Office of Educational Research and Improvement.

Elmore, R. F. (1990, September). *Reinventing school leadership* (pp. 62-65) [Working memo prepared for the Reinventing School Leadership Conference]. Cambridge, MA: National Center for Educational Leadership.

Elmore, R. F. (1999, September). *Leadership of large-scale improvement in American education.* Paper prepared for the Albert Shanker Institute.

Erickson, D. A. (1977). An overdue paradigm shift in educational administration, or how can we get that idiot off the freeway. In L. L. Cunningham, W. G. Hack, & R. O. Nystrand (Eds.), *Educational administration: The developing decades* (pp. 114-143). Berkeley, CA: McCutchan.

Erickson, D. A. (1979, March). Research on educational administration: The state-of-the-art. *Educational Researcher, 8*, 9-14.

Evans, R. (1991, April). *Administrative insight: Educational administration as pedagogic practice.* Paper presented at the annual meeting of the American Educational Research Association, Chicago.

Evans, R. (1998, Summer). Do intentions matter? Questioning the text of a high school principal. *Journal of Educational Administration and Foundations, 13*(1), 30-51.

Evers, C. W., & Lakomski, G. (1996a, August). Postpositivist conceptions of science in educational administration: An introduction. *Educational Administration Quarterly, 32*(3), 341-343.

Evers, C. W., & Lakomski, G. (1996b, August). Science in educational administration: A postpositivist conception. *Educational Administration Quarterly, 32*(32), 379-402.

Goldring, E. B., & Rallis, S. F. (1993). *Principals of dynamic schools: Taking charge of change.* Newbury Park, CA: Corwin Press.

Greenfield, T. B. (1988). The decline and fall of science in educational administration. In D. E. Griffiths, R. T. Stout, & P. B. Forsyth (Eds.), *Leaders for America's schools* (pp. 131-159). Berkeley, CA: McCutchan.

Greenfield, W. D. (1995, February). Toward a theory of school administration: The centrality of leadership. *Educational Administration Quarterly, 31*(1), 61-85.

Griffiths, D. E. (1985). Administration as decision-making. In A. W. Halpin (Ed.), *Administrative theory in education.* Chicago: University of Chicago, Midwest Administration Center.

Griffiths, D. E. (1988). *Educational administration: Reform PDQ or RIP* (Occasional paper, no. 8312). Tempe, AZ: University Council for Educational Administration.

Griffiths, D. E. (Ed.). (1991). Special issue: Non-traditional research methods in educational administration. *Educational Administration Quarterly, 27*(3).

Griffiths, D. E. (1995). Theoretical pluralism in educational administration. In R. Donmoyer, M. Imber, & J. J. Scheurich (Eds.), *The knowledge base in educational administration: Multiple perspectives* (pp. 300-309). Albany, NY: SUNY Press.

Griffiths, D. E. (1997, October). The case for theoretical pluralism. *Educational Management and Administration, 25*(4), 371-380.

Hallinger, P. (1990). *Reinventing school leadership* (pp. 75-78) [Working memo prepared for the Reinventing School Leadership Conference]. Cambridge, MA: National Center for Educational Leadership.

Hallinger, P., & Hausman, C. (1994). From Attila the Hun to Mary Had a Little Lamb: Principal role ambiguity in restructured schools. In J. Murphy & K. S. Louis (Eds.), *Reshaping the principalship: Insights from transformational reform efforts* (pp. 154-176). Newbury Park, CA: Corwin Press.

Harlow, J. G. (1962). Purpose-defining: The central function of the school administrator. In J. A. Culbertson & S. P. Hencley (Eds.), *Preparing administrators: New perspectives* (pp. 61-71). Columbus, OH: University Council for Educational Administration.

Hart, A. W. (1993). A design studio for reflective practice. In P. Hallinger, K. Leithwood, & J. Murphy (Eds.), *Cognitive perspectives on educational leadership* (pp. 218-230). New York: Teachers College Press.

Hart, A. W., & Bredeson, P. V. (1996). *The principalship: A theory of professional learning and practice.* New York: McGraw-Hill.

Hartzell, G. N., Williams, R. C., & Nelson, K. T. (1995). *New voices in the field: The work lives of first-year assistant principals.* Newbury Park, CA: Corwin Press.

Hoy, W. K. (1996, August). Science and theory in the practice of educational administration: A pragmatic perspective. *Educational Administration Quarterly, 32*(3), 366-378.

Institute for Educational Leadership (2000, October). *Leadership for student learning: Reinventing the principalship.* Washington, DC: Author.

Johnson, S. M. (1996). *Leading to change: The challenge of the new superintendency.* San Francisco: Jossey-Bass.

Kerchner, C. T. (1993). The strategy of teaching strategy. In P. Hallinger, K. Leithwood, & J. Murphy (Eds.), *Cognitive perspectives on educational leadership* (pp. 5-20). New York: Teachers College Press.

Kliebard, H. M. (1995). *The struggle for the American curriculum 1893-1958* (2nd ed.). New York: Routledge.

Leithwood, K., & Stager, M. (1989, May). Expertise in principals' problem solving. *Educational Administration Quarterly, 25*(2), 126-151.

Lincoln, Y. S., & Guba, E. G. (1985). *Naturalistic inquiry.* Beverly Hills, CA: Sage.

Louis, K. S., & Murphy, J. (1994). The evolving role of the principal: Some concluding thoughts. In J. Murphy and K. S. Louis (Eds.), *Reshaping the principalship: Insights from transformational reform efforts* (pp. 265-281). Newbury Park, CA: Corwin Press.

March, J. G. (1978, February). American public school administration: A short analysis. *School Review, 86,* 217-250.

Marshall, C. (1992). *The assistant principal: Leadership choices and challenges.* Newbury Park, CA: Corwin Press.

McCarthy, M. M., Cambron-McCabe, N. H., & Thomas, S. B. (1998). *Public school law: Teachers' and students' rights.* Boston: Allyn and Bacon.

Monk, D. K., & Plecki, M. L. (1999). Generating and managing resources for school improvement. In J. Murphy and K. S. Louis (Eds.), *Handbook of research on educational administration* (2nd ed.) (pp. 491-510). San Francisco: Jossey-Bass.

Moorman, H. (1990, September). *Reinventing school leadership* (pp. 98-103) [Working memo prepared for the Reinventing School Leadership Conference]. Cambridge, MA: National Center for Educational Leadership.

Murphy, J. (1992). *The landscape of leadership preparation: Reframing the education of school administrators.* Newbury Park, CA: Corwin Press.

Murphy, J. (1999). *The quest for a center: Notes on the state of the profession of educational administration.* Columbia, MO: University Council for Educational Administration.

Murphy, J., Beck, L. G., Crawford, M., Hodges, A., & McGoughy, C. L. (2001). *The productive high school: Creating personalized academic communities.* Thousand Oaks, CA: Corwin.

Osin, L., & Lesgold, A. (1996, Winter). A proposal for the reengineering of the educational system. *Review of Educational Research, 66*(4), 621-656.

Osterman, K. F., & Kottkamp, R. B. (1993). *Reflective practice for educators: Improving schooling through professional development.* Newbury Park, CA: Corwin Press.

Powell, A. G., Farrar, E., & Cohen, D. K. (1985). *The shopping mall high school: Winners and losers in the educational marketplace.* Boston: Houghton Mifflin.

Prestine, N. A. (1994). Ninety degrees from everywhere: New understandings of the principal's role in a restructuring Essential School. In J. Murphy and K. S. Louis (Eds.), *Reshaping the principalship: Insights from transformational reform efforts* (pp. 123-153). Newbury Park, CA: Corwin Press.

Rowan, B. (1995, February). Research on learning and teaching in K-12 schools: Implications for the field of educational administration. *Educational Administration Quarterly, 31*(1), 115-133.

Sergiovanni, T. J., & Starratt, R. J. (1988). *Supervision: Human perspectives* (4th ed.). New York: McGraw-Hill.

Sergiovanni, T. J. (1989). Value-driven schools: The amoeba theory. In H. J. Walberg & J. J. Lane (Eds.), *Organizing for learning: Toward the 21st century* (pp. 31-40). Reston, VA: National Association of Secondary School Principals.

Sergiovanni, T. J. (1991). *The principalship: A reflective practice perspective* (2nd ed.). Boston: Allyn & Bacon.

Silver, P. F. (1986, Summer). Case records: A reflective practice approach to administrator development. *Theory into Practice, 25*(3), 161-167.

Silver, P. F. (1987). The Center for Advancing Principal Excellence (APEX): An approach to professionalizing educational administration. In J. Murphy & P. Hallinger (Eds.), *Approaches to administrative training in education* (pp. 67-82). Albany, NY: SUNY Press.

Spillane, J. P., Diamond, J. B., & Loyiso, J. (2000, April). *Leading classroom instruction: A preliminary exploration of the distribution of leadership practice.* Paper presented at the annual meeting of the American Educational Research Association, New Orleans.

Starratt, R. J. (1991, May). Building an ethical school: A theory for practice in educational leadership. *Educational Administration Quarterly, 27*(2), 185-202.

Sykes, G., & Elmore, R. F. (1989). Making schools more manageable. In J. Hannaway & R. L. Crowson (Eds.), *The politics of reforming school administrations* (pp. 77-94). New York: Falmer Press.

Wallace, R. C. (1996). *From vision to practice: The art of educational leadership*. Thousand Oaks, CA: Corwin Press.

Weick, K. E. (1976). Educational organizations as loosely coupled systems. *Administrative Science Quarterly, 21,* 1-19.

Willower, D. J. (1998, September). Fighting the fog: A criticism of postmodernism. *Journal of School Leadership, 8*(5), 448-463.

Young, I. P., Place, A. W., Rinehart, J. S., Jury, J. C., & Baits, D. F. (1997). Teacher recruitment: A test of the similarity-attraction hypothesis for race and sex. *Educational Administration Quarterly, 33*(1), 86-106.

Zeichner, K. M., & Tabachnich, B. R. (1991). Reflections on reflective teaching. In B. R. Tabachnich & K. M. Zeichner (Eds.), *Issues and practices in inquiry-oriented teacher education*. London: Falmer Press.

CHAPTER 5

School Improvement Processes and Practices: Professional Learning for Building Instructional Capacity

JAMES P. SPILLANE AND KAREN SEASHORE LOUIS

The belief that the school is the key unit of change has become something of a mantra among scholars and practitioners over the past 20 years. Hence, efforts to understand the process of school improvement, as well as a variety of interventions that focus on school improvement, have flourished. Our goal in this paper is not to undertake an exhaustive review of the literature on school improvement, but rather to frame or perhaps reframe this work. Specifically, we stand back from scholarship that falls under the school improvement rubric and develop a conceptual scaffold for thinking about this line of research and its relation to teaching and learning in schools.

We begin by arguing that the bottom line for school improvement initiatives is student learning. Hence, school improvement has to be about improving students' opportunities to learn in order to improve both easily measurable and subtler achievement. While that may be an obvious point, in much of the literature relations between the process of school improvement and students' opportunities to learn remain implicit or blurred. Our central task in this chapter is to develop a framework for making relations between the process and practice of school improvement and students' opportunities to learn more explicit. Because classroom instruction is the proximal cause of students' opportunities to learn, we begin by adopting a perspective on instruction that anchors our model of the school improvement process. We argue that absent such a framework, it is difficult to explicate relations between school improvement and students' opportunities to learn. Next, adopting a "backward mapping" strategy (Elmore, 1979) we work backwards

Karen Seashore Louis is Professor of Educational Policy and Administration in the College of Education and Human Development at the University of Minnesota and Director of the Center for Applied Research and Educational Improvement. James Spillane is Associate Professor in the School of Education and Social Policy and Faculty Fellow at the Institute for Policy Research, Northwestern University.

from instruction to the classroom community and the school's professional community as sites for teacher learning, without which classroom opportunities for students cannot improve. Next, we consider organizational learning as the bridge that connects these two sites for teacher learning. Then we consider the challenges to school leaders. Drawing on a variety of literatures, including those that fall under the rather inclusive rubric of school improvement, we develop a framework for thinking about the school improvement process that is closely linked to classroom instruction.

Instruction and Its Improvement

What students come to know and understand about mathematics, reading, and other subjects depends in important measure on their opportunities to learn. *What* gets taught is a strong predictor of student achievement. How the curriculum is taught is equally important (Newmann & Associates, 1996). But students within the same school do not all have an equal opportunity to learn. Research consistently finds that there is more variability in student learning within schools than between them. Much of this is due to factors that cannot easily be affected by the school, such as students' socio-economic backgrounds. There is also evidence, however, that much of this within-school variation in learning is due to variation in the classroom settings experienced by students (Education Trust, 1999). Hence, teachers' performance is critical in efforts to improve instructional capacity.[1]

We borrow a formulation of instruction and instructional capacity from David Cohen and Deborah Ball, who argue that instruction is a function of what teachers know and can do with particular students around specific material (both physical and intellectual material) (Cohen & Ball, 1998). Instruction is constituted in the interaction of teacher, students, and material—three elements in what Cohen and Ball term an "instructional unit." Teachers' intellectual resources (e.g., subject matter knowledge) influence how they understand and respond to materials and students. Students' experiences, understandings, dispositions, and commitments influence what they make of teacher direction and materials. Materials (e.g., books, curricula), as well as the intellectual tasks, mediate teacher and student interactions. With respect to instructional improvement, Cohen and Ball argue that "instructional capacity—the capacity to produce worthwhile and substantial learning—is a function of the interaction among elements of the instructional unit, not the sole province of any single element" (p. 5).

Instructional capacity does not, as many reform efforts would have us believe, reside only in improving teacher knowledge or in design and development of better educational materials.

This conceptualization of instructional capacity as interactive has implications for our efforts to model the process and practice of school improvement. To begin with, while intervening in any one element of the instructional unit can potentially affect other elements, these other elements also mediate such interventions. Thus, new curricular materials will influence teachers and students, but their potential to effect change in students' opportunity to learn is also dependent on the teachers and students who use the materials. Further, "If instructional capacity is a property of interactions among teacher, students, and materials, then interventions are likely to be more effective if they target more interactions among more elements of instructional units, rather than focusing on one element in isolation from others" (Cohen & Ball, 1998, p. 10).

By adopting a model of instructional capacity that specifies key elements of instruction and relations among these elements, we are in a better position to untangle the relations between school improvement efforts and classroom instruction. The instructional unit framework suggests several pathways for thinking about relations between the school improvement process and instructional innovation. It suggests, for example, that school improvement initiatives should involve a variety of integrated tasks that target students (e.g., parent support or in-school discipline), teachers (e.g., evaluation, professional development), and materials (e.g., curriculum development, technological resources). The instructional unit framework provides a way of thinking about the relations among the multiple processes and practices of school improvement and their relations to instructional capacity building.

Finally, this framework allows us to put aside the many debates about different conceptions of "good" instruction and curriculum, debates we view as important but a distraction from the goal of *school improvement*. The framework is applicable to improvement efforts based on conventional didactic conceptions as well as constructivist conceptions of instruction. Similarly, it is applicable regardless of whether one views teaching as routine, inspiration, or craft. Different conceptions of instruction are likely to suggest different approaches to school improvement (Rowan, 1991), and our framework must accommodate these different conceptions.

For clarity we will consider each element of the instructional unit separately, but readers should bear in mind that in the instructional unit model instructional capacity is a function not of any single element but rather of the interaction of all three elements.

EDUCATIONAL KNOWLEDGE

Over the past quarter century, research on teaching, student learning, and teacher learning has generated substantial knowledge about instruction and its improvement. Advancement in the field is, in part, based on identifying the knowledge that is necessary in order to teach. Shulman (1987) specifies five types of teacher knowledge, including content knowledge, general pedagogical knowledge, content-specific pedagogical knowledge, curricular knowledge, and knowledge of learners. *Content knowledge* refers to the knowledge, understanding, skills, and disposition of a discipline that are to be learned by students, including both the substantive structure (i.e., organization of the principles of a discipline) and syntactic structure (i.e., ways in which truth or falsehood are established). *General pedagogical knowledge* includes principles and strategies of classroom management and organization that transcend subject matter. *Content-specific pedagogical knowledge* relates to the pedagogy that is appropriate to a specific discipline and focuses on how particular concepts and issues are organized, represented, and adapted to the diverse interests and abilities of learners (p. 8). *Curricular knowledge* involves the programs designed for the teaching of particular subjects and topics at a given level, the instructional materials available, and the characteristics that serve as both the indications and contraindications for the use of particular curriculum or program materials in particular circumstances. *Knowledge of learners* and their characteristics concerns students' cultural backgrounds and interests and is important for making representations interesting to students (Kennedy, 1991).

The instructional unit framework and a sizable literature on teacher learning remind us that this teacher knowledge has to be tailored to the particular teaching instance or situation. It can rarely be imported and used without modification by teachers in their classrooms—tailoring is imperative in most situations. Further, teachers' beliefs, dispositions, and knowledge about students, subject matter, and teaching, as well as their prior practice—in other words, their "mental models" about teaching and learning—influence how and what they learn about instruction (Schwille et al., 1983; Toole, 2001). Thus, while knowledge about teaching has a clearer scientific basis than it did several decades ago, the importance of "clinical judgment" in how to apply that knowledge is as relevant for teachers as for physicians.

One important issue in all of this is the subject matter. Teachers do not just teach, they teach particular subjects. Subject matter provides an important perspective for teachers' work (Little, 1993; McLaughlin & Talbert, 1993; Siskin, 1994). Even at the elementary level, where teachers do not have well defined content specializations, subject matter appears to be an important context for their work (Stodolsky, 1988). Furthermore, subject matter is an important context in elementary school teachers' efforts to reform their teaching, because teachers' identities as teachers and as learners can differ from one subject to the next, influencing their efforts to reconstruct their practice in these subjects (Drake, Spillane, & Hufferd, 2000).

STUDENTS AS LEARNERS

The increasing research on cognitive development has generated a sizable body of knowledge about student learning. What students make of new information has much to do with the knowledge, expertise, and prior experiences that they already possess, i.e., the schemas or script for a particular topic that they use to filter and interpret new information. Individuals assimilate new experiences and information through their existing knowledge structures (Piaget, 1970). Knowledge and learning, in this view, includes reflection (Brown, 1997), conceptual growth and understanding, problem solving (Newall & Simon, 1972), and reasoning. Knowing, the development of new understandings of phenomena, involves making sense of experience using existing mental schemas. Rather than absorbing new knowledge or information, we use our existing knowledge and schemas to construct new understandings. Hence, learning involves the active reconstruction of the learner's existing knowledge structures, rather than passive assimilation or rote memorization (Anderson & Smith, 1987; Confrey, 1990).

While cognitive scientists tend to dwell on finding common or universal patterns in human cognition—"cognitive universalism"—the social or situated dimensions of student learning are also important (Resnick, 1991). An extensive literature underscores the social and cultural dimensions of teaching and learning, and family background has consistently been linked to children's educational attainment (Coleman et al., 1966). Scholars have identified how structural forces such as the correspondence between work, family, and school environments (Bowles & Gintis, 1976), cultural capital (Lareau, 1987), the persistence of racial stratification (Ogbu, 1994), and institutional practices such as tracking (Oakes, 1985) and low teacher expectations influence students' opportunities to learn in school (Good & Brophy, 1987).

One way that family background is thought to influence children's educational outcomes and attainment is through differences in parent involvement, with low-income parents less actively involved than their middle-income counterparts (Schneider & Coleman, 1993). Another way is through student engagement in school, with poor students and students of color often engaging in passive or active resistance in school (Anyon, 1981).

TEACHER BELIEFS

Teachers' beliefs and expectations are also critical, because they may influence the ways in which classroom opportunities to learn are mobilized. Teachers' perceptions of low-income, Black, and female students' intellectual capacity are lower than those they hold for middle- and upper-income White male students (Farkas, Grobe, Sheehan, & Shaun, 1990). Believing that children of poverty are incapable of handling instruction beyond the basics, and that they need highly controlled classrooms to learn basic skills, teachers assign these students more structured and often less demanding academic work (Good & Brophy, 1987). In particular, teachers who assume that the children in their classroom bring with them disadvantaging conditions (behavior or motivation) that cannot be overcome are less likely to engage in more open-ended forms of pedagogy that focus on creating knowledge (Talbert & McLaughlin, 1993).

Teachers' assumptions may be rooted in cultural mismatches between teachers and students, which lead to teachers' misinterpreting the cognitive skills and abilities those students bring to school (Heath & Mangiola, 1991). Linguistic differences between social classes and cultures also play a significant role in how students are perceived to complete assignments and how they are assessed by teachers (Bernstein, 1971). Central to these arguments is the belief that student behaviors, rooted in family background and racial or ethnic differences, can lead teachers to mold their expectations and thereby cause them to engage in practices that contribute to social reproduction.[2] Teachers' low expectations reduce students' self-image, cause them to exert less effort in school, and lead teachers themselves to give certain students less challenging coursework (Rist, 1970).

To summarize our argument, we contend that if school improvement is to make a difference for children, it has to be in fundamental ways about improving teaching and learning. Improving instructional capacity has to be the central target of school improvement initiatives. We have also argued for a view of instructional capacity as a multi-faceted, dynamic, and situated activity, one that is constituted in the interaction of teachers with particular students around particular intellectual materials. Changes in any of these constituent elements are likely to have important consequences for instructional capacity.

School Improvement Structures and Processes

Improving our understanding of how school improvement initiatives contribute to improved student achievement requires exploring relations between improvement efforts and the instructional unit. In this section, we consider how school improvement structures, processes, and practices might contribute to improving instructional capacity. We know a considerable amount about the organizational structure and processes of "effective" or improving schools (Hallinger & Heck, 1996; Newmann & Wehlage, 1995; Teddlie & Reynolds, 2000). Several established lines of inquiry, such as effective schools and professional community, identify and describe school-level structures and processes that are thought essential for instructional innovation (Firestone & Corbett, 1988; Gousha, 1986; Leithwood & Montgomery, 1982; Louis, Toole, & Hargreaves, 1999; Teddlie & Reynolds). Among other things, we know that schools with shared visions and norms of instruction, norms of collaboration, and a sense of collective responsibility for students' academic success create incentives and opportunities for teachers to improve their practice (Bryk & Driscoll, 1985; Newmann, King, & Rigdon, 1996).

A selective synthesis of this research suggests several structures and processes that are necessary (if not sufficient) conditions for school improvement:

- Developing an instructional vision that is shared by members of the staff;
- Developing and managing a school culture, or collective belief system, that is conducive to conversations about instruction by building norms of trust, collaboration and academic press[3] among staff;
- Procuring and distributing resources for improvement, including materials, time, support, and compensation;
- Supporting teacher growth and development, both individually and for the faculty;
- Providing both formative and summative monitoring of instruction and of the implementation of innovation that focuses on collective responsibility for student learning.

These processes and structures have been identified by multiple studies as important ingredients for school improvement. We concur, noting that the above list suggests a minimal set of requirements to make schools environments in which teachers can learn about improving their own practice.

However, lists such as this one that identify critical processes and structures for improvement pose two problems. First, they shed little light on relations between the school improvement process and classroom instruction. Second, the interaction among the various ingredients in the school improvement process remains something of a mystery. For example, how does monitoring instruction and innovation implementation relate to building norms of trust and collaboration among staff? In order to make relations between school improvement practice and instructional capacity more transparent, we will organize our discussion by mapping outward from the classroom as a site for teacher learning to teachers' professional community and to school structures.

THE CLASSROOM AS A SITE FOR TEACHER LEARNING

Student success is a primary source of rewards for teachers (Lortie, 1975), although it is an uncertain one in school settings where many students struggle (Louis & Smith, 1991). When teachers are asked about accountability, they are most likely to point to themselves and their students rather than professional colleagues or other agencies (Newmann, King, & Rigdon, 1996). Thus, school incentive systems are filtered through teachers' orientation to students' performance and engagement rather than to salary and other external motivators (McLaughlin & Yee, 1988). Student performance and engagement can also serve as powerful incentives for either preserving the status quo or promoting instructional change (Metz, 1994). But they are a lever for change that is rarely utilized by school reformers, who tend to focus exclusively on curriculum and external standards.

In North America, teachers spend almost all of their work time in classrooms. Yet, classroom instruction is seldom considered as a potentially rich area for teacher learning, in spite of the efforts of advocates of teacher action research and peer coaching. Instead, both scholarly and practical views of teacher learning are more likely to center on opportunities to learn that lie beyond the classroom. Sadly, efforts to create classroom-based learning are often poorly supported, or bureaucratized to the extent that they do not stimulate genuine conversations about improvement (Hargreaves, 1994).

Teachers are the key agents when it comes to changing classroom practice, since they are the final brokers of school improvement or reform initiatives (McLaughlin & Talbert, 1990; Schwille et al., 1983). Efforts to improve instruction—policy, school reform initiatives, and professional development—are filtered through teachers' personal beliefs, knowledge and extant instructional practices (Toole, 2001). Teaching is often viewed as telling, learning is equated with remembering, and a didactic teacher-centered pedagogy dominates most schools. Students appear to develop similar perspectives on teaching and learning. Unless school improvement efforts entertain and engage with teachers' and students' beliefs and practices, they are unlikely to contribute to basic improvement in classroom instruction. To improve practice fundamentally, teachers have to question, unlearn, and discard much of their current, deeply rooted understandings of teaching, learning, and subject matter—a complex and troubling process (Cohen & Barnes, 1993). Changing instruction requires enabling teachers to take charge of their own practice, providing opportunities for them to examine and reconstruct not only that practice but also the beliefs and justifications that support it (Richardson, 1990).

There is striking, albeit limited, evidence of how powerful the classroom can be as a site for teacher learning and the transformation of instruction. A number of studies suggest that teachers can, under the right circumstances, learn a tremendous amount from examining and reflecting on their practice. For example, work on teachers' implementation of mathematics reforms illuminates how teachers can develop knowledge of content, teaching, and learning by focusing on and examining their students' thinking about mathematics in the context of trying out new programs and approaches (Wood, Cobb, & Yackel, 1991). Teachers can also learn about their students, unlearning and relearning what their students can do and developing a new appreciation for the resources students bring to the instructional situation.

Important knowledge for teaching can be generated by teachers inside the classroom (Cochran-Smith & Lytle, 1993). A critical challenge for school improvement is how this daily learning might be channeled in the cause of fundamental change in instruction. A number of case studies in mathematics, science, and literacy document how teachers who implement more inquiry-based approaches open up opportunities for students to share their knowledge, thus creating conditions that challenge their own knowledge and practices (Hufferd-Ackles, 1999; Reiser et al., 2000). For example, in trying out new instructional approaches and observing their students' academic success, teachers in these studies generated evidence that their "disadvantaged" students were capable of handling more demanding intellectual content. They began to see their students' resources, not just their deficiencies, and to see how these resources enabled them to learn more intellectually rigorous mathematics, language arts, and science. These teachers also found convincing evidence that their "disadvantaged" students were interested in learning and motivated to learn. As teachers tried out more challenging pedagogy and engaged students in talking about intellectual ideas, they developed a better appreciation for students' resources for learning and in the process created the learning conditions that challenged their own convictions and knowledge about "disadvantaged" students.

Relatively few classrooms appear to support the sort of teacher learning necessary for fundamental change in classroom instruction. The case studies mentioned above suggest that the extent to which the classroom becomes a site for teacher learning depends largely on connections to people outside the classroom and the school. It depends on deprivatizing classroom practice, bringing us to the next salient context—teachers' professional community.

TEACHERS' PROFESSIONAL COMMUNITY

An increasing body of research suggests that real change in schools requires the development of strong professional communities. A school culture that emphasizes professionalism is both "client oriented and knowledge based" (Darling-Hammond, 1990), and also communitarian and personally supportive (Louis, Kruse, & Associates, 1995). While, as Furman-Brown (1999) points out, these definitions evoke a positive emotional response, they beg the question of why professional communities matter to instructional improvement. The immediate question facing school improvement research is whether the social organization of teachers within a school makes a significant difference for classrooms and student learning.

In the U.S., teachers' practice and learning environments are most typically characterized by an "egg-carton" school structure, in which each teacher's classroom is sacrosanct; they provide limited opportunities for teachers to develop professional community and learn from each other (Lortie, 1975). Comparative studies indicate that North American teachers have less time for collective work on school improvement than those in many other developed countries (OECD, 1999) because they have proportionately fewer hours in the work week that are not directly involved in classroom work. There is considerable variation in the degree to which teachers experience strong collegial relationships within schools (Bakkenes, deBrabander, & Imants, 1999), and there can be significant variations in professional community among U.S. schools in the same district (Bryk, Camburn, & Louis, 1999).

In spite of limited opportunities for professional interaction, a strong relationship among teachers within a school can have a significant effect on conversations about school improvement (Little, 1993; Newmann & Wehlage, 1995), classroom practice (Louis, Marks, & Kruse, 1996) and student achievement (Marks & Louis, 1999). Bender-Sebring, Bryk, and Easton (1995) found that Chicago elementary schools in the top and bottom quartiles of a professional community index varied substantially in teaching and student learning, while Louis & Marks (1998) showed that "reforming schools" with higher levels of schoolwide professional community also showed improved instruction and student learning. Toole (2001) indicates that professional community is an important factor in sustaining instructional innovation within a school. Based on these findings, we conclude that teachers who have found a network of colleagues with whom they can discuss their professional practice—either inside or outside their school—are more likely to be engaged in improving their practice in ways that have the potential to affect student learning.

The concept of professional community is important to school improvement not because it is novel, but because it provides a basis for synthesizing the conceptions of a variety of writers on education. For example, we know from research on staff development that cooperative, job-embedded learning has the greatest potential for improving teacher performance and, eventually, student performance (Sparks & Hirsch, 1997). This kind of professional growth requires that staff be able to engage in serious discussions about the fundamental aspects of their teaching (reflective dialogue and sharing of practice), with at least a minimal level of agreement about the purposes of teaching and learning in their school (goal consensus). We also know from several decades of research on effective schools (Teddlie & Reynolds, 2000) that schools must have high expectations for all students, and that teachers need to believe that they have the capacity to teach all students (focus on student learning; collective responsibility for student learning). As we have noted, fundamental change in teaching practice is a personally painful process (Ball & Rundquist, 1993) that often requires replacing traditional and deeply embedded views of cognition and school social relations with more constructivist ones (Brooks &

Brooks, 1993). More than a half-century of research on individual and group change suggests that these shifts are unlikely to occur without socially supportive and (positively) pressuring environments (Huberman & Miles, 1994; Schmuck & Runkel, 1985). Thus, professional community should be viewed not as an "add-on" to an already long list of panaceas for school improvement, but as a mechanism that can bring together what we already know about how change in teachers and schools occurs. Professional community—however defined—is nothing more or less than a shorthand term for the kinds of adult relationships in schools that can support individual change in classrooms.

Professional community is also a broader tool that can lead to changes outside of the classroom that benefit students. The school effectiveness research, for example, suggests that safe, orderly schools become so because of clear agreements about student and teacher behavior that go beyond rules to consensus about how people treat each other (Teddlie & Reynolds, 2000). Agreements about curriculum and pedagogy that provide consistency of student experience across classrooms and teachers may also be important. Marks and Louis (1999) suggest that where teachers collectively make decisions about such school-specific "policies" under conditions of professional community, students will benefit—presumably from consistency of expectations. Strong teacher professional community also appears to be associated with students' perceptions that they are taught in a caring and communal environment (Louis & Marks, 1998). Teacher caring without academic motivations to succeed does not necessarily translate into student learning gains, but where caring is an outgrowth of teachers' consensus about what students need to learn there are positive effects.

Professional communities can exist in relatively inauspicious environments, where they may be fostered by a variety of conditions— many of which are "cost free" in terms of direct financial commitments.[4] Research suggests that social and human resources in the school are the most critical resources. Beyond the obvious need for competent and well-prepared teachers, the social conditions of the school are important. In studying Chicago schools, Bryk, Camburn and Louis (1999) found that of all the facilitating factors for professional community, *social trust* was "by far" the strongest. Trust and respect acted as a foundation on which collaboration, reflective dialogue, and deprivatization of practice could occur. Trust refers to all relationships in the school: among colleagues and between teachers and the principal, but also between teachers and students and their families.

In summary, in spite of limited policy support, many schools have managed to create settings in which teachers are engaged in systematic, collaborative work on the improvement of their classrooms, and the development of more thoughtful (even research-based) forms of improvement that can affect student learning. The fact that educational policy typically defines "teaching" as limited to student contact hours inhibits but does not prevent the development of professional communities that support teacher learning and, ultimately, student learning.

Organizational Learning: The Bridge

What else might connect student learning with professional community and school improvement? One recent theme in school improvement research emphasized the importance of organizational learning, which we view as a bridge between research on teaching and research on school improvement. Organizational learning resembles individual learning; it is a process the outcome of which is new knowledge, skills, or tools for increasing learning. But organizational learning transcends the aggregated learning of individual organizational members. It takes place among the individuals as a collective; it is "in between" (Salomon & Perkins, 1998) organizational members. Engaged in a common activity in a way that is uniquely theirs, the members of an organization learn as an ensemble possessing a distinctive culture that supports innovation (Cook & Yanow, 1993).

Current educational literature on organizational learning and high performance organizations has recently borrowed from the business literature, where the topic has a relatively longer history (Senge, 1990). Organizational learning theories assume that until members move beyond preoccupation with power, and toward issues of shared vision and inquiry, collectively held models, and increased (professional) mastery of work, they will consistently arrive at the wrong solutions to the wrong problems (Wheatley, 1992). In education, organizational learning is generally associated with a school's ability to consider and incorporate external and internal information that has implications for short- and long-term decisions about organizational and classroom improvement. An organization that learns, according to the theory, works efficiently, readily adapts to change, detects and corrects error, and continually improves its effectiveness (Argyris & Schon, 1974).[5]

Although the concept of organizational learning is popular in education (Senge et al., 2000), systematic investigations of organizational learning in schools have emerged slowly. One example (Huberman,

1994) involved looking at successful collaborations between university researchers and school practitioners, where sustained interaction and mutual influence were critical to finding improvement effects. Many of the empirical publications on organizational learning in schools have been based on case studies (Leithwood & Louis, 1998; Wohlstetter, Smyer, & Mohrman, 1994). There have been fewer studies that are based on larger samples of schools, and these have not been organized around a clear intervention (Bryk et al., 1999). To date, however, few of these analyses have linked schools' organizational capacity to learn with improvements in student learning (for an exception, see Marks & Louis, 2000). Nevertheless, the literature suggests a number of characteristics of learning in organizations that can be readily adapted to enhance student learning.

According to limited existing educational research, organizational learning may be a powerful vehicle for school improvement. Organizational learning harnesses the literature on professional community (focusing on the effects of adult relationships in the schools) with instructional improvement (focusing on conceptual tools that enable critical analysis of school and classroom activities and processes that affect student learning). Organizational learning, which emphasizes both group and individual growth (Senge, 1990), should not be confused with a simply technological prescription for school improvement. It focuses on the full complement of conditions described above: professional community, conditions supporting professional community and adult learning in schools, and processes within the organization that may engender changes in both teaching practice and the mental models that affect the daily work of teachers (Marks & Louis, 2000; Senge et al., 2000).

Challenges to School Leaders and the Leadership Profession

Our model of school improvement suggests a number of challenges for school leaders and the leadership profession, including anchoring leaders' work and preparation in learning and teaching, promoting a distributed understanding of leadership, nurturing the development of social trust, and facilitating the development of professional networks.

To begin with, a key challenge involves reorienting the profession to teaching and learning. Generating and sustaining the conditions that support the development of classrooms and schools as sites for teacher and administrator learning is not easy; it requires that those who lead in schools know something about teaching and learning. Without an understanding of the knowledge necessary for teachers to teach well—content knowledge, general pedagogical knowledge, content-specific pedagogical knowledge, curricular knowledge, and knowledge of learners—school leaders will be unable to perform essential school improvement functions such as monitoring instruction and supporting teacher development. Even if school leaders rely on external providers for their school's teacher development needs, they will still need a sophisticated understanding of teaching and learning in order to make wise selections. Central issues for both leader preparation and leadership research will involve figuring out what school leaders need to know about teaching and learning in particular subject areas in order to perform key school improvement tasks. The argument that school leaders will need rich content and pedagogical knowledge of each subject domain is too general and establishes unrealistic and unattainable expectations for the profession. For example, we cannot expect every school principal to develop the sort of rich content and pedagogical knowledge that teachers would need to teach sixth grade mathematics. This issue is further complicated by the fact that the sort of content and pedagogical knowledge that leaders will need will have to be tailored to their leadership work. Specifically, school leaders will need to grasp content and pedagogical content knowledge in ways that enable them to support educating teachers. A critical challenge for the profession, then, involves figuring out what sort of content and pedagogical knowledge leaders will need to have in order to lead effectively.

If, as we have argued, we have to map backwards from classroom instruction in order to understand the school improvement process, then those who work to initiate and sustain this process would have to acquire a vast array of skills and expertise. It is unlikely that any one individual could master all these skills and all this knowledge. No one individual can master knowledge of instruction, adult development and learning, and organizational development and learning, along with skills such as budgeting and scheduling. A principal practicing solo is unlikely to successfully enact the school improvement processes discussed in this chapter. A distributed understanding of leadership is therefore imperative if school leaders are to practice effectively and maintain their sanity and the profession is to be successful in attracting recruits (Spillane, Halvorson, & Diamond, 2001).

A distributed perspective on leadership will help considerably in determining how school principals might manage the daunting task of school improvement and supporting organizational learning—particularly when the core improvement processes involve detailed knowledge of cutting-edge pedagogy and content in multiple disciplines, as well as an understanding of adult development and social factors, inside and outside the school, that affect student learning. Both the researcher and practitioner communities too often equate leadership with principal leadership. Assistant principals, curriculum specialists, and teacher leaders can, and indeed do, play a role in the enactment of school improvement tasks. In light of our model of the school improvement process and leadership preparation, a distributed view of leadership that incorporates the activities of multiple individuals in a school (Gronn, 2000; Spillane et al., 2001) is essential, and development programs need to reflect this perspective. As a practical matter, school principals who cannot engage others in leading will be unable to spread and mobilize the expertise necessary for school improvement in their schools; they are thus unlikely to be very effective.

While the distributed perspective gives cause for optimism, it also complicates the notion of leadership expertise. We have a reasonably good fix on the principal leadership skills that are associated with school innovation, but the ways in which these skills might be distributed among school leaders, as well as the manner in which other knowledge and expertise might be distributed, are less well understood. Specifically, to the extent that particular leadership tasks are distributed among school leaders, it will be important to analyze a particular leader's knowledge and beliefs in relation to those of his or her fellow leaders in a given school. Thus, the question of what school leaders need to know about literacy, mathematics, and science instruction is likely to depend in some important measure on others in their school who share responsibility for executing the same school improvement task. Because the expertise necessary for the enactment of essential school improvement processes is spread over multiple leaders, the individual cannot be the sole focus of research on expertise. Rather, the school may be the most appropriate unit for thinking about the development of expertise.

A third and related challenge for school leaders involves the development of social trust, which is critical for both individual and organizational learning. While research evidence suggests that social conditions are the most important preconditions for creating professional community, structural features of the school (e.g., scheduling, meeting times) are not far behind, and opportunity to develop professional communities is always the most important issue. *Administrative leadership* is critical—at least in the North American context—for the development of social trust. Leithwood (1995) and Leithwood & Jantzi (1990) show that teachers are more likely to pursue their collective and individual learning when there are supportive conditions in the school—particularly *effective leadership*. How can leaders effectively develop social trust? How can we prepare leaders so that they have the skills necessary to perform this task?

One factor that appears in all studies that look at professional community is *time to meet and talk*. Schools address this issue in different ways: affluent schools or those that have special grants provide release time or retreats; those that do not have these luxuries use scheduling changes, overtime work, or, at worst, catch-as-catch-can. In addition, many schools that have strong professional communities have encouraged *interdependent teaching roles* through co-teaching, team structures, peer coaching, or other strategies. Where these work—where they create opportunities for serious discussion—they are powerful, because they focus on immediate teaching decisions and responsibilities in ways that encourage reflection and collaboration. Site based management that permits strong *teacher voice* in the development of policies that affect learning conditions and classrooms is also important (Marks & Louis, 1999), while *school size and complexity* may inhibit the development of community by segregating teachers in separate "wings" and limiting common meeting spaces that bring all teachers together.

A fourth challenge to leaders involves the cultivation of professional networks for themselves and their staff that extend beyond the schoolhouse. *Access to expertise* and the "ombudsman" role of the outside is important. Huberman (1993) argues that teachers often think of themselves as artisans, tinkerers or instructional handymen. What stimulates real change is sustained interaction between teachers and an outsider who uses research to question conventional practice. Teachers' involvement with professional networks that extend beyond the school can be potent sources and supports for instructional improvement (Talbert & McLaughlin, 1994). We are not referring to episodic state or regional conferences, which are marginally useful according to the above research, but to discipline- and project-focused networks that research suggests engage teacher commitment. Unfortunately, most of these networks involve externally funded and/or organized enterprises. A key challenge to school leaders is to develop and sustain these networks and, most important, ensure that they support ongoing rich deliberations about teaching and learning.

Conclusion

In this chapter we have developed a framework that makes relations between the processes of school improvement and students' opportunities to learn more explicit. Anchoring our model of the school improvement process in a particular perspective on instruction, we mapped backwards from instruction to the classroom, the professional community, and school organization and leadership, examining how each might support learning from and about instruction. We argued that if school improvement is to make a difference for children, it has to be fundamentally focused on improving the "core technology" of schools, that is, instruction. Instructional improvement depends on instructional capacity, which, in turn, depends on both individual and organizational learning in the school. Our account points to a number of challenges to leaders and the leadership profession that deserve both further inquiry and action research.

NOTES

1. We define the classroom setting very broadly to include any activity organized by the school and teachers to promote student learning. There is increasing evidence that opportunities outside the physical boundaries of the classroom, such as service learning, may provide important learning opportunities.

2. We emphasize race and class because the evidence of gender-based social reproduction effects in schooling, at least in the U.S. today, are more debatable.

3. "Academic press" denotes the extent to which school staff value and place emphasis on academic performance and goals.

4. We do not intend to imply that budgetary resources are not important, because there is increasing evidence that even in a resource-rich environment like North America, they are. However, we have observed strong professional communities in settings in districts with dramatic differences in per-student funding.

5. Organizational learning is thus related to theories of continuous improvement (sometimes known as total quality management). Because it is assumed to emerge from within the organization (even when it is in response to external demands), it is quite distinct from educational policies that emphasize systemic reform, standards based reform, or other accountability-based and regulatory efforts to make schools function better.

References

Anderson, C., & Smith, C. (1987). Teaching science. In V. Richardson (Ed.), *Educator's handbook: A research perspective*. New York: Longman.

Anyon, J. (1981). Social class and school knowledge. *Curriculum Inquiry, 11*(1), 3-42.

Argyris, C., & Schon, D. (1974). *Theory in practice: Increasing professional effectiveness*. San Francisco: Jossey-Bass.

Bakkenes, I., de Brabander, C., & Imants, J. (1999). Teacher isolation and communication network analysis in primary schools. *Educational Administration Quarterly, 35*(2), 166-202.

Ball, D. L., & Rundquist, S. S. (1993). Collaboration as a context for joining teacher learning with learning about teaching. In D. K. Cohen, M. W. McLaughlin, & J. E. Talbert (Eds.), *Teaching for understanding: Challenges for policy and practice* (pp. 13-42). San Francisco: Jossey-Bass.

Bender-Sebring, P. B., Bryk, A. S., & Easton, J. Q. (1995). *Charting reform: Chicago teachers take stock*. Chicago: Consortium on Chicago School Research.

Bernstein, B. (1971). *Class, codes and control* (Vol. 1). London: Routledge and Kegan Paul.

Bowles, S., & Gintis, H. A. (1976). *Schooling in capitalist America*. New York: Basic Books.

Brooks, J. G., & Brooks, M. G. (1993). *In search of understanding: The case for constructivist classrooms*. Alexandria, VA: ASCD.

Brophy, J. E., & Good, T. L. (1973). *Teacher-student relationships: Causes and consequences*. New York: Holt, Rinehart, and Winston.

Brown, A. L. (1997). Transforming schools into communities of thinking and learning about serious matters. *American Psychologist, 52*(4), 399-413.

Bryk, A., Camburn, E., & Louis, K. S. (1999). Professional community in Chicago elementary schools: Facilitating factors and organizational consequences. *Educational Administration Quarterly, 35*, 751-781.

Bryk, A., & Driscoll, M. E. (1985). *An empirical investigation of the school as community*. Chicago: University of Chicago Press.

Cochran-Smith, M., & Lytle, S. L. (Eds.). (1993). *Inside/Outside: Teacher research and knowledge*. New York: Teachers College Press.

Cohen, D. K., & Ball, D. L. (1998). *Instruction, capacity and improvement* (RR-42). Philadelphia: Consortium for Policy Research in Education, University of Pennsylvania.

Cohen, D. K., & Barnes, C. A. (1993). Pedagogy and policy, and Conclusion: A new pedagogy for policy? In D. K. Cohen, M. W. McLaughlin, & J. E. Talbert (Eds.), *Teaching for understanding: Challenges for policy and practice* (pp. 207-276). San Francisco: Jossey-Bass.

Coleman, J., Campbell, E. Q., Hobson, C. J., McPartland, J., Mood, A. M., Weinfield, E. D., & York, R. L. (1966). *Equality of educational opportunity*. Washington, DC: U.S. Government Printing Office.

Confrey, J. (1990). A review of the research on student conceptions in mathematics, science and programming. In C. Cazden (Ed.), *Review of research in education* (Vol. 16). Washington, DC: American Educational Research Association.

Cook, S. D., & Yanow, D. (1993). Culture and organizational learning. In M. D. Cohen & L. Sproull (Eds.), *Organizational learning* (pp. 430-459). Thousand Oaks, CA: Sage.

Darling-Hammond, L. (1990). Teacher professionalism: Why and how. In A. Lieberman (Ed.), *Schools as collaborative cultures: Creating the future now* (Vol. 3). Bristol, PA: The Falmer Press.

Drake, C., Spillane, J., & Hufferd, K. (2000). Storied identities: Teacher learning and subject matter context. *Journal of Curriculum Studies, 33*(1), 1-43.

Education Trust. (1999). *Achievement in America*. Washington, DC: Education Trust.

Elmore, R. (1985). Forward and backward mapping: Reversible logic in the analysis of public policy. *Political Science Quarterly, 94*, 606-616.

Farkas, G., Grobe, R., Sheehan, D., & Shaun, Y. (1990). Cultural resources and school success: Gender, ethnicity, and poverty groups within an urban school district. *American Sociological Review, 55*(1), 127-142.

Firestone, W. A., & Corbett, H. D. (1988). Organizational change. In N. Boyan (Ed.), *Handbook of research on educational administration* (1st ed.). White Plains, NY: Longman.

Furman-Brown, G. (1999). School as community: Editor's foreword. *Educational Administration Quarterly, 35*(1), 6-12.

Good, T. L., & Brophy, J. E. (1987). *Looking in classrooms.* New York: Harper and Row.

Gronn, P. (2000). Distributed properties: A new architecture for leadership. *Educational Management and Administration, 28*(3), 317-338.

Hallinger, P., & Heck, R. (1996). Reassessing the principal's role in school effectiveness: A research of the empirical research. *Educational Administration Quarterly, 32*(1).

Hargreaves, A. (1994). *Changing teachers, changing times: Teachers' work and culture in the postmodern age (Professional development and practice).* New York: Teachers College, Columbia University.

Heath, S. B., & Mangiola, L. (1991). Children of promise: Literate activity in linguistically and culturally diverse classrooms. Washington, DC: National Education Association.

Huberman, M. (1993). The model of the independent artisan in teachers' professional relations. In J. W. Little & M. W. McLaughlin (Eds.), *Teachers' work: Individuals, colleagues, and contexts* (pp. 11-50). New York: Teachers College, Columbia University.

Huberman, M. (1994). Research utilization: The state of the art. *Knowledge and Policy, 7*(4), 13-33.

Huberman, M., & Miles, M. (1994). *Innovation up close: How school improvement works.* New York: Plenum.

Hufferd-Ackles, K. (1999). *Learning by all in a math-talk learning community.* Unpublished doctoral dissertation, Northwestern University, Evanston, IL.

Kennedy, M. (1991). *An agenda for research on teacher learning* (Special report). Lansing, MI: Michigan State University.

Lareau, A. (1987). Social class differences in family-school relationships: The importance of cultural capital. *Sociology of Education, 60*(1), 73-85.

Leithwood, K. (1995). Cognitive perspectives on school leadership. *Journal of School Leadership, 5*(2), 115-135.

Leithwood, K., & Jantzi, D. (1990). Transformational leadership: How principals can help reform school cultures. *School Effectiveness and School Improvement, 1*(4), 249-280.

Leithwood, K., & Louis, K. S. (Eds.). (1998). Organizational learning in schools. Lisse, Netherlands: Swets and Zeitlinger.

Leithwood, K., & Montgomery, D. (1982). The role of the elementary school principal in program improvement. *Review of Educational Research, 52*(3), 309-339.

Little, J. W., & McLaughlin, M. W. (Eds.). (1993). *Teachers' work: Individuals, colleagues, and contexts.* New York: Teachers College, Columbia University.

Lortie, D. C. (1975). *Schoolteacher: A sociological study.* Chicago: University of Chicago Press.

Louis, K. S., Kruse, S., & Associates. (1995). *Professionalism and community: Perspectives on reforming urban schools.* Thousand Oaks, CA: Corwin Press.

Louis, K. S., & Marks, H. (1998). Does professional community affect the classroom? Teachers' work and student work in restructuring schools. *American Journal of Education, 106*(4), 532-575.

Louis, K. S., Marks, H., & Kruse, S. (1996). Teachers' professional community in restructuring schools. *American Educational Research Journal, 33*(4), 757-798.

Louis, K. S., & Smith, B. (1991). Restructuring, teacher engagement and school culture: Perspectives on school reform and the improvement of teachers' work. *School Effectiveness and School Improvement, 2*(1), 34-52.

Louis, K. S., Toole, J., & Hargreaves, A. (1999). Rethinking school improvement. In J. Murphy & K. S. Louis (Eds.), *Handbook of research on educational administration* (2nd ed., pp. 251-275). San Francisco: Jossey-Bass.

Marks, H., & Louis, K. S. (1999). Teacher empowerment and the capacity for organizational learning. *Education Administration Quarterly, 35*(5), 751-781.

McLaughlin, M. W., & Talbert, J. E. (1990). *The contexts of teaching in secondary schools: Teachers' realities.* New York: Teachers College, Columbia University.

McLaughlin, M. W., & Talbert, J. E. (1993). *Contexts that matter for teaching and learning: Strategic opportunities for meeting the nation's education goals.* Stanford, CA: Center for Research on the Context of Secondary School Teaching, Stanford University.

McLaughlin, M. W., & Yee, S. (1988). School as a place to have a career. In A. Lieberman (Ed.), *Building a professional culture in schools.* New York: Teachers College Press.

Metz, M. H. (1994). Desegregation as a necessity and a challenge. *Journal of Negro Education, 63*(1), 64-76.

Newall, A., & Simon, H. (1972). *Human problem solving.* Englewood Cliffs, NJ: Prentice-Hall.

Newmann, F. M., & Associates. (1996). *Authentic achievement: Restructuring schools for intellectual quality.* San Francisco: Jossey-Bass.

Newmann, F. M., King, B., & Rigdon, M. (1996). *Accountability and school performance: Implications from restructuring schools* (Deliverable to OERI). Madison, WI: Center on Organization and Restructuring of Schools.

Newmann, F. M., & Wehlage, G. G. (1995). *Successful school restructuring: A report to the public and educators.* Madison, WI: Center on Organization and Restructuring of Schools, Wisconsin Center for Education Research, University of Wisconsin.

Oakes, J. (1985). *Keeping track: How schools structure inequality.* New Haven: Yale University Press.

OECD. (1999). *Education at a glance.* Paris: Organization for Economic Cooperation and Development.

Ogbu, J. (1994). Racial stratification and education in the United States: Why inequality persists. *Teachers College Record, 96*(2), 264-298.

Piaget, J. (1970). *Science of education and the psychology of the child.* New York: Orion Press.

Reiser, B. J., Spillane, J. P., Steinmuller, F., Sorsa, D., Carney, K., & Kyza, E. (2000). *Investigating the mutual adaptation process in teachers' design of technology-infused curricula.* Paper presented at the International Conference of the Learning Sciences, Ann Arbor, MI.

Resnick, L. (1991). Shared cognition: Thinking as social practice. In L. Resnick, J. Levine, & S. Teasley (Eds.), *Perspectives on socially shared cognition* (pp. 1-20). Washington, DC: American Psychological Association.

Richardson, V. (1990). Significant and worthwhile change in teaching practice. *Educational Researcher, 19*(7), 10-18.

Rist, R. (1970). Social class and teacher expectations: The self-fulfilling prophecy in ghetto education. *Harvard Educational Review, 40,* 411-451.

Rowan, B. (1991). Commitment and control: Alternative strategies for the organizational design of schools. *Review of Educational Research* (Vol. 16). Washington, DC: American Educational Research Association.

Salomon, G., & Perkins, D. (1998). Learning in wonderland: What do computers really offer education? In S. T. Kerr (Ed.), *Technology and the future of schooling. Ninety-fifth yearbook of the National Society for the Study of Education. Part II.* Chicago: National Society for the Study of Education.

Schmuck, R., & Runkel, P. (1985). *Organization development in schools* (3rd ed.). Palo Alto, CA: Mayfield Publishing Co.

Schneider, B., & Coleman, J. (Eds.). (1993). *Parents, their children, and schools.* Boulder, CO: Westview Press.

Schwille, J., Porter, A., Floden, R., Freeman, D., Knappen, L., Kuhs, T., & Schmidt, W. (1983). Teachers as policy brokers in the content of elementary school mathematics. In L. Schulman & G. Sykes (Eds.), *Handbook of teaching and policy* (pp. 370-391). New York: Longman.

Senge, P. M. (1990). *The fifth discipline: The art and practice of the learning organization* (1st ed.). New York: Currency Doubleday.

Senge, P. M., Cambron-McCabe, N., Lucas, T., Smith, B., Dutton, J., & Kleiner, A. (2000). *Schools that learn: A fifth fieldbook for educators, parents, and everyone who cares about education* (1st ed.). New York: Doubleday.

Shulman, L. S. (1987). *Knowledge and teaching: Foundations of the new reform.* Harvard Educational Review, 57(1), 1-22.

Siskin, L. S. (1994). Is the school the unit of change? Internal and external contexts of restructuring. In P. P. Gimmett & J. Neufeld (Eds.), *Teacher development and the struggle for authenticity: Professional growth and restructuring in the context of change* (pp. 121-140). New York: Teachers College, Columbia University.

Sparks, D., & Hirsh, S. (1997). *A new vision for staff development.* Alexandria, VA: Association for Supervision and Curriculum Development.

Spillane, J., Halvorson, R., & Diamond, J. (2001). Investigating school leadership practice. *Educational Researcher, 30*(3), 23-28.

Stodolsky, S. (1988). *The subject matters.* Chicago: University of Chicago Press.

Talbert, J. E., & McLaughlin, M. W. (1993). Understanding teaching in context. In D. K. Cohen, M. W. McLaughlin, & J. E. Talbert (Eds.), *Teaching for understanding* (pp. 1-10). San Francisco: Jossey-Bass.

Talbert, J. E., & McLaughlin, M. W. (1994). Teacher professionalism in local school contexts. *American Journal of Education, 102*(2), 123-153.

Teddlie, C., & Reynolds, D. (2000). *The international handbook of school effectiveness research.* New York: Falmer.

Toole, J. (2001). *Mental models, professional learning communities, and the deep structure of school change: Case studies of service learning.* Minneapolis, MN: University of Minnesota.

Wheatley, M. J. (1992). *Leadership and the new science: Learning about organization from an orderly universe.* San Francisco: Berrett-Koehler Publishers, Inc.

Wohlstetter, P., Smyer, R., & Mohrman, S. A. (1994). New boundaries for school-based management: The high involvement model. *Educational Evaluation and Policy Analysis, 16*(3), 268-286.

Wood, T., Cobb, P., & Yackel, E. (1991). Change in teaching mathematics: A case study. *American Educational Research Journal, 28*(3), 587-616.

CHAPTER 6

Leadership for Democratic Community in Schools

GAIL C. FURMAN AND ROBERT J. STARRATT

In his recent monograph on the quest for a new "center" for educational leadership, Joseph Murphy (1999) identifies "three powerful
synthesizing paradigms" (p. 54) embedded in the "shifting landscape"
of the field—*democratic community, social justice, and school improvement.*
While suggesting that each offers the potential "to re-culture the profession of school administration" (p. 54), Murphy chooses school
improvement as *the* center, arguing that "it will be the most effective
of the three . . . in rebalancing the relationship between the academic
and practice wings of the profession" (p. 55). In this chapter we consider a different choice: What would it mean for democratic community to be *the* center for educational leadership in schools, and how
would this choice re-culture the profession?[1] We are interested in this
undertaking not only as a natural extension of our respective writings
on the relationships among community, democracy, ethics, and leadership in schools, but also as a response to the growing concern that current directions in public school policy, including initiatives associated
with "school improvement," actually threaten democracy in schools
and society (Berliner, 2001; Elshtain, 1995). We will say more about
this concern in a later section of this chapter.

Murphy's (1999) selection of *democratic community* as one of the
"synthesizing paradigms" of the field reflects the increasing use of this
term in educational writing in recent years. However, the concept is
not new, with much of the current work finding its grounding in
Dewey's ideas promulgated more than 80 years ago. Kahne's (1996)
rendition of democratic community is a good example, as he uses concepts derived directly from Dewey when he contrasts "traditional communitarians," who value traditional roles, responsibilities and norms,
with "democratic communitarians," who follow Dewey and consider

Gail Furman is Associate Professor in the Department of Educational Leadership
and Counseling Psychology at Washington State University in Pullman, Washington.
Robert J. Starratt is Professor of Educational Administration at the Lynch School of
Education at Boston College.

democracy as a "way of life" in which "community norms and values [are] continually held open to informed critique" (p. 27), diversity is recognized, and change is expected. In Kahne's Deweyan-influenced terms, democratic community may be defined as a participatory way of life, a "process, not a stagnant end" (p. 34), in which individuals are committed to "the full and free interplay" (p. 34) of ideas in working for the common good.

Apple and Beane (1995), in a similar vein, discuss the foundations for a "democratic way of life" (p. 6) and how it might be enacted in schools. The "central concerns of democratic schools" include:

1. The open flow of ideas, regardless of their popularity, that enables people to be as fully informed as possible;
2. The use of critical reflection and analysis to evaluate ideas, problems, and policies;
3. Concern for the welfare of others and "the common good";
4. Concern for the dignity and rights of individuals and minorities. (pp. 6-7)

Apple and Beane suggest the systemic scope of the challenge involved in "enacting" these conditions in schools when they state that it involves "two lines of work"—the creation of "democratic structures and processes," and the creation of a "democratic curriculum that will give young people democratic experiences" (p. 9).

From these and other discussions of democratic community in schools (e.g., Crow & Slater, 1996; Maxcy, 1995; Reitzug & O'Hair, in press; Rusch, 1998), some common themes begin to emerge regarding the nature or character of democratic community:

• Democratic community is based on open inquiry, the "full and free interplay of ideas" suggested by Dewey;
• Democratic community members work for the common good;
• In democratic community, the rights of all, including the less powerful, are respected;
• Creating democratic community in schools is a systemic challenge, involving structures, processes and curriculum.

The concept of democratic community derived from Dewey's progressivism—the basis for these common themes—has been questioned recently by Mitchell (2001) for its continued relevance in a period of "transnational" and "cross-border" movements. Mitchell argues that Dewey's take on democracy and its contemporary interpretations are inextricably bound up with the idea of the nation-state and with the American version of democracy. She writes:

It is worth pondering the connections between education and democracy in the contemporary period of increasing cross-border movements, transnational processes, and the accelerated flow of capital, commodities, culture, and people. What are the effects of these globalizing forces on conceptions of democratic citizenship? How should children be educated within (and for) an increasingly global context? (p. 52)

Our purpose here is to extend this emerging work on democratic community through a fuller and deeper analysis of the linkages between democratic community and leadership in schools. In approaching this task we are confronted with conceptual and practical problems. First, notwithstanding the common themes that are beginning to emerge from writings on democratic community, as noted above, the concept remains theoretically ambiguous and open to critique, partly because it is a composite of two other poorly defined or "contested" terms, *community* and *democracy*. *Community*, for example, is used in multiple ways in the education literature, sometimes referring to professional community among educators, sometimes to "learning community" among students, and sometimes to community "of difference" in multicultural settings (Shields, in press). Further complicating the theoretical understanding of community, it is a term with anachronistic meanings drawn from classical sociological theory (e.g., Tönnies, 1957), theory that was developed in the context of social conditions far different from the postmodern world of the 21st century (Furman, 1998). Similarly, *democracy* is interpreted in various ways in education, and its common meanings may also be anachronistic, as the earlier reference to Mitchell (2001) noted. Maxcy (1995) states, "The meanings of democracy are so varied that political regimes from the most authoritarian to the most anarchistic invoke the term in their self descriptions" (p. 57).

Given these conceptual issues, the first task in this chapter is to unpack democratic community by problematizing the key concepts of community and democracy, then to repackage it based on our analysis. A second conceptual problem is to analyze the linkages between our repackaged concept of democratic community and leadership theory and practice in education. The ensuing practical problem to consider is the *Realpolitik* of implementing democratic community in schools in view of current directions in school reform, which some have critiqued as inimical to democracy and community (Berliner, 2001; Murphy, 1996).[2]

Problematizing Community

We choose to problematize the concept of *community* in regard to two concerns. The first is that current understandings of community in education tend to reflect anachronistic understandings of community in assuming that the social conditions underpinning earlier theories of community can be recreated in contemporary schools and societies. As several authors have noted in recent years (e.g., Calderwood, 2000; Furman, 1998; Shields, in press; Strike, 1999), understandings of community in education tend to emphasize *commonalities* among community members, and implicitly, distinct community *boundaries*, which determine those who are included or excluded from the community. For example, much of the education literature on community cites Tönnies' (1957) seminal work on the gemeinschaft/gesellschaft distinction. Tönnies delineated three types of community (gemeinschaft), all based on "sameness" among the members: community of kinship (same family), community of place (same neighborhood), and community of mind (same values or lifestyle). Discussions of community in schools have reflected this "sameness" assumption by calling variously for "shared values and visions" or "a sense of place" as the basis for community (e.g., Sergiovanni, 1994).

The problem with this "sameness" assumption of traditional theory and its contemporary manifestations in educational thought is that contemporary Western society and public institutions like schools offer few opportunities to gather with those who are "like us." The extended family (kinship) groups that tended to live out their lives in the same location in former times, and the towns and villages (place) with stable populations who were interdependent economically, are practically extinct. Fewer people are participating in civic groups and clubs with like-minded citizens (mind), and even churches, the traditional bastions of "community of mind," reveal continuing arguments over theological interpretations and pastoral practice. Furthermore, contemporary adults tend to experience community, if at all, in memberships in multiple organizations, each with a specific focus or purpose. Membership in these communities is frequently temporary and tentative, due to the rapid transformation of many of these organizations, the increased mobility of families and the fast pace of life. This leads to a much more transitory and pragmatic experience of community, often created and improvised by people on the move with other people who share only one narrow interest. Hence, community tends to be invented on the spot, to last a relatively brief time, and to serve relatively superficial human needs. Even the viability of nation-state identity as a basis for a broader sense of civic community has been questioned (Mitchell, 2001). As public institutions, schools mirror this diversity and fragmentation of contemporary, "postmodern" society. It is difficult and potentially destructive to attempt to create a sense of community in schools through emphasizing traditional commonalities. Indeed, the overemphasis on commonalities as the basis for community leads to balkanizing solutions such as voucher systems and charter schools, in which those who think alike are encouraged to gather together. Kahne (1996) analyzes this problem of attempting to recreate "traditional communitarian" values in schools in a postmodern world:

. . . many hope to create publicly funded schools or programs with distinct cultural and/or religious orientations . . . Efforts to promote coherent communities in schools . . . can lead to a number of problems. Placing students, especially young students, in schools that endorse particular cultural norms and values may deny them access to alternative perspectives and constrain their ability to consider different visions of "the good." In addition, school cultures that grant primacy to one set of values constrain, if not oppress, those who hold alternative views. Such settings may have effects that extend beyond the school as well. They may lead mainstream students to develop and feel comfortable expressing contempt for those with other perspectives. (p. 31)

We argue that a new understanding of community is needed for schools, one that sheds the "sameness" connotations of traditional theory and is compatible with the context of postmodern diversity. The "community of difference" or "otherness" concept (Furman, 1998; Shields, in press) offers a model in its focus on "acceptance of difference with respect, justice and appreciation and peaceful cooperation within difference" (Furman, p. 312) as a basis for community cohesion.

The second problematic issue, related to the first, is that some of the renditions of community in education tend to create an impression of the school as an isolated, "stand-alone" community, in which heroic educators strive for cohesion amidst a sea of chaotic outside forces that threaten the school's educational values. For example, the literatures on professional community among educators (e.g., Louis & Kruse, 1995) and on community among students (as reviewed by Osterman, 2001) tend to this narrow rendition of school community. While another major strand of "school-community" literature in education explicitly addresses school-community linkages, such as shared governance, coordinated services for children, and parent involvement (Merz &

Furman, 1997), this literature also reflects a relatively atomized view of the school. For example, the coordinated services movement, which intends to better meet the needs of children and families through stronger collaborative linkages between schools and other community agencies, generally reflects a mindset of educational "professionals" providing services to "clients" within the community (Furman & Merz, 1996). This mindset and its manifestations in other areas of "school-community" literature overemphasize the distance or differences between the professional culture of the school and the culture of the outside community, while neglecting the interdependence of the two. However, as Driscoll and Kerchner (1999), Mawhinney (in press), and others are beginning to point out, this isolationist perspective is dysfunctional to the extent that it derives from a deficit view of the cultural capital of the surrounding community along with a tacit assumption of the superiority of the professional educational culture of the school, and fails to acknowledge the strong ties of students to their home cultures and the various "communities" to which they already belong. This developing literature offers an alternative "ecological" view of school community in which the school is seen as integrally embedded in the surrounding community, relying on the community's unique assets (as opposed to trying to fix its deficits) and contributing, in turn, to the development of the community's social capital. In other words, this literature is surfacing and exploring the fundamental *interdependence* of school and local community. Furman (1998) takes this idea further by calling for a vision of community that is based on a sense of *global* interdependence in regard to ecological sustainability and global survival. This developing literature suggests that the concept of community in schools has been artificially truncated by too narrow a focus on the school itself. For a sense of community to prosper in schools, the sense of interconnectedness, interdependence and cultural capital exchange between community and school needs to be recognized and nurtured.

Problematizing community around these two issues leads to the recognition that "community" as it is envisioned for schools in contemporary society needs to be redefined, and this redefinition will then inform the idea of democratic community. This new understanding of community must be based on acceptance and celebration of difference rather than a futile and nostalgic striving for sameness and homogeneity, and it will focus on the integral linkages between the school, the surrounding community, and the larger global community rather than on the isolated community within the school walls. We argue that key concepts on which to build this new concept of community are *interdependence* and *the common good*. In other words, an understanding needs to be developed that, within the diversity of the school population, all are interdependent in regard to achieving the common good of the school; that the school and surrounding community are also interdependent—culturally and economically—with the school being a key contributor to the community's cultural capital and common good; and that ultimately, all people, and the school communities to which they belong, are interdependent and interconnected in contributing to the common good of humankind.

Problematizing Democracy

There is no question that public schools in American society are expected to represent democratic values and prepare students for participation in a democratic society. This understanding is so ingrained in the American way of thinking about schooling that it is "common sense." But beyond this common sense understanding, the agreement ends. What is the best way to prepare students for a democratic society? How much democracy must there be in schools themselves to accomplish this? What do we really mean by democracy in our increasingly transnational and multicultural societies? A flurry of publications over the last 20 years has addressed these fundamental questions and debates about the meaning of democracy in our time (e.g., Allen & Regan, 1998; Barber, 1984; Bellah, Madsen, Sullivan, Swidler & Tipton, 1985, 1991; Guinier, 1994; Gutmann, 1987; MacIntyre, 1984; Marty, 1997; Mitchell, 2001; Sandel, 1998; Selznick, 1992).

To approach a reconstructed notion of democratic community in schools, we choose to problematize democracy around two related issues that are embedded in these questions. The first is that the practice of democracy in schools has been minimal; in other words, democratic practices such as freedom of choice and expression are seldom experienced in schools. The second issue is that a dominant understanding of democracy, an understanding that can be traced back to the founders (Barber, 1984; Shklar, 1991) and that continues as the dominant understanding and practice of democracy today, tends to emphasize the freedom to pursue individual self-interest, with citizen participation in government reduced to electing representatives who will promote policies that serve the pursuit of that self-interest. This position has tended to hold sway over the other view of democracy—that it is government by the people, of the people, for the people, where citizen participation involves debating issues concerning the common good of the community and enacting policies and legislation that serve the common good. The first view of democracy tends to be the typical understanding of democracy, both within schools and within the larger society.

DEMOCRATIC MINIMALISM IN SCHOOLS

We agree with Maxcy (1995) that democratic "minimalism" (p. 60) has dominated the history of American public education during the last century. Both within the school and in regard to local control or governance, the scope of democratic decision making and freedom of choice and expression has been extremely narrow. While the issue of local control will be discussed later in the section on *Realpolitik*, minimalism in regard to the practice of democracy *within* schools is relevant here.

Why is democracy minimally practiced in schools? Maxcy (1995) explains a common fear that "democracy cannot be extended fully into classrooms without risk" (p. 60). The perceived risks of democracy are apparently chaos and loss of control. As Crow and Slater (1996) state, "democratic organizations tend to be disorderly because they leave the solution of the problem of social order largely up to individual choice and will" (p. 7). To head off potential chaos, students and educators are expected to conform to hierarchically imposed decisions about what they study and teach and when, what the outcomes of instruction should be (in spite of persuasive constructivist theory of learning), how they behave and talk, and even how they look. Notwithstanding the recent wave of interest in "service learning" as an "experiential" path to learning democracy (Eisenhower Leadership Group, 1996), learning about democracy may be one of the least experiential aspects of K-12 curricula. Democracy is typically taught through the indoctrination of prescribed social studies curricula about governance and legal systems. It is assumed that students will "learn" what democratic participation means so they will be prepared to exercise it when they gain their full rights as citizens. The problem with such learning is that it is "abstract," or unconnected with real life. Slater (2000) explains this problem:

Abstract education bears little plausible relation to life. It makes little effort to inform the here and now. It is learning without having a readily apparent reason to learn. It is education motivated mainly by authority and command . . . it does not give children access to the full meaning of the present nor to experiences in democratic living. Abstract civic education, for example, does not give children any kind of experience that might be associated with democratic community but simply *ideas and information* about democracy and government. (p. 4, emphasis in the original)

We argue that the "democracy" of democratic community cannot exist in schools dominated by this minimalist, "abstract" approach to learning *about* democracy. Quite simply, democratic community must be *practiced*, a point we will develop in more detail later.

THE "MODERN" LIBERAL VIEW OF DEMOCRACY

The second issue regarding democracy is that current understandings of democracy are still shaped by "early 20th-century modern liberalism" (Maxcy, 1995, p. 58), which emphasizes individual rights and self-interest. As Maxcy states,

Modern liberalism conceived of a society in which the emphasis was on private individuals. Institutions of government were means by which these isolated individuals were governed by elected representatives . . . The public interest was taken to be the sum total of all individual interests, forming an endless calculation of self-interest. (p. 58)

Strike (1999) calls this "thin democracy," which

sees society as composed of individuals and groups who have their own conception of a good life and who have a right to pursue it without undue interference from others. These individuals and groups, however, live in a society with other individuals and groups with other conceptions of the good, with whom they must interact and cooperate. Thus, they will need to make some decisions collectively. Democratic decision making is viewed by thin democracy as the fairest way in which to make these collective decisions. (pp. 59-60)[3]

Strike contrasts this "thin" democracy with "thick" democracy, which

agrees that democratic practices promote fair decision making, but its value goes well beyond this. Thick democracy attaches significant value to such goods as participation, civic friendship, inclusiveness, and solidarity. Thick democracy tolerates significant diversity in conceptions of the good as well . . . (p. 60)

While some of the contemporary writing on democratic community in schools approaches this "thick" or "deep" version of democracy (e.g., Maxcy, 1995), the "thin" version is also highly visible in discussions of schooling and democracy. Crow and Slater (1996), for example, focus on rational decision making when they write that democracy is "rule by the many," in which

Decision-making is not confined to one or to a few people but becomes the work of many. In organizations, this work essentially comes down to the work of defining problems, setting goals for solving the problems, identifying alternative strategies for achieving the goals that have been set, choosing from among these alternatives definite courses of action to be pursued . . . (p. 5)

This second issue—the prevalence of the classical liberal notion of democracy—is linked to the first—the minimalist practice of democracy in schools. If democracy is viewed as democratic election of representatives who arbitrate the demands of self-interested groups of citizens, then teaching *about* it is perhaps sufficient. It requires little experience to learn to "vote" when one's individual preferences conflict with the preferences of others. But this version of democracy is problematic for the postmodern context of diversity, fragmentation, and transnationalism. Democracy focused narrowly on the rights of individuals concerned primarily with their own self-interest will not lead to mutual understanding and a sense of interdependence in working for the common good in a multicultural, diverse and increasingly cross-national society. Rather, this limited practice of democracy likely will perpetuate and increase misunderstandings and conflict between balkanized groups operating in their own self-interest, will leave power in the hands of the "majority," and will perpetuate the marginalization of the less powerful (Guinier, 1994).

Further, democracy cannot be just about national economic interests. As national boundaries are increasingly permeated by regional and global alliances, democracy as a national political order is giving way to a regional and a global political order. In terms of the environment, our participation in the setting of national and local policy must take account of the effects of our decisions on those nations to the north and south of us, and indeed to all the nations of the globe. Similarly with economic policy, with trade policy, with health policy, with migration policy, with military policy, and with space policy, we can no longer govern ourselves in isolation from, or worse, in positive disregard for the rest of the peoples of the earth. We are becoming more aware that our common survival as a human race depends on mutual cooperation among all nations.

RECONCEPTUALIZING DEMOCRACY

Problematizing democracy around these issues leads to a reconceptualization of democracy and how it may be practiced in schools. Because of the increasingly pressing need for cross-cultural, cross-national dialogue and understandings in regard to the common good, we argue that democracy needs to incorporate the values of "postmodern liberalism"

(Maxcy, 1995, p. 58) or civic republicanism (Bellah et al., 1985; Sandel, 1998) or "deep" democracy and civic participation as advocated by Gutmann (1987) and others, and as extended by more current analyses of transnationalism (Mitchell, 2001). These values include:

- The worth and dignity of individuals and the value of their participation;
- Reverence for free and open inquiry and critique;
- The responsibility of individuals to participate in open inquiry, collective choices and actions in the interest of the common good;
- The recognition that "postmodern" democratic participation transcends understandings of democratic principles associated with specific nation-states.

Starratt (2001) sees this democratic participation as the sharing of our "stories" in the interest of mutual understandings:

[Our] common space is productively occupied by our stories, not by our rationalizations of our convictions about theories of democracy. We will find common ground in stories about our lives and our communities, stories that will generate bonds of affection and sentiment. Instead of seeking to become a community in which we share uniform commitments to common goals, values, and cultural expression, we might seek a more modest goal of accommodation and acquiescence so that we can collectively get on with our public lives. (p. 6)

Another way to say this is that democracy implies a *social morality*, not simply of elementary justice, but the more subtle morality of sociality itself. Such a morality involves acting *for* others as well as with others, in the interest of the common good. It necessarily (though not inevitably) stretches the interests of citizens beyond national interests to whatever binds human beings in a fuller and more fruitful association.[4]

Rethinking Democratic Community for Schools

Rethinking the concept of democratic community for 21st-century schools requires leaving behind the comfortable but naive image of community in which a sense of belonging is achieved through identification with people who are "like us." While such "gathered" communities will always have an important place in our lives (e.g., in churches), it is an inappropriate notion for public schools in a postmodern society characterized by diversity, fragmentation and transnationalism. Indeed, the foundational principles of the "common school" system in the United States rejected the idea of specialized or "gathered" school communities, so it is doubly ironic that much of the contemporary work on community in schools tends to be regressive in its focus on sameness. Our repackaged concept of democratic community is informed by the idea of "community of difference" in which difference is celebrated but interdependence is recognized, and the common good, locally and globally, is the glue. Similarly, rethinking the concept of democratic community requires a transformed notion of democracy, one that challenges the traditional equation of democracy with majority-vote governance procedures that allow self-interested individuals in a nation-state to make collective decisions binding on all. Instead, our repackaged concept of democratic community is informed by a "deep" or "thick" version of democratic participation in which all citizens have a respected voice, and communal action is determined through high levels of participation in free and open inquiry.

In bringing together these ideas of community and democracy, we argue that contemporary concerns about the limits of democracy and the limits of community can be overcome through a synthesis of the strengths of democracy and the realities of contemporary community. The traditional formula "E pluribus unum" may now capture a new dynamic both for the school and for the polity. Scholars who have struggled with the meaning of *community* in postmodern times and scholars who have struggled with the meaning of *democracy* have dealt with the same issues of diversity, societal fragmentation and globalization. As they have worked toward new "theories" for each, they have achieved a remarkable convergence. It becomes clear that any sense of community within the context of postmodern diversity depends on the kind of intentional civic participation with a deep respect for difference that is the essence of "deep democracy." Likewise, the kind of civic participation expected in deep democracy will be motivated only by a communitarian sense of interdependence in seeking the common good. In this sense, the reconstructed concept of democratic community is more than the sum of its parts, as it both extends and resolves some of the theoretical struggles in both of these lines of inquiry. Our reconstructed concept of democratic community may be stated:

Democratic community is processual and moral. It is the enactment of participatory processes of open inquiry in working for the common good in regard to both local and global concerns; it is guided by a social morality that recognizes the worth of individuals *and* the social value of community (however temporal and provisional), celebrates difference, and understands the ultimate and pragmatic interdependence of all.

At this point, to approach an analysis of the linkages between this repackaged concept of democratic community and leadership practices, we should translate this theoretical abstraction into a sketch of what a democratic community in a school might look like. Since we agree with Apple and Beane (1995) that enactment of democratic community is a systemic challenge involving structures, processes, and curricula, we offer the following as an "ideal" portrait and will discuss the *Realpolitik* of its implementation later. Schools with this focus would center on two major concerns—the *processes* of democratic participation and the *morality* of democratic community—and both of these major concerns would be reflected in the core work of schools, curriculum and instruction.

THE PROCESSES OF DEMOCRATIC PARTICIPATION

Schools that build a democratic community would establish structures and procedures that allow all members of the school community to participate and have a respected voice in decisions and policies that affect them. Recognizing the interdependence of the school and the surrounding community, and the "assets" that any community offers, these structures and procedures would include a variety of community members and be open to *community-initiated* participation. Structural size becomes an important matter, as school community advocates have long recognized, since meaningful participation requires being heard in face-to-face settings. Meier and Schwarz (1995) capture the essence of this participatory component in describing Central Park East Secondary School:

We knew we had to be small, multi-aged, intimate, and interesting . . . Family and school would need to be allies . . . We created a structure in which people—students, students and teachers, and teachers and teachers, and their families—could think aloud together and jointly make decisions. (p. 29)

This "thinking aloud together" does not always involve formal mechanisms, such as committee structures and site-based councils. As Meier and Schwarz note, much of the intimacy of community is created through informal, spontaneous interactions. It is the smallness and openness of structures that allow these interactions to take place.

Taking these ideas to a more concrete level, in a democratic community students at the classroom level would work *with* teachers to "engage in collaborative planning, reaching decisions that respond to the concerns, aspirations, and interests of both" (Apple & Beane, 1995, p. 9). Students and teachers might engage in meetings guided by a four-stage process of democratic deliberation articulated by Gibbs (1994): (1) information sharing; (2) reactions; (3) ideas and strategy development; and (4) debriefing. Meetings such as these are not restricted to instructional/curricular decisions, but can address a variety of classroom issues and be used to continuously deliberate about the *morality* of democratic participation, as discussed below. Educators can follow the same basic procedures in their deliberations about teaching, curriculum, democratic participation, and other issues. School structure and schedules need to allow the time and space for this common planning and meeting time. Significant parent involvement and broad-based community participation also need to be nurtured through creative ideas in regard to shared governance, communication and meeting structures that are equitable and inviting and that promote understanding across groups and individuals who might clash in their values. Peterson (1995) provides an example of these creative initiatives at La Escuela Fratney in Milwaukee, Wisconsin:

We did three things to try to counter this [racial] imbalance [in parent involvement] and foster broader parental involvement. First we established quotas for our site-based management council, so that African American and Latino parents were ensured seats. Second, we decided to redirect money from our budget to hire two part-time parent organizers, a Mexican American and an African American. Finally, . . . we paid 15 parents to participate in a six-week evening workshop in which they discussed school issues . . . parents who didn't usually participate in school activities were encouraged to participate. (pp. 74-75)

Democratic participation requires more than forums, however; it also requires the *ability* to listen, understand, empathize, negotiate, speak, debate and resolve conflicts in a spirit of interdependence and working for the common good. As Maxcy (1995) states, "Communication forms one of the criterial methods of this new democracy. Dialogue and conversation are pledged to the value of continuous discussion and debate, not only regarding the ends but also regarding the means of reaching goals" (p. 129). Shields and Seltzer (1997) use the term "discursive communities" to center the importance of communication in "communities of difference," while Hemmings (2000) and Schultz, Buck and Niesz (2000) provide research-based examples of classroom dialogic processes.

A promising idea regarding communication and cross-cultural understanding that is emerging in recent literature is dialogue theory (e.g., Sidorkin, 1999) as informed by Bakhtin's concept of the dialogic as the center of human existence. Dialogue theory centers more on understanding than on decision making and "best arguments." While dialogue theory is complex, and what we say here is merely a gloss, as a practice dialogue is usually taken to mean that each person in a communicative space has the chance to openly express her or his thoughts and feelings, that these are received without argument or judgment, and that this process repeats until larger understandings are achieved within the space. Proponents of dialogue argue that it is an end in itself, rather than an instrument to other ends, yet it can produce the "satisfaction" associated with "good" schools that effectively create communities of difference. Sidorkin writes:

A good school is that with which students, parents, and teachers are sincerely satisfied, and which does not serve one group or class exclusively, at the expense of others. This condition is at the heart of the contemporary issues around the notion of inclusion, which in turn is a manifestation of the problem of difference . . . The way a school handles the difference without exclusion to a large extent defines the character of the school. How do we make so many people happy together if it is different things that make them happy? A solution is possible if a school possesses certain qualities that make dialogical relations possible and more likely to occur. In other words, people are happy in a school that is dialogical. In some way, whether a school is good has nothing to do with its organizational structure, curriculum and instruction . . . and so on. A school is good if your voice is included in that polyphonic act of assessing whether the school is good. (p. 111)

Regarding this "criterial" necessity of meaningful communication, then, democratic community schools would attend to continual training and practice in the skills of democratic deliberation and dialogue. The importance of "learning" deliberation is reflected in Smith's (2000) recent analysis of common themes in works about moral education for children, in which she found that

the best option for preparing young people to become virtuous adults and citizens is to educate them to engage in reasoned deliberations . . . In light of this view, the primary question for moral and civic education is not necessarily "What values should be cultivated in young people?" . . . [but] "What capacities are necessary?" (pp. 412-413).[5]

THE MORALITY OF DEMOCRATIC COMMUNITY

Inseparable from the type of communication and dialogue needed in democratic community is the moral sense or ethos that guides the community. This moral sense has several facets or dimensions, as implied throughout our discussions:

- A social morality that values sociality itself, that is, that values coming together in the communicative spaces in which dialogue can occur in the interest of the common good;
- A reverence for open inquiry and critique within these common spaces, in pursuit of the common good;
- A respect for individuals and for the "assets" they bring to communities, with a view toward celebrating difference;
- A sense of responsibility that acknowledges the interdependence of all in achieving the common good.

We recognize that, in making this claim about a strong moral sense as a basic component of democratic community, we are suggesting commitment to a "thick" set of values of the type that Strike (1999) claims violates the "liberal inclusiveness" of American democracy. In other words, adoption of this moral center may, paradoxically, "marginalize" other sets of values. However, we see no way out of this paradox, as we believe that survival of any sort of civic cohesiveness and of a sense of community within postmodern diversity is dependent on these basic tenets of sociality and civility. Further, because this "center" is about respect and celebration of difference, its basic purpose is *not* to marginalize but to commit to civility and collective action *within diversity*. Schools that practice democratic community, then, would need to continually promote these values. Educators would both model and discuss behaviors that represent respect, sociality, empathy, compassion, acceptance of difference, forgiveness, generosity, and teamwork. Older students could serve as big brothers and sisters for younger students, helping them to develop these basic habits of caring for fellow members of the school community. The interdependence of all might be a foundational moral "theme" for such a school community.

CURRICULUM AND INSTRUCTION

A democratic school would have a curriculum that is compatible with the processual and moral dimensions outlined above. As we have noted elsewhere (Furman, 1998; Starratt, 2001), curriculum is curiously absent from most discussions of school community and democracy, though how curriculum is chosen, what it consists of, and how it is delivered are part and parcel of the culture and ethos of the school. A curriculum compatible with democratic community would be "open" to multiple ideas and sources of information and to critique of this information. It would help students recognize that most sources of information are written from a certain point of view. It would be carefully scrutinized for tendencies to marginalize, disenfranchise or essentialize certain groups. As Apple and Beane (1995) state,

> Those committed to a more participatory curriculum understand that knowledge is socially constructed, that it is produced and disseminated by people who have particular values, interests, and biases. . . . In a democratic curriculum . . . young people learn to be "critical readers" of their society. When confronted with some knowledge or viewpoint, they are encouraged to ask questions like these: Who said this? Why did they say it? Why should we believe this? And who benefits if we believe this and act upon it? (pp. 13-14)

A democratic curriculum would also be based in the theme of interdependence. Particularly in its presentation of history, science, and government, the curriculum would help students understand the fundamental "ecological" interconnectedness of human life across cultures and with nature. Postmodern curriculum theorists have proposed just such an approach in their calls for a curriculum focused on interdependence and ecological sustainability. For example, Slattery (1995) states,

> The emerging postmodern holistic and ecological models of curriculum dissolve the artificial boundary between the outside community and the classroom. Postmodern teaching celebrates the interconnectedness of knowledge, learning experiences, international communities, the natural world, and life itself. (p. 169)

Needless to say, the enactment of democratic community in schools would require changes in teaching and classroom practice. The processes of democratic deliberation, which are the heart of democratic community, are not meant to be compartmentalized into specific classroom "meetings" or decision-making situations. Indeed, this segregation of democratic processes from instruction would constitute a parody of democracy rather than its enactment. In a democratic community, classroom management might involve a prior discussion among class members and consensus about appropriate behavior and sanctions for violations. Collaborative learning would take on a different tone. Peer teaching and coaching would become more common. Classroom debates of differing perspectives would teach respect for different points of view as well as provide for learning how to conduct such debates in public, following rules of civility and respect, as well as logic and evidence gathering.

This sketch of a "democratic community" school highlights the systemic nature and challenge of enacting democratic community in schools. Clearly, leadership is an important concern. We turn next to a consideration of the implications for leadership in schools.

Leadership for Democratic Community in Schools

Apple and Beane (1995) remind us that "democratic schools . . . do not happen by chance. They result from explicit attempts by educators to put in place arrangements and opportunities that will bring democracy to life" (p. 9). We define leadership for democratic community in this way, as explicit attempts by educators to "bring to life" democratic community. Starratt (2001) refers to this as "cultivation." He states,

By this I mean that democratic leadership is primarily concerned to cultivate an environment that supports participation, sharing of ideas, and the virtues of honesty, openness, flexibility, and compassion. Democratic educational leadership should be focused on cultivating school environments where . . . richer and fuller humanity is experienced and activated by people acting in communion. . . . (p. 7)

Research offers very few examples of these "explicit attempts" to "cultivate" democratic community in schools. Rusch (1998) provides a rare exception in her analysis of the leadership of seven principals who "foster and sustain democratic practices" in their schools, here defined primarily as participatory decision-making practices. Rusch found that the principals' *values* were more salient than actual practices in sustaining democratic community. These values included the idea of "mutual influence" in regard to leadership in a number of critical areas (e.g., teaching and learning, information access) and the valuing of "hard work" in the service of caring, resolving conflicts, and maintaining democratic practices. Rusch's study supports the notion of moral commitment on the part of educators involved in creating democratic communities but provides little in the way of specific practices. Informed by Rusch's research and other works on democratic community, what follows are our working hypotheses regarding the leadership practices that would help create and sustain democratic community in schools, followed by our analyses of the linkage between our repackaged notion of democratic community and leadership theory.

Leadership for democratic community in schools is, in fact, *democratic* and *communal*. It is not the purvey of persons in specific administrative roles but a communal responsibility shared by all participants at a particular school site. Rusch's (1998) research-based finding of "mutual influence" pertains here. However, it also needs to be recognized that some participants are at various times in more favorable positions than others to influence the school's structure, processes, curriculum and instruction. For example, a school principal may be in a better position to research solutions and suggest structural arrangements that allow for smaller, more intimate groupings of teachers and students. Curriculum directors or committees may critically analyze curriculum in regard to concerns and offer alternatives for adoption by teachers. In general, however, the implications for leadership that follow pertain to all participants in the democratic community.

Since democratic community is *processual*, leadership practice attends to the creation and maintenance of democratic processes and structures that nurture "thinking aloud together." Leadership in this regard is intentional and opportunistic. All decisions and issues that substantively affect school community members should be open to democratic deliberation. Thus, leaders need to attend with sensitivity to the continuous flow of concerns and decision opportunities within the life of the school, and those in the surrounding community that affect the school. They need to invite democratic deliberation in regard to these issues and decisions and make it clear that participation is open, welcome and appreciated. They need to work to "institutionalize" structures, forums, and communication processes that promote participation. They need to both model and provide training in deliberative processes such as dialogue.

For example, a school principal might become aware early in the year that something needs to be done about the school's discipline policy. Some of the teachers have continually expressed dissatisfaction with the current policy, feeling that it does nothing to change problem student behavior. Various students who have been disciplined have complained bitterly about the unjust nature of their punishments. The "no tolerance" policy on contraband has generated several appeals to the school board and even a lawsuit. Clearly, this is a substantive issue that affects all members of the school community. The principal decides to initiate a democratic process to consider the policy. She first invites all interested teachers to a series of open discussions about discipline in the school, asking for volunteer facilitators and recorders to summarize the meetings in writing. In these meetings, she suggests and models the ground rules for "dialogue" in which all may speak without judgment of their comments. She asks for any follow-up written comments by a certain date. Following these meetings, she provides a written summary to the entire staff and invites teachers to "get involved" in determining a process for revising the policy. This process, democratically determined by the staff participants, might include classroom meetings with students to discuss the discipline policy, what behaviors should be valued or proscribed in the school community, and how a just system of handling behavior problems might look. It might include open forums with parents and other community members in regard to the same questions. All of these meetings would generate written summaries and comments. Ultimately, any new policy would emerge from and take into account these various discussions and recommendations. Over time, through the continual modeling and repetition of these democratic processes, a "structure" that promotes these processes can become a routine part of the school.

What this vignette illustrates is the creative, opportunistic, messy and idiosyncratic nature of leadership for democratic community in schools. Since decisions about the processes themselves are open to democratic deliberation, there is no replicable "model" of democratic community that can be infused into schools, nor is it possible to prescribe specific practices. Instead, leadership for democratic community involves a stance or intentionality, a commitment to the moral sense of democratic community.

Since democratic community is *moral*, leadership practices proceed from this moral sense. It is intentional leadership aimed at enacting the values of democratic community: sociality for its own sake; open inquiry in pursuit of the common good; a deep respect for individuals; celebrating difference; and a sense of interdependence with all life. As we said earlier, we approach this argument for "thick" values (and, by extension, for these "thick" value dispositions on the part of educators) with some trepidation but also with some hope. We are mindful that advocating a particular set of values smacks of "indoctrination" or "social control," of "centers" and their marginalizing tendencies. However, we are also mindful that we all need a sense of community, and we need to live together in sustainable and ethical ways, particularly in public institutions like schools. In advocating a particular stance in regard to these needs, we join the ranks of "affirmative" or "constructive" postmodernists (Maxcy, 1995), who "seek to build a new worldview, a way to live in harmony with nature and with each other as the postmodern age unfolds" (Furman, 1998, p. 306).

How can leadership practice enact the values of democratic community in schools? First, the assumption is that those practicing leadership are, in fact, committed to these values. As we have noted earlier, democracy is practiced "minimally" in schools, so transforming schools into places of commitment to democratic community is obviously a tall order. While addressing this issue in any depth is beyond the scope of this discussion, we can suggest that there are major implications here for recruitment and preparation programs for both teachers and administrators. Assuming that educators at a particular school site are committed to these values, enactment would entail modeling, practice and training. Note again the vignette of the principal and the discipline policy. When inviting others to participate and demonstrating dialogue techniques, the principal is modeling not only the processes of democratic deliberation but also the values of respecting difference, open inquiry and pursuit of the common good, in ways that can be replicated in teacher meetings and in classrooms. Through iterations of these meetings, the principal is engaging both herself and her staff in practicing these processes and the enactment of these values. As participants become more interested in how these values and processes affect their lives in school, they may request more training in communication skills, listening, teamwork, dialogue and issues of diversity and multiculturalism. As Maxcy (1995) states, "the first step in becoming what you aspire to be is to purchase the uniform. By the daily habitual practice, you will become what you aspire to be" (p. 68).

CONNECTIONS WITH LEADERSHIP THEORY

In regard to leadership theory, our analyses of democratic community and leadership practices suggest a convergence of four leadership concepts or paradigms: moral leadership, critical-humanist leadership, constructivist leadership, and leadership as an art form. Leithwood and Duke (1998), in a recent analysis of the "conceptual models" of leadership in education, define moral leadership as including "normative, political/democratic, and symbolic concepts of leadership" (p. 36). They state,

During the 1990s, the normative dimension of leadership has been one of the fastest growing areas of leadership study . . . Those writing about moral leadership argue that values are a central part of all leadership and administrative practice . . . Moral leadership assumes that the critical focus of leadership ought to be on the values and ethics of leaders themselves. (p. 37)

They go on to cite Lees' (1995) claim that "leadership in a democratic society entails a moral imperative to promote democracy, empowerment, and social justice" (p. 37). Our rendition of leadership for democratic community echoes Lees' notion of "moral imperative." Thus, leadership for democratic community joins a growing body of work in the field on what leadership is *for*, rather than what leadership *is*, *how* it is done and by *whom*, all the primary subjects of study during "the theory movement" in educational leadership from the 1950s to the 1980s (Leithwood & Duke, 1998).

Our rendition of democratic community also reflects a critical-humanist perspective on leadership (Slater, Bolman, Crow, Goldring, & Thurston, 1994), which involves a commitment to social change. As described by Burrell and Morgan (1979), the critical humanist paradigm "emphasizes the importance of overthrowing or transcending the limitations of existing social arrangements" (p. 32). Clearly, working for democratic community in schools involves "overthrowing or transcending" existing structures, processes and power relationships that tend to minimize democratic practice.

Our concept of democratic community also fits nicely with the constructivist perspective on leadership (Slater et al., 1994), particularly as articulated by Lambert (1995) and her colleagues. Drawing from constructivist learning theory, Lambert defines constructivist leadership as "the reciprocal processes that enable participants in an educational community to construct meanings that lead toward a common purpose about schooling" (p. 29). Distinguishing constructivist leadership from the traditional leadership "paradigm," which is "hierarchical, individualistic, reductionistic, linear, [and] mechanical" (p. 32), Lambert states that constructivist leadership is "manifest within the relationships in a community" and emerges from "being real and vulnerable with each other in ways that engage us in genuine conversations" (pp. 32-33). Thus, constructivist leadership according to Lambert is distributed across all participants, based in communication, and aimed toward purpose which "emerges from conversation" (p. 47). Lambert's ideas and the implications for leadership practice proposed here are essentially in agreement and complement each other.

Finally, leadership for democratic community may be viewed as an "art form" in which leaders engage in "aesthetic and experimental behaviors" to "design" a new school order. Maxcy (1995) argues persuasively for this "moral artistry" in restructuring schools for democracy. He states,

If we think of the moral school as an artist's studio, we are able to use pragmatic metaphors to better approximate a revolution in thinking about the organization and function of schools. Take, for example, the school as a weaver's studio in which the artist-educator comes to inquire into and understand competing values—people's desires, needs, and goals—as threads of experience that must be interwoven into a tapestry of meaning. The educator qua artist is able to take the point of view of others with their interests and desires and to seek a harmonious whole—a moral ideal space within which competing interests become harmonious. (p. 169)

The convergence of these four concepts of leadership—moral, critical-humanist, constructivist, and artistic—seems to capture the essence of our concept of leadership for democratic community in schools. It is an "art" that facilitates the construction of meaning within diversity, aimed at the moral purpose of transforming schools into democratic communities.

The Realpolitik *of Enacting Democratic Community in Schools*

Berliner (2001) argues that democracy in schools and society is threatened by current policy directions dominated by "privileged" business interests. According to Berliner, business is so influential and privileged that it is shaping the curriculum taught in schools. It is "narrowing and intensifying" the curriculum under the assumption that knowledge is "instrumental" and must be linked to "productivity." Berliner argues that business is so dominant because when public discourse declines, the powerful take over. There is no longer any effective civic opposition to the takeover by business corporations. Apple and Beane (1995) agree with Berliner in stating,

The idea of democratic schools has fallen on hard times . . . All around us, we can see the signs . . . Local decision making is glorified in political rhetoric at the same time that legislation is introduced to put in place national standards, a national curriculum, and national tests . . . the needs of business and industry are suddenly the preeminent goals of our educational system. (p. 3)

The difficulty of enacting democratic community in schools in the face of these anti-democratic forces is illustrated by Peterson's (1995) description of the "struggle" to establish La Escuela Fratney—a democratic school governed by parents and teachers—in Milwaukee, Wisconsin. He states:

We have encountered significant problems that reflect how our society, despite its democratic rhetoric, is in many ways undemocratic. Among the problems: A central office wedded to autocratic methods of leadership, a school system structured to inhibit collaborative teaching practices, parents and teachers tied to the authoritarian habits of their own schooling, students conditioned by a mass-media culture that values individual consumption over the common good, and a socioeconomic system that places little value on urban schools and the families served by them. (p. 60)

The *Realpolitik* of school governance suggests that enacting democratic community in schools faces many challenges. Chief among these is overcoming the "rational/technical/instrumental" (Furman, in press) assumptions about schooling and learning, which have been increasingly shaped by business interests over the last several decades. These assumptions include the following:

- The purpose of schools is *instrumental*—to serve national economic interests by preparing students for the work force;
- The success of schools in achieving this instrumental purpose can be rationally determined by *measurable student achievement*;
- The individual's motivation for learning in schools is *instrumental*—to succeed on individual measures of student achievement, in competition with other students, to secure future financial prosperity;
- Teaching is a *technical* problem and teachers/schools can be held *accountable* for measurable student achievement.

Among the results of this mindset are that competition and individualism are valued over cooperation and interdependence; striving for personal success crowds out a sense of the common good; the myths of meritocracy are privileged over social justice; students are valued as academic "performers" rather than as unique and valuable individuals; and democratic processes are minimally practiced in schools.

Given this mindset about schooling, coupled with hierarchical, authoritarian traditions of school leadership, leadership for democratic community in schools requires opportunistic action at the local level as well as intentional and proactive leadership on the part of state and national leaders to affect policy directions. The research of Oakes, Quartz, Ryan, and Lipton (2000) on schools that attempted to wed

school renewal with the promotion of civic virtue indicates how difficult it is to bring the dream into reality. Leaders of these efforts—
administrators, teachers, parents—encountered passionate resistance
due to local political agendas, traditional perspectives on curriculum
basics, misunderstandings and arguments about the meaning of
democracy and community, resistance to diversity issues, and so forth.
Even under the best of circumstances, forming democratic communities in schools by its very nature implies public debate and disagreement. In proposing democratic community as a centerpiece theme for
shaping the agenda for educational leadership for the next several
decades we recognize that this ideal will not be easily enacted. We end
with a perspective offered by Cornell West (1999):

To be part of the democratic tradition is to be a prisoner of hope. And you
cannot be a prisoner of hope without engaging in a form of struggle that
keeps the best of the past alive. To engage in that struggle means that one is
always willing to acknowledge that there is no triumph around the corner, but
that you persist because you believe it is right and just and moral. (p. 12)

Conclusion

In considering democratic community as *the* center for educational
leadership, we make these claims:

- Democratic community is not a "marginalizing" center for the
  field because it is based on acceptance and appreciation of difference.
- Democratic community "recultures the profession" by focusing
  on what leadership is *for*—serving the common good in a multicultural society and world.
- Democratic community is the most appropriate focus for school
  leadership in the "postmodern" world of diversity, fragmentation and cross-nationalism.

NOTES

1. We recognize that the idea of a "center" for the field is problematic in itself. As
Murphy (1999) states, "the very concept of a core carries the potential to privilege certain ideas while marginalizing others." However, at this point in our discussion, we will
skirt this issue, with the goal of demonstrating later how "democratic community" is
perhaps the *least* marginalizing of centers that could be adopted for educational leadership.

2. Throughout this discussion, we are concerned with democratic community in
comprehensive K-12 public schools. The issues of community-building and democracy

in private schools differ markedly from those in public schools since private school student populations are likely to be more homogeneous than in public schools and attendance is voluntary. Thus, private schools are inherently "gathered" or "valuational" communities (Furman, 1998) that do not fully reflect the diversity of postmodern society.

3. Contemporary labels of "conservative" and "liberal" can be confusing. Today's conservatives can be viewed as the "modern liberals" who are interested in "conserving" their individual rights and freedoms from the encroachments of government, while today's liberals view strong government involvement as necessary to guarantee equality.

4. See Strike (1999), however, for a counter-argument that "thick" democratic community is a "distinctive vision of the good" and therefore violates the liberal inclusiveness foundational to American democracy. In addition, Starratt (2001) has argued elsewhere that any theory of democratic leadership is perhaps futile because it is doubtful that "any theory would receive broad based scholarly or professional acceptance" in conditions of postmodernity, in which "it is simply no longer possible to find a common ground in rational argument" (p. 9).

5. We acknowledge, however, that the notion of cross-cultural dialogue has been contested recently in regard to the "problematic imperialist assumptions that often underlie it" (Jones, 1999, p. 299). In other words, however well intentioned, the idea of cross-cultural dialogue is itself culturally biased in its assumption of the desire to engage verbally with "others." As Jones puts it, "What if the 'other' fails to find interesting the idea of . . . empathetic understanding of the powerful, which is theoretically demanded by dialogic encounters?" (p. 299).

References

Allen, A. L., & Regan, Jr., M. C. (1998). *Debating democracy's discontent: Essays on American politics, law, and public philosophy.* New York: Oxford University Press.

Apple, M. W., & Beane, J. A. (Eds.). (1995). *Democratic schools.* Alexandria, VA: Association for Supervision and Curriculum Development.

Barber, B. (1984). *Strong democracy.* Princeton, NJ: Princeton University Press.

Bellah, R. N., Madsen, R., Sullivan, W. M., Swidler, A., & Tipton, S. M. (1985). *Habits of the heart: Individualism and commitment in American life.* New York: Harper Collins.

Bellah, R. N., Madsen, R., Sullivan, W. M., Swidler, A., & Tipton, S. M. (1991). *The good society.* New York: Alfred A. Knopf.

Berliner, D. (2001, April). *Democracy and education: Losing the battle.* Paper presented at the meeting of the American Educational Research Association, Seattle, WA.

Burrell, G., & Morgan, G. (1979). *Sociological paradigms and organizational analysis.* London: Heinemann Educational Books.

Calderwood, P. (2000). *Learning community: Finding common ground in difference.* New York: Teachers College Press.

Crow, G. M., & Slater, R. O. (1996). *Educating democracy: The role of systemic leadership.* Fairfax, VA: National Policy Board for Educational Administration.

Dewey, J. (1937). Democracy and educational administration. *School and Society, 45,* 457–462.

Driscoll, M. E., & Kerchner, C. T. (1999). The implications of social capital for schools, communities, and cities: Educational administration as if a sense of place mattered. In J. Murphy & K. S. Louis (Eds.), *Handbook of research on educational administration* (2nd ed., pp. 385–404). San Francisco: Jossey-Bass.

Eisenhower Leadership Group (1996). *Democracy at risk: How schools can lead.* College Park, MD: Center for Political Leadership & Participation.

Elshtain, J. B. (1995). *Democracy on trial.* New York: Basic Books.

Furman, G. C. (1998). Postmodernism and community in schools: Unraveling the paradox. *Educational Administration Quarterly, 34,* 298–328.

Furman, G. C. (Ed.). (in press). *School as community: From promise to practice.* Albany, NY: SUNY Press.

Furman, G. C., & Merz, C. (1996). Schools and community connections: Applying a sociological framework. In J. Cibulka & W. Kritek (Eds.), *Coordination among schools, families and communities: Prospects for educational reform* (pp. 323–347). Albany, NY: SUNY Press.

Gibbs, J. (1994). *Tribes: A new way of learning and being together.* Santa Rosa, CA: Center Source Publications.

Guinier, L. (1994). *The tyranny of the majority: Fundamental fairness in representative democracy.* New York: The Free Press.

Gutmann, A. (1987). *Democratic education.* Princeton, NJ: Princeton University Press.

Hemmings, A. (2000). High school democratic dialogues: Possibilities for praxis. *American Educational Research Journal, 37,* 67–91.

Jones, A. (1999). The limits of cross-cultural dialogue: Pedagogy, desire, and absolution in the classroom. *Educational Theory, 49,* 299–316.

Kahne, J. (1996). *Reframing educational policy: Democracy, community, and the individual.* New York: Teachers College Press.

Lambert, L., Walker, D., Zimmerman, D. P., Cooper, J. E., Lambert, M. D., Gardner, M. E., & Slack, P. J. (1995). *The constructivist leader.* New York: Teachers College Press.

Lees, K. A. (1995). Advancing democratic leadership through critical theory. *Journal of School Leadership, 3,* 380–390.

Leithwood, K., & Duke, D. L. (1998). Mapping the conceptual terrain of leadership: A critical point of departure for cross-cultural studies. *Peabody Journal of Education, 73*(2), 31–50.

Louis, K. S., & Kruse, S. D. (1995). *Professionalism and community: Perspectives on reforming urban schools.* Thousand Oaks, CA: Corwin Press.

MacIntyre, A. (1984). *After virtue: A study in moral theory* (2nd ed.). Notre Dame, IN: University of Notre Dame Press.

Marty, M. E. (1997). *The one and the many: America's struggle for the common good.* Cambridge, MA: Harvard University Press.

Mawhinney, H. B. (in press). The microecology of social capital formation: Developing community beyond the schoolhouse door. In G. Furman (Ed.), *School as community: From promise to practice.* Albany, NY: SUNY Press.

Maxcy, S. J. (1995). *Democracy, chaos, and the new school order.* Thousand Oaks, CA: Corwin Press.

Meier, D., & Schwarz, P. (1995). Central Park East Secondary School: The hard part is making it happen. In M. W. Apple & J. A. Beane (Eds.), *Democratic schools* (pp. 26-40). Alexandria, VA: Association for Supervision and Curriculum Development.

Merz, C., & Furman, G. C. (1997). *Community and schools: Promise and paradox.* New York: Teachers College Press.

Mitchell, K. (2001). Education for democratic citizenship: Transnationalism, multiculturalism, and the limits of liberalism. *Harvard Educational Review, 71,* 51-78.

Murphy, J. (1996). *The privatization of schooling: Problems and possibilities.* Newbury Park, CA: Corwin Press.

Murphy, J. (1999). *The quest for a center: Notes on the state of the profession of educational leadership.* Columbia, MO: University Council for Educational Administration.

Oakes, J., Quartz, K. H., Ryan, S., & Lipton, M. (2000). *Becoming good American schools.* San Francisco: Jossey-Bass.

Osterman, K. F. (2001). Students' need for belonging in the school community. *Review of Educational Research, 70,* 323-367.

Peterson, B. (1995). La Escuela Fratney: A journey toward democracy. In M. W. Apple & J. A. Beane (Eds.), *Democratic schools* (pp. 58-82). Alexandria, VA: Association for Supervision and Curriculum Development.

Reitzug, U. C., & O'Hair, M. J. (in press). From conventional schools to democratic school communities: The dilemmas of teaching and leadership. In G. Furman (Ed.), *School as community: From promise to practice.* Albany, NY: SUNY Press.

Rusch, E. A. (1998). Leadership in evolving democratic school communities. *Journal of School Leadership, 8,* 214-250.

Sandel, M. J. (1998). *Liberalism and the limits of justice* (2nd ed.). Cambridge, U.K.: Cambridge University Press.

Schultz, K., Buck, P., & Niesz, T. (2000). Democratizing conversations: Racialized talk in a post-desegregated middle school. *American Educational Research Journal, 37,* 33-65.

Selznick, P. (1992). *The moral commonwealth: Social theory and the promise of community.* Berkeley, CA: University of California Press.

Sergiovanni, T. J. (1994). *Building community in schools.* San Francisco: Jossey-Bass.

Shields, C. M. (in press). Thinking about community from a student perspective. In G. Furman (Ed.), *School as community: From promise to practice.* Albany, NY: SUNY Press.

Shields, C. M., & Seltzer, P. A. (1997). Complexities and paradoxes of community: Toward a more useful conceptualization of community. *Educational Administration Quarterly, 33,* 413-439.

Shklar, J. N. (1991). *American citizenship: The quest for inclusion.* Cambridge, MA: Harvard University Press.

Sidorkin, A. M. (1999). *Beyond discourse: Education, the self, and dialogue.* Albany, NY: SUNY Press.

Slater, R. O. (2000). *Schools, schooling, and democratic community in the postemotional society: A case for inquiry-creativity schools.* Unpublished manuscript.

Slater, R. O., Bolman, L., Crow, G. M., Goldring, E., & Thurston, P. W. (1994). Leadership and management processes: Taxonomy and overview. In W. K. Hoy (Ed.), *UCEA Document Base*. New York: McGraw-Hill.

Slattery, P. (1995). *Curriculum development in the postmodern era*. New York: Garland.

Smith, S. (2000). Morality, civics, and citizenship: Values and virtues in modern democracies. *Educational Theory, 50*, 405-418.

Starratt, R. J. (2001, April). *Democratic leadership theory in late modernity: An oxymoron or ironic possibility?* Paper presented at the Annual Conference of the American Educational Research Association, Seattle, WA.

Strike, K. A. (1999). Can schools be communities? The tension between shared values and inclusion. *Educational Administration Quarterly, 35*, 46-70.

Tönnies, F. (1957). *Community and society* (C. Loomis, Ed. & Trans.). East Lansing: Michigan State University Press. (Original work published as *Gemeinschaft und Gesellschaft*, 1887).

West, C. (1999). The moral obligation of living in a democratic society. In D. Batstone & E. Mendieta (Eds.), *The good citizen*. New York: Routledge.

CHAPTER 7

Leadership for Social Justice

COLLEEN L. LARSON AND KHAULA MURTADHA

> The goal of a true democracy such as ours, explained simply, is that any baby born in these United States, even if he is born to the blackest, most illiterate, most unprivileged Negro in Mississippi, is, merely by being born and drawing his first breath in this democracy, endowed with the exact same rights as a child born to a Rockefeller. Of course it's not true. Of course it never will be true. But I challenge anybody to tell me that it isn't the type of goal we should try to get to as fast as we can.
>
> Thurgood Marshall, Chief Justice
> United States Supreme Court

Social justice eludes many people in the United States. City newspapers are filled with stories of racism, discrimination, sexual harassment, and gay bashing in society at large as well as in our places of work. Our institutions mirror our society. Police departments across the United States are defending themselves against charges of racial profiling and ethnic violence, while boardrooms and corporate executives are fighting, and often losing, lawsuits pertaining to discriminatory practices in hiring and promotion. The people charged in these lawsuits are often surprised by them. Because injustice has endured for so long in this prosperous nation, many people no longer see blatant injustice as unjust. Many educators, too, have come to believe that injustice in society, as well as in public institutions like schools, is natural, inevitable, and entirely unalterable.

If injustice in schools is natural and unalterable, then there is nothing either researchers or administrators can do about persistent inequalities in education. However, if inequity has been institutionalized in the theories, norms, and practices of our society, and if researchers and administrators reify inequity and injustice by failing to examine, question, and redress the inequities they see, then there is much to be

Colleen Larson is Associate Professor of Administration, Leadership and Technology at New York University. Khaula Murtadha is Executive Associate Dean and Associate Professor, School of Education, Indiana University, Indianapolis.

done. Researchers in educational administration who believe that injustice in our schools and communities is neither natural nor inevitable loosely coalesce under an umbrella of inquiry called leadership for social justice.

Increasingly, researchers are embracing the language of social justice research by invoking terms like equity, opportunity, and justice. Many researchers tout principles of justice as a laudable goal for public education; however, most of this research fails to articulate or advance these principles within the theories, frameworks, or methodologies employed.

To social justice theorists, lofty visions of equality and opportunity are important, but not sufficient for bringing greater educational equity into being. Like Martin Luther King, Jr., they understand that justice has never "roll[ed] in on the wings of inevitability" (Carson & Shepard, 2001, p. x). Throughout history, creating greater social justice in society and in its institutions has required the commitment of dedicated leaders. Like Thurgood Marshall, social justice theorists believe that all men and women who provide leadership for public educational institutions within a democratic society must continually reach for greater opportunity and justice for all children.

Like King and Marshall, social justice theorists are unapologetic about developing theories and strategies for redressing enduring norms of injustice in education. They believe that university professors have an obligation to provide independent criticism of this society and its institutions and to generate theories and policies that enhance the public good. If researchers do not challenge theories and practices that historically have poorly served people at the marginalized edges of our school communities, they ask, who will? And if administrators or teachers do not believe that promoting equity and justice through the policies and practices they enforce in schools is their job, whose job is it?

The fact that many researchers and practitioners in educational leadership abdicate responsibility for questioning or redressing the numerous inequities they see in education provides significant evidence of the overtly technical-rational orientation of a profession largely rooted in the corporate ethos of business management theory and practice (Larson, 1997). Social justice researchers reject business management theory as a viable model for leaders in education to emulate. Rather than seeing and leading schools as business organizations, social justice theorists emanate from a long tradition of scholars who view schools as social institutions that exist to serve the public good (Bellah,

Madsen, Sullivan, Swidler, & Tipton, 1991; Dewey, 1916; Tyack, 1974; Tyack & Hansot, 1982). Researchers and leaders for social justice, then, seek to define the theories and practices of leadership that are vital to creating greater freedom, opportunity, and justice for all citizens—citizens who, through public education, are better able to participate in and sustain a free, civil, multicultural, and democratic society.

BACKGROUND AND PURPOSE

In this chapter we examine the landscape of literature on leadership for social justice in educational administration as well as in fields of study where these issues have been studied over longer periods of time. Collectively, this body of research articulates the images, dispositions, and practices of leadership necessary for enhancing social justice in education. Our discussion of this literature is guided by two primary questions: How has leadership theory for social justice been defined and advanced in educational leadership? And according to this literature, what does leadership for social justice within a context of inequity require?

As critical research in leadership and policy studies has progressed over the past 30 years, researchers have posed questions that have motivated notable shifts in the study of leadership for social justice. These shifts have moved social justice research through three overlapping but progressive strands: 1) deconstructing existing logics of leadership; 2) portraying alternative perspectives of leadership; and 3) constructing theories, systems, and processes of leadership for social justice. Each strand of research has been vital to advancing leadership for social justice in education. As the field has progressed, so too has the work of individual scholars whose writings have cut across two or even all three strands of inquiry. Today, scholars are increasingly concerned with articulating the connections between their theoretical understandings of leadership for social justice and the everyday practices of school leaders. Therefore, the third and heretofore least developed strand of inquiry promises to articulate theories of leadership that can guide leaders and policy makers who are struggling to enhance equity, opportunity and justice through education.

As critical scholars strive to generate practical theory for leaders concerned with issues of social justice, they are finding themselves on new theoretical, epistemological and methodological ground. Educational researchers, however, are not alone in their efforts to develop theories and strategies that can enhance social justice in this society and in its public institutions. The research of scholars in other disciplines holds considerable promise for extending the work of leadership theorists interested in fostering greater social justice in education. Therefore, in the third strand of inquiry we discuss writings on social justice found in community organizing and social activism (e.g., Freire, 1970), economics (e.g., Sen, 1992, 1999), and law and ethics (e.g., Nussbaum, 1999, 2000). Through this interdisciplinary reading of social justice literature, leadership theorists may find insights that help them to articulate the theories, policies and practices of leadership that give direction to leaders who encounter injustice in their school communities.

Leadership for Social Justice: Overview of Literature

In this section we present the themes, questions, and insights that have emerged through three overlapping but distinct strands of research on leadership for social justice: 1) deconstructing existing logics of leadership; 2) portraying alternative perspectives of leadership; and 3) constructing theories, systems, and processes of leadership for social justice.

STRAND 1: DECONSTRUCTING ESTABLISHED LOGICS IN LEADERSHIP THEORY AND PRACTICE

In the first strand of critical inquiry, researchers sought to understand how dominant assumptions within the field maintained inequity through theory and practice. Thomas Greenfield began his critique of mainstream leadership theory almost 30 years ago (1975, 1982, 1986). He challenged the scientific assumptions underpinning research in the field. Informed by the phenomenological assumptions of critical humanism, Greenfield argued that organizations are not objective systems; rather, they are products of human construction. To Greenfield, institutions such as schools unavoidably reflect the values, perspectives, and interpretations of the people who create and sustain them.

Since Greenfield's early criticism of research in educational leadership, other writers have challenged the ostensibly neutral and apolitical stance of mainstream research (Anderson, 1990; Astuto, Clark, Read, McGree, & deKoven Pelton Fernandez, 1994; Bates, 1980, 1983; Foster, 1980, 1986). By deconstructing dominant theory, critical scholars have shown that an enduring allegiance to theories of leadership oriented toward maintaining stability through universal theories and hierarchical visions of schooling has maintained inequity in education. These traditional principles of leadership stemmed from the belief that our educational systems were inherently good and just for all children. Critical, feminist and poststructuralist writers challenged this belief.

Through this first strand of inquiry, researchers argued that societies and institutions, like schools, achieve stability not through consensus but through constraint, and that schools remain stable not through universal agreement but through the coercion of some by others. Critical theorists have shown that functionalist images of leadership as control have become powerful ideological casts for theories of leadership and the roles and expectations of school leaders (Hodgkinson, 1991). Researchers have also found that our enduring belief in stable, universal, and difference-blind systems of education has contributed to the profession's failure to challenge inequality based on class, race, ethnicity, and gender (Foster, 1986; Larson, 1996; Lomotey, 1994, 1997; Reyes, 1994; Shakeshaft, 1989, 1999).

The growing presence of women in university preparation programs during the 1980s stimulated greater interest in issues of equity and gender within the field. Shakeshaft's (1989, 1999) research on how discriminatory standpoints, stereotypes and masculine biases limited women's progress and potential for promotion in school leadership illuminated the structured systems of gender embedded in the theories and taken-for-granted norms of the profession. Arguing that women view leadership quite differently from their male colleagues, feminist scholars offered sophisticated critiques of the assumptions that underpinned and biased mainstream research. They argued that mainstream leadership was mired in metaphors emerging from male experience, particularly those gleaned from the military, athletics, and business (Rusch & Marshall, 1994; Shakeshaft, 1989). Women's limited involvement in these organizations led many conventional scholars and practitioners to assume that women were ill suited for positions of leadership. The widespread absence of women in leadership roles allowed these gender biases to remain intact in both theory and practice. Through feminist critique, however, researchers revealed how the profession's established images of leadership not only barred women from leadership roles, but also blocked researchers from envisioning theories of leadership that went beyond a White, middle-class, male standpoint.

More recently, social justice writers have embraced postmodern theory in an effort to expose the internal contradictions of the modernist meta-narratives underpinning leadership theory and practice. By deconstructing notions of language, knowledge, truth, and power, researchers are recognizing the deeply imbedded norms and expectations of modernist thought (Capper, 1993; English, 2000a, 2000b; Foster,

1992, 1995a, 1995b; Maxcy, 1994, 1995). Other scholars have invoked critical race theory and multicultural frameworks to reveal the racialized logics underlying both research and practice within the profession (Reyes, Velez, & Pena, 1993; Scheurich, 1997; Scheurich & Young, 1997).

Collectively, these deconstructionist scholars have provided powerful critiques of mainstream research. They have made particularly important contributions to researchers' understanding of the thinking that maintains multiple forms of inequity in education. However, as a whole, this strand of inquiry has been criticized for speaking to academics only (Capper, 1993; Robinson, 1994). By employing meta-theoretical critique, strand one researchers have largely focused on deconstructing mainstream research, often in language that is inaccessible to or seldom read by school leaders.

This strand of research was valuable in that it helped researchers to see previously ignored biases in leadership theory and practice. However, it stopped short of articulating the theories and practices needed to redress these biases in the corridors and classrooms of our schools (Anderson, 1989; Robinson, 1994). As the prejudices of mainstream research became more widely recognized, though, critical researchers' interest in developing alternative theories of leadership grew. These researchers sought to expand leadership theory by bringing previously silenced and marginalized voices to the fore. By listening to the experiences and perspectives of women and people of color in leadership positions, scholars ushered in the second strand of research.

STRAND 2: PORTRAYING ALTERNATIVE IMAGES OF LEADERSHIP THEORY AND PRACTICE

As more women and racial and ethnic minority populations entered the historically European American and masculine domain of educational administration, researchers became increasingly interested in studying the leadership of marginalized groups. This body of inquiry brought to light values and images of leadership that had been missing from mainstream leadership theory and practice.

Feminist images of leadership. Through feminist theory and critique, researchers found that the male voice has been privileged and embedded within theories of knowledge and research methodologies long accepted as universal and neutral. Feminist scholars of education administration have examined issues of gender and access to administrative roles, gender equity in administration, and alternative images of effective leadership.

By studying the leadership of women, researchers have found that women construct and enact leadership in ways that depart distinctively from those of their male colleagues (Blackmore, 1996; Dilliard, 1995; Grogan, 1996, 1999; Grogan & Smith, 1998; Marshall 1993a, 1993b, 1997; Marshall and Scribner, 1991; Skrla, Reyes & Scheurich, 2000; Shakeshaft, 1993; Tallerico & Burstyn, 1996). A range of perspectives, models and metaphors emerge from this literature. For example, through feminist inquiry, researchers have found that women leaders often enact an ethic of care rooted in concerns for relationships rather than roles. Feminist and critical race scholars have argued convincingly that if educational systems are to foster greater equity, we will have to recognize and revalue women's ways of understanding the nature of leadership as well as their ways of responding to moral dilemmas and civic responsibilities.

Nel Noddings (1992, 1999) and Lynn Beck (1994) have argued that an ethic of care is a fundamental starting point to reframe and reorganize schools away from hierarchical and role-based images of leadership. Noddings and Beck have argued that teachers and administrators respectively must see what they do in schools as entering relationships with people rather than as assuming roles within bureaucratic systems. This shift toward an ethic of care compels school leaders to attend to the needs and concerns of individuals rather than groups, and to recognize the very human consequences of the daily decisions they make on behalf of schools. Beck and Foster (1999) argue that in changing our understanding of leadership, we might look to moral and spiritual language. They suggest that "[w]ords like compassion, forgiveness, wisdom, humility and loyalty may be worthy of consideration and use, and images of home, church, and community may provide helpful ways for us to envision schools" (p. 355).

In a similar vein, Starratt (1997) talks about the importance of "administering community." He proposes combining ethics of care, justice and critique to provide a richer, more complete ethic of leadership. Like the threads of a tapestry, the themes of these ethics come together to form "a rich human response" (p. 57) to the many uncertain ethical situations that leaders in schools face each day. Similarly, Shapiro and Stefkovich (2001) view the ethics of care, ethics of critique and ethics of justice as complementary and valuable for developing a more humanly informed practice within the field.

These scholars are delineating the personal and professional codes of educational leaders, derived from life stories. These stories reveal how educational leaders have "grappled" with the diverse challenges of today's society. They explain: "By grappling, we mean that these educational leaders have struggled over issues of justice, critique, and care related to the education of children and youth, and through this process, have gained a sense of who they are and what they believe personally and professionally" (p. 21). Shapiro and Stefkovich argue that ethical issues like justice and fairness are central to a school leader's work. However, they lament that unlike law, medicine, dentistry and business, the field of educational administration does not have an ethics requirement.

African American scholars and leadership for social justice. As people of color entered educational research, they turned their attention to studying education in poor communities of color, communities that were long overlooked as important sites of inquiry. African American scholars, in particular, argue that the uncertainties of academic success and educational achievement for children of color highlight a need for leaders who understand Black family life and who can think beyond conventional parent and school community relationships.

Black scholars have engaged in a long tradition of activist leadership for social justice. Concern about inequity in education has been a rallying point for leaders whose skills, defined areas of competence, and stated life purposes are dedicated to achieving greater social justice in education.

Jackson (1999) points out that women of color have led under-resourced schools for years, and yet their narratives have not been a significant part of the reform literature in educational leadership. This omission limits our insight into how we might improve public schools serving poor children of color. Scholars developing this strand of inquiry note that women of color in positions of leadership are typically found in urban educational centers serving poor children and families of color. Jackson observes that these women bring to schools passion, energy and an unwavering belief that all children will experience educational success despite impoverished living conditions and other inhibiting factors. Lomotey (1989), too, found that African American principals in successful elementary schools have a sincere confidence in the ability of all African American children to learn, a strong commitment to the education of Black children, and a deep understanding of and compassion for the children and communities they serve.

African American principals often believe that their communities are at the heart of learning. For example, Murtadha and Larson (1999) found that the principals in their study view community involvement as a critical feature of leadership. These principals develop relationships with their communities and demonstrate a deep compassion for, commitment to, and understanding of the populations they serve. As Black principals working in institutions staffed by a predominantly White workforce, these women often find themselves standing with their communities and against institutionalized norms that are harmful to Black children.

Similarly, in a case study of an urban high school, Beck (1994) found that a nurturing, community-oriented culture exists when the principal is committed to accepting and respecting students and their families. This principal demonstrated a willingness to battle poverty and violence and sought educationally advantageous ways to build on students' cultural backgrounds. She exhibited a deep and profound caring for all members of the learning community—students, colleagues, families and others in the wider community. These examples show that by looking at school life as people of color experience it, researchers are expanding the profession's understanding of what leadership for under-resourced school communities and communities of color requires.

Spirituality, love and leadership. Another body of research that describes alternative images of leadership draws attention to the importance of spirituality in the work of educational leaders. There is a growing recognition of the vital role that spirituality plays in the lives and actions of many school leaders (Murtadha, 1999; Purpel, 1989; Sherr, 1999). Sherr points out, however, that despite the findings of this research, "education has a strong bias in favor of cognitive knowledge and, therefore, is suspicious of subjects associated with spirituality unless related to religious studies" (p. 12). She argues that the profession's failure to acknowledge and understand the spiritual as well as cognitive aspects of leadership is problematic, given that important educational questions, as well as central questions about life, are spiritual.

While there are many definitions of spirituality, social justice theorists note two general contemporary meanings. One characterizes spirituality as turning inward and withdrawing while attending to God, or spirit, and one's inner self. The other describes spirituality as a demanding, deep involvement and immersion in the world, "drawing on the belief that everything that is, is holy—although not yet completely so" (Sherr, p. 12). Research in this strand reveals that leaders who struggle for greater justice in our schools often speak to the role that spirituality plays in their work.

Spirituality is often the force that propels the activism of leaders for social justice in education. For example, Murtadha (1999) found that the spiritual strength of African American women leaders historically has spurred overt resistance to school practices that fail to educate or that miseducate black children. Anna Julia Cooper, Mary McLeod Bethune, and Nannie Helen Burroughs were "spirited sisters," fore-mothers of a long tradition of spirit-driven, activist leadership for education. These women fought injustice and led others to greater freedom, in part because of a deep spiritual strength that held forth hope and possibility for a better life for African American children and their families. They expressed a belief that God was involved intimately in their lives, driving their faith and lifting their people's spirit.

Keyes, Capper, Hafner and Fraynd (2000) examined the role of spirituality in the work of women leaders. The women portrayed in this study knew that their communities were living in conditions that defied any sort of justice. They assumed responsibility for seeking greater equity by building trust, taking risks, being fair, and extending love to the children and families of their community. In fact, love has become a topic of increasing discussion and debate within this strand of research.

In *All About Love: New Visions*, bell hooks (2000) states that many audiences attending her lectures about ending racism, poverty, and classism become uneasy when she speaks about the position of love in any movement for social justice. She asserts, "Indeed, all the great movements for social justice in our society have strongly emphasized a love ethic" (p. xix), while stressing "there can be no love without justice" (p. 19).

Engaging in a discourse of educational leadership and social justice that names love as an essential action, rather than as a privately held feeling, motivates many individuals who are committed to enhancing the lives of others. If we love those we lead, we willingly assume responsibility for, and accept accountability within, the relationships we enter. As leaders, we enter these relationships fully, not as individuals filling roles but as people caring for people. hooks notes that: "[t]he heart of justice is truth telling, seeing ourselves and the world the way it is, rather than the way we want it to be" (p. 33). This means we do not avoid seeing that which is difficult, or that which has no easy solution. Freire (1970), too, saw love as a vital force in the struggle for social justice. A social dialogue cannot exist, he argues, "in the absence of a profound love for the world and for people . . . No matter where the oppressed are found, the act of love is commitment to their cause—the cause of liberation" (p. 70).

Scheurich (1998) provides vivid examples of how love changes the way leaders work with the children and families they serve. By examining the practices of "loving principals," he illuminates the power of love to transform the educational experiences and academic outcomes as well as the hopes, dreams, and potential of poor children. Despite the findings of this growing body of literature, however, many scholars and administrators find talk of love and spirituality in their work disconcerting. Love requires forming connections and relationships, and spirituality seeks a greater good for all people. Neither of these values underpins conventional notions of role-based leadership. In recognizing the importance of relationships in leadership, many scholars suggest that if we hope to improve education in poor communities, we can no longer cling to objective, role-based images of leadership. Instead, we must recognize the need to accept responsibility for honest relationships and open communication. Leaders must recognize communities that have been marginalized in our schools and build trusting relationships with them, committing themselves to act out of love rather than fear, and to make decisions based on principles of care, human dignity, love, justice, and equity.

When the social justice theorists of strand two began studying the practices of unconventional school leaders, they were drawn into the dilemmas and daily realities confronting school administrators struggling to educate poor children and children of color in under-resourced schools. The findings of this body of literature are motivating researchers to articulate theories and practices of leadership that might eradicate multiple forms of injustice in school communities. Further, they challenge theories of leadership that have consistently separated the body from the mind, caring and feelings from rational judgment, spirituality from material reality, and conflict from images of effective schools. This literature shows that leaders who embrace equity and justice as central features of their practice enact relationships in ways that are quite different from their more mainstream colleagues.

Through the insights gleaned in this strand of research, scholars are developing alternative theories of leadership based on the practices and insights of men and women who are working in our most impoverished school communities.

STRAND 3: CONSTRUCTING THEORIES, SYSTEMS, AND PROCESSES OF LEADERSHIP FOR SOCIAL JUSTICE

Researchers who are developing the third strand of social justice research recognize that if critical research in educational leadership is to articulate theories and strategies for eliminating institutionalized inequities in our school communities, they will have to reconstruct the theories and systems they have so convincingly taken apart (Robinson, 1994).

In this section, we provide an overview of three promising paths within this strand: 1) rethinking leadership for marginalized school communities; 2) organizing multicultural communities through democratic leadership; and 3) developing human capacity and life chances through education. This body of research is notably the most recent and least developed strand within the social justice literature. Therefore, we discuss literature from other disciplines that may stimulate critical questions and advance inquiry along each path.

Rethinking leadership for poor and marginalized school communities. By examining the leadership of women and people of color in strand two, researchers came to see that strong leaders in poor school communities recognize rather than ignore the life world of the children and families they serve. By working with school leaders, researchers saw first-hand the chaos that poverty inflicts upon families and schools, as well as the ravaging effects of racism, sexism and homophobia in diverse school communities.

These powerful personal accounts of other people's lives helped researchers to see the importance of putting the life world of children and families at the core of leadership theory and practice. Capper (1993), for example, argues that educational administration must place opposition to suffering and oppression at the center of practice. She argues for a commitment to empowerment and transformation, aggressive advocacy on behalf of students and an emphasis on, rather than avoidance of, values in schools. Expressing a similar concern, Grinberg (2001) argues that leadership for social justice must interrupt the relationship of dependency that is typically reinforced through the conventional hierarchical theories, policies, and practices of school leaders. For example, top-down decision making in current school reform efforts is taking decisions about education out of the hands of local communities and putting them into those of school leaders and state governments. Further, escalating pressures for higher test scores are silencing debates about what children across the nation ought to know and be able to do.

The United States is moving toward adopting universal standards and high stakes testing in many states. As a result, the belief that poor children and children of color ought to know and be able to do the same things as their more privileged peers has not received serious scrutiny. The adoption of high stakes testing has silenced discussions of curriculum and closed school doors to the insights, concerns and needs of the children and families served by public schools. Paulo Freire recognized the need to reject such top-down approaches to education over 30 years ago.

In *Pedagogy of the Oppressed* (1970) Freire argues that education for poor and disenfranchised populations ought to be about human and community development, not about the acquisition of a preset bank of knowledge. He contends that the adoption of a predefined knowledge bank that all children ought to possess (the "banking approach") is typically designed to meet the needs of privileged children; therefore, it badly serves poor and disenfranchised populations. To Freire, education for marginalized populations requires a dialogical process that puts the primary needs, interests and concerns of poor people at the center of their own learning and liberation.

Freire's treatise on educating oppressed populations has been used widely in curriculum theory; however, leadership theorists have largely overlooked it. Nevertheless, Freire's arguments are as relevant to leadership as they are to teaching and learning. *Pedagogy of the Oppressed* offers social justice theorists in education a vivid description of what leadership for poor and disenfranchised populations requires.

Freire's image of effective educational leadership aligns with that of feminist/womanist and poststructural scholars who argue that knowledge is not something that can be determined by or delivered from a superior position, nor is it a gift that can be bestowed by those "who consider themselves knowledgeable upon people they consider to know nothing" (p. 58). Still, educational leaders often position themselves as superiors, "projecting an absolute ignorance onto others, a characteristic of the ideology of oppression" (p. 58).

Freire contends that oppressed populations must pave the road to their own economic and educational empowerment. However, he is not suggesting that leadership is unnecessary; rather, he is arguing that if a developmental process of learning is to flourish—one that leads poor populations to their own liberation—leaders will have to reject both top-down, hierarchical theories of leadership and banking approaches to education.

Larson and Ovando (2001) point out that many well-intentioned leaders maintain institutionalized inequity because they are committed to hierarchical logics that not only fail to question established norms, but keep economically impoverished citizens out of decision making.

Freire suggests that people who wish to empower oppressed populations will have to engage in what he calls "revolutionary leadership" (p. 56). Revolutionary leaders reject banking education and embrace what he calls "problem-posing education" (p. 56). Problem-posing education, according to Freire, raises critical consciousness, simultaneously transforming and educating both leaders and the marginalized populations with whom they work. He contends that without establishing this ongoing dialogical, educational process, leaders of school communities can quickly find themselves falling into the controlling logic of the oppressor.

Because poor and minority populations have learned to mistrust many public leaders, well-intentioned school leaders often have difficulty earning their confidence and cooperation. Freire explains that the lack of trust poor communities show to those who lead public institutions can be interpreted by some as an "inherent defect" in poor people, "evidence of their intrinsic deficiency" (p. 165). Since leaders need the cooperation of those they lead, educators can be tempted to resort to many of the same hierarchical and controlling practices used by dominant elites to oppress those they lead.

Leaders often rationalize their lack of confidence in the abilities of oppressed populations, and they often conclude that it is impossible to communicate with uneducated people. Like many leaders before them, they see themselves as the "ones who know" and opt for an antidialogical theory of leadership and action. To Freire, this is a mistake. He argues that "The role of leaders is to consider seriously the reasons for mistrust on the part of oppressed populations, and to seek true avenues of communion . . . helping the people to help themselves critically perceive the reality which oppresses them" (p. 163). To Freire, the purpose of dialogical leadership specifically, and of education in general, is to make it possible for the oppressed to make sense of and overcome injustice.

Freire asserts that as long as people are oppressed, internalizing the image of the oppressor, they alone cannot create a liberating theory of education. Similarly, leaders who do not understand oppression or the hardships of the oppressed cannot alone create a liberating theory of education. However, he suggests that every human being, no matter how uneducated or immersed in the "culture of silence," is capable of looking critically at his or her world through dialogical encounters with others. This insight has generated scholarly interest in reconceptualizing leadership as a democratic and dialogical process.

Organizing multicultural communities through democratic leadership.
Like Freire, social justice theorists in education argue that relationships
between school leaders and the communities they serve must change if
we are to improve the educational opportunities and life chances of
poor children and children of color. In recognizing the importance of
community to educational development, a growing number of scholars
are arguing that schools ought to be community centered. Therefore,
social justice theorists argue for less bureaucratic and more democratic
approaches to leadership and decision making. They seek to create
more open, community-based systems of education through inclusive
community-wide sensemaking processes (Furman, 1998; Maxcy, 1995;
Reitzug, 1994; Slater, 1994; Slater & Boyd, 1999; Strike, 1993).

Because democratic leadership is discussed separately in Chapter 6
(Furman & Starratt, this volume), we will not fully discuss that literature here. However, it is important to point out that not all research
focusing on democratic or community-based leadership advances issues
of equity and social justice in school communities. Social justice theorists note that the democracy literature is not always linked to questions of social justice and issues of equity. Inclusive discussions may
engage more people in open exchanges about educational issues, but
the accepted value of reaching agreement and consensus can quickly
silence issues of justice or equity (Blasé, Blasé, Anderson, & Dungan,
1995). Anderson and Grinberg (1998) argue that democratic contexts
can become contrived and inauthentic when more subtle forms of control, like self-regulating practices of "correct behavior," replace explicit
hierarchies of power.

Scholars advancing this line of inquiry contend that strong school-
community relationships in diverse communities require substantive
attention to building deliberative communities of difference for the
purpose of understanding culture, reducing prejudice, and learning to
talk across racial, ethnic, class, and gender differences (Larson &
Ovando, 2001; Young & Laible, 2000). They argue that issues of race,
class, and gender must be central to discussions about the purposes of
education and the needs of children and families in the school community. They note that ongoing dialogical processes between school leaders and their communities are vital to recognizing and interrupting
problematic institutionalized norms. They find that leaders working
within a context of inequity must be capable of and willing to confront
grave injustice in their school communities. Therefore, they argue that
the skills necessary for doing so must be at the heart of preparing strong
leaders for today's schools. Larson (1997) found that if administrators

are not capable of talking about the social, racial and economic disparities existing in their school communities, or if they are uncomfortable raising these issues, they will avoid conversations that are pivotal to creating greater equity in schools.

Bellah, Madsen, Sullivan, Swidler, and Tipton (1991) argue that greater inclusion in public institutions like schools is vital not only to creating better public institutions, but to maintaining a good society. They contend that leaders in public institutions today must recognize that American citizens suffer from a form of "radical individualism" (p. 154-155). They argue that people have turned inward to their own small neighborhoods, lives, and families. They have lost interest in and connection to their public institutions as well as to the broader society in which they live. Slater and Boyd (1999) suggest that the most striking sign of decline in American civil society is visible in the low rate of participation in our political process.

The United States ranks near the bottom of 11 key developed societies in voter turnout for national elections. In the 1992 presidential election only 55 percent of registered U.S. voters went to the polls, as compared to 64 percent in Hungary's 1990, 75 percent in Japan in 1993, 90 percent in Australia in that same year, and 93 percent in East Germany in 1990 (p. 329).

America's low rate of participation in electing its political leaders suggests a need to understand how the patterns of participation we have developed in our public institutions may be affecting the kind of society we are creating. Why are we not concerned, they ask, about the diminishing levels of participation that we are seeing in our political processes as well as in our public institutions?

Following the thinking of John Dewey and Walter Lippmann, scholars concerned about community participation in public institutions argue that a good society is a quest that must actively involve all its members, including leaders of government as well as leaders of public institutions, such as schools. In schools, this quest depends upon our capacity to enhance democracy, extend legitimate belonging, and increase intelligent public discourse and deliberation about issues that matter. Scholars advancing this strand of inquiry suggest that public discourse can make us all aware of our greater social responsibilities. Discourse on issues of public concern, they argue, can help school communities reach beyond the "radical individualism" apparent in the thinking and actions of many American citizens today—citizens who are directed more toward seeing and caring about only what is good for "me and my child."

Through this line of inquiry, scholars are recognizing that public deliberation is vital to broadening our individual and collective visions of what it takes to establish a good society. Further, they are seeing the important role that schools, as public institutions, play in sustaining both a society and institutions that are worthy of public support. However, given the top-down corporate ethos now flourishing in many public schools, and given the closed and hierarchical practices that this ethos is fueling, generating greater parental and community participation in schools, particularly in poor communities and communities of color, will be no easy task. Bellah and his colleagues remind us that:

> . . . responsible social participation, with an enlightened citizenry that can deal with moral and intellectual complexity, does not come about just from exhortation. It is certainly not enough simply to implore our fellow citizens to 'get involved.' We must create the institutions that will enable such participation to occur, encourage it, and make it fulfilling as well as demanding (1991, p. 15).

How might school leaders organize a school community to enhance the education and life chances of poor and minority children? Dantley (1990) suggests that principals must help teachers to develop an "articulation of hope" through processes that engage communities in creating a more just society. This may mean that leaders will have to recognize the wisdom of behaving less like corporate executives and more like community organizers.

Scholars and practitioners interested in developing this line of inquiry can learn a good deal about community organizing and political engagement from social activists. People like Dr. Martin Luther King, Jr., Gloria Steinem, and Nelson Mandela have organized communities around a shared cause and, in so doing, have achieved greater social justice in this nation. Through the stories of exceptional leaders who have worked for social change, we see that inspirational leadership, historically, has changed the world and the way we see it.

Researchers, however, do not often look to social justice activists for insight into how we might enhance leadership theory and practice in education. Purpel (1989) notes, for example, that prophets typically dislike the writings of academic political philosophers and political philosophers often reject the writings of social activists. They do so, in part, because they revere different languages. Purpel explains that the prophet, or social activist, is engaged in a battle to change the language of a society and its institutions. They are struggling to create a different epistemology out of which a more just society might emerge.

In schools, social justice activists often encounter resistance to their language of hope, compassion, ethics, equity and justice. He explains that this resistance arises because "the primary language [of schools] is the technical and bureaucratic one of control, task, and engineering" and he concludes that "this is a language of deficiency of serious proportions with important consequences to our society" (p. 25).

Throughout Purpel's work we encounter moving images of inspirational leaders like Gandhi, Jesus, Martin Luther King, and Rosa Luxemburg, leaders who sought to change the language of their societies. These people organized communities around shared concerns for creating greater compassion, equity and justice. Their stories portray the power of leadership emanating from a language of hope and a commitment to creating a more just world.

Developing human capacity and life chances through education. Social justice researchers argue that the purpose of education, particularly in oppressed communities, is to develop human capability so that people might break free of the hardships wrought by poverty. Freire's vision of education stands in direct contrast to current utilitarian efforts to close the achievement gap between poor children and their more privileged peers. Many school leaders confronted with increasing accountability for student performance on standardized tests are narrowing the curriculum to basic reading and math skills in an effort to improve lagging skills and competencies, particularly of poor children and children of color. School leaders are increasingly resorting to "teacher-proof" materials that drill students on skills that will be tested. In New York City, for example, school leaders are increasing the amount of time that "underperforming" students spend on learning these skills. Initiatives from schools and community-based organizations are extending the school day of largely poor and minority children into the evening hours, and summer school is now mandatory for students performing poorly on standardized tests. Some people argue that these strategies are positive efforts to create greater equity by increasing the educational competencies of school children. Others charge that these practices are resulting in little more than "killing through drilling," or what Lomotey (1994) calls "too much schooling and too little education."

In a recent study of high stakes testing in Texas, Linda McNeil (2000) points out the troubling irony of severely narrowing the curriculum to prepare children to pass high stakes tests. She asks, how is it possible that in these efforts to improve education we have given so little attention to all that we know about how children learn, and what they need in order to learn? And how is it possible that we have implemented a system of accountability and assessment that has narrowed rather than expanded the possibilities for children's growth, development and learning?

Freire argues that developing children's freedoms and capabilities to achieve must be central to any reform effort that seeks liberation and human development through education. He contends that serious efforts to increase the academic success of poor and minority children will require leaders who are capable of augmenting and developing children's and families' freedoms to achieve. Like Freire, leadership scholars also recognize that attaining greater equity in education will require much more than the current utilitarian pursuit of higher test scores and higher standards. However, what must we do if we hope to develop children's freedoms and capabilities to achieve? The work of Amartya Sen, a Nobel Prize-winning economist, might help advance the research of scholars interested in pursuing this important question.

In *Inequality Reexamined* (1992), Sen questions the rationality of universal public policies intended to achieve greater equity. In education, for example, he would question the current belief that all children of a certain age ought to achieve at the same level and pace despite vast disparities in students' freedom or ability to achieve. To Sen, such universal policies may serve a practical and political demand, but not a logical one.

Sen argues that if we seek greater equality, we must begin by asking, equality of what? The importance of the question "equality of what" is linked with "the empirical fact of pervasive human diversity" (p. xi). Sen argues that the advantages and disadvantages we possess can be judged in terms of many different variables, including income, wealth, utilities, resources, rights, quality of life, and so on. The choice of evaluative space, or which focal variables we choose to examine, is crucial to analyzing inequality as well as to developing good public policy.

Sen's thesis offers a methodological approach to examining issues of inequality and a substantive approach to assessing existing social arrangements in school communities. He argues that greater equality will require a decided shift away from utilitarian values, which concentrate on achievement while ignoring social, economic, and political disparities in freedoms to achieve. Researchers and school leaders could acquire a more sophisticated understanding of inequality by using observable data on achievement to identify the different freedoms enjoyed by different people. Sen's focus on freedoms to achieve, rather than on achievement or outcomes alone, marks a significant departure from standard utilitarian approaches to achieving equality.

Sen argues that when we concentrate on the freedom to achieve and not just on the level of achievement, we can shed light on the inequalities of freedom that different people enjoy. Leadership theorists and practitioners might develop more robust appraisals of inequality in poor and minority school communities by examining the link between individual capabilities and freedoms to achieve.

Sen also reminds us that the policy recommendations we choose are typically contingent upon feasibility. However, the recognition of poverty (and its impact on education) has to go beyond that. He suggests that the first step is to diagnose deprivation and determine what we should do *if we had the means.* Our actual policy choices, Sen argues, must be in line with the deprivations we see. In this sense, the descriptive analysis of poverty or inequality has to precede the policy choice we make.

In education, social justice theorists have shown how inequality is maintained through ostensibly neutral systems, policies and practices. However, we have too little insight into the specific forms of inequality that limit the life chances and educational opportunities of children. Researchers and school leaders alike differ in their abilities to recognize and respond to the inequalities existing in schools and communities. Sen's thesis provides a path for delineating spaces of inequality in education, and ultimately for developing theories of leadership that help school leaders not only to recognize inequality, but to address it.

In developing the aims of leadership for social justice, Sen's writing encourages us to identify the spaces of equality essential to human life and to achievement in education. Certainly, as Freire notes, considerable research already reveals many spaces of inequality in education. We know that many children enjoy privilege far beyond human need, while others live without the barest of human necessities. Our society, however, seems to have become numb to growing disparities between rich and poor. These disparities have been depicted in comparisons between the quality and forms of educational programs extended to children of wealth versus children of poverty.

Sen helps us to see that defining spaces of inequality is critical to developing freedoms to achieve. For example, we might ask: How do the various types of hardships that children and their families bring to school affect their freedoms to achieve? How are these hardships viewed by the school, the state, and the broader society? What social and educational policy emerges from the prevailing view of these hardships? How does this view affect the education/outcomes of those who bear these hardships? Sen argues that policymakers and the leaders who enforce policy typically deny and ignore these hardships in the belief that they are being "objective." However, Sen suggests that to ignore these hardships in policy and practice is "not so much to be super-objective, but to be super-dense" (p. 108).

Coming from an ethical rather than an economic approach, Martha Nussbaum (2000) argues that the capabilities approach to social justice theory plays a very practical role in sorting out our perplexing, often contradictory thoughts about greater equity and justice. Nussbaum's thesis is helpful to both researchers and practitioners who wish to eliminate "the sort of self-deceptive rationalizing that frequently makes us collaborators with injustice" (p. 36).

Nussbaum's theory of social justice offers a flexible framework for assessing students' quality of life. It helps leaders who struggle to understand and respond to the social and economic disparities they find in schools in a morally just way. Like Sen, Nussbaum argues that insufficient attention to cultural variety and the particular features of individual lives often leads to unjust and harmful policies and practices. Used as a benchmark, Nussbaum's theory of social justice compels researchers and practitioners to consider how the capability of each student ought to be supported. The core idea is that children and families are human beings first, not simply students and parents. Human beings need material support, and without such support people cannot come into full being.

The central question researchers and leaders of schools might ask from a capabilities perspective is, "What is child X actually able to do and to be?" Children and families vary greatly in their needs for resources and in their abilities to convert resources that institutions offer into valuable opportunities. Nussbaum argues that the structures of our social institutions should be chosen with an eye toward capabilities to achieve. For example, an individual should be able to live a human life of normal length, not dying prematurely or before one's life is "so reduced as to be not worth living." A person should be able to enjoy good health, good nutrition, and adequate shelter. If school leaders recognized the importance of these capabilities to the education and development of children and families, what would they do?

From a capabilities perspective, physical integrity and emotional comfort are essential. Yet current directions in school reform generally ignore issues of bodily and emotional integrity. Nussbaum contends that all children must have the capability to move freely from place to place, secure against assault, sexual abuse, and domestic violence. Children should also be able to use their senses, to imagine, think, and reason—and to do these things in a "truly human" way, informed and cultivated by an excellent education that spurs imaginative and critical thought in connection with experiencing and producing artistic, creative, and transformative works.

In assessing and supporting capabilities, Nussbaum also argues for valuing emotions—being able to develop attachments to things and people outside ourselves and to love those who love and care for us, to grieve at their absence, and to experience longing, gratitude, and justified anger. Not having one's emotional development blighted by overwhelming fear and anxiety, or by traumatic events of abuse or neglect, is critical to human well being.

Nussbaum suggests that a person should be capable of practical reason, being able to form a conception of the good and to engage in critical reflection about the planning of one's life. This also means being able to recognize and live with concern for other human beings, to engage in various forms of social interaction, to laugh, to play, to enjoy recreational activities, to imagine the situation of another and to have compassion for that person, and to have the capacity for both justice and friendship.

In this description of what children need to lead full and happy lives, we begin to see why many social justice theorists argue that reducing the curriculum of poor children to basic reading and math is highly problematic. Children and their families, no matter what their material circumstances in life, must have the social footing afforded by respect and by treatment as people of equal worth and dignity. To Nussbaum, supporting these capabilities entails, at a minimum, protections against discrimination on the basis of race, sex, sexual orientation, religion, caste, ethnicity, or national origin (2000, pp. 78-79).

For educational leaders, a focus on capabilities as worthy educational goals necessitates promoting a greater measure of equality than exists among most schools struggling with legacies of racism, sexism and classism. This approach suggests that if children receive educational and material support, they can become fully capable of human action and expression. Freedom from violence, unconditional support, and concern for health and nutrition are educational considerations that reach beyond today's hollow and entirely insufficient demands for improving academic achievement.

A capabilities approach to leadership involves assigning value to the actions that ought to be happening in the education of children. The capabilities approach to quality of life measurement poses disturbing questions about the broad context within which teaching and learning occurs, as well as about the nature of the society that our schools currently reflect.

Nussbaum (2000) points out that context and circumstances affect not only people's external options, but their choices and aspirations as well. The circumstances of people's lives affect "what they hope for, what they love, what they fear, as well as what they are able to do" (p. 31). If leaders and policymakers are serious about social justice, they must be willing to distinguish between the myths and realities they hold about the communities they serve (Reyes, Wagstaff, & Fusarelli, 1999) and the quality and kind of education they offer to poor children and children of color.

School leaders who believe that their schools are equitable for all children regularly enact programs and policies that they assume are fair and serve the academic and social interests of all students. But many are misguided, in part, because they are not sufficiently aware of the differences that limit children's and their families' freedoms to achieve. Many administrators assume that all children enter school on a level playing field and therefore should demonstrate the same capabilities. The reality, however, is that age-based expectations for performance have always privileged children of social and economic advantage.

For historically disadvantaged groups whose life choices can be severely limited by poverty, there is an economic divide in capabilities (Payne & Biddle, 1999). Of course, no single program or policy can ensure the life success of every child. However, attention to developing capabilities, as Nussbaum indicates, and using policy and practice to create greater freedoms to achieve, as Sen suggests, means supporting and enhancing the lives of children and their families. If leaders take Sen's and Nussbaum's theories seriously, they will recognize that they cannot educate the mind of a child if the body and spirit are threatened.

Such insights into how greater justice and equity ought to be defined and developed are encouraging the articulation of theories and policies of leadership that will enhance the practices of administrators working in our most economically impoverished school communities.

Conclusion

In this chapter we have examined the considerable research on leadership for social justice. Interest in this body of research is growing. Even when we look at the leadership literature more broadly, we find a wide array of scholars suggesting that leaders must be concerned about issues of social justice if we are to create meaningful educational reform. There is a vagueness, however, as to what all of this means to researchers and practitioners who are increasingly caught in the volatile winds of market-driven reform and test-based accountability.

Dissatisfaction with existing social arrangements is fueling a greater interest in and need for a leadership theory and practice that is robust enough to enhance social justice in education. Many of our schools are hungry for leaders who will stand with their communities and against policies that divert education and resources away from the real needs of children and their families.

Collectively, the research discussed in this chapter illustrates what leadership for social justice within a context of inequity requires. It delineates the methodologies and theories that will support researchers and school leaders in their efforts to make schools better places for more children. It recognizes the serious limitations of failing to connect leadership theory and practice to broader critical and social issues, such as economic deprivation and the chaos that deprivation creates in the lives of many children and their families.

The literature portrayed in this chapter takes leadership theory and practice into realities long ignored within the profession. Collectively, this body of inquiry provides important insight into the powerful role that leaders can and ought to play in advancing social justice in education.

Authors' Note

We would like to thank Darryl Stinchcomb, graduate student at New York University, who served as research assistant for this project.

REFERENCES

Anderson, G. L. (1989). Critical ethnography in education: Origins, current status, and new directions. *Review of Education Research, 59*(3), 249-270.

Anderson, G. L. (1990). Toward a critical constructivist approach to school administration: Invisibility, legitimation, and the study of non-events. *Educational Administration Quarterly, 29*(1), 38-59.

Anderson, G., & Grinberg, J. (1998). Educational administration as a disciplinary practice: Appropriating Foucault's view of power, discourse and method. *Educational Administration Quarterly, 34*(3), 329-347.

Astuto, T. A., Clark, D. L., Read, A., McGree, K., & deKoven Pelton Fernandez, L. (1994). Roots of reform: Challenging the assumptions that control change in education. Bloomington, IN: Phi Delta Kappa.

Bates, R. J. (1980). Educational administration, the sociology of science and the management of knowledge. *Educational Administration Quarterly, 16*(2), 1-20.

Bates, R. (1983). *Educational administration and the management of knowledge.* ESA Monograph 841. Victoria, Australia: Deakin University Press.

Beck, L. (1994). *Reclaiming educational administration as a caring profession.* New York: Teachers College Press.

Beck, L., & Foster, W. (1999). Administration and community: Considering challenges, exploring possibilities. In J. Murphy & K. S. Louis (Eds.), *Handbook of research on educational administration* (pp. 337-358). San Francisco: Jossey-Bass.

Bellah, R. N., Madsen, R., Sullivan, W. M., Swidler, A., & Tipton, S. M. (1991). *The good society.* New York: Vintage.

Blackmore, J. (1996). Breaking the silence: Feminist contributions to educational administration and policy. In K. Leithwood (Ed.), *International handbook of educational administration* (pp. 997-1042). Dordrecht, Netherlands: Kluwer Academic Publishers.

Blasé, J., Blasé, J., Anderson, G. L., and Dungan, S. (1995). *Democratic principals in action: Eight pioneers.* Thousand Oaks, CA: Corwin Press, Inc.

Capper, C. (1993). *Educational administration in a pluralistic society: A multiparadigm approach.* Albany, NY: SUNY Press.

Carson, C., & Shepard, K. (2001). *A call to conscience: The landmark speeches of Martin Luther King, Jr.* New York: Warner.

Dantley, M. (1990). The ineffectiveness of effective schools leadership: An analysis of the effective schools movement from a critical perspective. *Journal of Negro Education, 59*(4), 585-598.

Dewey, J. (1916). *Democracy and education.* New York: The Free Press.

Dilliard, C. (1995). Leading with her life: An African American feminist (re)interpretation of leadership for an urban high school principal. *Educational Administration Quarterly, 31*(4), 539-563.

English, F. (2000a). A critical interrogation of Murphy's call for a new center of gravity in educational administration. *Journal of School Leadership, 10*(5), 445-463.

English, F. (2000b). Psst! What does one call a set of non-empirical beliefs required to be accepted on faith and enforced by authority? [Hint: a religion, aka the ISLLC standards]. *International Journal of Leadership in Education, 3*(2), 159-167.

Foster, W. (1980). Administration and the crisis in legitimacy: A review of Habermasian thought. *Harvard Educational Review, 50*(4), 496-505.

Foster, W. (1986). *Paradigms and promises.* Buffalo, NY: Prometheus.

Foster W. (1992, October). Poststructuralist arguments in educational administration. Paper presented at the annual meeting of the University Council of Educational Administration, Minneapolis, MN.

Foster, W. (1995a, October). Postmodernist perspectives on leadership. Paper presented at the annual meeting of the University Council for Educational Administration, Salt Lake City, UT.

Foster, W. (1995b). Leadership: The contested terrain. *Journal of Management Systems,* 7(4), 1-33.

Freire, P. (1970). *Pedagogy of the oppressed.* New York: The Seabury Press.

Furman, G. (1998). Postmodernism and community in schools: Unraveling the paradox. *Educational Administration Quarterly, 34*(3), 298-328.

Greenfield, T. (1975). Theory about organization: A new perspective and its implication for schools. In M. Hughes (Ed.), *Administering education: International challenge* (pp. 71-99). London: Athlone Press.

Greenfield, T. (1982). Against group mind: An anarchistic theory of organization. *Journal of Education, 17*(1), 3-11.

Greenfield, T. (1986). The decline and fall of science in educational administration. *Interchange, 17*(2), 57-80.

Grinberg, J. (2001, April). Practicing popular social justice: Authentic participation and democratic critical leadership in the case of a community center in Caracas, Venezuela. Paper presented at the Annual Meeting of the American Educational Research Association, Seattle, WA.

Grogan, M. (1996). *Voices of women aspiring to the superintendency.* Albany, NY: SUNY Press.

Grogan, M. (1999). Equity/equality issues. *Educational Administration Quarterly, 35*(4), 518-536.

Grogan, M., & Smith, F. (1998). A feminist perspective of women superintendents' approaches to moral dilemmas. *Just and Caring Education, 4*(2), 176-192.

Hodgkinson, C. (1991). *Educational leadership: The moral art.* Albany, NY: SUNY Press.

hooks, b. (2000). *All about love: New visions.* New York: William Morrow & Company.

Jackson, B. (1999). Getting inside history—against all odds: African-American women school superintendents. In C. Brunner (Ed.), *Sacred dreams: Women and the superintendency* (pp. 141-160). Albany, NY: SUNY Press.

Keyes, M., Capper, C., Hafner, M., and Fraynd, D. (2000, October). Spiritual justice histories: The lives of two womanist leaders. Paper presented at the annual meeting of the University Council of Educational Administration, Albuquerque, NM.

Larson, C. (1996). Rethinking stability: The role of conflict in schools. *Planning and Changing, 27*(3/4), 130-144.

Larson, C. (1997). Is the Land of Oz an alien nation?: A sociopolitical study of school-community conflict. *Education Administration Quarterly, 33*(3), 312-350.

Larson, C., & Ovando, C. (2001). *The color of bureaucracy: The politics of equity in multicultural school communities.* Belmont, CA: Wadsworth.

Lomotey, K. (1989). *African American principals: School leadership and success.* New York: Greenwood Press.

Lomotey, K. (Ed.). (1994). *Going to school: The African-American experience.* Albany, NY: SUNY Press.

Lomotey, K. (1997). *Sailing against the wind: African Americans and women in U.S. education.* Albany, NY: SUNY Press.

Marshall, C. (1993a). The new politics of race and gender. In C. Marshall (Ed.), *The new politics of race and gender: The 1992 yearbook of the Politics of Education Association.* (pp. 1-6). Washington, DC: Falmer.

Marshall, C. (1993b). The politics of denial: Gender and race issues in administration. In C. Marshall (Ed.), *The new politics of race and gender: The 1992 yearbook of the Politics of Education Association* (pp. 168-174). Washington, DC: Falmer.

Marshall, C. (1997). Dismantling and reconstructing policy analysis. In C. Marshall (Ed.), *Feminist critical policy analysis.* London: Falmer Press.

Marshall, C., and Scribner, J. (1991). The micropolitics of education. *Education and Urban Society, 23*(4).

Maxcy, S. J. (1994). *Educational leadership: A critical pragmatic perspective.* New York: Bergin & Harvey.

Maxcy, S. J. (1995). *Democracy, chaos and the new school order.* Thousand Oaks, CA: Corwin.

McNeil, L. (2000). *Contradictions of school reform.* New York: Routledge.

Murtadha, K. (1999). Spirited sisters: Spirituality and the activism of African American women in educational leadership. In L. Fenwick (Ed.), *School leadership: Expanding horizons of the mind and spirit: Proceedings of the National Council of Professors of Educational Administration.* Lancaster, PA: Technomic.

Murtadha, K., & Larson, C. (1999, April). Toward a socially critical, womanist theory of leadership. Paper presented at the annual meeting of the American Educational Research Association, Montreal, Canada.

Noddings, N. (1992). *The challenge to care in schools: An alternative approach to education.* New York: Teachers College Press.

Noddings, N. (1999). Care, justice, and equity. In M. Katz, N. Noddings, & K. Strike (Eds.), *Justice and caring: The search for common ground in education* (pp. 7-20). New York: Teachers College Press.

Nussbaum, M. (2000). *Women and human development: A capabilities approach.* New York: Cambridge.

Payne, K. J., & Biddle, B. J. (1999). Poor school funding, child poverty, and mathematics achievement. *Educational Researcher, 28*(6), 4-13.

Purpel, D. (1989). *The moral and spiritual crisis in education.* Granby, MA: Bergin & Garvey.

Reitzug, U. C. (1994, October). Democracy, inquiry and inclusion: Lessons for principals and preparation programs. Paper presented at the annual meeting of the University Council for Educational Administration, Philadelphia, PA.

Reyes, P. (1994). Cultural citizenship and social responsibility: A call for change in educational administration. *UCEA Review, 35*(1), 11-13.

Reyes, P., Velez, W., & Pena, R. (1993). School reform: Introducing race, culture and ethnicity into the discourse (failing to address these issues in policy). In C. Capper (Ed.), *Educational administration in a pluralistic society.* Albany, NY: SUNY Press.

Reyes, P., Wagstaff, L., & Fusarelli, L. (1999). Delta forces: The changing fabric of American society and education. In J. Murphy & K. S. Louis (Eds.), *Handbook of research on educational administration* (pp. 183-201). San Francisco: Jossey-Bass.

Robinson, V. (1994). The practical promise of critical research. *Educational Administration Quarterly, 30*(1), 56-75.

Rusch, E., & Marshall, C. (1994, April). Gender filters. Paper presented at the annual meeting of the American Educational Research Association, San Francisco, CA.

Scheurich, J. J. (1997). *Research method in the postmodern.* London: Falmer.

Scheurich, J. J. (1998). Highly successful and loving public elementary schools populated mainly by low-SES children of color: Core beliefs and cultural characteristics. *Urban Education, 33*(4), 451-491.

Scheurich, J., & Young, M. (1997). Coloring epistemologies: Are our research epistemologies racially biased? *Educational Researcher, 6*(4), 4-16.

Sen, A. (1992). *Inequality reexamined.* Cambridge, MA: Harvard.

Sen, A. (1999). *Development as freedom.* New York: Anchor.

Shakeshaft, C. (1989). *Women in educational administration.* Newbury Park, CA: Sage.

Shakeshaft, C. (1993). Gender equity in schools. In C. Capper (Ed.), *Educational administration in a pluralistic society* (pp. 86-109). Albany, NY: SUNY Press.

Shakeshaft, C. (1999). The struggle to create a more gender inclusive profession. In J. Murphy & K. S. Louis (Eds.), *Handbook of research on educational administration* (pp. 99-118). San Francisco: Jossey-Bass.

Shapiro, J., & Stefkovich, J. (2001). *Ethical leadership and decision making in education: Applying theoretical perspectives to complex dilemmas.* Mahwah, NJ: Lawrence Erlbaum.

Sherr, M. (1999). Embracing spirituality: The inner journey of educational leaders. In L. Fenwick (Ed.), *School leadership: Expanding horizons of the mind and spirit: Proceedings of the National Council of Professors of Educational Administration.* Lancaster, PA: Technomic.

Skrla, L., Reyes, P., & Scheurich, J. (2000). Sexism, silence, and solutions: Women superintendents speak up and speak out. *Educational Administration Quarterly, 36*(1), 44-75.

Slater, R. J. (1994). Symbolic educational leadership and democracy in America. *Educational Administration Quarterly, 30*(1), 97-101.

Slater, R. J., & Boyd, W. (1999). Schools as polities. In J. Murphy & K. S. Louis (Eds.), *Handbook of research on educational administration* (pp. 323-335). San Francisco: Jossey-Bass.

Starratt, R. J. (1997). *Building an ethical school: A practical response to the moral crisis in schools.* Washington, DC: Falmer.

Strike, K. (1993). Professionalism, democracy, and discursive communities: Normative reflections on re-structuring. *American Educational Research Journal, 30*(2), 255-275.

Tallerico, M., & Burstyn, J. (1996). Retaining women in the superintendency: The location matters. *Educational Administration Quarterly, 32*(Supplemental), 642-664.

Tyack, D. (1974). *The one best system: A history of American urban education.* Cambridge, MA: Harvard University Press.

Tyack, D., & Hansot, E. (1982). *Managers of virtue.* New York: Basic Books.

Young, M., & Laible, J. (2000). White racism, antiracism and school leadership preparation. *Journal of School Leadership, 10*(5), 374-415.

Section Four
RESHAPING LEADERSHIP IN ACTION

CHAPTER 8

Exploring New Approaches to Teacher Leadership for School Improvement

MARK A. SMYLIE, SHARON CONLEY, AND HELEN M. MARKS

During the past 20 years teacher leadership has become an established feature of educational reform in the United States. In the mid-1980s, arguments began to appear in the scholarly and professional literatures asserting that teacher leadership was a crucial element of school improvement and the development and "professionalization" of the teacher work force. To some observers, it would be impossible to improve schools, attract and retain talented teachers, or make sensible demands upon school administrators without promoting teacher leadership (e.g., Little, 1988; Wasley, 1991). To others, creating opportunities for teacher leadership was a moral imperative, to give teachers their professional due and to provide all children with the quality of education they deserve (e.g., Barth, 2001; Maeroff, 1988).

It was not always seen this way. The planned change literature of the 1970s and early 1980s emphasized the importance of strong leadership for school improvement, but most of it focused on the principal or the superintendent (Fullan, 2001). More often than not, teachers were considered impediments to rather than leaders of improvement (Little, 1988). Even today, the subject of teacher leadership is cloaked in ambivalence. We look to teachers and their leadership to help solve

Mark A. Smylie is Professor of Education at the University of Illinois at Chicago. Sharon Conley is Professor of Education at the University of California, Santa Barbara. Helen M. Marks is Associate Professor of Educational Policy and Leadership at The Ohio State University.

today's educational problems, yet we consider teachers a primary cause of the problems that we call on their leadership to solve.

Of course, teacher leadership is not the product of recent educational reform. The literature has long recognized teachers' informal leadership in schools and classrooms (Smylie, 1997). For years, teachers have also assumed various formal leadership roles in union activity, as department chairs, and as members of advisory committees. Weise and Murphy (1995) remind us that the idea of teacher leadership as a means of reform dates back at least to the early 1900s, to progressive educators' calls to reshape schools as democratic communities.

Even though the idea of teacher leadership has been around for quite some time, our thinking about its form, its function, and its role in school improvement has evolved considerably. In the past 10 years several new approaches to teacher leadership have emerged. In this chapter, we explore three of these new approaches. We begin with a brief historical review describing the evolution of teacher leadership since the early 1900s. Then we examine teacher research as a form of teacher leadership. We explore several models of distributive school leadership. Finally we consider self-managed teams as means of teacher leadership and substitutes for administrative leadership. These new approaches depart from the individual empowerment, role-based models of teacher leadership that dominated the 1980s and early 1990s. They reframe teacher leadership as a more collective, task-oriented, and organizational enterprise. Are these new approaches more effective forms of leadership for promoting schoolwide improvement? We entertain this question and implications for teacher leadership development at the end of the chapter.

Teacher Leadership in Historical Perspective

It is difficult to think about the one-room schoolhouse of the 19th century and not also think about the teacher as an organizational leader (Fuller, 1989). It was not until the beginning of the 20th century, however, that we began to hear about teachers as leaders and the importance of teacher leadership to school reform. With the advent of the "professional" school administrator, the growth of centralized control, and the scientific management of schools in the early and mid-1900s, teacher leadership became an issue of workplace democracy. According to Weise and Murphy (1995), critics of these reforms argued that it would be virtually impossible for schools to promote a democratic society if they were not democratic communities themselves. Dewey (1903) argued, for example, that until public education was organized in such a way that "every teacher had some regular and representative way to register judgment upon matters of educational importance, with assurance that this judgment would somehow affect the school system, the assertion that the present system is not, from the internal standpoint, democratic seems to be justified" (p. 195).

Such critiques formed the foundation for the teacher council movement of the 1910s and 1920s and the democratic administration movement of the 1930s and 1940s (Weise & Murphy, 1995). These movements established new opportunities for teachers to participate in school- and district-level policy making (Conley, 1991). While these opportunities were not widespread, their aim was to "make all [teachers] students of the problems of the schools and proficient helpers in solving those problems" (Ortman, 1923, p. II). Beyond organizing teachers to help solve specific educational problems, the driving force behind these efforts was to "democratize" schools and increase their capacity to promote democratic society. In this regard, teacher participation in policy making was an expression of key democratic principles—self-determinism of teachers in their work and the "enfranchisement" of teachers in educational administration (Weise & Murphy).

Efforts to develop teacher leadership faded in the shadow of community control initiatives of the 1960s and 1970s, but they were renewed in the mid-1980s in response to the regulatory, bureaucratic reforms of the late 1970s and early 1980s (Murphy, 1990). By the late 1980s, nearly every American state had adopted or was studying some form of teacher leadership program or policy (Smylie, 1997). District-level initiatives abounded. Opportunities for teacher leadership came in the form of career ladder and mentor teacher programs, the appointment of master and lead teachers, and policies to decentralize and involve teachers in school- and district-level decision making.

While their association with workplace democracy was not completely lost, these teacher leadership initiatives followed from a different set of assumptions and objectives. First, teacher leadership was seen more specifically as an instrument of school improvement and of improvement of student academic learning. These initiatives would place teachers in positions of influence and decision-making authority, thereby increasing the human resources available for school improvement. Teacher leaders would break down "a backbreaking educational bureaucracy" that impeded reform and restricted teachers' ability to work according to their own notions of best practice (Lichtenstein, McLaughlin, & Knudsen, 1992, p. 37). This objective was consistent with literature of the late 1970s and 1980s that argued that educational improvement was best pursued at the school level, at the point closest to the problems to be solved (Bacharach & Conley, 1989; Firestone & Bader, 1992). It was also consistent with the logic that made paramount the involvement of people most instrumental to the solution of those problems—teachers.

Second, these teacher leadership initiatives were considered important means of "empowering" individual teachers, "professionalizing" the teacher workforce, and improving teacher performance (Lichtenstein et al., 1992). The teacher leadership initiatives of this period were closely associated with role-based theories and models of individual work redesign and job enhancement (Hart, 1990; Pounder, 1999). In general, they followed a logic that variation and expansion of teachers' work, including increased leadership responsibilities with commensurate recognition and compensation, would increase teachers' motivation, job commitment, satisfaction, and performance. New leadership roles would provide more effective incentives to attract and retain the best teachers in the profession. Moreover, these new roles would benefit not only the individual teachers who performed them, but also others in the school community, as teacher leaders applied their expertise to program development, decision making, and the professional development of their colleagues.

Today our thinking about teacher leadership is changing again. Since the mid-1990s there has been a shift away from individual empowerment and role-based initiatives toward more collective, task-oriented, and organizational approaches to teacher leadership. According to Leithwood and Jantzi (2000), many of the more ambitious role-based teacher leadership initiatives of the late 1980s and early 1990s have been abandoned. Indeed, one is hard pressed to find more than a few entries about these earlier forms of teacher leadership in scholarly and professional education literature published after the mid-1990s.

The reasons for this shift are not clear, but there are at least two possible explanations. First, the evidence on the effectiveness of the individual empowerment, role-based teacher leadership initiatives of the 1980s and early 1990s is equivocal at best. Much of what counted for teacher leadership at that time was the "appointment and anointment" of individual teachers to new "quasi-administrative" positions—rungs on career ladders, lead and mentor teachers, and membership on decision-making bodies—to share in managerial work (Bacharach, Conley, & Shedd, 1986; Pounder, 1999; Yendol Silza, Gimbert, & Nolan, 2000). Following the image of the "great man" in the principal's office, these positions embodied a "heroic" model of individual leadership. It was not always clear how teacher leaders were to perform their new roles. Moreover, these roles were not always focused on things that matter most to teachers—curriculum, instruction, and student learning (Little, 1988). These initiatives typically brought teachers into the "hierarchy" of administrative leadership. At the same time, ironically, they often failed to consider adequately the implications for principals and other school administrative leaders.

According to Smylie (1997), the research found that these initiatives produced mixed outcomes. Despite their tendency to focus on noncurricular and noninstructional matters, teacher leaders generally found that these roles provided new opportunities for professional learning and development. These roles were also associated with the development and adoption of innovations at the school and district levels, but they did little to promote the implementation of these innovations, particularly innovations aimed at promoting other teachers' professional development, improving classroom instruction, and increasing student learning. Overall, the research indicates that these teacher leadership initiatives did little to support school-level improvement.

The research was clear, however, that these teacher leadership initiatives could cause serious problems (Smylie, 1997). They could create work overload, stress, role ambiguity, and role conflict for teacher leaders as they tried to balance their new school-level responsibilities with their classroom responsibilities. The introduction of new teacher leadership roles could also create tension and conflict among teacher leaders, administrators, and other teachers. The research demonstrated that the organizational contexts of schools could exert substantial influence, often negative, on the performance and outcomes of these leadership roles. This evidence signaled clearly that it was not enough to think about teacher leadership solely in terms of roles and the individuals who occupy them. One also had to think about the organizational conditions necessary for teacher leadership to function effectively.

A second possible reason for the shift away from individual empowerment and role-based leadership is that we have learned a great deal about leadership and school improvement in the past 10 years, and these lessons point to potentially better ways to think about teacher leadership (Fullan, 2001). We understand that administrative leadership is crucial to school improvement, but we also understand that principals alone cannot provide all the leadership necessary to promote and sustain improvement over time (Donaldson, 2001). We have learned that school improvement and the improvement of teaching and student learning depend fundamentally on the development of teachers' knowledge, abilities, and commitments—their "will and skill" (Newmann & Wehlage, 1995). Moreover, we have come to understand that "restructuring" schools is not sufficient to improve them. The reform literature strongly suggests that improving teaching and student learning has less to do with structural changes in schools than with changes in what occurs within those structures (Elmore, Peterson, & McCarthey, 1996; Smylie & Hart, 1999). Structure certainly matters; however, changing structures is not synonymous with changing the social organization and cultures of schools (Fullan). These lessons and the research on the teacher leadership initiatives of the 1980s and early 1990s prompt us to expand our thinking about teacher leadership and school improvement.

New Approaches to Teacher Leadership

We now examine three new approaches to teacher leadership that have emerged during the past 10 years—teacher research as a form of teacher leadership; models of distributive leadership; and self-managed teams as sources of teacher leadership and substitutes for administrative leadership. Each of these new approaches has deep theoretical and philosophical roots. Each moves past the idea of leadership as manifested in individuals occupying formal positions to more dynamic, organizational views of leadership.

There is little empirical research to date that examines these new approaches "in action." Nevertheless, there is some initial evidence that these new approaches take us in positive directions. While the evidence is not conclusive, there are reasons to believe that these new approaches to teacher leadership are more conducive to school improvement than earlier ones.

It should be noted that it is difficult to discuss teacher leadership without saying something about leadership itself. Leadership has defied commonly accepted definition (Immegart, 1988). However, the new approaches to teacher leadership that we explore in this chapter are consistent with recent literature that defines leadership as a social influence process aimed at achieving some collective or organizational end (Bass, 1990; Yukl, 1998). As a social influence process, leadership permeates organizations rather than residing in particular people or formal positions of authority. As a result, leadership can come from and be exercised by a wide range of organizational participants. In schools, therefore, teachers, parents, and students, as well as administrators and others in formal positions, have potential for leadership in their relationships with others and through various aspects of their respective work. The first approach to teacher leadership sees leadership in teachers' efforts to develop new knowledge from inquiry into their own schools and classrooms.

TEACHER RESEARCH AS LEADERSHIP

The idea of teacher as researcher is almost a century old. In his brief historical account, Henson (1996) tells us that as early as 1908 concerted efforts were made to involve teachers in research. In 1910 the subject of teacher research appeared in the *Journal of Educational Psychology*. By the early 1900s teachers were recognized as the people best able to identify problems pertinent to teaching. They were charged with investigating solutions to those problems, although, according to Olson (1990), this work was never called research. Calls for teacher research to support school- and district-level curriculum development increased in the 1920s (Henson, 1996). In the 1950s teachers were urged to become researchers of their own classrooms. The most recent efforts to promote teacher research began in the late 1980s with a number of inquiry projects in the United States and Great Britain (Cochran-Smith & Lytle, 1999b). In 1994, the National Society for the Study of Education acknowledged the importance of teacher research by publishing a yearbook on the subject (Hollingsworth & Sockett, 1994).

Teacher research has been defined in many ways. We follow Cochran-Smith and Lytle (1999b) and adopt a broad definition of teacher research that encompasses all forms of teacher inquiry involving any systematic, intentional, and self-critical study of one's work, including inquiry referred to as action research, practitioner inquiry, teacher inquiry, and so on. For the most part, teacher research has been considered an individual activity geared toward teachers' personal professional development and improvement (Henson, 1996). In the past 10 years teacher research has also been viewed as a form of teacher leadership and a way to promote school improvement (Cochran-Smith & Lytle, 1998). Advocates of teacher research contend that it not only provides useful knowledge for teachers themselves; it also is an important source of knowledge about teaching for the larger educational community (Pappas, 1977). According to Cochran-Smith and Lytle (1999b), "the concept of teacher research carries with it an enlarged view of the teacher's role—as decision maker, consultant, curriculum developer, analyst, activist, school leader" (p. 17).

Central to the notion of teacher research as teacher leadership is the issue of influence. Its advocates argue that teacher research can "challenge the hegemony of a university-generated knowledge base for teaching" (Cochran-Smith & Lytle, 1999a, p. 282). As a source of "learning through doing" it can influence individual teachers' classroom practices. Moreover, because of its local nature and its close relationship to practice, teacher research may be a potentially powerful source of influence in efforts to improve schools (Cochran-Smith & Lytle, 1999a). By conducting research teachers may increase their sense of efficacy, enabling them to feel that they are better able to promote change (Henson, 1996). Teachers who are involved in research may become more reflective, critical, and analytical not just of their own teaching but of schooling practices around them.

Most studies of teacher research examine how it is conducted, factors that support or constrain its practice, and its implications for learning and change for teacher researchers themselves (see Henson, 1996; Zeichner, 1994). Relatively little has been written about teacher research as a form of teacher leadership or a means to promote change at the school level; however, the literature that has examined these functions of teacher research generally reports positive outcomes. Zeichner points to the work of the Boston Women's Teachers' Group and to other lesser-known cases in which teacher research has helped to shape schoolwide programs and policies. Tikunoff, Ward, and Griffin (1979) describe a model of school-based collaborative action research in which a researcher, a staff developer, and a group of teachers in a school worked together to identify a problem within the school, conducted research on it, and implemented a staff development program to address the problem. They found that this process led to considerable change in teacher practice schoolwide (see also Griffin, Lieberman, & Jacullo-Noto, 1983).

In another study Harris and Drake (1997) examined a high school that used schoolwide teacher research teams to develop teachers as change agents and to promote a more collaborative, reflective faculty culture. These teams were linked to a participative school-level decision-making structure that was to develop programs and policies from teacher research findings. Harris and Drake found that for the most part teachers perceived individual and organizational benefits from their work. They saw the group research experience as a source for their own professional development. Moreover, they believed that the research experience enhanced their ability to promote change at the school level. It is interesting to note that even though these teachers performed various leadership tasks as part of their work, and even though they considered themselves better able to promote school-level change, they did not see themselves as leaders. Instead, they reserved the concept of leadership for principals and others in formal administrative positions.

Additional evidence concerning teacher research and leadership comes from a study by Clift, Veal, Holland, Johnson, and McCarthy (1995) of a collaborative leadership project for school improvement. This project involved a partnership among five public schools and a team of university teacher education researchers. Clift and her colleagues describe the project not as action research where teachers and administrators jointly collected and analyzed data but as "action science," where university researchers took primary responsibility for data collection and analysis and teachers and administrators worked together to identify problems in their schools, set research agendas, and engaged in "public reflection" of findings. According to Clift and her colleagues, the project resulted in individual learning and growth among all project participants, teachers, administrators, and university faculty alike. Most notable for this discussion, they found that the project helped teachers develop a greater sense of individual and collective efficacy for leadership and a stronger ability to initiate and influence school-level improvement planning. As the project progressed and as participants studied the evidence that had been collected, teachers and administrators began "planning, arguing, and negotiating" desired changes in their respective schools (p. 23). Their joint deliberation around evidence resulted in new improvement plans in each school.

One of the more recent systematic studies of teacher research for leadership development and school improvement is the five-year evaluation of the Bay Area School Reform Collaborative (BASRC) (Center for Research on the Context of Teaching, 2000; Copland, 2001). BASRC was formed in the San Francisco Bay Area in 1995 as one of six initial local Annenberg Challenge projects. It provides grants to 86 Leadership Schools to implement a six-stage school-based Cycle of Inquiry for school improvement. The cycle begins with identifying a broad problem statement and proceeds to reformulating the problem statement and focusing effort, identifying measurable goals for student learning, building a concrete action plan, putting that plan into place, and collecting data and analyzing the results. The results should suggest new problems to investigate, and the cycle repeats. BASRC expects that this cycle will inform and motivate local school change through evidence and analysis (Center for Research on the Context of

Teaching). It provides a vehicle for sharing leadership functions among teachers and administrators and building leadership capacity throughout the school, as teachers are called upon to be leaders and authoritative decision makers. BASRC and its Cycle of Inquiry suggest a model of leadership defined less by the actions of single leaders than by a set of leadership tasks shared across a broad segment of a school community.

Longitudinal case studies and surveys of principals provide some evidence that the BASRC Cycle of Inquiry has helped to promote teacher leadership and school improvement. According to the principal survey data, teacher leadership had developed in 90% of the Leadership Schools (Copland, 2001). Case studies of 10 Leadership Schools show that the Cycle of Inquiry established a process that enabled teachers to assume leadership roles typically performed by administrators (Center for Research on the Context of Teaching, 2000). Across these cases, teachers worked on teams to develop goals for schoolwide improvement and to delegate problem solving to other groups within the school. They shared best practices with fellow teachers and, in some schools, led searches for new administrators. A number of these schools developed new leadership structures to support improvement activity, including a rotating system of lead teachers to replace the principal, the appointment of teachers to serve as co-principals, and new interschool partnerships that supported shared leadership. These and other examples of teacher leadership brought new expectations for principals to work more as professional colleagues of teachers than as their administrative superiors.

The cases suggest that BASRC's Cycle of Inquiry led to significant changes in school culture and core practices. They show that where strong cycles of inquiry developed, teacher professional community and professional development were strengthened. Teachers collaborated to evaluate student work, to develop new curricula and student assessments, to experiment with new teaching practices, and to solve classroom and school-level problems. The cycle helped teachers to develop shared knowledge, a common language, and a collective sense of efficacy that moved them deeper into school improvement efforts.

In summary, this literature suggests that teacher research can serve as a form of teacher leadership and as a source of influence for school improvement. It suggests that inquiry, particularly inquiry in collaborative contexts or "inquiry communities," can create new opportunities for teachers to learn and lead efforts to improve their schools (Cochran-Smith & Lytle, 1999a; Fullan, 2001). Moreover, the evidence suggests that the products of teacher research—the knowledge, the findings of inquiry—can provide an impetus and a direction for improvement planning and other organizational changes at the school level.

MODELS OF DISTRIBUTIVE LEADERSHIP

Another approach to teacher leadership comes through several emerging models of distributive leadership. In the mid-1990s the education literature began to discuss leadership that was exercised not only by people in formal positions of authority but also by people outside those positions. The literature stressed the importance to school improvement of leadership that was distributed and performed across roles. It called us to shift our attention away from individual and role-based conceptions of leadership and toward organizational and task-oriented conceptions of leadership.

Ogawa and Bossert (1995) traced these notions of distributive leadership back to ideas that were developed in the 1950s and 1960s. At that time, organizational and administration theorists were beginning to think of leadership not simply as a role-specific phenomenon but as an organization-wide phenomenon. For example, Barnard (1968) observed that the "authority of leadership" is not limited to those in executive positions. He implied that leadership might be exercised by any member of an organization. Similarly, Thompson (1967) argued that leadership flows throughout organizations, spanning levels and flowing both up and down organizational hierarchies. Others argued that leadership should be thought of as an organizational quality that could be measured and assessed organization-wide (e.g., Tannenbaum, 1962). Beginning in the 1970s, Griffiths (1979) and later others writing in the education literature (e.g., Haller & Knapp, 1985) began to direct our attention away from "leadership" to the acts of "leading." This distinction refocused attention beyond the person and the role to leadership tasks, behaviors, and functions.

Three related models of distributive leadership have emerged in the education literature since the mid-1990s. One model, articulated by William Firestone and his colleagues, views leadership as the performance of key tasks or functions rather than as the work of people in formal leadership roles (Firestone, 1996; Heller & Firestone, 1995). According to this view, leadership tasks in schools can be and often are performed by people outside of formal administrative positions, including teachers, parents, and students. When leadership is defined as certain kinds of work, it is more important that the work be done well than that it be performed by a particular individual.

In a series of studies, Firestone and his colleagues associated the success of complex innovations with the distributed performance of several key leadership functions: (a) providing and selling a vision; (b) obtaining resources; (c) providing encouragement and recognition; (d) adapting rules and procedures to support the innovation; (e) monitoring improvement; and (f) handling internal and external disturbances. In a study of elementary schools that had successfully institutionalized a new curriculum designed to help students develop and apply critical thinking and problem-solving skills, Heller and Firestone (1995) found these leadership functions well performed in each school. They also found that these functions were performed not by any "heroic" leader, such as the principal, but by a number of different people in a variety of overlapping roles, including principals, teachers, central office personnel, and outside consultants. In addition, they found that the same functions were often performed by people in different roles. This complementary redundancy enhanced the effectiveness of the functions and provided some insurance that the functions would be performed if there were turnover in personnel or if particular individuals failed to do their part. In a companion study of the inclusion of special education students in general education classrooms, Mayrowetz and Weinstein (1999) offered similar findings. In schools where special education inclusion had taken root, each leadership function was carried out by multiple individuals in different roles in a redundant, mutually-reinforcing manner. As Heller and Firestone found in their study, these individuals included school and central office administrators, teachers, aides, and parents.

Another model of distributive leadership has been described by Ogawa, Pounder, and their colleagues (Ogawa & Bossert, 1995; Pounder, Ogawa, & Adams, 1995). Rather than viewing leadership as the distributed performance of specific tasks or functions, they describe leadership as an organization-wide resource of power and influence. Drawing upon institutional perspectives of organizations, Ogawa and Bossert argue that leadership occurs not through the actions of individuals but through interaction among individuals. Because it occurs through interaction, influence that is exerted through leadership cannot be assumed to be unidirectional; it can flow up and down levels and between units of organizations. Ogawa and Bossert describe leadership as the multidirectional flow of influence through networks of roles that constitute organizations. Thus, as the flow of power and influence, leadership is not confined to certain roles but is distributed across roles, with different roles having access to different levels and types of power and influence. This view of leadership is consistent with political theory concerning power and influence among "lower" participants and the politics of upward influence in complex organizations (e.g., Mechanic, 1962-1963; Porter, Allen, & Angle, 1981).

As distributed across networks of roles, leadership can be considered an organization-wide phenomenon or an organizational quality. Pounder, Ogawa, and Adams (1995) examined the relationship of the leadership exercised by different individuals and groups in schools to four functions of effective organizations: (a) goal achievement; (b) ability to control relationships with the environment; (c) commitment among members to the organization; and (d) social solidarity among members. They also examined the relationship of leadership from different sources to several measures of school performance: (a) perceived organizational effectiveness; (b) student absenteeism; (c) academic achievement; and (d) faculty and staff turnover. Pounder and her colleagues defined leadership as the "amount of raw social influence" held by different individuals and groups in schools. They examined the amount of influence held separately by principals, teachers, secretaries, and parents and the sum of separately held influence as a measure of total leadership influence in a school.

This study found that total leadership influence in schools was associated with school performance through its effect on several organizational functions. Total leadership was directly and positively related to the level of goal achievement and commitment. High goal achievement was associated with low student absenteeism and higher achievement. Commitment was associated positively with members' perceptions of school effectiveness and was associated with low faculty and staff turnover. Rather than all actors possessing similar amounts of influence over the same things, Pounder and her colleagues found that individuals in different roles exerted influence on different organizational outcomes. For example, the leadership influence of principals and groups of teachers was positively related to organizational commitment, while parent leadership was associated with low student absenteeism and higher achievement. The study concluded that people in many different roles can lead and affect the performance of their schools in different ways.

Leithwood and Jantzi (2000) adopted a similar perspective to study the effects of principal and teacher leadership, separately and together, on school organizational conditions and student engagement with school. They examined the effects of leadership on (a) the clarity and awareness of school mission and goals; (b) collaborative school culture;

(c) the perceived effectiveness of school planning processes; (d) the school's instructional program; (e) structure and organization that support school mission and goals; (f) information collection and decision making; and (g) policies and procedures that support instruction, student learning, and teacher professional growth. They examined the effects of leadership on student engagement, taking into consideration as mediating factors these organizational conditions and "family educational culture" (i.e., assumptions, norms, values, and beliefs held by the family about intellectual work in general, school work in particular, and the conditions that foster both). Leithwood and Jantzi found that principal influence and teacher influence were both separately and positively related to school organizational conditions. Principal and teacher influence had an indirect relationship to student engagement through school organizational conditions.

Leithwood and Jantzi (2000) found that total leadership influence had a significant positive relationship to school organizational conditions, although this relationship was not as strong as the independent effects of principal influence and teacher influence. Like Pounder and her colleagues (1995), Leithwood and Jantzi conclude that both teacher leadership and principal leadership matter to school organizational functions and, through those functions, to student outcomes. And like Pounder and her colleagues, Leithwood and Jantzi contend that total leadership influence, as an indicator of the distribution of leadership influence across roles in a school, has a positive relationship to the quality and effectiveness of school organization.

A third model of distributive leadership, described by Spillane, Halverson, and Diamond (2000, 2001), builds upon task-oriented views of leadership and views of leadership as an organizational property. Drawing upon activity theory and theories of distributed cognition, Spillane and his colleagues argue that leadership practice is constituted in the interaction of school leaders, followers, and situations. The social distribution of leadership means more than the division or duplication of leadership tasks among formal and informal leaders. In their view, leadership is "stretched over" the practice of two or more leaders in their interactions with followers. As performed in the interactions among multiple leaders and followers, leadership practice occurs "in between" people (see also Donaldson, 2001). Leadership influence may therefore be multiplicative rather than additive because the interactions among two or more leaders in carrying out a particular leadership task may amount to more than the sum of the leaders' practices.

Previous research underscores the relational nature of leadership. It indicates that leaders not only influence followers but are also influenced by them and that leaders are dependent on those they lead (Dunlap & Goldman, 1991; Hollander, 1978). From a distributive perspective, the role of followers in leadership practice involves more than influencing the actions taken by formal leaders. Followers are an essential constituting element of the social interaction that is leadership activity.

Finally, Spillane and his colleagues argue that leadership is distributed in the dynamic web of people, interactions, and situations. Situation is not external to leadership activity but one of its core constituting elements. Leadership cannot be extracted from its organizational, structural, and social-cultural contexts. Thus, aspects of the situation can enable or constrain leadership activity at the same time that leadership activity can transform aspects of the situation over time. Situation is both constitutive and constituted of leadership practice.

To date, there are few reports of research that illustrates this third model of distributive leadership in action. In a preliminary report of their study of 13 Chicago elementary schools, Spillane, Halverson, and Diamond (2001) indicate that the performance of leadership tasks is often distributed among multiple leaders, including principals, teachers, assistant principals, counselors, and curriculum coordinators. Citing examples from case studies of these schools, they describe the co-enactment of leadership tasks by multiple leaders. These examples also illustrate how different areas of knowledge and expertise brought by different leaders can work interdependently in leadership task performance and can contribute to the effectiveness of leadership task performance in a way that is greater than the contribution any one leader might make alone. These findings are consistent with research related to the other two models of distributive leadership.

These three models of distributive leadership have several implications for teacher leadership. First, they indicate that teachers can and do perform important leadership tasks inside and outside formal positions of authority. The research suggests that school improvement is promoted by the distribution and the coordinated and redundant performance of leadership functions across roles, including teachers along with other members of school organizations. Distributed leadership requires mutual reliance among all school personnel even though, by virtue of their positions or knowledge and skills, different personnel might perform some leadership tasks better than others (Thurston, Zenz, Schacht, & Clift, 1995). Different teachers may lead from different strengths and lead in different ways (Wasley, 1991). Distributing leadership tasks among a number of people is important because the principal cannot "do it all." And while it is true that the division and distribution of labor may be important given the scope and fragmentation of principals' work (Fullan, 2001), the logic of distribution indicates that school leadership overall is ultimately enhanced by the different knowledge and skills brought by a variety of people and by the commitments that are developed among those who perform leadership tasks together.

Second, these models of distributive leadership suggest that teacher leadership may make both independent and, with leadership from other sources, additive or multiplicative contributions to school improvement and outcomes for students. Teacher leadership has "added value" to administrative leadership in schools. Depending on how one conceptualizes it, that "added value" may be equal to or greater than the sum of the parts.

Third, the argument that leadership is an organizational property reminds us that teacher leadership as a social influence process is a "given" in schools. Whether or not they occupy leadership roles, whether or not they perform particular leadership functions, teachers can exert influence by simply being part of the "webs" of relationships that define school organizations. We are reminded that influence in schools is exercised in all directions and among all participants. We are also reminded that relationships among leaders and followers are mutually influential and co-dependent. Even as "followers," teachers shape at the same time that they are shaped by other sources of leadership in their schools. Because leadership exists and functions in the relationships between leaders and followers, teachers as followers are by definition a constituting part of school leadership. Teachers are also key actors who shape the situations in which leadership relationships develop and are exercised.

LEADERSHIP OF TEAMS

In recent years there has been growing emphasis on self-managed teams for promoting teacher collaboration, improving teaching and student learning, and addressing problems of school organization (Fullan & Hargreaves, 1992; Pounder, 1998). Teams are small task groups in which members have a common purpose, interdependent roles, and complementary skills (Yukl, 1998). Self-managed teams are accorded considerable responsibility and discretion in how to perform their work. These work groups can be considered "intact social systems" whose members have the authority to handle internal processes as they see fit in order to perform their work (Hackman & Oldham, 1980, p. 164). In schools, teams may be created to increase teacher responsibility for group performance and outcomes and to expand opportunities for self-direction and management (Pounder, 1999). The logic of teams is that teachers' commitment, knowledge, and skills will be developed as they assume collective responsibility and as they work together to design their own methods for pursuing group objectives (Hackman, 1998).

In at least two ways, self-managed teams can be considered sources of teacher leadership. First, it is possible that these social units and the products of their work may promote improvement at the school level. Second, well-composed and well-functioning teams can exert substantial social and normative influence over their members, shaping their thinking, beliefs, and behaviors (Hackman, 1990; Yukl, 1998). Through their relationships and the work they perform together, teacher members can influence and lead one another. Group processes and the influence teachers may exert over one another in teams can provide some substitute for external administrative leadership, reducing the need for administrative initiative, guidance, and control (Bass, 1990; Kerr & Jermier, 1978; see also Pitner, 1988).

The management literature suggests that teams can improve organizational effectiveness; however, the evidence is mixed and much of it is based on weak research (Yukl, 1998). Hackman (1998) contends that what differentiates teams that "go into orbit and achieve real synergy from those that crash and burn" (p. 248) has much more to do with how teams are structured and supported than with any inherent virtues or liabilities of teaming itself (see also Yukl). His research found that teams benefit from being "set up right in the first place" (1990, p. 10). They require an organizational context that supports team performance through appropriate rewards, makes available relevant training and consultation, provides clear work requirements, and removes constraints on the team's work. Additional conditions of effectiveness include group composition appropriate to the task and work that is motivating to team members. Teams benefit from healthy interpersonal processes that increase the synergistic gains and reduce what Hackman calls "process losses" that result from lack of motivation and problems with coordination of activity.

Teams also require strong internal leadership to be effective (Hackman, 1990). This is another way that teams provide opportunities for teacher leadership. In a study of interdisciplinary teacher teams at the middle school level, Crow and Pounder (2000) found that teacher leadership skills and expertise were important aspects of "group composition" that enhanced team effectiveness. Teams with designated leaders generally functioned better than leaderless teams. Teams that exercised the greatest leadership in their schools were those that had strong leaders and a significant amount of member experience working in that particular school setting as well as in other team settings. These experiences gave teams expertise in "how things are done," helped them judge the implications of decision choices, and gave them confidence to try new ways of doing work.

In addition, teams require strong external leadership and support to be effective (Hackman, 1998). Crow's and Pounder's study (2000) found that lack of support from other teachers and administrators eroded team members' sense of efficacy, discretion, and autonomy. Lack of clarity from school administrators about what teams were to achieve also diminished members' sense that their teams were actually self-managing and compromised teams' work. Bauer and Bogotch (2001) also found that district administrative support and support from the building principal and building staff strongly influenced measures of team effectiveness and/or satisfaction with "site council" teams composed of teachers and others connected with the schools. We take up the issue of external leadership again in the conclusion of this chapter.

Given these conditions of effectiveness, what contributions can the leadership of teacher teams make to school-level improvement? Much like the management literature, the education research provides mixed answers. The education literature suggests that self-managed teams may be an effective way to accomplish particular tasks and promote collaboration and development of team members (Witziers, Sleegers, & Imants, 1999). In a comparative study of teachers on teams and in non-team work arrangements, Pounder (1999) found that teachers on teams reported significantly greater work motivation, job satisfaction, work efficacy, and professional commitment than their non-teaming counterparts. The research Pounder reviewed for that study reached similar conclusions. Erb's studies (1987, 1995) of interdisciplinary teacher teams found that teaming reduces teacher isolation and focuses teachers' attention and coordinated action on student learning. Erb found that teachers on teams were more likely than their non-team counterparts to develop coordinated curricular and instruction plans. Teachers on teams tended to address student problems earlier and more systematically. They communicated earlier and more frequently with parents. They were more proactive in changing their classroom practice to address problems. Teamed teachers spent more time talking about curricular and co-curricular issues and they were generally more knowledgeable about curricular and instructional matters than their non-teamed counterparts. In addition, teamed teachers were more likely than non-teamed teachers to integrate their instruction across subject areas. Other studies have demonstrated that in comparison with non-teamed teachers, teamed teachers tend to experience greater work satisfaction, sense of professionalism, and professional efficacy (Pounder, 1999). Teamed teachers also tend to have more knowledge of one another's work (Ashton & Webb, 1986) and provide more intellectual assistance and support to one another. Finally, teaming provides considerably more opportunities for direct and indirect involvement of teachers in decision making, including greater access to information (Kruse & Louis, 1997).

Studies of the effects of teacher teams on whole school improvement are not as encouraging (Donaldson, 2001; Witziers et al., 1999). In their study of high school departments as teams, for example, Herriot and Firestone (1984) found that departmental structure created barriers that hindered communication, collaboration, and curricular coherence across the larger school community. Interdisciplinary teams fared no better in promoting collaboration and collective decision making at the school level (Witziers et al., 1999). Kruse and Louis (1997) found that interdisciplinary teams undermined schools' ability to address schoolwide issues. In the middle schools they studied, the demands on teachers to deal with issues at the team level—from the management of team work to performing the work itself—minimized the opportunities that teachers had for engaging issues of teaching, student learning, and school organization across teams. Teaming appeared to inhibit the development of school-level reform agendas. Chrispeels' (1992) case studies of elementary schools also documented inconsistent influences of teams at the school level.

These findings are consistent with Yukl's (1998) assessment of the management literature that large organizations with many self-directed teams can experience serious problems coordinating activities and reaching agreement on strategic issues at the organizational level. This evidence does not necessarily mean that teacher teams cannot promote improvement at the school level. As Muncey and Conley (1999) pointed out, a shift to thinking, organizing, and planning around teaming may potentially provoke rethinking and experimentation about school structure, teaching strategies, and student learning—the central goals of educational reform (see Friedman, 1998). However, it may mean that strong external leadership is needed to set the direction for and to coordinate team work at the school level and to avoid organizational fragmentation (see Hackman, 1998). This conclusion is supported by the investigations of collective teacher research discussed earlier in the chapter.

Conclusion

In this chapter we explored three new approaches to teacher leadership. We began with a brief historical overview of the evolution of teacher leadership since the early 1900s, ending with a discussion of the individual empowerment, role-based initiatives of the late 1980s and early 1990s. We discussed teacher research as a form of teacher leadership, different models of distributive leadership, and the leadership of self-managed teacher teams. We argued that these new approaches to teacher leadership represent a substantial shift from earlier initiatives. Looking across these new approaches, we see that they emphasize the importance of collective versus individual leadership; leadership aimed at the level of the school, not just at the level of the classroom; leadership focused on developing important aspects of school organization, curriculum, and instruction, not simply on administrative tasks; and leadership organized around important functions, not simply people and positions. The evidence from research to date, while not fully developed, suggests that these new approaches to teacher leadership can promote school improvement and that they appear to be more effective in this regard than previous models. Our experiences with teacher leadership initiatives of the 1980s and early 1990s reveal the limitations of the teacher as "heroic leader." However, we see in these new approaches the greater capacity of teachers to influence. We see that school improvement may be better served by teacher leadership that does not act alone but is part of a broad system of leadership influences and tasks performed by multiple actors.

What are the implications for teacher leadership development, or for that matter, school leadership development more generally? First, the fact that these new approaches to teacher leadership appear to be more effective than formal leadership roles for individual teachers in promoting school improvement does not mean that the latter should necessarily be abandoned. Recent research on school improvement in Chicago elementary schools documented the important contributions that teachers hired into instructional coordinator positions made in promoting curricular, instructional, and organizational improvement in their schools (Smylie, Wenzel, & Fendt, in press). At the same time, this research showed that these coordinators were much more effective when they worked as members of a broader constellation of school leaders, including principals, other teachers, and sometimes parents, each performing complementary tasks aimed at school-level improvement. These findings suggest that although it may be very useful to develop formal teacher leadership roles, these roles should not be relied upon as the primary means for promoting school improvement. Instead, they might best be developed as part of a schoolwide network of leadership.

This leads to a second implication, that the development of school leadership should not be aimed primarily at individual leaders but at leaders collectively. It is no less the case with these new approaches that the performance and outcomes of teacher leadership hinge on teachers' capacity to perform their tasks well. The capacity to lead is a function of knowledge relevant to the task, knowledge of the context, and process knowledge and skills (Little, 1988). If school leadership functions as a system of work performed by multiple actors, it makes little sense to develop that leadership by focusing on knowledge and skills of individual leaders outside the context of that system. Instead, we need to consider ways to develop the collective capacity of teachers, principals, and others who perform tasks of leadership together at the organizational level.

That said, it is clear that principals play a crucial role in the performance and outcomes of teacher leadership, whether it is exercised individually or in a collective context (Barth, 2001; Bizar & Barr, 2001). It is a paradox of teacher leadership that it requires administrative leadership to be effective, even those forms of teacher leadership, such as self-managed teams, that serve as substitutes for administrative leadership (Bass, 1990). For teacher leadership to work well, principals may be required to provide examples, incentives, guidance, and support, as well as the means of accountability (Smylie & Hart, 1999). It may fall to them to keep teacher leadership focused on meaningful work (Little, 1988). Principals need to know how to develop, support, and manage these new forms of leadership. Their unique position in the school organization gives them the resources, the ability, and the authority to do this leadership management work well. It is the principal who may best be able to direct the work of self-managed teams toward broader organizational objectives. It is the principal who may best be able to support teacher research and link it to school-level improvement planning and decision making and to teacher professional development activity. It is the principal who may be needed to coordinate and manage the performance of distributed leadership tasks. It is the principal and/or district administrator who can clarify the goals and processes of teacher teams, participate in defining the parameters of their work, and set the goals for which they will be held accountable (Bauer & Bogotch, 2001). We cannot assume that principals and district administrators know how to do these things particularly well. So while it makes sense to develop school leadership collectively, the importance of developing administrators' capacity for supporting these new approaches to leadership cannot be overlooked.

Finally, as with previous initiatives, it is unlikely that these new approaches to teacher leadership will be effective if they are not supported by the broader organizational and institutional contexts in which they develop and function. In writing for the 89th NSSE yearbook on teacher professionalism, school restructuring, and leadership, Rallis (1990) argued that the challenge of school leadership generally, and teacher leadership in particular, is not to find "super" leaders but "to discover and to promote the conditions that allow the process of leadership to flourish" (p. 186). There is no reason to believe that the lessons from research on individual role-based models of teacher leadership are not applicable to new task-oriented, organizational forms of leadership. Lack of leadership precedent will constrain the development and exercise of any form of teacher leadership (Little, 1988). So will hostility or resistance from other teachers (Lieberman, Saxl, & Miles, 1992). And of course, there is the principal and the central office.

Donaldson (2001) describes the problems this way. He argues that schools have leadership-resistant architectures. There is no time to convene people to plan, organize, and follow through. Contact and the transaction of business are usually "on the fly" and communication is often haphazard. The culture and social norms of schools conspire against leadership development. Teacher rewards tend to be intrinsic and student-focused. Norms of individualism, autonomy, and privacy are pervasive. Teacher isolation and individualism and the history of hierarchical relationships in schools may doom collaborative effort. Donaldson concludes that school conditions can paralyze "action-in-common" because work is generally not conceived as interdependent, feedback on practice is scarce, and schools cannot stop the action long enough to understand the central adaptive challenges well enough to meet them. These are the very organizational problems that bedeviled previous efforts to develop teacher leadership (Smylie, 1997). Individual role-based models of teacher leadership were simply not strong enough to overcome them. However, the new forms of collective, task-oriented, organizational approaches to leadership we discussed in this chapter hold greater promise for overcoming these seemingly intractable problems. The initial evidence is encouraging, but more work needs to be done to experiment with these new approaches over an extended period of time and to study their implementation and outcomes systematically. Then we will have a much better idea whether these new approaches can fulfill their initial promise of promoting meaningful school-level improvement.

REFERENCES

Ashton, P. T., & Webb, R. B. (1986). *Making a difference: Teachers' sense of efficacy and student achievement.* New York: Longman.

Bacharach, S. B., & Conley, S. C. (1989). Uncertainty and decision-making in teaching: Implications for managing line professionals. In T. Sergiovanni and J. H. Moore (Eds.), *Schooling for tomorrow: Directing reform to issues that count* (pp. 311-329). Boston: Allyn & Bacon.

Bacharach, S. B., Conley, S., & Shedd, J. (1986). Beyond career ladders: Structuring teacher career development systems. *Teachers College Record, 87,* 563-574.

Barnard, C. I. (1968). *Functions of the executive.* Cambridge, MA: Harvard University Press.

Barth, R. (2001). Teacher leader. *Phi Delta Kappan, 82,* 443-449.

Bass, B. M. (1990). *Bass & Stogdill's handbook of leadership* (3rd ed.). New York: Free Press.

Bauer, S., & Bogotch, I. E. (2001). Analysis of the relationships among site council resources, council practices, and outcomes. *Journal of School Leadership, 11,* 98-119.

Bizar, M., & Barr, R. (2001). *School leadership in times of urban reform.* Mahwah, NJ: Lawrence Erlbaum Associates.

Center for Research on the Context of Teaching. (2000, May). *Assessing results: Bay Area School Reform Collaborative—Year 4.* Stanford, CA: Center for Research on the Context of Teaching, Stanford University.

Chrispeels, J. H. (1992). *Purposeful restructuring: Creating a culture for learning and achievement in elementary schools.* Washington, DC: Falmer.

Clift, R. T., Veal, M. L., Holland, P., Johnson, M., & McCarthy, J. (1995). *Collaborative leadership and shared decision making: Teachers, principals, and university professors.* New York: Teachers College Press.

Cochran-Smith, M., & Lytle, S. L. (1998). Teacher research: The question that persists. *International Journal of Leadership in Education, 1,* 19-36.

Cochran-Smith, M., & Lytle, S. L. (1999a). Relationships of knowledge and practice: Teacher learning in communities. In A. Iran-Nejad & P. D. Pearson (Eds.), *Review of Research in Education, 24* (pp. 249-305). Washington, DC: American Educational Research Association.

Cochran-Smith, M., & Lytle, S. L. (1999b). The teacher research movement: A decade later. *Educational Researcher, 28*(7), 15-25.

Conley, S. (1991). Review of research on teacher participation in school decision making. In G. Grant (Ed.), *Review of research in education, 17* (pp. 225-266). Washington, DC: American Educational Research Association.

Copland, M. A. (2001, April). *Shared school leadership: Moving from role to function in an inquiry-based model of school reform.* Paper presented at the annual meeting of the American Educational Research Association, Seattle, WA.

Crow, G. M., & Pounder, D. G. (2000). Interdisciplinary teacher teams: Context, design, and process. *Educational Administration Quarterly, 36,* 216-254.

Dewey, J. (1903). Democracy in education. *Elementary School Teacher, 4*(4), 193-204.

Donaldson, G. A. (2001). *Cultivating leadership in schools: Connecting people, purpose, and practice.* New York: Teachers College Press.

Dunlap, D. M., & Goldman, P. (1991). Rethinking power in schools. *Educational Administration Quarterly, 27,* 5-29.

Elmore, R. F., Peterson, P. L., & McCarthey, S. J. (1996). *Restructuring in the classroom: Teaching, learning, and school organization.* San Francisco: Jossey-Bass.

Erb, T. O. (1987). What team organization can do for teachers. *Middle School Journal, 18*(4), 3-6.

Erb, T. O. (1995). Teamwork in middle school education. In H. G. Garner (Ed.), *Teamwork models and experience in education* (pp. 175-198). Boston: Allyn & Bacon.

Firestone, W. A. (1996). Leadership roles or functions? In K. Leithwood, J. Chapman, D. Corson, P. Hallinger, & A. Hart (Eds.), *International handbook of educational leadership and administration* (Vol. 2, pp. 395-418). Dordrecht, The Netherlands: Kluwer.

Firestone, W. A., & Bader, B. D. (1992). *Redesigning teaching: Professionalism or bureaucracy?* Albany, NY: SUNY Press.

Friedman, V. J. (1998). Making schools safe for uncertainty: Teams, teaching, and school reform. *Teachers College Record, 99*(2), 335-370.

Fullan, M. (2001). *The new meaning of educational change* (3rd ed.). New York: Teachers College Press.

Fullan, M., & Hargreaves, A. (1992). Teacher development and educational change. In M. Fullan & A. Hargreaves (Eds.), *Teacher development and educational change.* London: Falmer Press.

Fuller, W. E. (1989). The teacher in the country school. In D. Warren (Ed.), *American teachers: Histories of a profession at work* (pp. 98-117). New York: Macmillan.

Griffin, G. A., Lieberman, A., & Jacullo-Noto, J. (1983). *Interactive research and development on schooling: Executive summary of final report.* Austin: University of Texas, Research and Development for Teacher Education.

Griffiths, D. (1979). Intellectual turmoil in educational administration. *Educational Administration Quarterly, 13*(3), 43-65.

Hackman, J. R. (1990). *Groups that work (and those that don't).* San Francisco: Jossey-Bass.

Hackman, J. R. (1998). Why teams don't work. In R. S. Tinsdale et al. (Eds.), *Theory and research on small groups* (pp. 245-267). New York: Plenum.

Hackman, J. R., & Oldham, G. R. (1980). *Work redesign.* Reading, MA: Addison-Wesley.

Haller, E., & Knapp, T. (1985). Problems and methodology in educational administration. *Educational Administration Quarterly, 21*(3), 157-168.

Harris, B., & Drake, S. M. (1997). Implementing high school reform through school-wide action research teams: A three year case study. *Action in Teacher Education, 19*(3), 15-31.

Hart, A. W. (1990). Work redesign: A review of literature for education reform. In S. B. Bacharach (Ed.), *Advances in research and theories of school management and educational policy* (Vol. 1, pp. 31-69). Greenwich, CT: JAI Press.

Heller, M. F., & Firestone, W. A. (1995). Who's in charge here? Sources of leadership for change. *Elementary School Journal, 96,* 65-86.

Henson, K. T. (1996). Teachers as researchers. In J. Sikula, T. J. Buttery, & E. Guyton (Eds.), *Handbook of research on teacher education* (pp. 53-64). New York: Macmillan.

Herriott, R. E., & Firestone, W. A. (1984). Two images of schools as organizations: A refinement and elaboration. *Educational Administration Quarterly, 20*(4), 41-57.

Hollander, E. P. (1978). *Leadership dynamics.* New York: Free Press.

Immegart, G. L. (1988). Leadership and leader behavior. In N. J. Boyan (Ed.), *Handbook of research on educational administration* (pp. 259-277). New York: Longman.

Kerr, S., & Jermier, J. (1978). Substitutes for leadership: Their meaning and measurement. *Organizational Behavior and Human Performance, 22,* 374-403.

Kruse, S. D., & Louis, K. S. (1997). Teaching teaming in middle schools: Dilemmas for a school-wide community. *Educational Administration Quarterly, 33,* 261-289.

Leithwood, K., & Jantzi, D. (2000). The effects of different sources of leadership on student engagement in school. In K. A. Riley & K. S. Louis (Eds.), *Leadership for change and school reform: International perspectives* (pp. 50-66). New York: Routledge/Falmer.

Lichtenstein, G., McLaughlin, M. W., & Knudsen, J. (1992). Teacher empowerment and professional knowledge. In A. Lieberman (Ed.), *The changing contexts of teaching. Ninety-first yearbook of the National Society for the Study of Education, Part I* (pp. 37-58). Chicago: National Society for the Study of Education.

Lieberman, A., Saxl, E. R., & Miles, M. B. (1992). Teacher leadership: Ideology and practice. In A. Lieberman (Ed.), *Building a professional culture in schools* (pp. 148-166). New York: Teachers College Press.

Little, J. W. (1988). Assessing the prospects for teacher leadership. In A. Lieberman (Ed.), *Building a professional culture in schools* (pp. 78-106). New York: Teachers College Press.

Maeroff, G. I. (1988). *The empowerment of teachers: Overcoming the crisis of confidence.* New York: Teachers College Press.

Mayrowetz, D., & Weinstein, C. S. (1999). Sources of leadership for inclusive education: Creating schools for all children. *Educational Administration Quarterly, 35,* 423-449.

Mechanic, D. (1962-63). Sources of power of lower participants in complex organizations. *Administrative Science Quarterly, 7,* 349-364.

Muncey, D. E., & Conley, S. (1999). Teacher compensation and teacher teaming: Sketching the terrain. *Journal of Personnel Evaluation in Education, 12*(4), 365-385.

Murphy, J. (1990). The educational reform movement of the 1980s: A comprehensive analysis. In J. Murphy (Ed.), *The educational reform movement of the 1980s: Perspectives and cases* (pp. 3-55). Berkeley, CA: McCutchan.

Newmann, F. M., & Wehlage, G. G. (1995). *Successful school restructuring.* Madison: Center on Organization and Restructuring of Schools, University of Wisconsin.

Ogawa, R. T., & Bossert, S. T. (1995). Leadership as an organizational quality. *Educational Administration Quarterly, 31,* 224-243.

Olson, M. W. (1990). The teacher as researcher: A historical perspective. In M. W. Olson (Ed.), *Opening the door to classroom research.* Newark, NJ: International Reading Association.

Ortman, E. J. (1923). *Teacher councils: The organized means for securing the co-operation of all workers in the school.* Montpelier, VT: Capital City Press.

Pappas, C. (1997). Making "collaboration" problematic in collaborative school-university research: Studying with urban teacher researchers to transform literacy curriculum genres. In J. Flood, S. B. Heath, & D. Lapp (Eds.), *Handbook of research on teaching literacy through the communicative and visual arts* (pp. 215-231). New York: Macmillan.

Pitner, N. J. (1988). Leadership substitutes: Their factorial validity in educational organizations. *Educational and Psychological Measurement, 48,* 307-315.

Porter, L. W., Allen, R. W., & Angel, H. L. (1981). The politics of upward influence in organizations. In L. L. Cummings & B. W. Staw (Eds.), *Research in organizational behavior* (Vol. 3, pp. 109-149). Greenwich, CT: JAI.

Pounder, D. G. (1998). Teacher teams: Redesigning teachers' work for collaboration. In D. G. Pounder (Ed.), *Restructuring schools for collaboration: Promises and pitfalls* (pp. 65-88). Albany, NY: SUNY Press.

Pounder, D. G. (1999). Teacher teams: Exploring job characteristics and work related outcomes of work group enhancement. *Educational Administration Quarterly, 35,* 317-348.

Pounder, D. G., Ogawa, R. T., & Adams, E. A. (1995). Leadership as an organization-wide phenomenon: Its impact on school performance. *Educational Administration Quarterly, 31,* 564-588.

Rallis, S. (1990). Professional teachers and restructured schools: Leadership challenges. In B. Mitchell & L. L. Cunningham (Eds.), *Educational leadership and changing contexts of families, communities, and schools. Eighty-ninth yearbook of the National Society for the Study of Education, Part II* (pp. 184-209). Chicago: National Society for the Study of Education.

Smylie, M. A. (1997). Research on teacher leadership: Assessing the state of the art. In B. J. Biddle et al. (Eds.), *International handbook of teachers and teaching* (pp. 521-592). Dordrecht, The Netherlands: Kluwer.

Smylie, M. A., & Hart, A. W. (1999). School leadership for teacher learning and change: A human and social capital development perspective. In J. Murphy & K. S. Louis (Eds.), *Handbook of research on educational administration* (2nd ed., pp. 421-441). San Francisco: Jossey-Bass.

Smylie, M. A., Wenzel, S. A., & Fendt, C. R. (in press). The Chicago Annenberg Challenge: Lessons on leadership for school development. In J. Murphy & A. Datnow (Eds.), *Leadership for school reform: Lessons from comprehensive school reform designs.* Thousand Oaks, CA: Corwin.

Spillane, J., Halverson, R., & Diamond, J. B. (2000). *Towards a theory of leadership practice: A distributed perspective*. Evanston, IL: Northwestern University, Institute for Policy Research.

Spillane, J., Halverson, R., & Diamond, J. B. (2001). Investigating school leadership practice: A distributed perspective. *Educational Researcher, 30*(3), 23-28.

Tannenbaum, A. S. (1962). Control in organizations: Individual adjustment and organizational performance. *Administrative Science Quarterly, 7*, 236-257.

Thompson, J. D. (1967). *Organizations in action*. New York: McGraw-Hill.

Thurston, P. W., Zenz, K., Schacht, M., & Clift, R. T. (1995). Exploring leadership. In R. T. Clift & P. W. Thurston (Eds.), *Distributed leadership: School improvement through collaboration* (pp. 155-177). Greenwich, CT: JAI.

Tikunoff, W. J., Ward, B., & Griffin, G. A. (1979). *Interactive research and development on teaching study: Final report*. San Francisco: Far West Laboratory for Educational Research and Development.

Wasley, P. A. (1991). *Teachers who lead: The rhetoric of reform and the realities of practice*. New York: Teachers College Press.

Weise, R., & Murphy, J. (1995). SBM in historical perspective, 1900-1950. In J. Murphy & L. Beck, *School-based management as school reform: Taking stock* (pp. 93-115). Thousand Oaks, CA: Corwin.

Witziers, B., Sleegers, P., & Imants, J. (1999). Departments as teams: Functioning, variations and alternatives. *School Leadership and Management, 19*, 293-304.

Yendol Silva, D., Gimbert, B., & Nolan, J. (2000). Sliding the doors: Locking and unlocking possibilities for teacher leadership. *Teachers College Record, 102*, 779-804.

Yukl, G. (1998). *Leadership in organizations* (4th ed.). Upper Saddle River, NJ: Prentice Hall.

Zeichner, K. M. (1994). Personal renewal and social construction through teacher research. In S. Hollingsworth & H. Sockett (Eds.), *Teacher research and educational reform. Ninety-third yearbook of the National Society for the Study of Education, Part I* (pp. 66-84). Chicago: National Society for the Study of Education.

CHAPTER 9

Reshaping the Role of the School Principal

GARY M. CROW, CHARLES S. HAUSMAN,
AND JAY PAREDES SCRIBNER

In his recent book on globalization, *The Lexus and the Olive Tree*, Thomas Friedman (1999) described two events that led not only to the title of his book but also to his realization of the tensions in our society. In the first instance, he described his visit to a Lexus plant in Tokyo City. The plant, with 66 human workers and 310 robots, manufactures 300 Lexus sedans each day. Friedman observed the process of applying rubber sealant to the windshields of the cars. "The robot arm would neatly paint the hot molten rubber in a perfect rectangle around the window. . . . When it finished its application there was always a tiny drop of rubber left hanging from the tip of the robot's finger. . . . This robot arm would swing around in a wide loop until the tip met a tiny, almost invisible metal wire that would perfectly slice off that last small drop of hot black rubber—leaving nothing left over" (p. 26). Friedman described how impressed he was with the planning, design and technology inherent in that automated process.

The second event occurred as he rode back to Tokyo aboard a "bullet train" travelling at 180 miles an hour. Reading a news story concerning the controversy over the right of return for Palestinian refugees to Israel, he realized the conflict was over who owned which olive tree. Friedman decided that the Lexus and olive tree are both apt symbols of our society. "Half the world seemed to be emerging from the Cold War intent on building a better Lexus, dedicated to modernizing, streamlining and privatizing their economies in order to thrive in the system of globalization. And half of the world—sometimes half the same country, sometimes half the same person—was still caught up in the fight over who owns which olive tree" (p. 27).

Gary Crow is Professor and Chair in the Department of Educational Leadership at the University of Utah. Charles Hausman is the Director of Research and Evaluation for the Salt Lake City, Utah School District. Jay Paredes Scribner is Assistant Professor of Educational Leadership and Policy Analysis at the University of Missouri–Columbia.

Friedman maintained that the fight over the olive tree is not an insignificant pursuit. Instead, olive trees "represent everything that roots us, anchors us, identifies us and locates us in the world—whether it be belonging to a family, a community, a tribe, a nation, a religion or, most of all, a place called home" (p. 27).

This tension between change and continuity is a useful way to describe the context in which the role of the principal is being reshaped. Principals perform their roles in the school, an institution that, for many people, represents their roots—a place where their children live for a sizeable portion of the day, a place that many reformers argue can and should serve as the center of the community. Yet schools are also places that confront some of the most intractable forces of our society and that are called on to prepare the next generation of Lexus designers. To reshape the principalship is to venture into a place where tensions exist—between change and continuity, between complexity and routines, between the global and the home.

In our somewhat presumptuous attempt to discuss reshaping the principal's role, we acknowledge these tensions. We also acknowledge that, as Peter Drucker (1999) warned, forecasting the future—especially of an "information revolution"—is difficult, if not foolhardy. What this information revolution will look like in 10 or 20 years, much less, 50 years, is blurred at best. And what work roles such as the principalship will look like is also difficult to forecast.

Reshaping the principal's role is not a passive process happening to principals. Admittedly, the changing nature of work and the larger society in which schools exist is affecting how principals enact their role and how they are being pressured to change that role. But any discussion of how the principal's role is being, or should be, reshaped also must acknowledge that principals themselves in their daily routines, conversations, and actions shape and reshape their roles. Reshaping the principal's role involves principals themselves in this process.

Although there are perils in this discussion of reshaping the principalship, we pursue the discussion because not only are there ample criticisms of the current way the principalship is enacted and how principals are prepared (Guthrie & Sanders, 2001), but there is also ample evidence of the importance of the principal in contributing to the learning community of schools (Bryk, Camburn & Louis, 1999). We present this discussion in the hope that it will stimulate continuing debate over how stakeholders, including principals themselves, can work together to reshape a role that will make schools better places for learning and working.

This chapter begins with an identification of how work roles have changed, and are changing, in the 21st century. This change is represented primarily by greater complexity in how work is performed. In light of this change, the remainder of the chapter focuses on the internal and external complexities that contribute to reshaping the principal's role.

Changing Work Roles in the 21st Century

In this section we will discuss how work roles are changing in the 21st century. We will do so by first describing what they are changing from and then moving to features of work roles in the future.

THE NATURE OF WORK IN INDUSTRIAL SOCIETY

Jerald Hage and Charles Power (1992), in their discussion of post-industrial work roles and relationships, suggested that work before this period emphasized rationality. By rationalization they mean "the tendency to streamline and simplify which relies on knowledge being implanted in organizational processes or machines" (p. 47). Work during the last century involved processes aimed at diminishing human error and decreasing ambiguity.

These authors identified several components that characterized work roles during the Industrial Age. Since we live in a transition between industrial and post-industrial society, these components are still reflected in some aspects of work roles. First, procedures are standardized. Standard operating procedures are important rules used to decrease error and diminish ambiguity. The first rule of conduct for new role incumbents is to learn the policy book. For school administrators, this is the bible. Frequently, administrators are admonished to follow district policies so they can avoid lawsuits, grievances, and complaints. When a problem arises, the first response is to check district or school policies.

The second characteristic of this emphasis on rationality is a de-emphasis on human agency. Much of work during the Industrial Age has been mechanized and routinized (Taylor, 1911). Although mechanization in schools typically has not involved the use of physical automation, e.g., robots, as it has in manufacturing sectors, mechanization still is present. Most of us remember as children eyeing the teacher's edition of the textbook and noticing that it was larger than student editions and had shaded pages. When we peeked at the teacher's edition, we found scripts telling the teacher how to introduce material, what activities to use, and, in some cases, what to say.

A third characteristic of this rationality is limited contact with other roles. Mohrman and Cohen (1995) described the traditional organization of the last century as consisting of boxes and lines, e.g., the typical organizational chart. Individual work is confined to one box or one role. Usually a box is connected by a line to only one other box. These authors also suggested that the relationships within these traditional work settings are primarily mediated by the boss. The typical architectural arrangement of most schools clearly reflects this limited contact with other roles. The typical "egg crate" school emphasizes one teacher in a self-contained room with her/his students. The principal typically mediates any contact among teachers. Moreover, very little contact among principals is apparent. Schools are primarily self-contained units separated from the external world, in some cases by fences and frequently by signs that instruct visitors to check in at the office. A major role for principals in these contexts is to buffer teachers from external contacts, pressures, and disruptions.

The fourth characteristic of rationality is an emphasis on efficiency and quantity of work as criteria for effectiveness (Callahan, 1962). Moreover these criteria are primarily assessed in terms of individual achievement. This individual focus is reflected not only in how we assess students, but also in how we assess teachers. The principal, either by scheduled visit or surprise drop-by, observes the teacher on an infrequent basis to evaluate the teacher's actions based on a district script—a set of standardized appraisal items. In terms of curriculum, the primary assessment is typically based on the amount of content covered.

Standardization of procedures, de-emphasis on human agency, limited contact with other roles, and individual assessment based on efficiency and quantity of work have characterized work roles in the past century (and still characterize many roles) that emphasize rationality and attempt to decrease ambiguity. One could argue that in an industrial age these characteristics of work served society, and schools in particular, well. They allowed the spread of the common school movement and probably helped parents feel more confident about releasing their children to "strangers." However, they also had pitfalls, among them increased rigidity and segmentation (Mohrman & Cohen, 1995), which, as we will see, are dysfunctional in a post-industrial society.

THE NATURE OF WORK IN POST-INDUSTRIAL SOCIETY

We have entered what Bell and others (Bell, 1973; Touraine, 1971) referred to several years ago as post-industrial society. This society, instead of being based on the inventions, processes, and machines of the Industrial Revolution, is now influenced more by the Information Revolution. Knowledge explosion and globalization are among the characteristics of this society. Hage and Powers (1992) argued that an explosive growth in knowledge is the defining feature of post-industrial society, and they identified various institutional failures, new institutional forms, and the recognition of change as evidence that we are in a new era.

Instead of the emphasis on rationality that was characteristic of work roles in the past century, Hage and Powers (1992) point to the emphasis on complexity in post-industrial work roles. Complexity means that work is more "driven by the accumulation of additional knowledge and the adding in of more demanding activities. . . . (This) means more and more skills and education are required of the typical worker, which means ongoing learning. It also means constant change in the definition of roles" (p. 50). This rapid growth of knowledge has affected almost every occupation, and we should not expect that principals, in institutions where the core technology is teaching and learning, could escape these post-industrial changes.

According to Hage and Powers (1992), complexity influences several characteristics of work roles and relationships. First, instead of standardization of procedures, work roles in post-industrial society emphasize customized responses. Within a more dynamic environment, the ability to respond to new problems is critical. No one with any exposure to contemporary schools would deny the increasing number of new challenges that educators face with students. For example, educators encounter students with a greater number of at-risk conditions, new diagnoses of learning problems, and multiple ways of learning. Developing a static set of standardized procedures to address the contingencies of this dynamic environment is impossible. Instead of simply categorizing at-risk students, for example, we develop individualized education plans. The principal's role in such a dynamic environment requires the ability to create or facilitate the creation of innovative customized responses.

The second characteristic of work roles in this climate of complexity is a greater emphasis on human agency and information search (Hage & Powers, 1992). Complex environments, because they do not lend themselves to scripts and rules, require ongoing learning—search for information—by individuals. The jobs that can be performed by routinization have been automated or relocated to less expensive environments. What is left requires human discretion and judgment and the ability to quickly and continually search for information to solve problems. Relying on specific knowledge and skills acquired in previous training is no longer adequate to meet these challenges. One estimate suggests that a physician's knowledge is outdated every five years (Hage & Powers). Although we have no such estimate of the principal's knowledge, we should expect that similar obsolescence is present, given changing demographics, new understandings of learning, and modern technologies for teaching, as well as the changing political, legal, economic, and organizational features of schools that principals encounter.

The third characteristic is increased and continuing contact with other roles. Instead of the simple box and line organization where individuals act autonomously and their relationships with other individuals are limited and mediated by the boss, a more lateral organization exists (Mohrman & Cohen, 1995). Roles in this type of organization are continually interacting and networking in order to solve complex problems. One form this organization is taking involves self-managed teams where individual members play a variety of roles and interact continually with each other. In this type of organization, leadership is shared, and the official leader plays both a leadership or management role and a technical role. Interdisciplinary teacher teams in middle schools are one example of this lateral organization (Crow & Pounder, 2000).

The fourth work role characteristic in a complex post-industrial society is the emphasis on innovation and creativity as criteria for assessment. Hage and Powers (1992) suggested that individuals in post-industrial society need "creative minds" and "complex selves." Because scripts are not available for the complex situations individuals will face, they must be able to imagine scenarios that have not yet occurred. "In industrial society the emphasis was on learning rules that make situations unambiguous by making them standard. In PI [post-industrial] society the emphasis must be on transforming rules in order to individualize cases" (p. 69).

In addition, Hage and Powers (1992) argued that individuals must have complex selves that allow independent thought while working with others. In this work they must be able to acknowledge and use others' perspectives. Post-industrial individuals are also more likely to have several identities within the work organization. The day of being able to conceive work identity by attaching one category, label, or job description is over. Individuals perform their work by doing multiple tasks. The same goes for management. Mohrman and Cohen (1995) quoted Handy (1989): ". . . in the organization of the future everyone will have to be a manager, and no one will be able to afford being only a manager" (p. 391).

Instead of assessment based on individual accomplishments, evaluation of individuals will be based on how they contribute to the group endeavor. Hackman (1990) and Pounder (1998) suggested that for monitoring purposes teams be treated as a group rather than as a collection of individuals. A greater emphasis on collective work rather than individual work changes the way we look at the effectiveness of teachers and administrators and the way we assess their performance.

The nature of work in post-industrial society is characterized by customized responses, an emphasis on human agency and information search, increased contact with other roles, and innovation and creativity as criteria for assessment. These characteristics are based on understanding work roles as emphasizing complexity rather than rationality. In his work on the leader as medium, Weick (1978) suggested that instead of decisiveness and firmness, we may find that flexibility and sensitivity to the complex environment around them are more effective and more desirable characteristics of leaders. In post-industrial society, the principal's role will necessitate the ability to respond to complexity in ways that are very different from those required by the principal's role in the last century.

Hage and Powers (1992) suggested that in post-industrial society workers will have to have the flexibility and imagination to continually redefine their roles to match the complex environment in which they live and work. In the case of the principalship, that complex environment involves the kinds of tensions we suggested earlier in this chapter. Principals will need the ability to redefine their roles in ways that address the rapidly changing environment but acknowledge the expectation that schools are communities.

In the next two sections we identify two major areas of complexity in which the principal's role will need to be reshaped. First, we examine the internal complexity that principals face and how that complexity reshapes the principal's role as a leader of a learning community. Second, we examine the external complexity of the principal's role in terms of accountability, markets, and civic capacity.

Internal Complexity and the Principal's Role

The societal tensions represented by the Lexus and the olive tree metaphors are also occurring in education policy arenas, school districts, and school buildings throughout the U.S. At the risk of oversimplifying the comparison—Lexus builders seek to increase school effectiveness and efficiency through standardized measures that account for the work of school professionals and students. Those who defend the olive tree strive passionately to maintain the freedom to meet educational challenges defined at the local level through homegrown creativity and innovation. At the school level principals and teachers are strained by these competing philosophies of education and educational change. However, one fact is becoming clear. Successful schools are able to meet the unique and context-specific realities they each face by organizing in ways that fully utilize the bank of knowledge and skills available within the school. School leadership plays a vital role in this type of organizational learning, but it does so in ways different from past conceptions of leadership. Principals' orientations toward leadership must expand. And their rules of thumb that guide day to day practice must be reconsidered.

PROFESSIONAL COMMUNITY: BALANCING THE FORCES OF CONTINUITY AND CHANGE

As the forces of organizational change have created new images of workplace structures and roles across the professions (Kleiner, 1996), so too have these change forces influenced our images of schools and schooling. The past decade has witnessed a concerted effort to shift the organizational metaphors of schools from hierarchical and rigid bureaucracies to an image of networks of professionals in constant interaction (Sergiovanni, 1994). Borrowing from Brown and Duguid (1991), schools as "communities-in-practice"—places where learning and innovation occur through work—require leaders capable of building strong social networks in ways that harness the organization's cumulative capacity to improve.

In education, schools as professional communities represent the kinds of communities-in-practice that Brown and Duguid (1991) described. Most research on professional community has emphasized similar dimensions that define the nature and organization of teacher work (e.g., Cohen et al., 1993; Hord, 1997; Louis et al., 1996; Murphy, Beck, Crawford, & Hodges, 2001). In general, this body of literature has conceptualized professional communities in terms of three concentric circles representing dynamic and complex relations among people. Within the innermost circle is the community that exists between teachers and children—where learning occurs. The outermost ring represents the nature of relationships between school personnel and the community at large. The middle ring—the focus of this portion of the chapter—represents relations among the professional staff within a school (including faculty and their principal).

With our focus squarely on the middle ring, strong professional communities are those that foster collaboration among teachers, use constructive dialogue to critically examine individual teacher practices in group settings, commit to and take responsibility for a shared vision, and rely on a shared commitment to student learning to guide their work (Smylie & Hart, 2000). Furthermore, in strong professional communities teachers do not work in isolation; on the contrary, they team-teach, model and work in other ways that bring teachers together to focus on curriculum and the quality of the work produced (Scribner, Hager, & Madrone, 2000).

Clearly, establishing professional community presents at least a couple of challenges to school leaders. First, professional communities require a shift in perspective away from leadership via chain of command and rigid hierarchies. They also require a broadening of notions such as that of the principal as instructional leader. To innovate quickly and soundly, principals of tomorrow will not have the luxury of adopting canned reform models that apparently succeeded in other contexts. Rather, principals will have to guide the development of indigenously developed school improvement models that, while based on solid research, are tailored to their own school contexts. To achieve this type of school environment, principals will also have to be open to leadership that emanates from anywhere in the organization and thus create learning opportunities for teachers. For as Mack and Hord (2000) stated, strong professional communities are not well defined programs but rather infrastructures that organize school professionals in specific ways. Therein lies the potential of professional community.

Studies have shown that schools with strong professional communities demonstrate important outcomes for students and school professionals. For instance, Bryk et al. (1999) found that professional community could flourish in urban elementary schools. Specifically, they found that in schools with strong professional communities educational achievement inequities among students were diminished. In a study of elementary, middle and high schools, Newmann and Wehlage (1995) associated strong professional communities with gains in math, reading and science achievement. Professional community has also been shown to have important outcomes for teachers. In a study of high schools, for example, Bryk and Driscoll (1988) found that teachers working within strong professional communities held higher expectations for their students. In another high school study, Scribner et al. (2000) discovered that strong professional community appeared to foster healthy teacher-principal relationships that supported responsible risk-taking and professional learning among teachers.

It appears that these important organizational outcomes may be attributable to professional community for several reasons (Newmann, 1994; Newmann & Wehlage, 1995), each of which bears important implications for the role of principal. First, schools characterized by an imbalance towards teacher autonomy and away from professional community can lead to "reduced teacher efficacy when teachers can't count on colleagues to reinforce [school] objectives" (Newmann & Wehlage, p. 31). Second, teacher collaboration can enhance teacher learning, thus improving teachers' technical skills and propositional knowledge. And third, Newmann and Wehlage found that strong professional communities bind teachers together through a common commitment and responsibility for high quality achievement for all students. The principal's role as a facilitator of professional community is evident. Principals must nurture and use the intellectual capacity of their faculty as opposed to seeing themselves as the primary source and disseminator of knowledge. Principals also must help teachers develop a common vision and mission for the school and take a leadership role in advocating for and maintaining the course of the school in the face of external challenges. Finally, leadership should be shared throughout the school to foster the creative forces and tap into the intellectual power of teachers.

CHANGING ORIENTATIONS OF SCHOOL LEADERSHIP

In an environment in which organizations rely on dynamic social processes not only to survive, but also to thrive, principals play an indispensable role in transforming schools into organizations that learn (Leithwood, Jantzi, & Steinbach, 1998; Leithwood, 2000). In the broadest sense, the successful school principal will be able to foster social relations among teachers (and between teachers and administrators) that promote the types of professional interaction described above. Thus, rather than limiting principal leadership to activities designed, for example, to control teacher classroom behaviors, principals will need to influence the nature and intensity of teacher relations, foster meaningful collaboration among teachers, and cultivate values that promote concern for children (McLaughlin, 1993).

From this perspective, it is clear that the principal's role has evolved beyond that of the instructional leader steeped in behaviorist traditions, or even the leader "in the center," a more recent image. In either case, the challenge remains the same. Whether leading from the top or from the center, the principal remains the focal point. Although he or she will always play a critical role in school improvement, the principal at the apex or at the hub perpetuates an image in which it is difficult to envision others in the school taking on initiative (which is what it takes to be creative and innovate) in any meaningful way. Given the context within which schools now operate—i.e., the need for customized responses, emphasis on human agency and continuous learning, increased contact with others, and an emphasis on creativity and innovation—empowering forms of leadership are replacing controlling ones.

Perhaps school leadership, and the principal's role within that concept, should be imagined as a web of social relationships. With that vision in mind, principals would take more responsibility in maintaining the vibrancy and health of the web's social relationships among teachers, administrators, and others. In particular, three orientations toward leadership are congruent with an image of professional community as a web of social relationships: interactional, collaborative, and democratic leadership.

Smylie and Hart (2000) described the interactional principal, the broadest of the three orientations, as one who attends to the social relations within the school, especially among teachers. Interactional principals constantly work within the social network of the school "to broker information and promote relations among disconnected groups in ways that are mutually beneficial" (p. 429). The interactional principal's relationship to the web of social relations is clear as she or he continuously assesses the nature of teacher work, bringing teachers together to have conversations they would not have had otherwise. The influence of the interactional principal can transform traditional top-down patterns of communication into more constructive patterns of social relations that support the spread of innovative ideas and healthy values towards teaching and learning.

Collaborative leadership also contributes to the image of principals as leaders within webs of social relations (Crow, 1998). Like interactional leaders, collaborative leaders understand their role "as a relationship [that] involves looking beyond formal authority as the source of leadership" (p. 136). As Crow described, emphasis on social dimensions of school leadership requires attention to the political dynamic of collaborative school leadership. In other words, to foster the social relations among staff that create strong professional communities, principals must acknowledge, work to understand, and even embrace the inevitable conflict that arises when people engage over teaching and learning matters. As with tightly knit families, as the social relations among teachers grow stronger, the potential for destructive internal politics increases (Achinstein, 2000). Put differently, perceived acts of betrayal among individuals or groups in strong professional communities can lead to damaging politics that rip apart once healthy relationships and limit the school's ability to meet the needs of children. By attending to the political nature of school professional communities, principals will be better positioned to help teachers negotiate the tensions that arise from intrinsic motivations to act with professional autonomy and from schoolwide pressures to improve as a whole (Scribner et al., 2000).

Finally, democratic leadership makes explicit the moral dimension of school leadership. The moral imperative inherent in democratic leadership is indispensable within the internal complexity of the school and in building professional communities out of bureaucratic organizations. Starratt (2000) argued that democratic leadership is important precisely because lack of consensus, burgeoning information and its misuse, and constant challenges to formal authority are typical challenges facing principals. The strengths that the democratically minded principal would bring to the school are an emphasis on cultivating professional openness and honesty, full participation in the development and sharing of ideas, and compassion. As Starratt described, an important part of the principal's role will be to help teachers with the deconstruction of

meanings, values, and assumptions—the analysis of their negatives and their positives, of what is to be rejected and what kept—*and* a reconstruction, and invention of new meanings, new metaphors, new organizational dynamics, new institutional processes which will carry the playing of school into a more humanly satisfying and morally fulfilling story. (p. 20)

Thus, the democratically oriented principal sees her position as more than managing tasks or influencing behaviors; rather, she believes it is her responsibility to tap into the intrinsic motivation of others and imbue meaning, a moral imperative, and a commitment to inclusiveness in the schoolhouse (Starratt, 2000).

Together, these three leadership orientations underscore the evolving nature of school leadership. Rather than seeking to maintain control over schools and schooling through administrative means, principals must improve the educational experiences of children by facilitating collaboration, minimizing the destructive nature of internal school politics, and using inclusive and open approaches to leadership.

CHANGING APPROACHES/ACTIVITIES OF PRINCIPALS

The leadership orientations mentioned above need to be reflected in the daily activities of principals. Given that interactional, collaborative, and democratic leadership styles together can help guide principals toward developing a strong professional community, some specific approaches are worth mentioning. Principals must view their teachers as change agents. Many teachers will need to learn the skills of reflective practice, group participation, action inquiry, and problem solving. In this regard, the principal must be willing and able to foster teacher leadership throughout the school and to instill in teachers the value of not only student learning but also teacher learning. The latter effort will not be easy, given the long history of misguided attempts to develop teachers professionally.

Because of the extraordinary complexity of the school as workplace, principals would be well advised to consider leadership as an organizational quality. As Ogawa and Bossert (1995) noted, acts of leadership can occur at any given time and place in a school, and within any configuration of personnel. In fact, given our description of post-industrial society, school cultures that associate leadership with formal positions, and "followership" with those who are not in formal leadership positions, will be unable to innovate quickly enough to thrive in their environments. It is therefore imperative that principals adopt a "broader conception of school leadership, one that shifts from a single person, role-oriented view to a view of leadership as an organizational property shared among administrators, teachers and perhaps others" (Smylie & Hart, 2000, p. 428). Principals who see leadership as an organizational quality will be better positioned to foster school cultures of strong professional communities and learning organizations, for example, through shared decision-making arrangements. Principals who foster cultures where individual and group decisions are driven by issues directly related to student learning, where teachers challenge each others' basic assumptions about teaching and learning, and where teachers collaborate are more likely to see strong professional communities take root. With this perspective, principals can foster leadership throughout the school network, encouraging teacher leadership throughout the organization.

However, if leadership is to become a true organizational quality, investments of time, energy and resources in the human capital of teachers (e.g., to develop a spirit of human agency) are required. Clearly, too many resources have been spent on teacher learning activities that do not meet the needs of teachers or the students they serve. In order to lead schools in the manner we suggest, principals will have to restore teachers' commitment to their own learning in ways that contribute to individual and organizational learning. Principals are uniquely positioned to ensure that professional development in their schools addresses teacher and student needs. They will need to provide full support for teacher professional learning (Bredeson & Johansson, 2000; Senge, 2000). Bredeson and Johansson conceptualized the principal's role, in this regard, as that of a steward of professional learning, while Senge described the role as modeling a learner-centered (as opposed to an authority-centered) approach to education. Bredeson and Johansson argued that principals, as stewards, must communicate the value of professional development in meeting school and teacher goals and the professional responsibility of teachers to engage in acts of self-renewal and professional growth. They suggested that principals can foster these values by participating in professional development themselves—thus demonstrating that they, too, find the time worthwhile.

Another dimension of the principal's role as professional development facilitator is modeling desired behaviors. Through modeling—for instance, modeling what it means to interact, collaborate, and critically reflect—principals show not only their support for certain behaviors, norms and values, but also how to enact them. Fortunately, evidence suggests that principals do not need to know everything to gain the credibility of their teachers or to ensure student success. But Stein and D'Amico (2000) suggested that effective principals must have "leadership content knowledge," a deep understanding of one content area and accompanying pedagogy, and the ability to use that knowledge to help teachers identify problems and resolve them accordingly. Finally, to further strengthen the web of social relations among teachers, principals should see as one of their primary responsibilities the validation of local expertise within the school by nurturing and tapping into veins of local knowledge that exist in most schools. In this way, principals can strengthen the professional community and overall performance in their schools by enabling teachers to share with one another effective strategies that are working with students in specific local school contexts.

External Complexity and the Principal's Role

In the previous section we described how the internal complexity of schools is resulting in the emergence of new conceptions of principal leadership. Central to these new roles is the ability to facilitate the development of professional community, which research indicates leads to improved outcomes for students and teachers. In this section we argue that while such a focus on the internal complexity of schools is critical, educators should not become distracted from the complexity of the larger environment in which schools operate. This view of schools as open systems has equally important implications for principal leadership, as well as for principals' ability to nurture community within *and* beyond their schools. We examine the external complexity of the principal's role in terms of accountability, markets, and civic capacity—emphasizing the influence of these constructs on school community.

ACCOUNTABILITY

The majority of states have articulated core standards for student learning, and these standards are becoming increasingly linked to high stakes tests. Simultaneously, research has repeatedly identified instructional leadership as a characteristic of effective schools (Bossert et al., 1982; Hallinger & Murphy, 1985). However, the popularity of and interest in the instructional leadership role of the principal has diminished—this despite the fact that the principal remains the central figure who will be held accountable at the school, the primary business of which is teaching and learning. Although leadership should and must be shared, effective principals still must serve as instructional leaders, especially in an era of increasing standards and accountability. From our perspective, instructional leadership encompasses those behaviors and processes principals implement with the explicit goal of improving educational outcomes. Furthermore, instructional leadership is a shared responsibility and does not imply that principals are directive, unilateral decision-makers. On the contrary, principals who enact interactional, collaborative, and democratic leadership do so to improve outcomes for students and teachers. Thus, they are serving as instructional leaders in a broadened sense.

As instructional leaders, effective principals rely on empirical rather than anecdotal data to facilitate curricular and instructional decisions. Moreover, effective school leaders consistently analyze the consequences of these decisions and make time to reflect on and learn from them. As a result, they are more aware of their values and allocate time in a manner consistent with them. Finally, these principals help create the norm that teaching and learning are the shared responsibility of all stakeholders.

At a rhetorical level, it is difficult to oppose the case for standards and accountability. Who is not in favor of high expectations and achievement for all children? However, policy as intended and policy as implemented are rarely the same. Therefore, it is important to assess how the standards and accountability movement may influence the complexity of work roles and relationships.

On one hand, it can be argued that accountability policies are increasing the complexity of schooling and the principalship. From this perspective, principals must find solutions to persistent challenges or face such threats as fiscal cuts, school probation, or even closure. On the other hand, the accountability movement may actually be reducing the complexity of work roles. In reference to Hage's and Powers' (1992) criteria for work roles in a more complex climate, state standards and high stakes testing may actually define and delimit the work of teachers and principals, reducing innovation and decreasing human agency as a result of teaching to the test.

MARKETS

A movement to more market-oriented views of schooling has taken place at the same time as the standards movement, with both resulting in part from a desire for greater accountability. Market theory posits that competition among schools will lead to improvement. On the "demand side" of the market, parents and students are assumed to be rational and motivated consumers who will shop around for the school that best meets their needs. On the "supply side" schools will be compelled to improve in order to attract and retain students, or face going out of business. Presumably, since principals of schools of choice do not have access to guaranteed student enrollments, they must market their schools to attract students, and become more responsive to families in order to retain those students.

As predicted by the theoretical frameworks of Crow (1992) and Kerchner (1988), experimental data have confirmed the premium placed on entrepreneurial leadership in the market environment of education. Hallinger and Hausman (1993) reported that principals in schools of choice spend increased time marketing the school's program and services. Specifically, the principals in this study allocated additional time to parent tours, informational meetings, and creation of marketing tools such as brochures.

School choice, by expanding external boundaries, also alters the relationships between schools and their constituencies after parents have chosen a school. Schools are part of a more open system and must interact more frequently with their external environments, thus magnifying the complexity of work relationships. A large body of evidence demonstrates that environmental management functions of the principal are enlarged as a consequence of school choice initiatives, particularly those affording parents greater influence. Specifically, school principals are being urged to expand parent outreach efforts, empower parents in the decision-making process, and garner additional community resources. These responsibilities have been labeled boundary spanning (Goldring, 1990) and environmental leadership (Hallinger & Hausman, 1993). These more frequent interactions with the external community and pressures to sell the school to attract and retain students compel effective principals in a choice context to exercise highly-developed public relations skills. It remains to be seen whether these increased demands for external relationships will come at the expense of time allocated by principals to the internal leadership of the school.

Finally, little is known about how enhanced market forces will influence the ability of principals to build community. In fact, the link between school choice and community has only recently emerged. In their study of private schools, Coleman and Hoffer (1987) found that a sense of membership in a value community may be created under conditions in which parents choose schools based on similar values and expectations. Similarly, Smrekar (1996) found that school choice may be an important factor in developing a strong sense of school community. Hausman and Goldring (2000) reported that the levels and types of community found in schools of choice vary with their structures. Specifically, they found that whole school magnets exhibited higher levels of internal community (e.g., goal congruence, teacher commitment) than programs within school magnets, and both types of magnets were characterized by low levels of external community (e.g., home-school relations). Additional studies are needed to ascertain the influence of more aggressive choice strategies (e.g., vouchers) on school community—both internal and external indicators. Will teachers choose to work in schools of choice because they share similar values? Are families from different geographic neighborhoods who choose the same school—as opposed to functional communities—able to generate community? Will they be involved as often with the school community when they live further apart? What can principals who lead such schools of choice do to enhance school community? What can principals of traditional schools do to prevent schools of choice from creaming the brightest and most motivated students?

Will the competition resulting from market forces have unintended consequences for community (e.g., competition between teachers and between schools that decreases contact and collegiality among educators)? These are only a few of the questions needing attention in this emerging line of research.

CIVIC CAPACITY

Educators have long argued that schools alone often lack the capacity to address the multiple social problems facing students in urban schools, especially as pivotal indicators of social well-being continue to decline. Students arrive at school each day with a myriad of sociological and psychological challenges. In America, 18.7% of children under the age of 18 live in poverty (Bennett & Lu, 2000). Dryfoos (1994) reported that one in four children "do it all—use drugs, have early unprotected intercourse, are truant and fall far behind in school" (p. 3). These children are not likely to have access to adequate family supports, health care, and social networks that are crucial for success in school. As a result of these social changes, schools have been relegated several new roles—social worker, health care provider, character developer, and more.

Reformers continue to claim that schools should be placed at the focal point of entire communities to increase the potential for schools to meet these diverse needs of students, especially those most at risk for failure. Relying on notions about the ecological perspective of schooling (Bronfenbrenner, 1979), some educators emphasize the importance of social linkages between children and adults across different environments and structures. Support systems that reach multiple contexts for children often act as "immunizing" factors against adversity (McLaughlin, 1994; Wang, 1997). We argue that alterations in the social fabric of the United States must place a premium on principals, as key leaders at the school site, to serve as builders of civic capacity— "the ability to build and maintain an effective alliance among institutional representatives in the public, private, and independent sectors to work toward a common community goal" (Henig, 1994). A principal can accomplish this by forming partnerships to obtain additional resources from the business community and by serving as a central member of key stakeholder groups. Principals must work closely with community and social agencies that assist students and their families. Broad-based coalitions must be formed with civic responsibility to rejuvenate neighborhoods where schools are located. Education takes place in the context of communities, not just in a school building.

Much has been written about the challenges of collaboration in education (Pounder, 1998). These challenges often focus on incompatible roles, lack of resources, inconsistent cultures, and contradictory structures. Principals often confront similar challenges of control, uncertainty, and accountability as they collaborate with teachers, parents, and community agencies (Crow, 1998). The concept of civic capacity extends considerably beyond notions of partnering or collaborating. It requires a new mental model of schooling. While collaboration and interdependence are necessary for school improvement, they are not sufficient.

Educators, service providers, youth development specialists, and others join forces to collaborate because of enlightened self-interest. Self-interest means, for example, that principals invest time, energy, and resources in community and family work because they know that they and their schools cannot be successful without them. They are self-interested but not selfish. They are also enlightened because they choose their involvement strategically with an eye toward building supports for children and schools. (Lawson, in press, p. 12)

Since principals are expected to "do it all," this enlightened self-interest and awareness is critical if principals are going to allocate time and energy to building civic capacity.

Conclusion

Reshaping the principal's role takes place in a context where the future struggles with the past. More important, this role reshaping takes place as part of the tension between continuity and change. Schools are not simple organizations pliable to the latest fashion. They are increasingly complex settings where people's lives and hopes come face to face with societal injustices, uncertainties, and demands.

Everyday, principals are reshaping their roles in light of this complex environment. This reshaping takes place within the internal school environment, where professional community is being fostered or hindered, and within the external environment, where accountability, markets, and civic capacity are demanding attention. Reshaping the principal's role brings both a stressful bombardment of demands and expectations and an exciting opportunity for change and growth. Principals today find themselves in a complex setting between change and continuity—between the Lexus and the olive tree.

REFERENCES

Achinstein, B. (2000). *The micropolitics of teacher collaborative reforms: Conflict, borders, and ideology in teacher professional communities.* Paper presented at the annual conference of the American Educational Research Association, New Orleans, LA.

Bell, D. (1973). *The coming of post-industrial society.* New York: Basic Books.

Bennett, N. G., and Lu, H.-H. (2000). *Child poverty in the states: Levels and trends from 1979 to 1998.* Child Poverty Research Brief 2. New York: National Center for Children in Poverty.

Bossert, S. T., Dwyer, D. C., Rowan, B., and Lee, G. V. (1982). The instructional management role of the principal. *Educational Administration Quarterly, 18*(3), 34-64.

Bredeson, P. V., & Johansson, O. (2000). The school principal's role in teacher professional development. *Journal of In-Service Education, 26*(2), 385-401.

Bronfenbrenner, U. (1979). *The ecology of human development.* Cambridge, MA: Harvard University Press.

Brown, J. S., & Duguid, P. (1991). Organizational learning and communities-of-practice: Toward a unified view of working, learning, and innovation. In M. D. Cohen & L. S. Sproull (Eds.), *Organizational learning* (pp. 58-82). Thousand Oaks, CA: Sage.

Bryk, A., Camburn, E., & Louis, K. S. (1999). Professional community in Chicago elementary schools: Facilitating factors and organizational consequences. *Educational Administration Quarterly, 35* (Supplemental), 751-781.

Bryk, A. S., & Driscoll, M. E. (1988). *The high school as community: Contextual influences and consequences for students and teachers.* Madison, WI: National Center on Effective Secondary Schools.

Callahan, R. E. (1962). *Education and the cult of efficiency.* Chicago: University of Chicago Press.

Cohen, D. K., McLaughlin, M. W., & Talbert, J. E. (Eds.). (1993). *Teaching for understanding: Challenges for policy and practice.* San Francisco: Jossey-Bass.

Coleman, J., & Hoffer, T. (1987). *Public and private high schools: The impact of communities.* New York: Basic Books.

Crow, G. (1992). The principal in schools of choice: Middle manager, entrepreneur, and symbol manager. *The Urban Review, 24*(3), 165-74.

Crow, G. (1998). Implications for leadership in collaborative schools. In D. G. Pounder (Ed.), *Restructuring schools for collaboration: Promises and pitfalls* (pp. 135-153). Albany, NY: SUNY Press.

Crow, G. M., & Pounder, D. G. (2000). Teacher work groups: Context, design, and process. *Educational Administration Quarterly, 36*(2), 216-254.

Drucker, P. F. (1999). Beyond the information revolution. *The Atlantic Monthly,* 47-57.

Dryfoos, J. (1994). *Full-service schools.* San Francisco: Jossey-Bass.

Friedman, T .L. (1999). *The Lexus and the olive tree.* New York: Farrar Straus Giroux.

Goldring, E. (1990). Elementary school principals as boundary spanners: Their engagement with parents. *Journal of Educational Administration, 28*(1), 53-62.

Guthrie, J. W., & Sanders, T. (2001, January 7). Who will lead the public schools? *The New York Times, Education Supplement,* p. 46.

Hackman, J. R. (1990). *Groups that work (and those that don't): Creating conditions for effective teamwork.* San Francisco: Jossey-Bass.

Hage, J., & Powers, C. H. (1992). *Post-industrial lives: Roles and relationships in the 21st century.* Newbury Park, CA: Sage.

Hallinger, P., & Hausman, C. (1993). The changing role of a principal in a school of choice. In J. Murphy and P. Hallinger (Eds.), *Restructuring schooling: Learning from ongoing efforts* (pp. 114-42). Newbury Park, CA: Corwin Press.

Hallinger, P., & Murphy, J. (1985). Assessing the instructional management behavior of principals. *The Elementary School Journal, 86*(2), 217-47.

Handy, C. B. (1989). *The age of unreason.* London: Business Books.

Hausman, C., & Goldring, E. (2000). School community in different magnet program structures. *School Effectiveness and School Improvement, 11*(1), 80-102.

Henig, J. (1994). *Rethinking school choice: Limits of the market metaphor.* Princeton, NJ: Princeton University Press.

Hord, S. M. (1997). *Professional learning communities: Communities of continuous inquiry and improvement* (ED410659).

Kerchner, C. (1988). Bureaucratic entrepreneurship: The implications of choice for school administration. *Educational Administration Quarterly, 24*(4), 381-92.

Kleiner, A. (1996). *The age of heretics: Heroes, outlaws, and the forerunners of corporate change.* New York: Doubleday.

Lawson, H. A. (in press). Two new mental models for schools and their implications for principals' roles, responsibilities, and preparation. *Bulletin,* National Association of Secondary School Principals.

Leithwood, K. (2000). *Understanding schools as intelligent systems.* Stamford, CT: JAI Press, Inc.

Leithwood, K., Jantzi, D., & Steinbach, R. (1998). Leadership and other conditions which foster organizational learning in schools. In K. Leithwood & K. S. Louis (Eds.), *Organizational Learning in Schools.* Lisse, Netherlands: Swets and Zeitlinger.

Louis, K. S., Kruse, S. D., & Marks, H. M. (1996). Schoolwide professional community. In F. M. A. Newmann (Ed.), *Authentic achievement: Restructuring schools for intellectual quality.* San Francisco: Jossey-Bass.

Mack, P. M., & Hord, S. M. (2000). A community of professional learners. *Catalyst for Change, 29*(3), 5-8.

McLaughlin, M. W. (1993). What matters most in teachers' workplace context? In J. W. Little & M. W. McLaughlin (Eds.), *Teachers' work: Individuals, colleagues, and contexts* (pp. 79-103). New York: Teachers College Press.

McLaughlin, M. W. (1994). *Urban sanctuaries: Neighborhood organizations in the lives and futures of inner-city youth.* San Francisco: Jossey-Bass.

Mohrman, S. A., & Cohen, S. G. (1995). When people get out of the box: New relationships, new systems. In A. Howard (Ed.), *The Changing Nature of Work* (pp. 365-410). San Francisco: Jossey-Bass.

Murphy, J., Beck, L., Crawford, M., & Hodges, A. (2001). *The productive high school: Creating personalized academic communities.* Thousand Oaks, CA: Corwin Press.

Newmann, F. M. (1994). *School-wide professional community* (No. 6). Madison, WI: Center on Organization and Restructuring of Schools.

Newmann, F. M., & Wehlage, G. G. (1995). *Successful school restructuring: A report to the public and educators.* Madison, WI: Center on Organization and Restructuring of Schools.

Ogawa, R. T., & Bossert, S. T. (1995). Leadership as an organizational quality. *Educational Administration Quarterly, 31*(2), 224-243.

Pounder, D. G. (Ed.). (1998). *Restructuring schools for collaboration.* Albany, NY: SUNY Press.

Scribner, J. P., Hager, D., & Madrone, T. R. (in press). The paradox of professional community: A tale of two high schools. *Educational Administration Quarterly.*

Senge, P. M. (2000). *Schools that learn: A fifth discipline fieldbook for educators, parents, and everyone who cares about education.* New York: Doubleday.

Sergiovanni, T. J. (1994). Organizations or communities? Changing the metaphor changes the theory. *Educational Administration Quarterly, 30*(2), 214-226.

Smrekar, C. (1996). *The impact of school choice and community: In the interest of families and schools.* Albany, NY: SUNY Press.

Smylie, M. A., & Hart, A. W. (2000). School leadership for teacher learning and change: A human and social capital development perspective. In J. Murphy & K. S. Louis (Eds.), *Handbook of Research on Educational Administration* (pp. 421-441). San Francisco: Jossey-Bass.

Starratt, R. J. (2000, November). *Democratic leadership theory in late modernity: An oxymoron or ironic possibility?* Paper presented at the annual conference of the University Council for Educational Administration, Albuquerque, NM.

Stein, M. K., & D'Amico, L. (2000, April). *How subjects matter in school leadership*. Paper presented at the annual meeting of the American Educational Research Association, New Orleans, LA.

Taylor, F. W. (1911). *The principles of scientific management*. New York: Harper & Row.

Touraine, A. (1971). *The post-industrial society: Tomorrow's social history: Classes, conflicts, and culture in the programmed society*. New York: Random House.

Wang, M. (1997). Next steps in inner-city education: Focusing on resilience development and learning success. *Education and Urban Society, 29*(3), 255-276.

Weick, K. (1978). The spines of leaders. In M. W. McCall, Jr. & M. M. Lombardo (Eds.), *Leadership: Where else can we go?* (pp. 37-61). Durham, NC: Duke University.

CHAPTER 10

Shifts in the Discourse Defining the Superintendency: Historical and Current Foundations of the Position

C. CRYSS BRUNNER, MARGARET GROGAN, AND LARS BJÖRK

Murphy (1999) asserts that in response to 21st century exigencies, the work of educators during this current "era of ferment can be characterized as a search for a much needed, defining center for the profession" of educational leadership (p. 3). He observes that the search for a "new center for the profession may grow from the seed of school improvement and social justice" (p. 3). In the same vein, Larson and Ovando (2001) suggest that educational leadership in the public schools needs to be founded more securely upon hearing the disparate voices within our diverse communities. They advocate putting the public back into public education. This notion, however, raises questions about the most recent search for the re-centering of the superintendency. Is there evidence that it will grow from the seed of school improvement and social justice—will it reflect the concerns of the greater public? And what nourishes this new seed? Will it be sustained by the beliefs and expectations of the past?

We are interested in these questions. In this chapter, we seek answers by examining the discourse of the superintendency to try to determine what has shaped the role previously and what is likely to shape it in the future. Kress (in Davies, 1994) defines discourse as "a systematically organized set of statements which give expression to the meanings and values of an institution" (p. 17). Such an institution as education has incorporated many different values and beliefs over time. Discourses change according to the social, political and economic forces at work during any given period. Thus, we begin with a

Lars Björk is co-director of the UCEA Joint Center for the Study of the Superintendency and Associate Professor in the Department of Administration and Supervision at the University of Kentucky. C. Cryss Brunner is co-director of the UCEA Joint Center for the Study of the Superintendency and Associate Professor at the University of Minnesota. Margaret Grogan is the co-director of the UCEA Center for the Study of Leadership and Ethics and Associate professor in the Department of Leadership, Foundations and Policy at the Curry School, University of Virginia.

documentation of the historical shifts in the superintendency, in order to determine the nature of those values and beliefs. Next, we trace what we believe is the most recent shifting in the discourse. Finally, inspired by Larson's and Murphy's assertions, we wish to identify the nature and directional focus of this currently forming discourse of the superintendency.

Discursive Stages: Historical Analysis (1820-1980)

Although this is not a new idea, we will begin with the chronicling of historical stages of the superintendency. Chronicling has typically identified the *developmental stages* of the superintendency. However, in this chapter, we are *not* describing developmental stages—although many of the same issues are highlighted—but rather *discursive stages* that not only determine the rhetoric of the superintendency, but also tend to drive the responsibilities, priorities, and activities of superintendents. Development implies a maturation or growth from one step to the next. The reason we do not see such an orderly progression is that each discursive stage is not necessarily built on the strengths of the previous one.

In our view, the first and second discursive stages basically coincide with the first and second developmental stages identified by historians. There is some disagreement among historians and researchers, however, about the inclusive dates for each of these developmental stages. For example, Carter and Cunningham (1997) identify the first developmental stage as the years 1820-1850, Tyack and Hansot (1982) use the years 1820-1890, and Griffiths (1966) chooses the years 1837-1910. A closer read reveals that Carter and Cunningham and others break the years identified by Tyack and Hansot (1982) and Griffiths (1966) into two developmental stages. In our own work, we find that the number of discursive stages is significantly greater than the number of developmental stages.

FIRST DISCURSIVE STAGE (1820-1850)—SUPERINTENDENTS
AS CLERKS SERVING A REDEEMER NATION

Although public schools were first established as early as 1640, the position of superintendent of schools did not exist until the mid-1800s (Griffiths, 1966). The reluctance of Americans, during the earliest years of public schooling, to appoint what are now called superintendents stemmed from a strong anti-executive tradition that existed among the American colonists. This attitude was evident in state constitutions adopted between 1775 and 1800 (Griffiths, 1966). The earliest formal superintendency was not a clearly defined position that was created to address a specific need. Instead, it could be said that during the years 1820-1850, clerks were used to assist boards of education with the day-to-day activities related to schooling (Campbell et al., 1985; Carter & Cunningham, 1997; Norton, Webb, Dlugosh, & Sybouts, 1996). The accepted need for a clerk of the board eventually led to the non-paid appointment of the first superintendent—whose assigned job was that of school inspector—in 1837 in Buffalo, New York (Carter & Cunningham, 1997; Norton et al., 1996).

In contrast to the modest beginnings of the position of superintendent of schools, the educational discourse of the times was grand. For it was "[w]ith great fervor, determination, and conviction, [that] crusaders worked to establish public education" (Brunner, 1998a, p. 247). As Tyack and Hansot (1982) remind us,

Many of the public school promoters were convinced that America was literally God's country, the land He had chosen to bring about the redemption of mankind. The version of the millennialism they most commonly shared was . . . the gradual creation of the kingdom of God on earth and the triumph of Christian principles in the government and society. The common-school crusaders regarded themselves as God's chosen agents. (p. 37)

Thus, the rhetorical themes of the common-school movement were primarily based on Protestant-republican ideology and discourse, with connections to economic and political arguments as well. For as Brunner (1998a) notes in citing Kaestle (1983), "In 'God's country,' it was implied, strong believers should be properly educated political citizens, individually and collectively enjoying the economic rewards appropriate for an educated God-centered citizenry." Without a doubt the schools were viewed as a force to serve national unity even while they were controlled by thousands of local communities (Cremin, 1951; Crowson, 1992; Kaestle; Tyack & Hansot, 1982; Vallance, 1973).

In 1837, the same year that the first superintendency position was created, one of the best known common-school crusaders, Horace Mann, was appointed to direct the public schools of Massachusetts. His and other crusaders' persuasive message helped move Americans' faith in education into support for public schools (Bailyn, 1960; Eby, 1957). As was true in Mann's case, it was not unusual for the crusaders to become directly involved in the work of public schools, and, therefore, quite naturally their discourse permeated the nascent superintendency.

All schoolmen were to *serve* the redeemer nation—as clerks or in other tasks of service—by supporting the education of the nation's youth to the end that they became God-fearing citizens who deserved the economic rewards afforded God's people.

While the strength of the crusaders' message was evident in the establishment of public schools, the same message instilled in local citizens the belief that *they* had the responsibility and power to meet the goals of the redeemer nation through the education of their youth. Citizens' sense of responsibility and power was played out in the government bodies that controlled the first community schools. Membership in these bodies included wardens, overseers, and grandjurymen (Gilland, 1935; Griffiths, 1966). As communities grew, boards were established specifically to run the local schools, but they continued to rely on their city councils for direction in decision making (Norton et al., 1996). It is clear that most boards intended to maintain citizen control and authority over education in their communities and, thus, continued to be reluctant to appoint superintendents to direct the schools. Instead they appointed subordinate clerks to take care of the practical chores required to conduct the education of youth.[1]

Certainly the early superintendency was not a powerful position, but rather one that served the redeemer nation by way of serving the local board of education. Thus, the discourse of the first discursive stage established several important themes for education broadly and for the superintendency in particular. Leaders of education—as inspired by the crusaders—were to be concerned with the development of Protestant citizens of the republic who would prosper economically. Further, superintendents were to serve by accommodating the practical educational needs, views, and wishes of the local community and by supporting the common good of the nation.

SECOND DISCURSIVE STAGE (1850-1900)—SUPERINTENDENTS AS POLITICAL MASTER EDUCATORS OR INSTRUCTIONAL LEADERS

Two major shifts in the education and superintendency discourse occurred during the second discursive stage. First, Catholic and Jewish immigrants began to strongly oppose the discourse and practices that connected public schools to pan-Protestant teachings. This opposition led to debate-filled meetings of the National Teachers Association and other political gatherings during the second half of the 1800s.

Tyack and Hansot (1982) write that "urban 'politicians' in general—led the assault on religion in public education. Priests and party bosses catering to the new immigrants sought to dampen controversy by eliminating all religious teaching from the schools" (p. 75). As the debate reached the national level "in the 1870s and 1880s, [it] divided the Republican and Democratic parties . . . Republicans favored homogenization while Democrats embraced a tolerance for cultural differences" (Tyack & Hansot, pp. 76, 81). These general partisan positions held across other debates—like ones over the use of languages other than English in the public schools—that occurred during this period. Most often, however, the Republican favoring of homogenization won out. For example, compulsory education laws were passed during this stage, and it is highly likely that they were a Republican initiative (Tyack & Hansot, p. 103).

Indeed, Horace Mann's rhetoric supporting public schools helped calm the feud when he claimed that education would eliminate the secular concerns of delinquency and crime (Eby, 1957). The discourse of superintendents and other leaders of education began to turn from overt religious references to a discourse that upheld the "common school [as] a symbol of patriotism, an emblem of a government rooted in the virtue of free individuals" (Tyack & Hansot, 1982, p. 77).

Not coincidentally, the second major shift in the discourse of education and the superintendency was a result of a strengthening of the political connections between public schools and state and national governments. In fact, the view of public schools as symbols of patriotism gained prominence, for as Brunner (1998a) notes, "it was thought that democratic government could survive only if citizens were educated properly" (p. 253). Further, "[t]his political argument for schooling" gathered strength "when the responsibility for funding of schools shifted to local and state governments" (Brunner, 1998a, p. 253). In addition, federal aid in the form of federally owned land given to states for the promotion and building of schools (e.g., the Morrill Act of 1862) soon became part of the funding package for public schools. Further evidence of the strengthening of federal involvement in public schools came with Congress's establishment, in 1867, of the Department of Education. This new federal department "became the single most important source of educational information during the rest of the nineteenth century" (Hillesheim & Merrill, 1980, p. 334).

At the macro level, discourse on the superintendency during the second discursive stage was shifting from one that reflected Protestant religion to one that, because of economies, more strongly reflected patriotism and other state and national agendas. At the micro level—where superintendents were doing their daily work—discourse was heavily focused on the tasks at hand. This strong task orientation continued from the first discursive stage of the superintendency because local school boards still directed the work of superintendents. In fact, Gilland's (1935) analysis of the tasks and responsibilities of city superintendents (the majority of whom were appointed after 1850) revealed that most were related to instruction and the fewest were related to finance. School board members generally attended to finances and considered themselves more capable than the superintendent in this area (Gilland). Superintendency discourse at the time reflected, among other things, the fact that the superintendent's role—because it was related to instruction[2]—was that of master educator or scholar.

During the last half of the 19th century school board/superintendent relations changed, apparently because of action taken by both superintendents and boards. First, in 1870 the Department of Superintendence was formed as part of the National Education Association. This new organization was the predecessor of the American Association of School Administrators (AASA) (Norton et al., 1996). Papers presented at the annual meeting of the Department of Superintendence during the late 19th century "indicate the efforts of the superintendents to utilize the machinery of their organization to accomplish a common goal: Namely (to) acquire enough power to be effective as an executive" (Young, 1976, p. 157).

Next, as a result of the publication of Joseph Mayer Rice's research in 1893, a committee of prominent school administrators was appointed by the Department of Superintendence to study, among other things, the organization of city school systems. In its resulting report, the famous "committee of fifteen" did not recommend the elimination of school boards but came very close to it. The committee believed that administrative duties could be separated into two broad categories: business management and supervision of instruction. The committee also stated that the legislative or policy function of the school should be handled by a small board of education, elected at large, while the executive function, including instruction, should be assigned to the superintendent. These recommendations were made in part in an effort to emancipate the schools from partisan politics and excessive decentralization. The committee viewed political corruption as the prime cause of the inefficiency of education in large cities; "indeed, many politicians at that time regarded the schools as a useful support for the spoils systems and awarded jobs and contracts as political favors" (Wirt & Kirst, 1972, p. 6). As a result, the rhetoric surrounding the nature of the position of superintendent became pointedly apolitical in spite of the reality of (1) the schools' connection to the recognizable political system of state and national government, and (2) the ongoing local politics of resource allocation and use. And apparently, even though the rhetoric related to the superintendency became apolitical, superintendents were still focused on gaining more control and authority in their positions.

Finally, during this same period, boards became more accustomed to superintendents, and superintendents became more able and experienced. Board committees were reduced as greater numbers of tasks were assigned to the superintendent. Eventually, as board election processes changed and boards became smaller, superintendents were given the important instruction-related task or privilege of nominating teachers—something board members had once done in return for personal or political favors (Gilland, 1935). School boards dependent on city councils gained separation from city government (Norton et al., 1996) and at the end of this period, "[t]he board began to operate as a legislative body rather than both a legislative and an executive body: the executive functions were delegated to the superintendent, who came to be officially designated as the executive officer of the board of education. Operating in this new role, he [or she] assumed more responsibility for business management, finance, and school facilities" (Norton et al., p. 6).

The discourse of the superintendency had shifted again. At the end of the 1800s, limited control and authority began to shift from city councils and school boards to the superintendency. Thus, the second discursive stage defined the superintendency as that of the apolitical master educator or scholar whose new, yet modest, authority was to be used to ensure that the learner was endowed with (1) a non-sectarian moral character—according to Tyack and Hansot (1982) superintendents at the time appeared to read religious literature weekly—and (2) the kind of education that was deemed necessary for democratic citizenship and financial well-being.

THIRD DISCURSIVE STAGE (1900-1954)—SUPERINTENDENT AS EXPERT MANAGER

During the third discursive stage, several events of great significance drove the discourse and practice of superintendents. To begin, World War I increased the federal government's involvement in the economic affairs of the nation and promoted greater cooperation across organized labor, business, and government. In fact, the rise of business and industry in the United States had a profound impact on the education system as well as the nation. The goal of effective and efficient operations was targeted by reform efforts of the early 1900s. From 1911 to 1913 criticism mounted from sources like the *Saturday Evening Post* and *Ladies Home Journal* claiming that the schools were inefficient, ineffective, and a shame to America (Callahan, 1962). In this atmosphere, superintendents responded by embracing the values and beliefs of business and industry. Many attempted to apply Frederick Taylor's concept of "scientific management" to the educational enterprise as a solution to their problems (Callahan, 1962; Webb, Montello, & Norton, 1994, p. 8). Callahan (1962) notes that "[w]hat was unexpected was the extent, not only of the power of the business-industrial groups, but of the strength of the business ideology in the American culture on the one hand and the extreme weakness and vulnerability of schoolmen, especially superintendents, on the other" (p. iii).

Clearly, the core work of business and other large institutions— which were considered progressive—came to be the standard to which education was expected to aspire (Cuban, 1976). Under these influences, the self-image of the superintendent was changing from that of a scholar to that of a businessman (Callahan, 1962). In sum, the discourse of reform moved from a "revivalist Protestant-republican ideology to the language of science and business efficiency" and educational leaders worked to "shift decision making upward and inward in hierarchical systems of management" (Tyack & Hansot, 1982, p. 107). The shift in models of decision making followed the tenets of efficiency, and the once strong fear of centralization, while not forgotten, was largely set aside as attacks were waged daily on the rural schools of America (Tyack, Lowe, & Hansot, 1984).

Another significant influence on education was felt when, after World War I, the White House was returned to Republican Party control and conservative views prevailed. The political move to make school attendance compulsory reflected the strength of the Republican-dominated legislatures, for "in the states as well as the federal government, Republicans often took the lead in using government to coerce those who disagreed, departing from the older tradition of reform by persuasion. . . . [These laws] were at most a foreshadowing of a new state-dominated and bureaucratic educational order" (Tyack & Hansot, 1982, pp. 102-3).

The same conservative power wielders—in the main, White Anglo-Saxon Protestants—were concerned about the changing face of the nation and passed immigration restriction laws in 1921. In no small measure, the influx of immigrants during this discursive stage was viewed negatively by prominent leaders of education. For example,

Tyack and Hansot (1982) remind us that Ellwood P. Cubberly—who was the superintendent of schools in San Diego, California from 1896 to 1898, and who in 1898 accepted an appointment as assistant professor of education at Stanford University—believed that the "coming [of immigrants] . . . served to dilute tremendously our national stock and to corrupt our civic life" (p. 127). Cubberly's statement and others—such as his view that White students should be educated separately from Black students because he assumed that Blacks were mentally different if not inferior—were published as late as 1934 without fear that they would be considered objectionable ideas (Tyack & Hansot). This particular discourse about difference reinforced a belief in the inherent superiority of White, male, Anglo-Saxon, native-born Americans and left the schooling of others outside the intentions of educational reform. Clearly, valuing diversity was not a part of this discursive stage.

A third major influence of this period was the Great Depression—an event that brought industrial and agricultural production to a near standstill. As a result, organized labor increased in numbers and strength, and under the Roosevelt administration the whole political face of America was reshaped as the government moved slowly towards a welfare conception of the state (Butts & Cremin, 1953; Pulliam & Van Patten, 1995). Interestingly, school administrators who embraced the principles of business efficiency in the 1920s remained steadfast in their beliefs throughout the Depression, even as public opinion turned against big business (Urban & Wagoner, 1996). In no small measure, the economy recovered with the onset of World War II, and education felt the impact of yet another significant historical event. Two notable and direct results of the Second World War, beyond the resurgence of industry, were the focusing of curriculum on military training for national defense and the improvement of teachers' working conditions.

Close to the time of the transition from the third to the fourth discursive stages, then, the superintendency appeared to be founded on business principles. This focused definition of the superintendency was evident in the core of training programs for superintendents, as these programs were almost exclusively concerned with the routine, technical, and business aspects of the position (Griffiths, 1966). Although the public became somewhat disenchanted with business leadership during the Great Depression, because of the capitalist foundations of the United States and the strength of the economy after World War II, business and industry continued to influence superintendency discourse. This strong business focus, combined with the prevailing conservative views of the third stage, created a superintendency discourse dense with the language of efficiency and effectiveness and sparse with the language of social justice.

Along with the rest of education in the United States during the second half of the 20th century, the superintendency discourse underwent yet another shift. As Carter and Cunningham (1997) note,

The call in American education was for leadership, political savvy, reform, community responsiveness, and improved education. As a result, the superintendent serves as the professional advisor to the board, leader of reforms, manager of resources, and communicator to the public. (p. 24)

Although superintendents were to be, among other things, communicators to the public, beginning in the 1950s the public began to express greater dissatisfaction over declining student achievement. This dissatisfaction made evident the civil-rights desire to use public education "to resolve the contradiction between racism and those democratic and egalitarian values which Gunnar Myrdal called an 'American Creed.' In its historic decision on school desegregation in the *Brown* case in 1954 the United States Supreme Court sought to align educational policy with that creed and thereby gave impetus to a campaign that mobilized citizens, both black and white, to recreate American education" (Tyack & Hansot, 1982, p. 214).

Political challenges (e.g., teachers unions—National Education Association and American Federation of Teachers; a more involved citizenry and school board) and legislative challenges (e.g., Civil Rights Act; Economic Opportunity Act; Elementary and Secondary Education Act of 1965) to superintendents' traditional role as expert advisor became more common, and at times superintendents were criticized when schools were not appropriately responsive (Wirt & Kirst, 1997). To be sure, superintendents had major external pressures with which to contend. Besides desegregation and declining achievement, superintendents were faced in 1957 with the impact of the Soviet Union's success of the Sputnik launch. Not surprisingly, "[o]ur government studied this significant blow to the American ego and decided that there was only one institution to blame: American schools. The resulting political activity led to congressional passage of the National Defense Education Act (NDEA) in 1958, which placed much greater emphasis on mathematics, science, and foreign languages" (Carter & Cunningham, 1997,

p. 24). The need to educate youth at high levels in math and science to maintain national security strengthened the influence of scientific management theory and the ideology of business and industry. Thus, the discourse broadened to include new knowledge and skills while it shifted emphasis towards the superintendent as district spokesperson. Grogan (2000) states that

[a]ccording to a 1968 pamphlet, 'Selecting a School Superintendent' (p. 6), published by the American Association of School Administrators (AASA) and the National School Boards Association, the expanded nature of the position was clearly defined. Superintendents were to be responsible for such functions as planning and evaluation; organization; management of personnel, business, buildings, and auxiliary services; provision of information and advice to the community; and coordination of the entire school system." (p. 121)

During this discursive stage, superintendents were perhaps expected to be more responsive to community members (including school boards), legislation, and other political pressures. At the same time, the rhetoric that superintendents be "communicators to the public" granted them the positional power to determine what, when, how, how much, and to whom they communicated or provided information.

FIFTH DISCURSIVE STAGE (1970-1980)—SUPERINTENDENT AS ACCOUNTABLE: LIVING WITH CONFLICT

Carter and Cunningham (1997, p. 26) assert, "The 1970s heralded widespread concern that American schools were insensitive to the desires of communities, parents, and students." The discourse of the superintendency became focused on an early notion of "accountability" (p. 26). They continue:

The mission of most schools became: "All children will learn." Money was lavished on special programs for students having trouble learning (they were later to be called "at-risk" students). A new US cabinet-level position, secretary of education, was created on September 2, 1979. . . . The new cabinet position was a response to fulfilling a hopeful promise, coming out of the 1976 presidential campaign, to the National Education Association to improve relations with America's teachers. (p. 26)

In the 1970s, superintendents were under great pressure to respond to various types of organizations and interest groups and to adhere to mandates from state legislators who were assuming more responsibility for education. Specifically, "[p]arent advisory councils and national assessment were two major initiatives that gained headway during this decade. A major concern of the period was to provide equal opportunity for all individuals in American society" (Carter & Cunningham, p. 26). School boards and community members representing various values and interests pushed superintendents to adopt their agendas. Tyack and Hansot (1982) comment that "[a]n article [in 1974] in the *New York Times* reported that 'the American school superintendent, long the benevolent ruler whose word was law, has become a harried, embattled figure of waning authority.' " (p. 238).

Thus, the superintendency was no longer able to maintain the facade that it was removed from politics (Boyd, 1974; Cuban, 1976; both cited in Grogan, 2000), and the vulnerability of the position increased. This increased vulnerability was due, in part, to the fact that when the school board that appointed a superintendent was replaced with new board members who held different views, more often than not the superintendent was removed (Lutz & Iannaccone, 1978). As the fifth discursive stage ended, the superintendency discourse reflected political conflict. The ongoing issue of who had control over education was becoming more hotly contested.

Current Discursive Stages (1980s and Beyond)

In this section, we trace the most recent shifts in the discourse of the superintendency. The section is divided into two additional discursive stages, one that highlights events and influences of the 1980s, and a second that outlines issues of the 1990s and beyond.

SIXTH DISCURSIVE STAGE (1980-1990)—SUPERINTENDENT AS POLITICAL STRATEGIST FOCUSED ON EXCELLENCE

By the 1980s, the discourse reveals that the superintendency had grown to include multiple functions. In fact, if we review the nature of the position through its various iterations, it appears that more recent stages include aspects of past discursive stages. In general, while its primary focus has changed over time, the superintendency discourse has added discursive layers reflecting responsibility, capability, and accountability. In the 1980s the discourse continued to emphasize efficiency and corporate leadership skills combined with political maneuvering. The superintendency was often described in the literature as a powerful position embedded in politics (Blumberg, 1985; Iannaccone, 1967; Kimbrough & Nunnery, 1988; McCarty & Ramsey, 1971). In a work that received much attention, Blumberg, echoing Boyd (1974) and Cuban (1976), further developed the notion of the superintendent as "educational statesman" or "political strategist," or a combination of both. He also reinforced the image of the superintendent engaged in high politics and added a morally disturbing element. He drew on Burlingame (1981), who argued that the best tactics a superintendent should use to retain power include deliberate mystification, cover-up, and tactical rules. Blumberg admitted that at times a superintendent's ethics are subordinated to the "higher goal of keeping the system in balance and peaceful" (p. 68; cited in Grogan, 2000, p. 121). Apparently, Blumberg's strategies for balance and peace did not work, because during this time teacher dissatisfaction, along with the stress of reconciling diverse interests and initiatives, reached a breaking point. Reform proposals and policies were being advanced from all sectors of society. Indeed, "[m]uch of the 1980s school reform literature pointed a finger at superintendents as the culprits who stand in the way of true reform" (Glass, 1997, p. 24).

In 1983, in the midst of this public outcry, *A Nation at Risk* was released. A more dramatic narrative was introduced into discussions about education in general, and about the superintendency specifically. As a result of this report, education and the superintendency became politicized; politicians were suddenly heavily focused on large-scale educational programs meant "to improve the quality (or 'excellence') of schools" rather than on equality of educational opportunity (Wirt & Kirst, 1997, p. 17). Educators at all levels were to focus on "setting higher standards; strengthening the curriculum in core subjects; increasing homework, time for learning, and time in school; more rigorous grading, testing, homework, and discipline; increasing productivity and excellence; and providing more choices regarding education" (Carter & Cunningham, 1997, p. 28).

Since 1983, successive waves of educational reform have contributed to shifting policy initiatives away from accountability toward teacher professionalism and toward more complex issues associated with learning and school restructuring. Individually and collectively, these changes challenged conventional assumptions about schooling, leaders, and leadership (Björk, 1996). As a consequence of reformers' heightened interest in large-scale, systemic reform and questions about superintendents' contributions to school performance, a resurgence of scholarly inquiry helped describe the changing landscape of superintendents' work and lay the groundwork for redefining their role in school reform (Björk, 2000). Björk, Lindle, and Van Meter (1999) discuss changes in the field of educational administration over time (1957-1999), reflected in changes in the discourse on the super-intendency in terms of "knowing about," "knowing for," "knowing how," and "knowing why" (p. 659).

During the first wave of educational reform (1982-1986), demands for educational accountability and performance standards underscored the importance of formal knowledge or "knowing about" administrators' work, and craft knowledge focused primarily on "knowing for" managing and improving schools. During the second wave of educational reform (1986-1989), new expectations for school and district leadership shifted emphasis from organizational efficiency and management issues to student learning, teacher professionalism, and decentralization. These policy initiatives underscored the importance of superintendents' educational and instructional leadership roles (Björk, 1993). Thus, "knowing how" to improve learning, teaching, and student performance, as well as distributing leadership and generating broad-based community support, became increasingly prominent aspects of job performance expectations.

With the proliferation of policy specifically directed at the role and responsibilities of superintendents, the superintendency was not only drawn into the political arena, it was—in much larger part—under the thumb of policymakers. Under these conditions, political strategies articulated by superintendents were less about the superintendency's maintaining positional power and more about superintendents' personal survival. Thus, by 1989,

. . . school reform was developing within the most ideologically conservative political climate of recent times. In this setting, President George Bush and the nation's governors came together at a historical education summit in Charlottesville, Virginia. All agreed that "the time has come for the first time in the United States' history to establish clear national performance goals, goals that will make us internationally competitive" (U.S. Department of Education, 1991, p. 2). There was a clear call for a "renaissance in education." The meeting of the president and governors was clearly a response to the perception of a rising economic challenge from highly productive industrialized nations. (Carter & Cunningham, 1997, p. 29)

The fact that the education summit basically excluded educators was further evidence that the superintendency as a position had lost its political clout and was expected to respond to power wielders at national and state levels. Clearly, significant control of and responsibility for public education had moved into the hands of state and local bureaucracies. Diminished positional power and the need to be responsive to multiple and diverse external pressures resulted in another shift in the focus of superintendency discourse.

SEVENTH DISCURSIVE STAGE (1990S AND BEYOND)—SUPERINTENDENT AS COLLABORATOR

With diminished positional power, superintendents were faced with the need to work with others if they intended to implement what has been referred to as the third wave of reform (1989-2001). This particular wave of reform placed emphasis on the notion that all children can learn and promoted systemic restructuring focused on schools organized as professional hubs of integrated service systems embedded in communities (Björk, 1996; Murphy, 1990). Carter and Cunningham (1997) describe the superintendents' dilemma:

With the alienation of teachers, communities, and children came formal recognition of the importance of collaborative relationships among diverse groups in order to improve schools and ultimately student learning. The push was to achieve greater understanding through exchange of information and ideas among both internal and external groups; the goal was to ensure that all the groups that were needed to support public education were full partners in the process. The Goals 2000: Educate America Act, which was passed in 1993, encourages 'communities to develop their own reform plans and provided seed money to support these efforts' (Riley, 1994). The law requires innovation in teaching and learning, increased parental and community involvement, professional development of teachers, and reduction in educational bureaucracy. (p. 31)

The increased public exposure required that superintendents have the ability to understand and explain the importance of school reform for the preservation of both a sound economy and a democratic society. Thus, the discourse of "knowing why" became indispensable to their success (Björk, 1996). In fact, when facing the issues confronting schools, superintendents not only are expected to know and articulate why reforms are needed but also must be willing to use their position to change school structures, practices, and relations with the broad community. These circumstances accentuated political and moral dimensions of their leadership role in changing the nature of schooling and schools. In the past, conventional management practices of superintendents were built on notions of corporate values of efficiency, scientific management and hierarchical, apolitical, professionalism (Callahan, 1967; Iannaccone, 1982; Tyack & Hansot, 1982).

During recent years the confluence of a number of factors is altering the landscape of American education. They include expanding social diversity in ethnicity and race; increasingly complex expectations for schooling; political environments whose intensity is being heightened by interest groups and alliances as well as conflicts internal to schools and school districts (Malen, 1995), and all are redefining superintendents' work.

Above all, the most recent shift in the discourse encourages superintendents to be collaborators, working with others and sharing leadership. This shift is reflected in the literature on leadership itself. The language of educational leadership has changed over the past 10 to 15 years. Leadership in the superintendency, in particular, is now associated with words such as collaboration, community, cooperation, teams, and relationship-building. Leadership used to be framed by words like control, power, authority and management. This indicates a major discursive shift in the thinking about leadership.

Interestingly, one of the main reasons for this new emphasis lies in the renewed focus on instruction in the rhetoric surrounding the superintendent's position. Scholars and practitioners alike have begun to view a superintendent's leadership from the perspective of working with and through others rather than commanding others. Certainly, the word "follower" appears to have fallen out of favor. In its place is the notion of distributed leadership (Elmore, 1999; Houston, 2001; Neuman & Simmons, 2000).

According to Elmore (1999), "in a knowledge-intensive enterprise like teaching and learning, there is no way to perform these complex tasks without widely distributing responsibility for leadership . . . among roles in the organization" (p. 27). This means drawing on individuals' particular skills, knowledge, and expertise for the guidance and direction the organization will need to enable it to achieve its shared goals. Most important in this notion of leadership is the creation of a common culture to "make . . . distributed leadership coherent" (p. 27). And to create the common culture, with a common set of values binding the group together, Elmore encourages an emphasis on collaboration among the various stakeholders. Elmore has deliberately removed the word "control" from his definition of educational leadership. He states simply that "Leadership . . . [is] the guidance and direction of improvement in public schools" (p. 3). He does this because leadership could not be distributed if it were about control. His focus is on the improvement of teaching and learning that is to be facilitated by many members of the organization. Superintendent John E. Deasy (2000) expressed the same idea when talking about his own district, which operates collaboratively. He calls it moving from a "paradigm of oversight to one of insight" (p. 15). He now views the job of superintendent as one of guidance. "Rather than seeing my job as a powerful and directive management position, I see it as providing support for developing professional, collaborative communities" (p. 15). The notion of support here echoes the first discursive stage of the superintendency, which emphasized service.

Further, in his discussion of the 21st century superintendent, Paul Houston (2001) goes so far as to say, "We must begin to identify a new cadre of leaders who see the role as one of collaboration, rather than command, and mentor them into the jobs" (p. 433). Like the others who use the term "distributed leadership," Houston is motivated by an emphasis on learning. He argues that future superintendents must be "leaders who focus on the organic and holistic qualities of learning and who structure learning that speaks to the hearts and minds of learners" (p. 432). Influenced by the standards based reform movement, Elmore (1999) *equates* leadership with improvement of learning. His definition "focuses leadership on instructional improvement and defines everything else as instrumental to it . . . [because] most of the knowledge required for improvement must inevitably reside in the people who deliver instruction, not in the people who manage them" (p. 26). Neuman and Simmons (2000) believe that none of the traditional leadership roles have "had at [their] core a focus on student achievement" (p. 10). "This traditional system has institutionalized the appointing and anointing of formal leaders, often marginalizing those with more flexible leadership styles and discouraging teachers and district personnel from assuming significant but informal leadership roles" (p. 10). Instead, distributed leadership resides "in the entire education community, and learning becomes the focus and primary value for every member" (p. 12).

It appears that the idea of shared or distributed leadership is gaining some credence in the discourse of education in general. In addition, many works on district governance and leadership underscore the increased role of the community in future conceptions of the superintendency. Owens and Ovando (2000) make the case for a superintendent's leading through the community in his or her district. Strategies for involving the community in a meaningful way include: soliciting community input; extending the school into the community; focusing the community on the benefits of a strong educational system; inviting community members into the school; opening school facilities for community use; initiating programs for the community; and providing volunteer assistance to the community (pp. 125-130).

Building community capacity to enhance learning in schools is a related concept. Drawing on Sergiovanni (1994), Sewall (1999) argues that community capacity building is an important responsibility of superintendents and central office personnel. She also advocates active pursuit of community involvement. "[T]he concepts of ownership in the process of participation and planning and decision making can be helpful tools for establishing trust and credibility on the part of the school and district personnel" (p. 143). Sewall also points out that recognizing the importance of community means remembering the roles of teachers and other district employees. As community members, these people can be powerful sources of positive outreach into other groups situated farther from the schools. In sharing the leadership for learning, teachers and staff members help generate community capacity building. Community support for reform efforts has long been considered a vital factor in their success (Annenberg Institute for School Reform, 1998; Portz, 2000; Sirotnik, 1991). Because superintendents are seen as leading reform in their districts, it is no wonder that much of the current literature in this era of high reform highlights the relationship between superintendents and their communities.

Another departure from the past, although not about leadership per se, is the identification of bureaucratic mechanisms characterized by Murphy (2000) as a *hindrance* rather than an asset to school governance. This idea represents a loss of confidence in a bureaucratic approach to schooling, and it will surely have an impact on the discourse of the superintendency. Defining governance as about control—about "who drives the educational bus" (p. 57), Murphy considers a number of future possible control processes in his rethinking of school governance in the postindustrial world. He argues that "bureaucracies may be working well for those that run them but . . . they are not serving children well" (p. 68). Reporting various reasons for this criticism of the time-honored system of school governance, Murphy synthesizes the major ones as having to do with preventing children from learning. Not only do bureaucratic structures constrict educators in the system, but they also make it difficult to achieve the kind of community involvement advocated earlier. Murphy outlines five different governance options to replace the flawed current one: state control, citizen control, professional control, community control, and market control. In addition, he considers five ideological foundations of an emerging governance structure: localization or decentralization; a replacement of representative governance with more populist conceptions; a rebalancing of the governance equation in favor of lay citizens; the ideology of choice; and democratic professionalism. All of these chip away at the notion of a powerful superintendent in charge of the system.

It is interesting to note that while Murphy still frames his discussion in terms of control, he concurs with Elmore's (1999) prediction of a changing role for teachers. Murphy states that "the call for an enhanced voice for teachers is . . . likely to become a key pillar in school governance for tomorrow's schools" (p. 79). Central to the concept of distributed leadership is the respect for and reliance on teacher expertise. Not since the very early days of public education have we seen much in the discourse of the superintendency about the role of teachers in school governance.

Most recently, the literature includes ideas for a reconception of the superintendency. For example, a volume edited by Brunner and Björk (2002), *The New Superintendency: Advances in Research and Theories of School Management and Educational Policy*, contains several suggestions for reframing the position. In one chapter, "A New Balance Between Superintendent and Board: Clarifying Purpose and Generating Knowledge," Shibles, Rallis, and Deck posit that superintendents' new roles will involve being "clarifiers," "data-bearers," "facilitators," and "knowledge generators." In another chapter, "The New Superintendency as Guardian of Justice and Care," Patricia First persuasively critiques the contentious and litigious conceptualization and handling of the problems that involve children and families. She advocates that the new superintendency be focused on the transformation of school districts through wise use of the law and a sense of justice and caring for children.

In addition, Grogan's (2000) article offers five approaches that might lay the groundwork for a new superintendency. This trend corresponds to Murphy's (1999) call for a re-centering of the profession of educational leadership. It certainly emerges from our immersion in the "era of ferment" he identifies. As stated earlier, public confidence in education has waned, legislator enthusiasm for high-stakes testing has reached fever pitch, and compensation for the position has not kept pace with similar executive positions in business and industry (Cunningham & Sperry, 2001). In short, the need to find a new foundation for the superintendency is a reflection of several converging factors: the demands for the organization of schooling to educate *all* students to high levels (Larson and Ovando, 2001); public scrutiny of an intensely political post (Houston, 2001); perceived loss of depth in the candidate pools for the position (Glass, 2000; Houston, 1998); and increased disruptive conflict between boards and superintendents (Björk & Lindle, 2001).

Challenges Facing the Newly Defined Superintendency

While the changing language of leadership indicates some agreement with Grogan's (2000) notions for a reconception of the superintendency, not all of the five approaches she advocates—working through others; being comfortable with contradiction; appreciating dissent; developing a critical awareness of how children are being served; and adopting an ethic of care (p. 132)—are found in the current literature on superintendents and district governance. While there are encouraging signs in the literature and certainly progress towards embracing these values, there are still some embedded beliefs and attitudes associated with the superintendency that inhibit full acceptance of their worth. In this section, we briefly mention literature that seems consistent with each approach and then talk about what needs to occur if the new discourse of the superintendency is to address current demands.

The emphasis on distributed leadership and shared governance is aligned with Grogan's first approach, working through others or along with others, especially when that approach includes opportunities for "others to own their own ideas . . . and for shared decision-making, which take[s] a bottom-up approach" (Grogan, 1996, p. 162). Working through others means empowering others, allowing them to take the credit for the success of their ideas. It takes the nominal leader out of the limelight and stresses the relational approach to leadership. This approach also emphasizes the development of others' capacity to learn, to teach, to lead, and to serve students as well as possible. Elmore (1999) asserts that individuals should "frame their responsibilities in terms of their contribution to enhancing someone else's capacity and performance" (p. 56). In an organization where distributed leadership is the norm, each administrator, including the superintendent, is *evaluated* on the basis of how well he or she facilitates this capacity building. This seems to be quite a departure from the earlier concepts of leading from the front. Kelleher (2001) also stresses collaborative strategies to enhance others' work when he writes about the need for superintendents to transform the system to improve student achievement. He argues, "Testing does not improve student achievement. Teaching does." (p. 2). Houston (2001) agrees and advocates "leading by sharing power and by engaging members of the organization and community in the process of leading" (p. 430).

The related invitation, in much of the literature, to involve stakeholders in decision-making and to work with community is consistent with Grogan's second and third notions of being comfortable with contradiction and appreciating dissent—especially when these notions are coupled with shared leadership instead of control. It is not easy or simple work. The moral imperative to create and administer community found in the work of Starratt (1994, 1997), Sergiovanni (1994), Beck and Foster (1999), and others establishes the worth of collaborating with all stakeholders for the good of the children in every district. Beck and Foster highlight the tension inherent in simultaneously building community and administering high-stakes tests. Working towards a collective good collides with a system that emphasizes individual achievement. To appreciate dissent in such environments is to live with contradictions. The key here is to legitimate the opposing values so that stakeholders are encouraged to coalesce around common goals instead of fighting to have their voices heard. The notion of valuing dissent is contrary to the idea of striving for consensus at all costs. While it is important for superintendents to seek common goals to provide direction, it is also important that they make space for dissenters. Brunner's (1998b, 1999) work reinforces the idea that superintendents who use power "with" others instead of "over" others are far more likely to get wide participation in their endeavors.

One could also argue that the focus on student learning derives from Grogan's fourth approach of adopting an ethic of care. But unless it is framed by her fifth notion of a critical awareness of how children are being served, such a focus could reinforce business as usual. Much rhetoric surrounds the cry for increased student achievement and the superintendent's role in leading the charge. Superintendents both on the way into and on the way out of their jobs are assessed in terms of their success or failure in raising student achievement (Johnston, 2000; Reid, 2000; Stricherz, 2001). For instance, Rod Paige's tenure of nearly seven years in the Houston Independent School District is attributed to his management improvements and rising student achievement (Johnston). Similarly, Dennis Chaconas, superintendent of the Oakland Schools, California, has been praised recently for his plan to give top school administrators bonuses tied to test scores (Stricherz). And there is acclamation for some of the non-educator superintendents who have also aggressively attacked the problem of student achievement (Mathews, 2001).

To adopt an ethic of care, framed by a critical awareness of how children are being served, suggests a more activist role for the superintendent than is found in the traditional literature. This is true especially if the superintendent pays attention both to the elimination of the test-score gaps and to the education of the whole child. It is similar to the idea of creative courage Brunner (2000) identifies and Kelleher (2001) advocates. An extension of this idea is to encourage superintendents to speak "in one voice to enlighten politicians about both the benefits and pitfalls of standards" (Kelleher, p. 4). An ethic of care prompts superintendents to use their collective energies to convince state policymakers to refine their testing systems so that they are fair and appropriate.

To be sure, the signs of a new foundation for the superintendency can be detected in the literature. But there is work yet to be done. It is a stretch for certain superintendents to give up some of the power and control that the traditional discourse affords them. Appreciating dissent and living with contradictions are very difficult for superintendents who believe that they must steer the ship unaided. Despite Houston's (2001) embrace of collaborative approaches he still argues that superintendents "have to know how to take the pulse of the public and how to sell their ideas" (p. 432). There is something contradictory about believing that "persuasion is the ultimate tool for a superintendent of education" although "[l]eadership is not about exerting a superintendent's will" (p. 432). Kelleher (2001) articulates a similar fear when he states that superintendents must "[find] the balance between listening to others and asserting our convictions in developing the new vision. (The danger of not involving others is that we become leaders without followers. The danger of only facilitating and listening is that we lose our advocacy)" (parentheses in the original, p. 3). To highlight these tensions is not to suggest that superintendents should abdicate their responsibilities for providing direction. Instead, in listening to others and gaining insight into the pluralistic contexts within which they operate, superintendents will find direction in resisting solutions that reinforce the status quo.

These are enormous challenges for superintendents who are motivated to collaborate with other district stakeholders in the best interests of the students. While the discourse suggests that working through others and forming coalitions are effective strategies, there is little agreement on what are the best interests of students. We argue that this is where most work still needs to be done. No child must be left behind. Significant human and material resources must be devoted to eliminating inequities in the quality of schooling available to children disadvantaged by ethnicity, race, gender, disability, sexual orientation, language or other marginalizing factors. Although the current literature on the superintendency offers much evidence supporting the need to raise achievement scores, there is not enough emphasis on how this approach works for students outside the mainstream. Exceptions include some mention of Rod Paige's success in raising minority test scores in Houston (Reid, 2000) and Stanford's and Olchefske's similar success in

Seattle (Mathews, 2001). In this frenzy of high-stakes testing, there is also little attention to the futures of students in vocational tracks or those who will not graduate from high school under the new accountability systems in many states. Thus, while there is more focus on how well students are being served, it is not yet a critical awareness. Murphy (1999; this volume) writes of social justice as one of the three key concepts providing new anchors for the profession of educational administration. It is to be hoped that this includes a critical sense of who is not served well by educational policies and practices. School improvement, another suggested anchor for the profession, must be founded on the knowledge that policies and practices are not neutral, no matter how well intentioned.

In addition, although the word "community" is used often in the current literature, it, too, needs further scrutiny. Grogan's (2000) idea of working with the community in order to gain "a better understanding of pluralistic contexts" (p. 133) is premised on the kind of horizontal relationships formed by superintendents who do not "manage" community involvement so much as seek it. Issues of social, racial, cultural and moral disagreements among community members must be openly addressed. Larson and Ovando (2001) observe that "For too long, educators . . . have interpreted complex situations through the clouded lens of their own received views, life histories, and personal experiences" (p. 206). For all superintendents, sharing leadership with communities includes working with groups they are part of and with groups quite apart from themselves. Since most superintendents have been White males, community has a particular connotation for them, which might be an inhibiting factor when they attempt to work with the community as encouraged by the discourse. Larson and Ovando talk of "imagined communities . . . collective notions of minority communities that many white educators have absorbed from the mass media or from ubiquitous societal stereotypes" (p. 8). It appears that working successfully with the kinds of diverse communities found across America requires an ability to abandon learned behaviors and to rethink assumptions. For superintendents to be effective, a passionate commitment to equity must form the basis of such endeavors.

Conclusion

In sum, we believe that the current discourse of the superintendency, influenced by a change in the demands of leadership, does reflect recognition of the need for social justice and school improvement as Murphy (1999; this volume) advocated. While it is not as critical as it could be, the discourse at least offers the possibility that all students could be better served. At the heart of today's superintendency is a renewed focus on teaching and learning in the schools. This harkens back to earlier discursive stages, where instruction was uppermost in the mind of the superintendent, whose energies went into the support and facilitation of others' work. However, new layers of meaning enter the current discourse that have not been previously expressed. The call for sharing power with communities, with teachers, with principals, and most challenging of all, with state legislators, does diminish the role of superintendent in some people's eyes. Will the position lose its current strength? Or will the position gain respect as one in which individuals use their collective power to effect major social change? We believe that the future of the superintendency lies in the promise of the current discourse, which may encourage more superintendents to embrace the concept of power "with" instead of power "over" (Brunner, 2001).

NOTES

1. Although a full discussion lies beyond the scope of this chapter, we note that at least four types of superintendencies were established during the first discursive stage: state superintendents, who were appointed at the state level as early as 1812 with the charge to intervene in educationally resistant areas on behalf of the children; county superintendents, a position created to assist state superintendents in the distribution of funds and in oversight functions; and district and city superintendents, who were appointed by rural or city school boards when the tasks grew too numerous (Blount, 1998). The last two superintendencies, district and city, are the focus of this chapter.

2. During the second discursive stage, superintendents were considered master educators because they were primarily in charge of instruction-related tasks—most often reported to be "the making of an annual report and supervision and visitation of the schools" (Norton et al., 1996, p. 4). This description of master educator in the second discursive stage seems to translate into a role currently labeled "instructional leader." This is not necessarily an appropriate translation, however, for as Leithwood (1995) points out, "the meaning of 'instructional leadership' has never been well defined." He adds that he uses the phrase to denote "a form of leadership that is designed to affect classroom instruction quite directly, through, for example, supervision, coaching, staff development, modeling and other such means of influencing teachers' thinking and practice" (p. 3). He goes on to articulate what instructional leadership is not: "Leadership that indirectly constrains teachers' choices or frames their work needs to be called something else" (p. 3).

REFERENCES

Annenberg Institute for School Reform. (1998). *Reasons for hope, voices for change: A report of the Annenberg Institute on public engagement for public education.* Providence, RI: Author.

Bailyn, B. (1960). *Education in the forming of American society: Needs and opportunities for study.* Chapel Hill, NC: University of North Carolina Press.

Beck, L., & Foster, W. (1999). Administration and community: Considering challenges, exploring possibilities. In J. Murphy and K. Seashore Louis (Eds.), *Handbook of research on educational administration* (pp. 337-358). San Francisco: Jossey-Bass.

Björk, L. (1993). Effective schools—effective superintendents: The emerging instructional leadership role. *Journal of School Leadership 3*(3), 246-259.

Björk, L. (1996). The revisionists' critique of the education reform reports. *Journal of School Leadership, 7*(1), 290-315.

Björk, L. (2000). Personal characteristics. In Glass, T., Björk, L., & Brunner, C. C. *The study of the American superintendency 2000: A look at the superintendent in the new millennium* (pp. 15-32). Arlington, VA: American Association of School Administrators.

Björk, L., & Lindle, J. C. (2001). Superintendents and interest groups. *Educational Policy, 15*(1), 76-91.

Björk, L., Lindle, J. C., & Van Meter, E. (1999). A summing, up. *Educational Administration Quarterly, 35*(4), 657-663.

Blount, J. (1998). *Destined to rule the schools: Women and the superintendency, 1873-1995.* Albany, NY: SUNY Press.

Blumberg, A. (1985). *The school superintendent: Living with conflict.* New York: Teachers College Press.

Boyd, W. (1974). The school superintendent: Educational statesman or political strategist? *Administrator's Notebook, 22*(2), 21-26.

Brunner, C. C. (1998a). The legacy of disconnection between the public schools and their communities: Suggestions for policy. *Educational Policy, 12*(3), 244-266.

Brunner, C. C. (1998b). The new superintendency supports innovation: Collaborative decision making. *Contemporary Education, 69*(2), 79-82.

Brunner, C. C. (1999). Power, gender, and superintendent selection. In C. C. Brunner (Ed.), *Sacred dreams: Women and the superintendency* (pp. 63-78). Albany, NY: SUNY Press.

Brunner, C. C. (2000). *Principals of power: Women superintendents and the riddle of the heart.* Albany, NY: SUNY Press.

Brunner, C. C. (2001, April). Supporting social justice: Power and authentic participatory decision making in the superintendency. Paper presented at the annual meeting of the American Educational Research Association, Seattle, WA.

Brunner, C. C., & Björk, L. (Eds.). (2002). *The new superintendency: Advances in research and theories of school management and educational policy.* Oxford, London: Elsevier Press.

Butts, R., & Cremin, L. (1953). *A history of education in American culture.* New York: Holt, Rinehart & Winston.

Callahan, R. E. (1962). *Education and the cult of efficiency.* Chicago: University of Chicago Press.

Callahan, R. E. (1967). *The superintendent of schools: An historical analysis.* Final report, S-212. Washington, DC: U.S. Office of Education (HEW).

Campbell, R. F., Cunningham, L. L., Nystrand, R. O., & Usdan, M. D. (1985). *The organization and control of American schools* (5th ed.). Columbus, OH: Merrill.

Carter, G., & Cunningham, W. (1997). *The American school superintendent: Leading in the age of pressure.* San Francisco: Jossey-Bass.

Cremin, L. A. (1951). *American common school: An historical conception.* New York: Columbia University Teachers College.

Crowson, R. L. (1992). *School-community relations under reform.* Berkeley, CA: McCutchan.

Cuban, L. (1976). *Urban school chiefs under fire.* Chicago: University of Chicago Press.

Cunningham, W., & Sperry, J. (2001). The underpaid educator. *American School Board Journal* (April), 38-42.

Davies, B. (1994). *Poststructuralist theory and classroom practice.* Geelong, Victoria, Australia: Deakin University Press.

Deasy, J. (2000). Moving from oversight to insight: One community's journey with its superintendent. *Phi Delta Kappan, 82*(1), 13-15.

Eby, F. (1957). *The development of modern education.* Englewood Cliffs, NJ: Prentice Hall.

Elmore, R. (1999, September). *Leadership of large-scale improvement in American education.* Paper prepared for the Albert Shanker Institute.

Gilland, T. M. (1935). *The origins and development of the powers and duties of the city-school superintendent.* Chicago: University of Chicago Press.

Glass, T. E. (1997). The superintendency: Yesterday, today, and tomorrow. In C. H. Chapman (Ed.), *Becoming a superintendent: Challenges of school district leadership* (pp. 19-39). Columbus, OH: Merrill.

Glass, T. E. (2000, November 8). The shrinking applicant pool. In *Education Week on the Web* [On-line]. Retrieved May 30, 2001 from http://www.edweek.org/ew/ewstory.cfm?slug=10glass.h20

Glass, T., Björk, L., & Brunner, C. C. (2000). *The study of the American superintendency 2000: A look at the superintendent in the new millennium.* Arlington, VA: American Association of School Administrators.

Griffiths, D. E. (1966). *The school superintendent.* New York: The Discourse for Applied Research in Education, Inc.

Grogan, M. (1996). *Voices of women aspiring to the superintendency.* Albany, NY: SUNY Press.

Grogan, M. (2000). Laying the groundwork for a reconception of the superintendency from feminist postmodern perspectives. *Educational Administration Quarterly, 36*(1), 117-142.

Hillesheim, J. W., & Merrill, G. D. (1980). *Theory and practice in the history of American education: A book of readings.* Washington, DC: University Press of America.

Houston, P. (1998, June 3). The ABCs of administrator shortage. In *Education Week on the Web* [On-line]. Retrieved May 30, 2001 from http://www.edweek.org/ew/ewstory.cfm?slug=38houst.h17

Houston, P. (2001). Superintendents for the 21st century: It's not just a job, it's a calling. *Phi Delta Kappan, 82*(6), 428-433.

Iannaccone, L. (1967). *Politics in education.* New York: The Center for Applied Research in Education, Inc.

Iannaccone, L. (1982). Changing political patterns and governmental regulations. In R. Everhart (Ed.), *The public school monopoly: A critical analysis of education and the state in American society* (pp. 295-324). Cambridge, MA: Ballinger.

Johnston, R. (2000, October 4). Boosters call Houston's chief 'a good thing and we know it'. In *Education Week on the Web* [On-line]. Retrieved May 30, 2001 from http://www.edweek.org/ew/ewstory.cfm?slug=05paige.h20

Kaestle, C. R. (1983). *Pillars of the republic: Common schools and American society, 1780-1860.* New York: Hill and Wang.

Kelleher, P. (2001, March 28). Implementing high standards. In *Education Week on the Web* [On-line]. Retrieved May 20, 2001 from http://www.edweek.org/ew/ewstory.cfm?slug=28kelleher.h20

Kimbrough, R. B., & Nunnery, M. Y. (1988). *Politics, power, polls and school elections.* Berkeley, CA: McCutchan.

Larson, C., & Ovando, C. (2001). *The color of bureaucracy: The politics of equity in multicultural school communities.* Belmont, CA: Wadsworth/Thompson Learning.

Leithwood, K. (Ed.). (1995). *Effective school district leadership: Transforming politics into education.* Albany, NY: SUNY Press.

Lutz, F., & Iannaccone, L. (1978). *Public participation in local schools: The dissatisfaction theory of American democracy.* Lexington, MA: Lexington Books.

Malen, B. (1995). The micropolitics of education. In J. D. Scribner & D. H. Layton (Eds.), *The study of educational politic: The 1994 commemorative yearbook of the Politics of Education Association (1969-1994)* (pp. 147-167). Philadelphia: Falmer Press.

Mathews, J. (2001, June). Nontraditional thinking in the central office. In *The School Administrator Web Edition* [On-line]. Retrieved May 30, 2001 from http://www.aasa.org/publications/sa/2001_06/feature_mathews1.htm

McCarty, D., & Ramsey, C. (1971). *The school managers: Power and conflict in American public schools.* Westport, CT: Greenwood Press.

Murphy, J. (1990). Educational reform of the 1980s: A comprehensive analysis. In J. Murphy, *Educational reform of the 1980s: Perspectives and cases* (pp. 3-56). Berkeley, CA: McCutchan.

Murphy, J. (1999). *The quest for a center: Notes on the state of the profession of educational leadership.* Columbia, MO: The University Council for Educational Administration.

Murphy, J. (2000). Governing America's schools: The shifting playing field. *Teachers College Record, 102*(1), 85-124.

Neuman, M., & Simmons, W. (2000). Leadership for student learning. *Phi Delta Kappan, 82*(1), 9-12.

Norton, M. S., Webb, L. D., Dlugosh, L. L., & Sybouts, W. (1996). *The school superintendency: New responsibilities, new leadership.* Needham Heights, MA: Allyn & Bacon.

Owens, J., & Ovando, M. (2000). *Superintendent's guide to creating community.* Lanham, MD: Scarecrow Press.

Portz, J. (2000). Supporting education reform, mayoral and corporate paths. *Urban Education, 35*(4), 396-417.

Pulliam, J., & Van Patten, J. (1995). *History of education in the United States* (6th ed.). Englewood Cliffs, NJ: Merrill.

Reid, K. (2000, September 6). Corporate-style team sought to take charge of Philly District. In *Education Week on the Web* [On-line]. Retrieved May 30, 2001 from http://www.edweek.org/ew/ewstory.cfm?slug=01philly.h20

Riley, R. (1994). Education and Goals 2000. Keynote address at the annual conference of the American Association of School Administrators, San Francisco.

Sergiovanni, T. (1994). *Building community in schools.* San Francisco: Jossey-Bass.

Sewall, A. (1999). *Central office and site-based management: An educative guide.* Lancaster, PA: Technomic.

Starratt, R. (1994). *Building an ethical school.* London: Falmer Press.

Starratt, R. (1997). *Administering meaning, administering community, administering excellence: The new fundamentals of educational administration.* New York: Merrill.

Sirotnik, K. (1991). Improving urban schools in the age of "restructuring." *Education and Urban Society, 23*(3), 256-69.

Stricherz, M. (2001, January 24). Top Oakland administrators to receive bonuses tied to test scores. In *Education Week on the Web* [On-line]. Retrieved May 30, 2001 from http://www.edweek.org/ew/ewstory.cfm?slug=19oakland.h20

Tyack, D., & Hansot, E. (1982). *Managers of virtue: Public school leadership in America, 1820-1980.* New York: Basic Books.

Tyack, D., Lowe, R., & Hansot, E. (1984). *Public schools in hard times: The Great Depression and recent years.* Cambridge, MA: Harvard University Press.

Urban, W., & Wagoner, J. (1996). *American education: A history.* New York: McGraw-Hill.

Vallance, E. (1973). Hiding the hidden curriculum: An interpretation of language of justification in nineteenth century educational reform. *Curriculum Theory Network, 4*(1), 5-21.

Webb, L. D., Montello, P. A., & Norton, M. S. (1994). *Human resources administration: Personnel issues and needs in education* (2nd ed.). New York: Merrill.

Wirt, F. M., & Kirst, M. W. (1972). *Political and social foundations of education.* Berkeley, CA: McCutchan.

Wirt, F., & Kirst, M. (1997). *The political dynamics of American education.* Berkeley, CA: McCutchan.

Young, H. S. (1976). *In pursuit of a profession: A historical analysis of the concept of "professionalization" for the American public school superintendency, 1865-1973.* Unpublished doctoral dissertation, The Pennsylvania State University.

CHAPTER 11

Repositioning Lay Leadership:
Policymaking and Democratic Deliberation

SHARON F. RALLIS, MARK R. SHIBLES, AND AUSTIN D. SWANSON

Communities in the 21st century are complex systems. They are composed of a number of interacting and constantly changing individuals and groups who hold diverse beliefs and values. The differences may be immense and obvious, or they may be small and subtle. The public schools of the community are charged with educating the youth who come from homes representing various perspectives of the community. Consequently, schools are elaborate, loosely coupled organizations (see Weick, 1976) with multiple goals and diverse technologies. The challenge for *professional leadership* is to synthesize the multiple voices within a frame of what is known about teaching and learning, to articulate a vision for teaching and learning, and to move the community's schools toward that vision. The challenge for *lay leadership* is to represent multiple voices (and to ensure that all voices are heard) while implementing state and federal mandates, and yet to agree on purpose and local policy for schooling. Because this task is deeply complex, nonlinear, and unpredictable, the lay leadership function operates with varying degrees of ambiguity within formal and informal structures. These structures serve as forums for democratic deliberation in which the multiple community values can surface and coalesce.

Our analysis categorizes control of education as a struggle among several broad categories of groups: individuals, families, and communities; the educating profession; and society at large (Swanson and King, 1997). Leadership from these groups is enacted in the venues of government, the market, and voluntary association (Murphy, 2000). To the extent that decisions are made through the market, consumers can maximize their personal choices within the limits of their economic

Sharon Rallis and Mark Shibles are Professors in the Department of Educational Leadership at the Neag School of Education of the University of Connecticut. They also work in the Northeast Center for Educational Policy and Leadership. Austin Swanson is a Professor in the Graduate School of Education, State University of New York at Buffalo, specializing in educational administration.

resources and according to individual value preferences, and professionals are free to provide or withhold services and to determine the nature of those services. But when decisions are made through the government, individuals and groups of varying value orientations must negotiate a single solution, and their value preferences are diluted in the process. Leadership through voluntary association can provide a middle ground having some attributes of the market and of government (Brown, 1998).

Other chapters of this volume have addressed leadership issues from the perspective of the educating profession. This chapter examines the fundamental leadership functions played by those outside that profession. Laypeople are elected to, appointed to, or volunteer for leadership positions within schools and school districts. We consider how professional leadership interacts with and responds to political and economic leadership that is independent of the schools, and how layperson participation can strengthen schools' capacity to meet the educational challenges before them. The chapter begins by examining the natural tensions that exist among groups, both lay and professional, that have different local, state, and national perspectives and responsibilities. It then explores the potential of lay volunteers in altering school culture for the better, and the role of laypeople in formally defined roles on school boards and advisory councils. The chapter concludes with a proposal for repositioning lay leadership to better meet the needs of our increasingly diverse public.

The Historical Paradox of Control

American schools, as artifacts of religion and democracy, belong to the public. The "old deluder" law of 1647 in Massachusetts (which required all towns to establish and maintain public schools so that people would not be ignorant of the scriptures and therefore would be less easily deluded by Satan) introduced the principle that education is a local responsibility. As the nation grew, states and territories required that communities provide for schools because education was seen as necessary for individual happiness and an educated population as necessary for democratic government. These early laws recognized both the public's need for education and the public's role in schools' existence.

Yet, the American public school has a paradoxical relationship with its public over issues of control. The first tension lies between local lay control and state or federal governmental control:

. . . while local school boards as the governing bodies of school districts are agents of the state responsible for local education, they are not free to exercise unfettered discretion on behalf of their local constituencies; they must act within the parameters established by law. (Russo, 1992, p. 3)

Thus, local lay boards are challenged to represent the interests of the local community as well as carry out the mandates of the larger society as expressed through state and federal legislation.

The second tension lies between lay control and professional control. Local lay boards were established for governance and oversight. As local education increased in size and complexity, lay leadership delegated much of its authority over daily operations of the schools to professional leadership, while officially retaining legal authority and policymaking. Yet, professional educators complain of micromanagement by lay leadership; boards have been called "collective management committees" instead of policymaking bodies (Twentieth Century Fund, 1992, p. 2). To add to the confusion, the courts have eroded local and lay authority as a result of rampant litigation, and through collective bargaining, boards have negotiated away their management prerogative.

The third tension lies in the discussion of whether community leaders should control decisions and policy or merely participate in decision making. Under the guise of devolution, parental involvement is institutionalized through partnerships and site councils. In some localities, these councils have assumed control of site budgets and made deep changes in school operations; in most, the councils have no control over site budgets, and thus their participation is more one of influence.

STATE VERSUS LOCAL CONTROL

The first schools in America were administered through town meetings, then town selectmen, then ward committees. As communities expanded and the task of governing them grew, separate school governing bodies were created that were independent of other local government entities. The Tenth Amendment to the Constitution, however, reserved for the states "all powers not delegated to the United States by the Constitution, nor prohibited by it to the states." Since the Constitution does not mention education, it falls under state control. While each state differs in the details, the local school board is a political subdivision of the state, empowered to administer the public school district. Whatever the origins of local lay/public leadership, "the local school board and the district in its charge are creatures of the state; they may be created or abolished by the will of the legislature" (Russo, 1992,

p. 70). Although elected or appointed locally, members of a school board are state officials, and they have no authority as individuals.

Yet because they are elected or appointed locally, residents of the district expect that board members will be responsive to their interests and needs. Confusion is exacerbated by the presence in most states of a state board that determines, along with its legislature and executive officers, what is in the best educational interests of the people of the state (Russo, 1992). The delegated powers of these boards are usually coextensive with the powers delegated to the local boards and cover those activities that are best practiced consistently across all districts throughout a state. The one exception to this division of powers is Hawaii, where the state board runs one system throughout the islands.

The move away from local decision making accelerated during the 1950s and through the 1970s as civil rights suits were successfully pursued in federal courts to correct the inequities that had resulted from local control (Levin, 1987). Litigation was followed by state and federal legislation that had the effect of making specific court decisions universal. Accordingly, decisions about the nature and distribution of educational services began to be made by national and state guidelines and mandates concerning pupil assignment and discipline, teacher employment, and curriculum.

Sarason (1994) links the opening challenge to the hegemony of local actors over education to the 1954 U.S. Supreme Court decision in *Brown v. Board of Education*. He argues that, in addition to ending the dual school system based on race, the decision signaled the existence of an external force influencing and monitoring educational decision making. The external force in this case was the Supreme Court's new interpretation of the 14th Amendment.

Another significant blow to the oligarchy of the educating profession was the 1975 Education for Handicapped Children Act. The act required all schools to eliminate the practice of automatically segregating children with disabilities from other children. Further, it delineated significant rights of parents to be involved in their children's program placement and also extended to them the right to appeal a school system's decision (Sarason, 1994).

External influence in the 1970s was expanded further with respect to the allocation of resources, once again through litigation followed by legislation (Berne & Stiefel, 1983; Guthrie, Garms, & Pierce, 1988, chap. 8). States increased their participation in financing school operations, school buildings and transportation. The federal role in school finance became a significant factor for the first time, coming in the form of categorical aid grants. State education departments and the U.S. Department of Education grew in size and influence, placing additional limits on the discretion of local school authorities. A perceived decline in student achievement, especially in urban centers, preceded a decline in the credibility of the teaching profession due to the profession's inability to address the challenge.

PROFESSIONAL VERSUS LAY LEADERSHIP

The early lay leadership of school committees set policy and managed the single school in its purview. As cities and towns grew and enrollments increased, communities contained more than one school and the district structure developed. The task of managing and supervising the day-to-day operations of the district became overwhelming for the laypeople serving on boards. Eventually, lay boards created a professional position, the superintendent of schools, at first to supervise instruction and evaluate the schools, later to assume more and more of the management functions of the district. In theory, the board makes policy and the superintendent implements it, but in practice the roles and responsibilities are not clearly delineated. Expectations and authority lines are blurred, and conflict often arises between professional and lay leadership (Guthrie & Kirst, 1988).

Paralleling this development, state boards of education appointed state superintendents to manage state departments of education. These departments are the professional arm of the state lay leadership, and they are charged with carrying out state policies. States became more involved by enacting compulsory attendance laws, setting certain basic standards for teacher certification, consolidating rural schools, and providing increasing amounts of financial aid. Tyack (1974) reported the impact on direct lay control of schools in rural and urban communities this way:

This movement to take control of the rural common school away from the local community and to turn it over to the professionals was part of a more general organizational revolution in American education in which laymen lost much of their direct control over the schools. In the cities schoolmen pioneered new bureaucratic patterns of educational organization. They sought to "free education from politics. . . ." (p. 25)

With the growing sophistication of the teaching profession, especially its administrators, professional control and bureaucratization grew substantially during the first half of the 20th century (Callahan, 1962; Tyack, 1993). Parents and community members, the laypeople, became more and more disconnected from the school and as a consequence exercised less and less control.

School reform and restructuring efforts of the past several decades have aimed to bring decision making and management back closer to the school site. Strengthening bonds between schools and neighborhoods is currently high on the American national agenda of school reform. In enacting the 1994 *Goals 2000: Educate America Act*, Congress declared the importance of building closer relationships with parents; the seventh goal states: "Every school will promote partnerships that will increase parental involvement and participation in promoting the social, emotional, and academic growth of children" (National Goals Panel, 1997, p. xvii). Objectives within this goal include: engaging parents and families in partnerships that support the academic work of children at home; shared decision making at school, enabling parents and families to ensure that schools are adequately supported; and holding schools and teachers to high standards of accountability.

Late 20th century reforms enhanced layperson control directly by mandating governing and advisory boards for some schools (e.g., site improvement councils, self-study committees for accreditation) and indirectly by increasing parents' options among schooling alternatives for their children (e.g., vouchers, charter schools). Sarason (1994) invokes the *political principle* in justifying a broadening of participation in education decision making: "When you are going to be affected, directly or indirectly, by a decision, you should stand in *some* relationship to the decision making process" (p. 7). Coons and Sugarman (1978) base their arguments for a broadened participation by laypeople, especially parents, on the philosophical *principle of subsidiarity*. This principle holds that responsibility for dependent individuals is better placed with the smaller and more intimate community to which the individual belongs, rather than a larger and more anonymous one:

A small community is more likely to listen to and respect constituent voices, to know individual interests, and to be motivated to serve them—particularly when it is so structured that all members are affected by its decisions about any member. Subsidiarity represents the impulse to preserve individualistic values within a collective. (p. 50)

Community control is recast as community participation in school site decision making through advisory bodies. Reformers expect that the renewal of lay participation and leadership in decision making will transform the nature of schools. Brown (1998) found that extensive use of laypeople ultimately affects the climate and organization of the school itself. Being dependent directly on parental and community contributions causes a school to become a collectivity with a shared ethos, informal and enduring social relationships, and diffuse roles. In the words of Coleman and Hoffer (1987, p. 3), such a school is "an extension of the family, reinforcing the family's values. . . . The school is, in this orientation, an efficient means for transmitting the culture of the community from the older generation to the younger."

Brown (1998) characterizes the typical public school in bureaucratic terms. There is:

a distinct division of adult labour, governance by rules, and affectively neutral treatment of students. The bureaucratic school has a relatively clear hierarchy of control, and boundaries that are not difficult to define. . . . If schools are seen largely as bureaucracies, then there is a clear separation between the school and its environment and particularly between the school and the families of those children who attend it. (p. 92)

Public schools have been organized as state agents to be standardized, to be impartial, and to have special knowledge to impart to students. As social instruments, they serve the interests of the larger society and not necessarily those of the parent—or the learner. When parents and other lay participants are kept at a distance, teachers and parents/volunteers have the potential to become natural adversaries as a consequence of their divergent interests regarding the child (Lortie, 1975; Waller, 1932).

Coleman (1990) notes that the shift from the more family-based, connected institutions he has labeled *primordial* toward *constructed* organizations has led to a change in incentives as well:

primordial social organization [generates] the incentive structure that brings into being actions on behalf of another, norms, trustworthiness, and other components of social capital. The constructed social organization purposively created by governments and other modern corporate actors undermines that existing incentive structure . . . and does not generate a comparable replacement. (pp. 653-4)

Coleman goes on to suggest that the interests of children may be served better by primordial institutions than by modern corporate actors because of the more personal and caring social structure of those institutions. A consequence of the dominance of schools by modern corporate actors has been the depletion of social capital for children—the collective knowledge, values, skills, and supporting relationships of a symbiotic community.

The bifurcation of personal versus collective social space has been characterized as *Gemeinschaft* and *Gesellschaft* (Tonnies, 1940); as primary and secondary groups (Litwak and Szelenyi, 1969); and as primordial institutions and corporate actors (Coleman, 1990). The personal is characterized by simple relationships between individuals within families and friendships. Actions are governed by love, understanding, and custom. The relationships between individuals are self-sustaining and become building blocks in forming a natural social environment of community (Brown, 1998). The collective involves calculated relationships in which all things, including people, are seen as means to ends; thus contracts are based on results alone. Collective, or constructed, institutions are wholly instrumental and do not require binary personal obligations and expectations as mechanisms for social success. The traditional public school falls into this category.

However, when a public school makes extensive use of lay volunteers, it moves somewhere between the extremes of a primordial institution and a constructed one (Brown, 1998). In contrast to the specialization of labor associated with schools as bureaucracies, the consolidation or overlap of spheres connects the interests of the family with those of the larger society. Public schools become bridging institutions. However, token membership on a school's community advisory committee is insufficient, because community members must be integrated fully into the school organization and culture if a fundamental change is to occur.

The extreme tension between the two social realms, and their outright incompatibility, inhibits democratic interaction. Over the past 500 years, corporate actors have gradually gained near supremacy over primordial institutions (Brown, 1998). According to Hewitt (1989, p. 119), ". . . modern society has disrupted, transformed, and in many cases simply destroyed the organic communities of the past, but it has not eliminated those human tendencies that were satisfied within those communities." Lay leadership in schooling can be seen as an effort to bridge the personal and the collective and to recognize value in the means as well as the ends.

The Realities of Lay Leadership

Lay leadership, offered as an antidote for the ills of bureaucratic control, is still merely an ideal. The ambiguity in the roles of lay leader groups, whether they be legally elected or appointed boards or volunteer advisory councils, is crippling. The groups' processes tend to be reactive rather than proactive. Lay members are not broadly representative of the school's community; often, individuals speak for special interests. Levels of participant commitment vary, and community members' lack of time to devote to the community's schools interferes with meaningful involvement. Perhaps most troubling is the inability of the board to fuse into a body with a unified vision. Still, legal as well as volunteer structures exist and function with defined responsibilities.

AMBIGUITY OF PURPOSE

While the purpose of the local school board is to administer the public district, the role of the board in accomplishing this is inherently ambiguous. Most sources agree that boards exist to hire the superintendent and to make policy, but few agree on what policies are to be made, and how (Wirt & Kirst, 1983). Boards use executive power when they enter into personnel or service contracts; they use legislative authority when they approve rules and regulations necessary to carry out the policies they have adopted; they function in a quasi-judicial manner when they hear appeals resulting from differing interpretations of implemented policies (Russo, 1992).

The ambiguity in roles is complicated by the relationship between local power and state control. From the state's point of view, the local board exists primarily to translate state and federal mandates into local policy. School boards spend more of their time on application of state regulation to local issues than on policy initiation. At the same time, however, local board members consider their allegiance to be to their constituencies (Campbell, Cunningham, Nystrand, & Usdan, 1985); thus, they may lack the will and capacity to support federal and state directives (Odden & Marsh, 1990).

Critics of centralized and bureaucratic control believe that "America has lost its way in education because America has disenfranchised individual local schools" (Guthrie, 1997, p. 34). The extant policy and governance infrastructure that places control outside the school is in direct conflict with devolution moves; local schools may be held accountable for outcomes, but they have no real authority for policymaking or implementing any local decisions. "A school-based governance system and state-formulated accountability measures are inherently contradictory" (Snauwaert, 1993, p. 98). "Talking about holding schools accountable is useless until schools have the political and lay leadership structures to be accountable" (John MacDonald, personal communication, 2001).

LACK OF SHARED VISION

Confusion about the role of local governance may be either the cause or the result of its lack of a shared vision. Few school boards have articulated what precisely they believe is in the best interest of the community's children, or how to provide access to favorable learning conditions for all the children in the community. To lead and govern schools, school boards need to understand the purposes of schools and what needs to be done to enable schools to fulfill these purposes. Lay advisory councils may also suffer from a similar lack of vision and clarity of values (Shibles, Rallis, & Deck, 2001).

Board or council members' views on the purposes of schooling are fundamentally shaped by their values and beliefs about human beings and learning. For example, individuals who see a person as having a defined place in the larger society will see schooling as a means to maintain that society and to teach people how to fill their role. Alternatively, those who see the individual as a unique contributor to a yet undefined society will see schooling as a means to develop the individual and her unique contributions (see Astuto et al., 1994 for a complete discussion of assumptions about the purposes of schooling). Whatever lay leaders see as the purpose of schooling drives decisions and policies on schooling. If group members do not share values and beliefs, they are unlikely to come together on these decisions and policies.

In reality, however, boards (or councils) seldom have or take the time to thrash out and clarify their beliefs and values regarding the purpose of schooling. Most have endorsed district mission statements, but few have agreed on and articulated what the embedded principles mean and look like in practice. Without this shared vision about purpose to drive board policies and actions, boards cannot forge a cohesive plan for educating all their children, nor can they make decisions about integrating federal or state mandates and policies into local policies (see, for example, Danzberger, Kirst, & Usdan, 1992). Without a shared vision, they cannot communicate their purposes, explain their actions to the community at large, and thus garner community support.

REACTIVE STANCE

Boards are legally empowered only as an organizational unit. But without clarified values, members cannot coalesce around shared purpose and vision, so they act individually. Usually elected or appointed to represent a specified jurisdiction, board members recognize and are influenced by their respective constituencies. Moreover, an individual

may run on a special interest platform and feel obligated to that con-
stituency. Hence, board decision making follows a pluralistic model
more often than the legally effective unitary model that sees the members as trustees of public welfare (Wirt & Kirst, 1982). When members act individually, they cannot operate proactively with purpose and
vision—they cannot demonstrate leadership.

Instead, they are reactive, considering issues on an ad hoc basis,
rather than in the context of defined goals and objectives, and without
in-depth analysis (Washington State House of Representatives, 1990).
School boards do not really determine their own agendas—things get
brought to them (Rallis, 1993). With no consistent focus, boards are
driven by the interests of particular constituencies of individual board
members or limited by externally established parameters.

Boards are especially sensitive to uninformed criticisms from their
publics (Leuker, 1992). Special interest groups and collective bargaining
units dominate and prevent all voices from being heard (Danzberger,
1992). These petitioners have an economic stake in decisions or "an
ideology that they are trying to have enshrined in policy" (Rosenthal,
1998, p. 201). In fact, special interests, whether they are collective bargaining units such as teachers' unions, grassroots community organizations, political action committees (PACs), or groups represented by
official lobbyists, are so intertwined in public policymaking that the line
between where one leaves off and the other begins is difficult to define.

NOT REPRESENTATIVE OF THE BROADER COMMUNITY

Lay leadership groups tend not to represent the entire breadth of
the community. The electoral process erroneously assumes a unitary
community voice in a pluralistic society. Yet, meta-analyses of significant studies on community involvement in school policy formulation
reveal that board opinions and actions reflect elite and professional values more often than the general public's opinion. Zerchykov (1984)
discovered that boards are unlikely to express, much less seek out, their
constituents' preferences in policy decisions. Because school boards are
an official arm of the government, they tend to represent those who
already hold power, and thus they serve to maintain the status quo.

Furthermore, school board elections traditionally draw a low voter
turnout (7-15% of registered voters). The Institute of Educational
Leadership (1986) study of school boards revealed massive public ignorance about the actual role and activities of boards. School board tenure
is brief, and many of those who run do so with a specific political
agenda—an ax to grind (IEL, 1986). Other structures, such as school site

councils and charter schools, arise as alternatives, but they too consist of special interests; members seldom have altruistic or unselfish motives.

MEETINGS AS RITUAL

Boards have been characterized as a body of independent members with little or no socialization who come together for the purpose of conducting board business (Rallis, 1993). Sharing no mutually established set of values and beliefs, they engage in a ritual activity of holding meetings during which they assimilate information, make motions, and vote upon them. The only meaning shared across the board may lie in the importance of the appearance. Board meetings become rituals, that is, familiar, systematic, and programmed routines where immediate concerns are addressed and special concerns are brought for consideration. Members do not appear to define their work; rather the work is defined for them through the ritual of the meeting. The ritual makes sense to all participants because it is familiar and predictable, with an agenda constructed by the superintendent; while each issue is itself unique, all fall into expected categories, for example, discipline, building concerns, personnel.

Members perceive themselves as community helpers (Leuker, 1992) more than as politicians; thus, a component of the ritual is listening and responding to community needs as expressed at the meeting. The ritual allows the board to take on symbolic importance—it is a place where folks can come with complaints and concerns; they believe they will be heard and their issues will be addressed because the board, composed of elected or appointed laypeople like themselves, belongs to them. Because the board meets, people are comforted and believe their voice will be heard. The governance structure of schools, then, is designed to support a "logic of confidence" between the public schools and their constituents (see Elmore, 2000). Decision making is actually "about the symbolism of mobilizing and consolidating political constituencies" (p. 8).

Despite limitations on their legal authority and practical ability to function effectively as a voice or trustee of the community welfare concerning its schools, local lay leadership can and often does have tremendous influence on the interpretation of policy and the operation of the district. Lay leadership's authority may primarily be its informal power, that is, its capacity to shape decisions by informal means or influence. As schools are often confronted with issues that spark local controversy and divide community groups, an effective board or advisory council can become a forum for democratic deliberation. Such deliberation brings out diverse opinions and gives them voice. Through its informal processes and formal rituals, the board can shape consensus that brings together disparate groups in a divided community. Board members become "stewards of the community conversation about schools" (Ramsay, 2000, p. 52). This democratic, albeit symbolic, authority is an important positioning for lay leadership of the 21st century.

Repositioning Lay Leadership in a Democratic Community

Governance is about control (Murphy, 2000), and school governance, like most forms of governance, operates as a complex system—nonlinear, contextual, interactive, emergent, and unpredictable (see Wheatley, 1994). Thus, the landscape of educational control is reshaping (Murphy, 2000). The Kettering Foundation's study *Is There a Public for Public Schools* (Mathews, 1996) warns that the public schools are becoming dangerously disconnected from the public, to the point where the public school system as we have known it may not survive.

What do site-based management programs, vouchers, charter schools, home schools, private schools, and state takeovers of "bankrupt" systems have in common? They all have to do with control of education. There are evidently a great many people who don't believe that the public schools are responsive to their concerns. So they are creating their own schools, trying to take back the schools, or putting someone in charge who will make schools respond to their priorities. (p. 741)

Restoring legitimacy to the public school system will require school leaders to see the public in a new light and to take advantage of lay leadership in ways that will reconnect the public with its schools. First recognizing that schools are political entities and that they naturally engage with and alter power relations is crucial (Oakes, 1995).

Schools are grounded in history and culture. The challenge lies in ensuring that decisions in this political world are made democratically, not merely to serve those in power already. Our view of democracy celebrates significant diversity of opinion as to what is considered good (Strike, 1999). At the same time we recognize the need for building a society of "people held together because they are working along common lines, in a common spirit, with reference to common aims" (Dewey, 1990, p. 14). People come together by sharing what Strike calls *constitutive values*, that is, values that forge common projects, values that are pursued cooperatively.

We believe, as did Dewey, that constitutive values and common purpose are achieved through "interchange of thought" (p. 14), and that "communication is the way in which [people] come to possess things in common" (Dewey, 1916, p. 5). We construe such interchange or communication as *democratic deliberation*. Dewey (1916) and Habermas (1996) indicate that deliberative discussion in the context of a democratic society is an ideal. The dialogue and argument of democratic deliberation yields fair decision making and justifies public authority (Ackermann, 1980).

Democracy is an organic, messy business. Governance structures like school boards endure because they tolerate ambiguity and multiple perspectives. Conflict is inherent in the interaction of groups within these structures. Democracy was built on conflict, so its practice should celebrate ambiguity and individual differences. In fact, the goals of democratic communities are contradictory and nonrational: democracy encourages expression of individual differences at the same time it aims to bind groups together into a larger whole; it fosters both independence and interdependence; it supports both the individual and the social organism (Barth, 1990; Lieberman, Falk, & Alexander, 1995; Starratt, 1997). People in democratic communities believe they can "influence members of the group and are themselves influenced by others" (Hobbs et al., 1984, p. 41).

These contradictions of democracy both demand and arise from the deliberative process that brings together divergent views, facilitates inquiry, and seeks resolution. Democratic deliberations serve as a forum both for sharpening people's understanding of human needs and for resolving conflicts between needs (Mark, Henry, & Julnes, 2000). But simple majoritarianism will not suffice (Cohen, 1997). Minorities' rights must be protected; minorities must be guaranteed both access and participation (Mark, Henry & Julnes). Values emerge through democratic deliberation—through critical analysis and reflection.

A robust democracy requires *inclusion, dialogue*, and *deliberation* (House & Howe, 1999). *Inclusion* ensures that all relevant groups have voice and that power imbalances are neutralized. Inclusion ensures that different points of view (House & Howe, p. 21) are heard and considered. *Dialogue* is the process of discovering and articulating real interests as opposed to perceived interests; participants introduce information, determining and weighing interests of individuals and groups. Individuals interpret each other's actions, so their responses are less a reaction to the action than an interpretation of the other's actions (Blumer, 1969). With this considered, they need safe and open opportunities to test their interpretations before they act. Inclusive dialogue is essential to this testing.

Deliberation is a cognitive process grounded in reason and evidence. "Collective deliberation requires a reciprocity of consciousness among participants and a rough equality of power if participants are to reach a state in which they deliberate effectively about their collective ends" (House & Howe, 1999, p. 102). Views and preferences are subjected to critique and rational analysis. Democratic structures usually employ some framework to facilitate the deliberative process.

The ritual of school board meetings (also lay advisory council meetings) offers one such framework for facilitating deliberation in a democratic community. It is not enough "that policy makers . . . decide what the views and preferences of participants are without conducting sufficient dialogue with those participants" (House & Howe, 1999, p. 12). The symbolic authority of the meetings allows the lay leadership groups to accomplish what professional leadership cannot. Free from the expectation that they be experts, they can explore the deep-seated values and beliefs of the community about their children and their children's learning; encourage minority views and consider alternative perspectives; take risks and make mistakes; and finally, build consensus. Meetings can be a forum that provides a ground for open and inclusive interpretation of political actions. Subjective opinions (those seen only through an individual perspective) transform into objective phenomena, that is, opinions of the public domain, shared across multiple perspectives (see Scriven, 1991, 1972 for discussions of subjective/objective phenomena).

When lay leadership group meetings—and school board meetings, in particular—function as opportunities for democratic deliberation, principles of "democratic localism" (Katz, 1971, p. 305) prevail. Such principles recognize the contextuality of political action and policy making. What makes sense in one location may look different elsewhere. Structures vary across communities. Rules made by those in power in one place are not likely to work elsewhere. External bureaucrats who generate rules and standards out of context have little touch with the reality of life in specific communities; their inventions mean little to parents and practitioners. The multiple and diverse value-bases across communities would mean that none could abide by the common rules or meet generalized standards. Specific rules and standards for structures and operations of lay leadership emerge locally.

Dangers do exist, however, in democracy without inclusion, dialogue and deliberation (Rosenthal, 1998). Laws, regulations, and procedures regarding school boards (and advisory boards) must support conditions for these three activities. First, the groups must be inclusive and practice equality. If elected boards do not draw from underrepresented constituencies, then the political infrastructure must be held accountable and must act. For example, in large urban centers, the mayor may need to appoint the board, or at least members to represent unempowered and underrepresented constituencies. Alternatively, participation of these groups could be encouraged by public funding for first-time candidates. Authentic inclusion also requires that all voices be heard. All board members need the knowledge and self-confidence to participate equally in policy discussions—hence the need for dialogue and deliberation. Boards also need opportunity to hear voices from the greater community as well—hence the need for public engagement.

Effective dialogue and deliberation require a certain framework in meetings to sort through the multiple and often conflicting and contentious views and practices. This framework has two components—law and ritual. While we argue that boards need legitimate local authority, this authority is necessarily limited by laws that establish clear and absolute principles for what a board may or may not do. Massachusetts law, for example, limits board activity to hiring a chief executive officer for the district and shaping policies to guide the CEO's actions; boards no longer have the power to make final decisions on personnel, and they may set only the bottom line on budgets. Such laws are essential because their boundaries promote board dialogue and deliberation about the meaningful and substantive policy issues that should be their focus.

The ritual of meetings serves as a framework to focus the board on policy decisions filtered through their shared beliefs about the purposes of schooling and the articulated mission. The framework relies on dialogue that addresses issues by revisiting goals and identifying criteria to judge information and goal attainment. Without shared purposes and mission, board members cannot agree on criteria for reasoned decision making. Criteria focus the next step, deliberation of the policy question; they provide a basis for analysis, the reasons for decisions, and development of a pattern of deliberation among board members and between the board and the superintendent and other constituents.

Deliberation—that is, collecting data, deciding what alternatives to consider, seeking stakeholder voices, determining what factors are relevant, assessing the interrelationships among the factors, and interpreting results to form policy—requires judgment. Judgment uses a clear and shared understanding of purpose as a foundation for criteria.

The dialogue explores various aspects of these questions, and the deliberation applies the criteria to evidence. The process is interactive and iterative. Multiple perspectives are voiced and re-voiced, altering slightly each time. Gradually, though not in a rational, linear fashion, a shared understanding emerges. The group reaches consensus.

Another important condition, then, is an environment in which board members can explore and clarify their purposes. A genuinely inclusive board is hardly structured to function as a cohesive unit. Board members need time and often facilitation to build trust and mutual respect, to become more than a mere collection of individuals. Some boards choose to find time and space for dialogue beyond regularly scheduled meetings, away from the constant press of controversy, away from narrow agendas, and away from political posturing (see McAdams, 2000 and Rallis & Deck, 1998, for illustrative examples). These sessions may be cast as training or retreats so the board deals not with policy or with making decisions but with the specific goal of nurturing internal relationships away from the media and interest-driven constituencies. The dialogue of these meetings articulates values and beliefs and builds shared purpose. From this more private dialogue, the board returns to the public eye and draws on shared criteria to deliberate on the information and issues confronting them.

Effective lay leadership requires the interlocking of purpose and policy, plus the ability to disseminate decisions in a clearly understandable form to constituents. Boards that have clearly articulated the criteria that guide their policy making are able to communicate their policies effectively. Without criteria, decisions seem mysterious, emerging from intuition or unknown factors rather than reason. Because board power is grounded in the symbolic, the ritual of regular meetings expresses purpose and criteria that the public can see and understand and thus enhances the board's credibility.

Challenges for Professional Leadership

Superintendents, the professional leaders who deal directly with boards of education (and at another level, principals who interact with site councils), operate at the forefront of this ritual and serve as links between deliberation and practice. To be most effective, they convert legitimate board-determined policy decisions into operational decisions grounded in professional knowledge and judgment. Superintendents ask: Where does the line fall between board decision making and administrative leadership? How can I ensure the board's support for my decisions on the implementation of its policies?

Boards have the power to hire and fire superintendents (and in some cases, site councils hire principals), so superintendents and principals work for their boards. But because the superintendent's (and principal's) job is to be the expert on the business of schooling and because they have access to information that board members do not, they must also guide their boards. The challenge lies in this paradox: the superintendent (and principal) is both leader and follower.

As professional school leaders, superintendents and principals set the tone that establishes and ensures democratic deliberation. Effective professional leaders encourage the board to spend time on clarification of values and beliefs, on articulating purpose, and on strategic planning—and they constantly remind board members of these shared values, beliefs, purposes, and plans. They provide board members access to multiple sources of information on various and relevant issues. They continuously feed their boards data about teaching and learning in the schools.

While superintendents (or principals) may not officially lead board meetings, they guide and influence by engaging fully in the meetings. They develop agendas and support dialogue by listening and questioning. They monitor inclusion of all community voices, including those often silenced or seldom heard. They foster deliberation by supplying data, suggesting alternatives, and reiterating criteria. They work with their board, expressing and upholding their shared purpose.

Effective superintendents and principals also recognize the board's legitimate authority. The product of their boards' regular deliberation is policy. As professional executives, they implement or enforce that policy. If they do not view the policy as congruent with the agreed-upon beliefs and purposes and cannot, or choose not to, implement or enforce it, both sides must consider the consequences. Both must revisit their shared understandings to see if these still hold and if their official relationship should continue.

At the same time, effective superintendents and principals recognize that the board's legitimate authority has limitations. Boards hire their superintendents to run the district and its schools according to established policy; in turn, boards should support their leadership with budgets and freedom for superintendents to do so. The challenge for professional leadership lies in enforcing these limits without offending board members who overstep the bounds, either inadvertently or intentionally. For example, boards are not meant to micromanage, but members often interfere with day-to-day operations when they receive calls from their constituencies about specific activities or personnel. As a result, the professional leader's job also involves the delicate balancing of board members' enthusiasm with role definition.

Conclusion

When states, territories, and counties established schools and school districts, control was vested in the laity through local boards of education. Lay control was meant to represent the interests of the community and to carry out the mandates of the larger society expressed through state and federal governments. The shape and scope of that control has altered over time, and tensions have arisen between the educating profession and the laity and between authorities in both camps at the local, state and national levels. Even definitions of community participation have been a bone of contention. Confusion and debate over the role of lay leadership dominated the final decades of the 20th century. Some suggest that lay leadership through boards of education be eliminated, while others call for stringent legislative limitations on board power. Most agree that the current governance structure impedes the exercise of both lay and professional leadership.

Still, local boards of education and lay advisory groups and volunteers are not going to disappear. They serve important symbolic and policymaking roles, and they can support authentic democratic deliberation. Since their inception, lay boards have tolerated ambiguity and multiple perspectives in the formulation of local policy. Their structure allows risk taking and excuses mistakes, since few decisions are irrevocable and members come and go with elections. Their localism honors the contextuality of political decisions and action, and membership does not require expertise, so anyone can participate. They meet regularly and usually in public, providing time and place for deliberation. Moreover, they are credible because the public can *see* and *hear* the deliberation and find comfort and safety in the bounded ritual. Remaining at the forefront is the challenge of clarifying the relationship between lay and professional leadership so that each may do its job well.

References

Ackermann, B. (1980). *Social justice in the liberal state.* New Haven: Yale University Press.

Astuto, T. A., Clark, D. L., Read, A., McGree, K., & Pelton Fernandez, L. d. (1994). *Roots of reform.* Bloomington, IN: Phi Delta Kappa Educational Foundation.

Barth, R. S. (1990). *Improving schools from within: Teachers, parents, and principals can make the difference.* San Francisco: Jossey-Bass.

Berne, R., & Stiefel, L. (1983). Changes in school finance equity: A national perspective. *Journal of Education Finance, 8,* 419-435.

Blumer, H. (1969). *Symbolic interaction.* Englewood Cliffs, NJ: Houghton Mifflin, pp. 78-89.

Brown, D. J. (1998). *Schools with heart: Voluntarism and public education.* Boulder, CO: Westview Press.

Callahan, R. E. (1962). *Education and the cult of efficiency: A study of the social forces that have shaped the administration of the public schools.* Chicago: University of Chicago Press.

Campbell, R. F., Cunningham, V. L., Nystrand, R. O., & Usdan, M. D. (1985). *The organization and control of American schools.* Columbus, OH: Charles E. Merrill.

Cohen, J. (1997). Deliberation and democratic legitimacy. In J. Bohman & W. Rehg (Eds.), *Deliberative democracy: Essays on reason and politics* (pp. 67-92). Cambridge, MA: MIT Press.

Coleman, J. S. (1990). *Foundations of social theory.* Cambridge, MA: Belknap Press of Harvard University Press.

Coleman, J. S., & Hoffer, T. (1987). *Public and private high schools: The impact of communities.* New York: Basic Books.

Coons, J. E., & Sugarman, S. D. (1978). *Education by choice: The case for family control.* Berkeley, CA: University of California Press.

Danzberger, J. (1992). School boards: A troubled institution. In The Twentieth Century Fund/Danforth Foundation, *Facing the challenge: The report of The Twentieth Century Fund Task Force on School Governance* (pp. 19-129). New York: The Fund.

Danzberger, J., Kirst, M., & Usdan, M. (1992). *Governing public schools: New times, new requirements.* Washington, DC: Institute for Educational Leadership.

Dewey, J. (1916). *Democracy and education.* New York: Macmillan.

Dewey, J. (1990). *The school and society.* Chicago: University of Chicago Press.

Elmore, R. F. (2000). *Building a new structure for school leadership.* The Albert Shanker Institute, winter.

Guthrie, J. W. (1997, October). The paradox of educational power: How modern reform proposals miss the point. *Education Week, 17*(7), 34.

Guthrie, J. W., Garms, W. I., & Pierce, L. C. (1988). *School finance and education policy: Enhancing educational efficiency, equality, and choice.* Englewood Cliffs, NJ: Prentice Hall.

Guthrie, J. W., & Kirst, M. W. (1988, March). *Conditions of education in California, 1988.* Policy Paper # 88-3-2. Berkeley, CA: Policy Analysis for California Education.

Habermas, J. (1996). Three normative models of democracy. In S. Benhabib (Ed.), *Democracy and difference: Contesting the boundaries of the political* (pp. 21-30). Princeton, NJ: Princeton University Press.

Hewitt, J. P. (1989). *Dilemmas of the American self.* Philadelphia: Temple University Press.

Hobbs, N., Dokecki, P. R., Hoover-Dempsey, K. V., Moroney, R. M., Shayne, M. W., & Weeks, K. H. (1984). *Strengthening families.* San Francisco: Jossey-Bass.

House, E. R., & Howe, K. R. (1999). *Values in evaluation and social research.* Thousand Oaks, CA: Sage.

Institute for Educational Leadership. (1986). *School boards: Strengthening grass roots leadership.* Washington, DC: Author.

Katz, M. B. (1971, Summer). From voluntarism to bureaucracy in American education. *Sociology of Education, 44* (3), 297-332.

Lieberman, A., Falk, B., & Alexander, L. (1995). A culture in the making: Leadership in learner-centered schools. In J. Oakes & K. H. Quartz (Eds.), *Creating new educational communities: Ninety-fourth yearbook of the National Society for the Study of Education* (pp. 108-129). Chicago: National Society for the Study of Education.

Leuker, G. (1992). *Roles and realities of the local school board member.* Unpublished doctoral dissertation, Peabody College of Vanderbilt University, Nashville, TN.

Levin, B. (1987). The courts as educational policy-makers in the USA. In W. L. Boyd & D. Smart (Eds.), *Educational policy in Australia and America: Comparative perspectives* (pp. 100-128). New York: The Falmer Press.

Litwak, E., & Szelenyi, I. (1969). Primary group structures and their functions: Kin, neighbors and friends. *American Sociological Review, 34,* 465-81.

Lortie, D. C. (1975). *School teacher: A sociological study.* Chicago: University of Chicago Press.

McAdams, D. R. (2000). *Fighting to save our urban schools . . . and winning! Lessons from Houston.* New York: Teachers College Press.

Mark, M. M., Henry, G. T., & Julnes, G. (2000). *Evaluation: An integrated framework for understanding, guiding, and improving policies and programs.* San Francisco: Jossey-Bass.

Mathews, D. (1996). *Is there a public for public schools?* Dayton, OH: Kettering Foundation Press.

Mathews, D. (1997). The lack of a public for public schools. *Phi Delta Kappan, 78,* 740-43.

Murphy, J. (2000). Governing America's schools: The shifting playing field. *Teachers College Record, 102*(1), 57-84.

National Goals Panel. (1997). *The national education goals report: Building a nation of learners, 1997.* Washington, DC: U.S. Government Printing Office.

Oakes, J. (1995). Normative, technical, and political dimensions of creating new educational communities. In J. Oakes & K. H. Quartz (Eds.), *Creating new educational communities: Ninety-fourth yearbook of the National Society for the Study of Education* (pp. 1-15). Chicago: National Society for the Study of Education.

Odden, A., & Marsh, D. (1990). Local response to the 1980s state education reforms: New patterns of local and state interaction. In J. Murphy (Ed.), *The educational reform movement of the 1980s: Perspectives and cases.* (pp. 167-186). Berkeley, CA: McCutchan.

Rallis, S. F. (1993, April). *School boards and school restructuring: A contradiction in terms?* Paper presented at the annual meeting of the American Educational Research Association, Atlanta, GA.

Rallis, S. F., and Deck, L. L. (1998). *Get out of the sunshine—For a while.* Unpublished monograph for the Center for the Support of Professional Practice in Education, Vanderbilt University, Nashville, TN.

Ramsay, J. G. (2000, October 4). A culture of questions. Commentary. *Education Week, 20*(5), 52, 30.

Rosenthal, A. (1998). *The decline of representative democracy.* Washington, DC: Congressional Quarterly Press.

Russo, J. C. (1992). The legal status of school boards in the intergovernmental system. In P. F. First & H. J. Walberg (Eds.), *School boards: Changing local control,* pp. 3-20. Berkeley, CA: McCutchan.

Sarason, S. B. (1994). *Parental involvement and the political principle: Why the existing governance structure of schools should be abolished.* San Francisco: Jossey-Bass.

Scriven, M. (1991). *Evaluation thesaurus* (4th ed.). Thousand Oaks, CA: Sage.

Scriven, M. (1972). Objectivity and subjectivity in educational research. In L. G. Thomas (Ed.), *Philosophical redirection of educational research: The seventy-first yearbook of the National Society for the Study of Education* (pp. 94-142). Chicago: National Society for the Study of Education.

Shibles, M. R., Rallis, S. F., & Deck, L. L. (2001). A new political balance between the superintendent and board: Clarifying purpose and generating knowledge. In C. Brunner & L. G. Bjork (Eds.), *Advances in research and theories of school management and education policy: The new superintendency* (Vol. 6). Oxford: Elsevier Press.

Snauwaert, D. T. (1993). *Democracy, education, and governance: A developmental conception.* Albany, NY: SUNY Press.

Starratt, R. J. (1997). *Administering meaning, administering community, administering excellence: The new fundamentals of educational administration.* New York: Merrill.

Strike, K. A. (1999, February). Can schools be communities? The tension between shared values and inclusion. In G. Furman-Brown (Ed.), *School as community: Educational Administration Quarterly, 35*(1), 46-70.

Swanson, A. D., & King, R. A. (1997). *School finance: Its economics and politics* (2nd ed.). New York: Longman.

Tonnies, F. (1940). *Fundamental concepts of sociology.* New York: American Book Co.

Twentieth Century Fund. (1992). *Facing the challenge: The 20th Century Fund TaskForce on School Governance.* New York: Twentieth Century Fund Press.

Tyack, D. B. (1974). *The one best system: A history of American urban education.* Cambridge, MA: Harvard University Press.

Tyack, D. B. (1993). School governance in the United States: Historical puzzles and anomalies. In J. Hannaway & M. Carnoy (Eds.), *Decentralization and school improvement* (pp. 1-32). San Francisco: Jossey-Bass.

Waller, W. (1932). *The sociology of teaching.* New York: Wiley.

Washington State House of Representatives. (November, 1990). *Report on an evaluation of Seattle public schools.* Seattle: Author.

Weick, K. (1976). Educational organizations as loosely-coupled systems. *Administrative Science Quarterly, 21,* 1-16.

Wheatley, M. J. (1994). *Leadership and the new science.* San Francisco: Berrett-Koehler Publishers.

Wirt, F. M., & Kirst, M. W. (1982). *Schools in conflict.* Berkeley, CA: McCutchan.

Zerchykov, R. (1984). *School boards and the communities they represent: An inventory of the research.* Boston: Research for Responsive Education. ED 251 920.

Section Five
RECASTING THE DEVELOPMENT
OF SCHOOL LEADERS

CHAPTER 12

Preparing School Leaders for School Improvement,
Social Justice, and Community

DIANA POUNDER, ULRICH REITZUG, AND MICHELLE D. YOUNG

Previous chapters in this volume have discussed the complex challenges of educational leadership at the beginning of the 21st century. These multiple conditions affecting school leadership emphasize the need to prepare leaders whose knowledge, skills, and dispositions are focused on school improvement, social justice, and democratic and collaborative professional community (Murphy, 1999). These three concepts or goals—school improvement, social justice, and democratic and collaborative professional community—involve important interrelationships. For example, it could be argued that building a democratic and collaborative community and focusing attention on issues of social justice are critical processes required to improve schools. That is, community and social justice are means to an end—school improvement that supports educational excellence and equity for all children. Or, it could be argued that a collaborative community and social justice are worthy goals in and of themselves—independent of school improvement. It could also be argued that effective schools enhance social justice and democratic community.

Diana Pounder is Professor of Educational Leadership and Associate Dean of the College of Education, University of Utah. Ulrich C. Reitzug is Professor and Chair of the Department of Educational Leadership and Cultural Foundations at the University of North Carolina at Greensboro. Michelle D. Young is the Executive Director of the University Council for Educational Administration and a former educational leadership professor.

We take the position that social justice and community are not just means that serve the end of overall school improvement, but rather are both means and ends. We believe that increases in student achievement or other learning outcomes are not the only indicators of school improvement; enhanced community and greater social justice are also essential indicators. We believe that these three goals support and reinforce one another and form a strong focus for the preparation of educational leaders.

The organizing framework for this chapter is school improvement, democratic and collaborative community, and social justice and how educational leadership preparation programs can meet these collective challenges. Specifically, the authors discuss the needed content and instructional focus of preparation programs, as well as various preparation program design elements, such as program structure, field experiences, and faculty and students.

Content and Instructional Focus of Educational Leadership Programs

If we are to achieve our goal of educational excellence and equity for all children, the content focus of educational leadership programs must shift. In the following sections, the authors describe and discuss the needed content of educational leadership preparation programs focused on school improvement, social justice, and democratic and collaborative professional community.

PREPARING LEADERS FOR SCHOOL IMPROVEMENT

Although there are many different topics that could be addressed in preparing leaders for school improvement, we believe that there are five key relationships that shape school improvement. Each of these relationships is supported by the literature on school improvement but may run counter to prevailing modes of school leadership practice. Although it is impossible to review all or even a reasonable portion of the literature in each of these areas in this chapter, we will cite a significant work or two to steer our readers in the right direction. The five relationships that define school improvement and on which educational leadership preparation programs must focus are:

- the relationship among school improvement, instructional leadership, and administrative work;
- the relationship among school improvement, high-stakes testing, and authentic pedagogy;

- the relationship between school improvement and schools as centers of inquiry and renewal;
- the relationship between school improvement and the democratic purpose of schools; and
- the relationship between school improvement and social justice.

THE RELATIONSHIP AMONG SCHOOL IMPROVEMENT, INSTRUCTIONAL LEADERSHIP, AND ADMINISTRATIVE WORK

The literature on the role of principals has long advocated that the focus of principals' work be not merely on the management of schools, but rather on instructional leadership. Indeed, Beck and Murphy (1993) in their analysis of the metaphors that have pervaded the principalship literature cite "the principal as instructional leader" (p. 148) as the dominant metaphor of the 1980s. They note,

> In every decade some attention has been paid to the principal's impact on teaching and learning processes . . . A dominant assumption of the eighties, conveyed in the language of this period, is that the principal can and should become directly involved with the teaching/learning process. Most often, the metaphor used in discussions of this assumption is that of the principal as instructional leader. (p. 149)

However, there has long been a disparity between the role advocated for administrators as instructional leaders and the way in which administrators spend their time. Although the literature argues for instructional leadership, it is common knowledge that principals spend most of their time in management tasks. Indeed, researchers have found that the types of activities in which effective principals engage are not much different from the activities of ineffective principals (e.g., Krug, 1992).

Researchers have also discovered that what distinguishes effective principals from less effective principals is the presence of a foundation of values and beliefs and the ability to see the relationship between daily activities and this foundation (Dwyer, Barnett & Lee, 1987; Krug, 1992). In essence, the work of both effective and ineffective principals is characterized by what has been described as an "undifferentiated jumble" of activities. But what has distinguished effective principals from their less effective colleagues is:

- the meaning they ascribe to their work;
- their ability to see the relationship between daily routine and nonroutine activities and their personal values, beliefs, and vision; and

- their ability to connect the "undifferentiated jumble" of activities to what Dwyer et al. call their "overarching perspectives" of schooling (p. 33).

Dwyer et al. note,

The success of these principals' actions for instructional management and leadership hinges on principals' capacities to connect them to their own overarching perspectives of the purposes of schooling and of the instructional systems of their schools. The principals we worked with tacitly held such overarching perspectives; most could articulate these perspectives when asked. Their perspectives were complex constellations of personal experiences and beliefs, community and district "givens," . . . and organizational variables that offered both direct and circuitous routes for principals to use to influence their schools and the experiences their students encountered daily. (p. 33)

Krug (1992) notes, "The essential differences between effective instructional leaders and others are less easily discerned in activities, behaviors, or actions than in the effective instructional leader's interpretations of those activities, behaviors, and actions" (p. 434). Thus, a central aim of school leadership preparation programs should be to help students build a foundation of belief and knowledge for their educational leadership—no matter whether they exercise that leadership as a principal, teacher, parent, or community member.

One way in which we have helped students develop a foundation of values is through the process of developing a covenant (Glickman, 1993). Rather than simply articulating trite, unexamined, and general beliefs about schooling, the process of developing a covenant requires students to address questions of knowledge, evidence, and perspective, and engage in analysis before deciding on what they truly value. In a sense, students are going beyond simply having beliefs—which do not necessarily require support in order to be beliefs—to having a set of supportable beliefs. The specific questions students examine are:

- What do we know from research and our documented experience about teaching, learning, curriculum, good classrooms and schools?
- What is our evidence?
- From whose perspective do we know this?
- What are the themes that run through what we know?
- What do we most value of the things we know?

Developing a covenant helps students form a meaningful set of supportable beliefs. The covenant serves as the foundation from which students and school leaders make decisions, develop policies, and discuss desirable practices. In essence, it serves as the foundation for an individual's or school's daily and ongoing study of their practice.

The process of developing a covenant also has value by itself. It leads to an enhanced understanding of what is important and valued to an individual. When done in groups, it gives students practice in defending their values as they discuss and debate among themselves. In addition, it simulates the process of working with the belief component of school renewal efforts.

While developing a grounded covenant of beliefs does not guarantee that students will always connect their beliefs to their daily practices as educational leaders, it does serve to provide them with a more rigorously developed and more explicitly articulated set of beliefs. In conjunction with ongoing opportunities throughout the preparation program to examine the congruency between their beliefs and their practices, they begin to develop the skill and capacity for such efforts. For example, preparation programs might have students use the covenants as a tool to assess school policy. Specifically, the covenants could be used to critically examine school policies in effect in the schools in which leadership students work and to illuminate how the policies are and are not congruent with the values contained in the covenants.

THE RELATIONSHIP AMONG SCHOOL IMPROVEMENT, HIGH-STAKES TESTING, AND AUTHENTIC PEDAGOGY

A recent development that has placed increasing pressure on principals to focus on school improvement and function as instructional leaders is the escalation of the stakes involved in state-level testing and accountability systems. For example, in North Carolina principals whose schools are categorized as low-performing based on standardized test scores may lose their positions, the schools are provided with assistance teams, and students who score poorly on the tests are not promoted to the next grade. High-stakes testing has placed political pressure on principals to be instructional leaders. Unfortunately, the result has been linear norms of principal instructional leadership that promote instructional strategies such as teaching to the test and aligning the school's curriculum with the test. In addition, the pressure to achieve high test scores has resulted in practices such as manipulating test scores by finding ways for students who are likely to score poorly not to take the tests, or by providing students and teachers with extrinsic rewards if test scores improve. Although the result may be higher test scores and there may be the perception of school improvement, the question of whether the school has really helped students learn more about things that matter remains an issue.

Unfortunately, principals and other school leaders are often not sufficiently knowledgeable about constructivist learning, authentic instruction, and the findings of brain research. This research suggests that the rote type of exercises and the accompanying behaviorist forms of teaching that typically constitute test-focused instruction run counter to what we know about how students learn. From brain research we know that in the learning process current knowledge serves as a filter for new information, helping learners connect new things that have learner meaning to those things the learner already knows (Bransford, Brown, & Cocking, 1999; Sousa, 2000). We also know that how the learner feels emotionally about a learning situation affects his or her ability to attend to it, as does the extent to which his or her senses are engaged in the experience.

Many of the findings of brain research are reflected in constructivist theory. Constructivism holds that learning is a process in which we construct knowledge. Rather than viewing students as empty vessels to be filled, constructivism holds that learners form knowledge and beliefs within themselves as they integrate new information and reframe what they already know. In addition, rather than expecting a teacher to tell students what something means (e.g., the interpretation of a painting, a passage, a story), constructivist philosophy believes that meaning is individual, with each learner interpreting information, and that interpretations vary from student to student. Unlike linear models of teaching (such as teaching to the test), constructivist-oriented teaching means embracing a greater degree of flexibility. Students may bring richer or less rich perspectives to classroom learning experiences than the teacher had anticipated, or they may respond in other unanticipated ways. Instead of adopting the formal curriculum and planned instructional methods prescribing teaching practice, teachers engage in ongoing decision making during teaching that modifies the decisions made during planning (see Resnick & Klopfer, 1989, and Walker & Lambert, 1995, for overviews of constructivist theory).

Growing out of our knowledge of constructivist learning is authentic pedagogy. Rather than adopting a didactic manner that focuses on the memorization of factual information, teachers engaged in authentic pedagogy design and facilitate learning experiences for students that:

- engage them in the personal construction of new knowledge;

- result in their conducting disciplined inquiry about the topic at hand; and
- have some value beyond the school (Newmann & Wehlage, 1995).

Authentic pedagogy treats students as individuals, recognizing that students bring different experiences to the classroom and that they construct knowledge in different ways, rather than assuming that all students are the same. In authentic pedagogy, lessons, skill learning, and problems are presented within a surrounding context that connects them to the real world. Teaching is geared not simply to scores on a test but to purposes that extend beyond the classroom.

Authentic practices require activities in which students study disciplinary content, organize information, consider alternatives, gather new information, and link the information and alternatives to what they already know (Newmann & Wehlage, 1995). This results in the construction of new knowledge. Teachers who use authentic practices frequently ask students to convey newly constructed knowledge by such means as elaborated written or oral communication. In addition, teachers are concerned that the learning experiences they design and facilitate for students have a value beyond school, that is, that learning experiences address problems connected to the world beyond the classroom, and that students have an audience beyond the school to whom or for whom they can "communicate their knowledge, present a product or performance, or take some action" (Newmann & Wehlage, 1995, p. 14). Most significantly, research has found a correlation between authentic pedagogy and high test scores. The Center for the Organization and Restructuring of Schools, in a study of over 1500 schools, found that not only did schools in which there was a high degree of authentic pedagogy score higher on standardized tests, but the gap between White students and students of color was less than it was in schools that had a lesser degree of authentic pedagogy (Newmann & Wehlage, 1995; Newmann & Associates, 1996).

Absent an in-depth grounding in brain research, constructivism, and authentic pedagogy, it is likely that principals and other school leaders will bend like willows to the political pressure of high-stakes accountability. Rather than serving as educational leaders who work to improve their schools through increased student learning, they are likely to embrace and perpetuate status quo strategies to address high-stakes testing. The result may well be students who score higher but know and care less, and teachers who have been disconnected from their creativity and professional dignity.

THE RELATIONSHIP BETWEEN SCHOOL IMPROVEMENT AND SCHOOLS AS CENTERS OF INQUIRY AND RENEWAL

A third dimension that has significant implications for schools is the research on effective and "good" schools that work well for students and adults who work in them. In the past, effective leadership was often equated with the supervision and evaluation of teachers and with providing staff development, typically through workshops or in-services. In a sense, effective leadership was an event that occurred periodically throughout the year and that was imposed upon teachers (Reitzug, 1997). What we know about schools that work well suggests a radically different conception of the principal's role in improving the school.

The research about good schools that work well for the students and adults who are part of their community suggests that these schools function as centers of inquiry and renewal (Little, 1982; Rosenholtz, 1989). They are characterized by ongoing study of the school's practices, frequent professional discourse, regular access to external expertise and new perspectives, extensive collaboration, daily instructionally-focused leadership by teachers and others, and collective responsibility for students. In addition, the shared values and core learning principles held by such schools serve as a foundation for the school's inquiry, the basis on which teachers and administrators evaluate decisions, policies, practices, and programs. Further, shared decision making structures and processes provide them with the power to ensure continuous school renewal (Glickman, 1993).

In order for schools to be centers of inquiry and renewal, they must have supportive principal leadership. It is the *nature* of this supportive principal leadership that is at issue here. Certainly, supportive principal leadership is not hierarchical, grounded in authority and perceived superior expertise, or event-oriented—as are traditional conceptions of instructional leadership (Reitzug, 1997). In addition, supportive principal leadership does not mean taking a passive or laissez-faire stance. To be supportive, principal leadership must be active, collegial, and participatory (Reitzug & O'Hair, in press). It involves:

- asking questions rather than peddling solutions;
- creating connective communication structures;
- initiating and stimulating inquiry and discourse; and
- facilitating school renewal processes such as the development of school charters and covenants (Glickman, 1993; Louis & Kruse, 1995; Reitzug, 1994, 1997).

The implications of what we know about schools as centers of inquiry and renewal for school leader preparation programs are that administration students must develop: (1) a thorough understanding of what we know about schools that work; (2) a personal vision of the purposes of schooling; (3) an understanding of how teachers develop professionally; (4) knowledge of school renewal processes and the skills to initiate and facilitate such processes; and (5) the disposition to continually see how inquiry and discourse fit with vision and values (see previous discussion regarding school covenants and policy analysis).

THE RELATIONSHIP BETWEEN SCHOOL IMPROVEMENT AND DEMOCRATIC SCHOOL PURPOSE

A fourth factor in school improvement and the principal's instructional leadership role is the long-standing purpose of schools to prepare students *for* democracy while functioning *as* democracies (O'Hair, McLaughlin, & Reitzug, 2000). As we have noted, school improvement does not simply refer to increased test scores or enhanced academic performance for students. School improvement also refers to broader social goals, such as developing schools that function *as* democracies and that prepare students *for* democracy.

The discourse about democratic schools has frequently concentrated on the governance of schools and specifically on increasing the participation of various stakeholders in school decision making through initiatives such as site-based management. Conceptualizing democratic schooling by focusing exclusively on a school's form of governance overlooks significant aspects of democratic schooling that are played out in school policy as well as in issues of daily practice.

Democracy is more than a form of governance, it is a *way of life*. The Center for Living Democracy (1998) describes democracy as "not what we have, but what we do." Democracy is a process and an ideal rather than a product and a structure, and it extends far beyond decision making and governance. Dewey (1916) notes that democracy includes a whole range of "associated living" and occurs in the various realms of social life (p. 87). Beane and Apple (1995) note that the following conditions undergird a democratic way of life:

- The open flow of ideas, regardless of their popularity, that enables people to be as fully informed as possible;
- Faith in the individual and collective capacity of people to create possibilities for resolving problems;
- The use of inquiry, critical reflection and analysis to evaluate ideas, problems, and policies;

- Concern for the welfare of others and "the common good";
- Concern for the dignity and rights of all individuals and groups;
- The organization of social institutions to promote and extend the democratic way of life.

Thus, democracy is not a state that can be achieved, but rather "an 'idealized' set of values that we must live and that must guide our life as a people" (Beane & Apple, p. 7).

While it is beyond the scope of this chapter to elaborate on all the specifics of democratic schools and the preparation of leaders for them, such schools have at their core ideals of inquiry and discourse, equity and justice, authenticity and caring, shared leadership, and service to community (O'Hair, McLaughlin, & Reitzug, 2000; Sergiovanni, 1992, 1996; Starratt, 1991). These democratic ideals should guide the hidden and formal curricula of schools, interpersonal interactions and school governance, and the delivery of administrator preparation programs.

THE RELATIONSHIP BETWEEN SCHOOL IMPROVEMENT AND SOCIAL JUSTICE

A fifth factor to be considered in examining the principal's role in school improvement is a social context that continues to be rife with inequity and school practices that are inequitable and lead to inequitable outcomes. How do principals stimulate and facilitate school improvement for children? What are the implications for administrator preparation programs? The next section of this chapter will explore this area in some detail.

PREPARING LEADERS TO PROMOTE SOCIAL JUSTICE

Most of those who choose to work in the field of education do so because they believe that they can make the world a better place for their students and their communities and that the students with whom they work will benefit from the instruction and care they provide. Unfortunately, this hope does not become a reality for all children. Literally millions of students, every year, are not served well by our schools. Schools across our nation in districts large and small with different resources and different student populations are failing to educate, failing to nurture, failing to develop, failing to protect, and failing to include all students. According to Capper and Young (2001), what is particularly significant about our schools' failure is that the students who are affected most are typically from marginalized groups (e.g., students of color, students with disabilities, low-income students, girls, and gay/lesbian students).

The failure of our schools to serve all children well is a complex problem, and it will require a complex response. Part of this response, as a number of scholars and practitioners have recently argued, must be social justice education for school and district leaders (Capper & Young, 2001; Young, 1999). Social justice education is an educational process that takes as its goal the absolute equal right of all individuals to live in and participate in a society that they help to shape and that also meets their needs (Adams, Bell, & Griffin, 1997). Thus, the goal of social justice education reflects the overarching belief system of our nation and constitutes one of the driving forces behind our nation's public schools.

THE IMPORTANCE OF SOCIALLY JUST LEADERSHIP

For well over a century, school and district leaders have worked to educate an increasingly diverse student population. Some have been successful and some, quite frankly, have not. At least part of the latter group's lack of success can be attributed to their preparation as educators and educational leaders. Few leaders will realize the widely touted goal of providing equal educational opportunities and outcomes for all students until they are adequately prepared to lead for social justice. While issues of equity have been part of the educational administration agenda for years, some have argued that few programs or professors working with present and future school leaders have taken the steps necessary to ensure that all leaders are prepared to support social justice. For example, studies which have reviewed the curriculum in educational administration have noted a severe lack of explicit emphasis on social justice (see, for example, Lomotey, 1989; Parker & Shapiro, 1992).

It is critical that we prepare educational leaders to promote and support social justice in their institutions. We must understand that leaders cannot fix the problems of society by leading better, nor can leaders alone transform the lives of the children in their schools, particularly if larger societal and institutional issues of oppression and inequity are not addressed. However, their work does have the potential to contribute to the improvement of schools, society, and the education of all of our children.

Underlying this idea is the understanding that leadership and education are fundamentally political activities. That is, there is no way to educate a child or to lead a school that is not value-laden. This is not to suggest that we politicize but rather that we recognize that education and leadership are already political (Bruner, 1996). Part of leading for social justice, then, is understanding that one is not just a leader but an activist for children, an activist who is committed to supporting educational equity and excellence for all children.

PREPARATION FOR SOCIALLY JUST LEADERSHIP

What is involved in preparing leaders to support social justice? First, leaders must develop an understanding of social justice and its implications for our nation's schools and school systems. Second, they must develop a clear understanding of how schools and schooling can both support and undermine social justice. Third, they must develop the ability to interrupt processes that undermine social justice while simultaneously building on processes that support it.

As demonstrated by Riehl (2000), there is a growing literature on how schools and school leaders can more effectively meet the educational and developmental needs of all students. This literature focuses on educational policy and law, school finance, the organization of schools and classrooms, relationships between schools and families, curriculum, pedagogy, teacher preparation, and administrator preparation. Of importance here is: (1) what insight this literature provides into what school and district leaders need to know and be able to do to promote social justice in their schools, and (2) what insight this literature provides into how programs can develop leaders to champion and support social justice.

Leadership for social justice requires that leaders understand that schools are not neutral grounds but contested political sites. Programs must ensure that future leaders understand that:

The structural inequities embedded in the social, organizational, and financial arrangements of schools and schooling help to perpetuate dominance for dominant groups and oppression for oppressed groups. Power, privilege, and economic advantage and/or disadvantage play major roles in the school and home lives of students, whether they are part of language, cultural, or gender majority groups or minority groups in our society. The history of racism and sexism in America and the ways "race" and "gender" have been constructed in schools and society are central, whether consciously or not, in the ways students, families, and communities make meaning of school phenomena as well as how they interact with school designates. Curriculum and instruction are neither neutral nor natural. The academic organization of information and inquiry reflects contested views about what knowledge is of most value; part of the curriculum is what is present or absent as well as whose perspectives are central or marginalized, and whose interests are served or undermined. (Cochran-Smith, 1999, p. 117)

As Cochran-Smith demonstrates, social justice is not limited in its concern to issues of diversity; rather, it addresses a broad array of factors that either support or impede absolute equality. The implication of social justice for our nation's school and district leaders, then, is that they must recognize the schooling process as political and value-laden and commit themselves to contributing to the improvement of schools, society, and the education of our nation's children.

In order to commit themselves to work for social justice, leaders must develop a clear understanding of how schools and schooling can both support and undermine social justice. Such an understanding can be developed by exposure to descriptive statistics, theory, and the results of school and district case study research, as well as by engagement in field-based inquiry and candid discussions of oppression and discrimination. For example, there is compelling empirical evidence that racism exists within our schools and school districts (see, for example, Donaldson, 1996). By carefully examining and discussing this evidence, future school leaders can learn how to recognize incidences of racism in their own schools.

Recognition can begin with the identification of stereotypes and then develop into a more sophisticated understanding of how oppression and discrimination operate on a series of levels. Spencer's (1986) research, which documented the stereotyping, low expectations, and overlooking of children of color by White teachers and administrators, is an excellent resource for information on stereotyping and other subtle forms of racial discrimination. In her study of women teachers, Spencer interviewed one African American teacher who claimed that most of the discipline problems she saw occurred in White teachers' classrooms. This teacher went on to explain that because the White teachers thought Black people simply acted that way, "they didn't see anything wrong with kids jumping up and down and climbing on the walls and walking across window sills. They actually believed that this is how these people are supposed to act" (p. 134). Expecting children of color to act in a destructive manner is racist, although educators who engage in such behavior may not intend to damage the children of whom they have low and incorrect expectations (Young & Laible, 2000).

The way discussions of racism and other forms of oppression and discrimination are developed and guided is vitally important to students' ability to critically reflect on their own participation in these social systems (Young & Laible, 2000). It is helpful to present oppression and discrimination as operating on a series of planes that extend from the individual level to the societal level (Scheurich & Young, 1997) and to engage students in identifying examples for each level. Presentation and discussion in this manner enables most students to see how deep and pervasive racism and other forms of oppression are. Furthermore, through discussions of this nature professors can intelligently demonstrate how individual and institutional discrimination and prejudice can have a powerful negative impact on both adults and children in our nation's schools, districts, and communities. This discrimination and prejudice may be evidenced in teaching, leadership, school policy, organizational norms and beliefs, school culture, and the explicit and hidden curriculum.

INTEGRATION OF SOCIAL JUSTICE AND LEADERSHIP CONTENT

The preparation of school and district leaders must tightly connect knowledge, interpretive frameworks, and experiences that promote a complex understanding of teaching, learning, leadership, professional development, organizations, and management, among other knowledge areas, with a commitment to social justice. The integration of these areas must enable leaders to identify practices, processes, beliefs, and other factors that work against: (1) high expectations for all children and faculty; (2) a curriculum that is rigorous, multicultural, and inclusive; (3) learning environments that scaffold and support individual learners; (4) a learning-focused and inclusive community; and (5) widespread commitment to unqualified equity.

A leader's work, however, involves more than identification, examination, and interpretation. It also involves problem solving, decision making and action. With regard to social justice, leaders must develop the ability to counteract practices, processes, beliefs, and other factors that undermine equity, while building conditions that support equity. There are no existing best practice models for developing this ability. Perhaps leading for social justice is better understood as inquiry-based praxis. According to Lather (1991, pp. 11-12), "the requirements of praxis are theory both relevant to the world and nurtured by actions in it, and an action component in its own theorizing process that grows out of practical political grounding." In other words, leading for social justice requires that one engage with and explore content, theory, and the problems of practice and, in the process, reconstruct and expand the theory, knowledge, and perspectives that drive one's practice.

PEDAGOGICAL APPROACHES TO PREPARING LEADERS FOR SOCIAL JUSTICE

If we accept the notion that inquiry-based praxis is integral to leading for social justice, then our preparation programs must operate from that understanding as well. We have available to us a number of pedagogical approaches that support and reflect inquiry-based praxis. For example, a number of programs already use problem-based learning strategies, cases, simulations, and action research. Integrative internships and field experiences that connect knowledge and interpretive frameworks with practical experiences and ideological commitments are another option. The work of Cochran-Smith (1999), who operates an inquiry-centered teacher education program, is also instructive. She places reflective writing at the center of her students' field-intensive preparation. Lather (1991), along with other scholars who support reflective practice (e.g., Hart, 1993; Osterman, 1990), argues that reflective writing and reflective practice provide a generative space where one can learn and grow. Furthermore, having students reflect on their experiences, practice, and lives facilitates their development as effective leaders (Young & Laible, 2000).

The role of the educational administration professor, then, would be to facilitate inquiry-based learning experiences. This would include enabling students to develop rich understandings of teaching, learning, leadership, professional development, organizations, and management, as well as diversity and social justice, and helping them to connect these content areas to authentic problems of practice.

One approach for equipping school and district leaders with the skills and knowledge to support all children would be focusing a preparation program thematically around social justice, scaffolding existing content emphasis on the theme of social justice. Another approach is to take a program "as is" and search for areas within the program where social justice preparation is needed. In this "integration approach" attention to social justice is integrated within the existing curriculum. Still another approach, although probably less desirable and less effective, might involve creating a stand-alone course that would be added to a list of stand-alone courses required for certification and graduation. Regardless of structure, social justice preparation for educational leaders can be organized around a set of principles that can be implemented differently in unique contexts. Those principles would include developing the knowledge, skills, and dispositions necessary to: (1) understand social justice and its implications for our nation's schools; (2) identify, challenge, and counteract discrimination and prejudice; (3) foster a culture of high expectations for all children and faculty; (4) facilitate the construction of a curriculum that is rigorous, multicultural, and inclusive; (5) support the development of socially just practices among one's faculty, staff, and student body; (6) develop learning-focused and inclusive communities; and (7) sustain widespread commitment to unqualified equity.

PREPARING LEADERS TO BUILD A DEMOCRATIC AND COLLABORATIVE SCHOOL COMMUNITY

In the past 10 years there has been a marked increase in scholarly attention to issues of democratic decision making and collaboration and professional community in schools. Literature and practice have repeatedly addressed participative or site-based management as a democratic decision-making model (e.g., Malen, Ogawa, & Kranz, 1990; Ogawa, 1994). This emphasis on democratic community reflects our valuing of democratic ideals and may enhance the quality of educational decisions, but it may sometimes come at the expense of organizational efficiency (Galvin, 1998). The scholarship on collaboration and professional community has addressed collaboration among teachers and other school professionals and inter-agency collaboration among school personnel and other human service professionals serving children (Pounder, 1998). In addition, schools have continued to emphasize the importance of building closer relationships with parents and seeking input from multiple community constituent groups to promote more responsive and democratic decision making (e.g., Bauch & Goldring, 1995; Ogawa, 1998).

The arguments for increasing collaborative working relationships in schools are many (Louis & Kruse, 1995; Pounder, 1998). Researchers reason that building a collaborative school community will enhance teachers' professional growth and development, resulting in enhanced student learning and other positive school outcomes. For example, collaborative work promises to tighten the connection between teachers' work and student outcomes, because work is focused more on students than on separate academic disciplines. Collaborative work among educators in multiple roles, parents, and human/social service workers outside the school is particularly likely to enhance teachers' understanding of "the whole child." This may be especially beneficial in secondary schools where educators' work and students' educational experiences are often splintered (Boyer, 1983; Goodlad, 1984; Sizer, 1984). Creating a collaborative work community also has been found to enhance educators' work lives and students' educational experiences. For example, teachers working in a school that has a strong sense of community report greater internal work motivation, growth satisfaction, general job satisfaction, work efficacy, and professional commitment, and less isolation than their counterparts (Pounder, 1999). Similarly, students in such schools report higher levels of social bonding with peers, teachers, and their schools (Arhar, 1992) and more satisfaction with their fellow students (Pounder, 1999); feel less anonymity and isolation (Clark & Clark, 1994); and have higher levels of self-concept (Stefanich, Wills, & Buss, 1991). Perhaps most important, in schools with high degrees of collaborative community, student learning and achievement levels are enhanced and student behavioral problems are reduced (Crow and Pounder, 2000; Felner et al., 1997; Smylie, Lazarus, & Brownlee-Conyers, 1996).

Given these conditions, how can we better prepare administrators to build democratic and collaborative professional communities in schools? What knowledge, skills, and dispositions should be developed? Or, to use Restine's (1997) framework, what conceptual, technical, and human skills are needed to build democratic and collaborative professional communities? The list below, though not exhaustive, is illustrative of the types of understandings that might be emphasized in pre-service preparation programs to enhance administrators' capacity to build democratic and collaborative school communities:

1. Understanding the multiple needs of school children and their families, especially those from disadvantaged socioeconomic and diverse backgrounds;
2. Understanding the roles, responsibilities, and cultures of other professionals working with school children and their families;
3. Understanding the organizational supports, work structures, and interpersonal processes associated with effective collaborative professional communities;
4. Understanding how to assess the effectiveness of a collaborative school community in terms of educational effectiveness, equity, and efficiency, and how to enhance the benefits of professional community while minimizing the costs and inefficiencies that can be associated with increased collaboration.

Understanding the multiple needs of school children and their families. Often the preparation of school administrators focuses largely on the functions, disciplinary knowledge bases, or roles associated with administrative work. However, if administrators are to be adequately prepared to influence and shape the core technology of schools—teaching and learning—they and other educators must first understand the backgrounds, cultures, needs, and conditions of the population served by public schools. It is particularly important to understand the multiple and complex needs of students and their families from disadvantaged socioeconomic and diverse backgrounds.

To develop this understanding, considerably more of the administrative preparation curriculum must focus on the learner and his/her family. To use a business/marketing comparison, it is unlikely that we can develop and deliver an appropriate service to our "clients" without understanding who they are and what they need. The kind of population we serve can shape both our instructional curriculum and our delivery methods. For example, students experiencing reading difficulty often come from homes where parents have limited literacy skills or where there is a lack of appropriate reading materials. School-based literacy programs for parents and students, offered at night, often have direct impact on families and on student learning. Similarly, parent education programs that focus on the development of effective parenting skills are often valued by a broad range of parents—especially as they see their children's growth, development, and behavior changing. To address the limited access to reading materials and computers, many communities benefit from extended evening hours for school libraries and computer laboratories. These efforts may reduce the "digital and resource divide" between lower income and higher income students. The kind of student population we serve can also shape the range and extent of auxiliary services we provide, such as before- and after-school programs, meal services, or health, counseling, and integrated social services. These are but a few examples of how our instructional and support efforts can be more effective when they are designed around the specific needs of the students and families we serve.

Understanding the roles, responsibilities, and culture of other professionals. Often, children from low income families and students with exceptionalities are served by multiple human service professionals. Some of these professionals work within schools (e.g., special educators, school counselors, school psychologists, and school social workers). Some of them work in other human service agencies (e.g., occupational therapists, health professionals, social service workers, and child protection agents).

One of the biggest challenges for school administrators and classroom teachers is to understand the roles and responsibilities of these other professionals and to learn how these multiple services can be effectively integrated and focused on individual students and their families. Because these diverse services are not always delivered from the school, service professionals are often unaware of available services being provided by others. Further, different professional cultures, coupled with ethical and legal constraints, often inhibit interprofessional communication and coordination of services (Galvin, 1998; Hart, 1998). Yet, well-integrated educational and support services to children and families have much greater promise for effective problem solving and intervention than uncoordinated efforts.

Understanding the organizational supports, work structures, and interpersonal processes associated with effective collaborative professional communities. Research on effective work groups and learning communities offers a rich knowledge base to enhance understandings of collaborative professional communities. One particularly comprehensive model of productive work groups is Hackman's and Oldham's Work Group Effectiveness Model (1980). This framework captures the major organizational supports, work structures, and interpersonal processes that enhance work group effectiveness. Collectively, these elements shape the degree of effort, the knowledge and skills, and the appropriateness of performance strategies utilized by work groups or collaborative school communities. Not only do prospective administrators need to understand these elements conceptually, but they also need the technical and human skills to facilitate the development of these effective work group elements in shaping a collaborative school community. For example, one important element in enhancing the amount of knowledge and skill applied to work is healthy work group dynamics that encourage members to share knowledge and balance inputs among members. This requires administrators to secure resources to provide appropriate training to school community members in how to develop these healthy interpersonal processes. It also requires that administrators be able to convince school board and community members to allow a portion of the school day or week for collaborative group meetings and to build school schedules that allow for shared work. To build a sense of community, administrators must be able to secure and effectively utilize resources—shared time being perhaps the most important—to enhance communication and coordination among school community members.

Understanding how to assess the effectiveness of a collaborative school community. It is critical to be able to assess the effectiveness and long-term viability of any significant school change initiative. This is especially true in our current climate of educational accountability. With the introduction of a collaborative school community, administrators must be able to assess how this initiative influences educational effectiveness, equity, and efficiency. For example, indicators of educational effectiveness could include enhanced student learning and achievement, student attendance, reduced behavioral problems, or other student-related outcomes. It may also be important to assess effectiveness outcomes related to teachers and families. These outcomes could include enhanced professional efficacy for teachers or increased comfort and degree of school communication for parents. Whatever indicators are evaluated, one of the key questions should be "To what degree does a collaborative school community enhance these effectiveness indicators relative to those of a traditional school structure and environment?" In other words, what is the "value-added" of a collaborative school community? Administrators should also be able to examine how the initiative influences equity within the school. Does a collaborative school community enhance outcomes for students—those from low achieving backgrounds as well as those from high achieving backgrounds, those from minority cultures as well as those from majority cultures, those with exceptionalities as well as those with no disabilities?

Even if the development of a collaborative school community favorably influences effectiveness and equity, these improvements may come at the expense of efficiency or liberty. Although most educators would argue that this is simply the price we must pay for school improvement, taxpayers and policymakers may not agree. For an initiative to be sustained over the long run, it must show a reasonable degree of efficiency. In the case of collaborative initiatives, often the greatest cost is the increased communication and coordination time and effort required of school and community members. These participants will be disinclined to continue the effort if the costs of collaboration exceed the benefits (Galvin, 1998) or if the working group burns itself out over time (Crow & Pounder, 2000; Hackman, 1990). Thus, both material and psychological costs must be assessed relative to benefits, and the resulting cost-benefit ratio compared to those of less collaborative school environments. These kinds of assessment strategies require administrators to have facility in understanding, using, and reporting and explaining simple descriptive statistics and qualitative data related to valued educational goals—school effectiveness, equity, liberty, and efficiency. Further, these skills must be used on a regular basis and integrated into the regular tasks and responsibilities of administrators to promote better school decision making and educational accountability.

Administrator Preparation Program Design

There are several elements of preparation program design that should be considered if the goal is to develop leader knowledge, skills, and dispositions that promote school improvement, democratic and collaborative school community, and social justice. The following section organizes this discussion around the elements of program structure, clinical and field experiences, and faculty and students.

PROGRAM STRUCTURE

Cohort program models have been quite popular during the past decade (Hart & Pounder, 1999; Milstein, 1993). Certainly it could be argued that cohort models provide excellent opportunities to build learning communities within the context of the preparation program itself. However, these cohort experiences and shared learning could be enhanced with the inclusion of other preparing professionals such as teachers, social workers, counselors, and school psychologists. Coursework and learning experiences focusing on the needs and characteristics of students and their families or on issues of social justice could be especially relevant for all of these human service workers, including administrators. These interprofessional cohort experiences may promote understanding of the multiple roles, responsibilities, and cultures of professionals working with school-age children and their families.

A second structural element of programs is curriculum organization. For many years, preparation program courses have been organized around functions (e.g., personnel administration), disciplinary knowledge bases (e.g., political science, sociology), and/or roles (e.g., principalship, superintendency) associated with school administration. However, administrative work requires administrators to synthesize and apply the understandings from these multiple disciplines to complex problems of practice. Few school or administrative problems can be framed as only economic problems, or only legal problems, or only human resource problems. Thus, it is important that the conceptual, technical, and human skills associated with these various disciplines be taught in a more integrated fashion and focused on the overlapping themes of school improvement, social justice, and democratic and collaborative school community. To organize the preparation program curriculum around these three major themes, there must be greater shared curricular planning and collaborative teaching across faculty with different areas of disciplinary expertise. Modular course experiences, problem-based learning, case method, or administrative simulation teaching approaches could enhance the integration and synthesis of administrative knowledge and skills. These techniques and others should be explored in order to reduce the "silo" structure of many administrative preparation programs and promote a more web-like program structure.

A third structural consideration is the sequencing of learning experiences in the preparation program. That is, how should content and experiential components of the program be arrayed to enhance student learning and administrative development? How should conceptual, technical, and human skill development experiences be scaffolded upon one another to enhance learning? Although it may be true that conceptual skills are a necessary foundation for building related technical and human skills, students may not clearly see the value of these conceptual skills without prior or concurrent immersion in actual field problems. Similarly, students may fail to understand the relationship between conceptual knowledge and associated technical and human skills unless they are immersed in skill development exercises or applications during or immediately after conceptual knowledge development.

FIELD AND CLINICAL EXPERIENCES

Although often relegated to a secondary role, field and clinical experiences might well serve as the core of the educational leadership preparation experience. Field experiences provide an opportunity for leadership preparation students to serve as apprentice administrators, educational leaders, inquirers, and change agents. During field experiences leadership students can practice and perhaps initiate or facilitate many aspects of school improvement, leadership for social justice, and the development of democratic and collaborative community that are discussed in this chapter.

A major objective of clinical and field experiences is to expose the tensions between the technical aspects of administration and schooling that maintain existing educational arrangements and the educational leader's responsibility for school improvement and change, particularly school improvement and change that fosters equity, social justice, democracy, and community. Field experiences provide opportunities for students to reflect critically on:

- the purposes and assumptions of education;
- the possibilities of school improvement;
- education's connections to the broader social context; and
- the realities of administrative practice.

Clinical and field experiences might consist of shadowing, participation, advocacy, and critical reflection. Experiences need not be limited to one setting; they could occur in a variety of settings and contexts that broaden the student's understanding of educational practice and how educational leaders can foster school improvement, equity, justice, and democracy. Ideally, students would take part in experiences that include:

- participation in a nonschool social service agency or other education-related community agency or initiative;
- participation in a school setting in a cultural context that is different from that with which the student is most familiar;
- participation in work for a "cause," that is, a significant, long-term initiative about which the student feels passionately and that works to change educational or social practice in a school, district, community, or state;
- participation in inquiry and planning that address real problems identified by a school district;
- interaction with a variety of school leaders at all levels of administration in the district, region, and state.

Field experiences should enhance habits of critical reflection and cultivate school leaders for whom activism focused on school improvement, community building, and social justice is integral to educational practice. Opportunities for critical reflection can be provided via university-based seminars and other activities such as: (1) student-initiated case studies of issues that occur during the internship; (2) faculty-initiated case studies that problematize issues in administrative practice; (3) critical analysis of the routines, structures, and other regularities that dominate administrative practice; (4) keeping a reflective journal; (5) debriefing student experiences during the internship; and (6) engaging in inquiry about issues that arise during the internship (including issues that arise in the local, state, national, and international educational environment).

Field experiences might be sequenced before, during, and after content coursework. For example, administrator preparation programs typically sequence content courses prior to a capstone field experience or internship. However, few programs begin with in-depth field experiences. Students might better appreciate the nature of administrative work or better understand the needs and characteristics of diverse and low income student populations if they participated in in-depth field experiences or service-learning activities upon entrance into their administrative preparation program. They might better see the relevance of their more formal academic/content coursework after having been immersed in an introductory administrative field experience. Greater juxtaposition of academic coursework with field experiences may better facilitate the synthesis of conceptual and technical skills and their application to problems of practice. These introductory and integrated field experiences are intended not to supplant in-depth immersion in a capstone clinical internship experience, but rather to gradually guild students' administrative knowledge, skills, and dispositions throughout the course of the preparation program (LaCost & Pounder, 1987).

STUDENTS AND FACULTY

The end of the 20th century brought numerous journal, magazine, and newspaper articles focused on leadership for the 21st century. Authors representing universities, professional organizations, government, and non-profit groups reflected on educational, social, economic, and demographic trends and predicted what these trends meant for the future of school leadership. What have been the results? Paul Houston (2001) of the American Association of School Administrators (AASA) argued that future leaders must be "courageous champions for children . . . willing and able to challenge the status quo, while acting as collaborative catalysts and working with others" (p. 432). Gerald Tirozzi (2001) of the National Association of Secondary School Principals (NASSP) argued that "understanding and assessing the demographic, social, economic, and educational trends on the horizon—and abandoning a commitment to the status quo—will make possible a successful transformation of America's secondary schools" (p. 435). Meanwhile scholars from universities across the globe have "offered eclectic and overlapping perspectives on what should be the focus of leaders' attention and how leadership manifests itself in practice" (Duke, 1999, p. 55).

Such perspectives present a challenge not just in terms of how we prepare leaders for the future but also with regard to whom we should prepare and who should do the preparing. The themes in much of the recent leadership literature and this chapter suggest that candidates for school leadership should be experienced and expert educators, advocates for social justice, and effective collaborators and communicators, and that they should reflect the community diversity within which they lead. Assuming that these are the characteristics that we desire in our future leaders, the question becomes "How do we identify and attract such leaders into educational leadership programs?"

One thing is certain: educational leadership faculty must be proactive. University faculty must work closely with local school district administrators to identify, recruit, and support future school leaders. In addition, entrance requirements and procedures should be designed to screen candidates for their strengths in the areas delineated above. For many programs, this will require a sharp departure from the norm (McCarthy, 1999).

Our themes on the future of educational leadership also hold implications for the faculty of educational leadership programs. First, faculty must be well grounded in education, school processes, and leadership. Second, faculty must have a collaborative orientation and a commitment to social justice. The continuous program enhancement that is necessary for program currency and quality will require that faculty be able to work together to develop and strengthen the program on an ongoing basis. This will also require that faculty maintain a connection to the schools and participate in the identification, development and promotion of a relevant knowledge base for the contemporary and future practice of education leadership. The instructional strategies we have described require that educational leadership faculty have strong teaching skills as well as opportunities to further develop their skills and content area knowledge over time. Such professional development opportunities are essential to continuous program enhancement.

The increased emphasis on collaboration between educational leadership programs and schools and the importance of an integrated and focused program require that well planned and well supervised field experiences have a critical mass of full-time faculty. These faculty, which in many universities will consist of a mixture of regular and clinical positions, must also represent the diversity of the populations with whom they work. In sum, programs must consciously seek to hire a diverse cadre of educational leadership faculty who are well grounded in education, educational leadership, and schooling processes and are committed to quality teaching, collaboration, continuous program enhancement, and social justice.

Conclusion

The purpose of this chapter was to articulate how preparation programs could better prepare educational leaders to develop the knowledge, skills, and dispositions necessary for school improvement, social justice, and democratic and collaborative professional community. One of the biggest challenges is for educational leadership faculty to move outside of their disciplinary, role-oriented, and administrative function "silos" to a more holistic, focused, and integrated preparation of school leaders.

References

Adams, M., Bell, L., & Griffin, P. (1997). *Teaching for diversity and social justice: A sourcebook*. New York: Routledge.

Arhar, J. M. (1992). Enhancing students' feelings of school membership: What principals can do. *Schools in the Middle, 1*(3), 12-16.

Bauch, P. A., & Goldring, E. B. (1995). Parent involvement and school responsiveness: Facilitating the home-school connection in schools of choice. *Educational Evaluation and Policy Analysis, 17*(1), 1-21.

Beane, J. A., & Apple, M. W. (1995). The case for democratic schools. In M. W. Apple & J. A. Beane (Eds.), *Democratic schools* (pp. 1-25). Alexandria, VA: Association for Supervision and Curriculum Development.

Beck, L. G. & Murphy, J. (1993). *Understanding the principalship: Metaphorical themes 1920s-1990s*. New York: Teachers College Press.

Boyer, E. L. (1983). *High school: A report on secondary education in America*. New York: Harper & Row.

Bransford, J. D., Brown, A. L., & Cocking, R. R. (1999). *How people learn: Brain, mind, experience, and school*. Washington, DC: National Academy Press.

Bruner, J. (1996). *The culture of education*. Cambridge, MA: Harvard University Press.

Capper, C., & Young, M. D. (2001). *Educational leaders for social justice*. Manuscript submitted for publication.

Center for Living Democracy (1998). *What is living democracy?* Brattleboro, VT: Author.

Clark, S. N., & Clark, D. C. (1994). *Restructuring the middle level school: Implications for school leaders*. Albany, NY: SUNY Press.

Cochran-Smith, M. (1999). Learning to teach for social justice. In G. Griffin (Ed.), *The Education of Teachers* (pp. 114-144). *Ninety-eighth yearbook of the National Society for the Study of Education*, Part I. Chicago: National Society for the Study of Education.

Crow, G. M., & Pounder, D. G. (2000). Interdisciplinary teacher teams: Context, design, and process. *Educational Administration Quarterly, 36*(2), 216-254.

Dewey, J. (1916). *Democracy and education*. New York: Macmillan.

Donaldson, K. B. (1996). *Through students' eyes: Combating racism in United States schools*. London: Praeger.

Dwyer, D. C., Barnett, B. G., & Lee, G. V. (1987). The school principal: Scapegoat or the last great hope? In L. T. Sheive and M. B. Schoenheit (Eds.), *Leadership: Examining the elusive* (pp. 30-46). Reston, VA: Association for Supervision and Curriculum Development.

Felner, R. D., Jackson, A. W., Kasak, D., Mulhall, P., Brand, S., & Flowers, N. (1997, March). The impact of school reform for the middle years: Longitudinal study of a network engaged in Turning Points based comprehensive school transformation. *Phi Delta Kappan*, pp. 528-532, 541-550.

Furman, G. C. (1998). Postmodernism and community in schools: Unraveling the paradox. *Educational Administration Quarterly, 34*(3), 298-328.

Galvin, P. (1998). The organizational economics of interagency collaboration. In D. G. Pounder (Ed.), *Restructuring schools for collaboration: Promises and pitfalls* (pp. 43-65). Albany, NY: SUNY Press.

Glickman, C. D. (1993). *Renewing America's schools: A guide for school based action*. San Francisco: Jossey-Bass.

Goodlad, J. I. (1984). *A place called school*. New York: McGraw-Hill.

Hackman, J. R. (Ed.). (1990). *Groups that work (and those that don't): Creating conditions for effective teamwork*. San Francisco: Jossey-Bass.

Hackman, J. R., & Oldham, G. R. (1980). *Work redesign*, Chapter 4. Reading, MA: Addison Wesley.

Hart, A. W. (1993). A design studio for reflective practice. In P. Hallinger, K. Leithwood, and J. Murphy (Eds.), *Cognitive perspectives on educational leadership* (pp. 213-230). New York: Teachers College Press.

Hart, A. W. (1998). Marshaling forces: Collaboration across educator roles. In D. G. Pounder (Ed.), *Restructuring schools for collaboration: Promises and pitfalls* (pp. 89-121). Albany, NY: SUNY Press.

Hart, A. W., & Pounder, D. G. (1999). Reinventing preparation programs: A decade of activity. In J. Murphy & P. Forsyth (Eds.), *Educational Leadership Programs: A Decade of Reform.* Columbus, MO: UCEA.

Houston, P. (2001). Superintendents for the 21st Century: It's not just a job, it's a calling. *Phi Delta Kappan, 82*(6), 428-433.

Krug, S. (1992). Instructional leadership: A constructivist perspective. *Educational Administration Quarterly, 28*(3), 430-443.

LaCost, B. Y., & Pounder, D. G. (1987, October). *The internship: An alternative model.* A paper presented at the University Council for Educational Administration Conference, Charlottesville, VA. [ERIC #ED 295 306].

Lather, P. (1991). *Getting smart: Feminist research and pedagogy with/in the postmodern.* New York: Routledge.

Leithwood, K., & Duke, D. (1999). A century's quest to understand school leadership. In J. Murphy and K. S. Louis (Eds.), *Handbook of research on educational administration* (2nd ed.). San Francisco: Jossey-Bass.

Little, J. W. (1982). Norms of collegiality and experimentation: Workplace conditions of school success. *American Educational Research Journal, 19*, 325-340.

Locke, J. (1960). *Two treatises of government.* New York: Cambridge University Press.

Lomotey, K. (1989). Cultural diversity in the school: Implications for principals. *NASSP Bulletin, 73*(521), 81-88.

Louis, K. S., & Kruse, S. D. (1995). *Professionalism and community: Perspectives on reforming urban schools.* Thousand Oaks, CA: Corwin Press.

Louis, K. S., Kruse, S. D., & Bryk, A. S. (1995). Professionalism and community: What is it and why is it important in urban schools? In K. S. Louis and S. D. Kruse (Eds.), *Professionalism and community: Perspectives on reforming urban schools* (pp. 3-22). Thousand Oaks, CA: Corwin Press.

Malen, B., Ogawa, R., & Kranz, J. (1990) What do we know about school-based management? A case study of the literature. In W. H. Clune & J. H. Witte (Eds.), *Choice and control in American education (Vol. 2). The practice of choice: Decentralization and school restructuring* (pp. 289-342). New York: Falmer Press.

McCarthy, M. (1999). The evolution of educational leadership preparation programs. In J. Murphy and K. S. Louis (Eds.), *Handbook of research on educational administration* (2nd ed.). San Francisco: Jossey-Bass.

Milstein, M. (1993). Changing the way we prepare educational leaders: The Danforth experience. Newbury Park, CA: Sage, a Division of Corwin Press.

Murphy, J. (1999). *The quest for a center: Notes on the state of the profession of educational leadership.* Columbia, MO: UCEA.

Newmann, F. M., & Associates (1996). *Authentic achievement: Restructuring schools for intellectual quality.* San Francisco: Jossey-Bass.

Newmann, F. M., & Wehlage, G. G. (1995). *Successful school restructuring.* Alexandria, VA: Association for Supervision and Curriculum Development.

Ogawa, R. T. (1994). The institutional sources of educational reform: The case of school-based management. *American Educational Research Journal, 31*(3), 519-548.

Ogawa, R. T. (1998). Organizing parent-teacher relations around the work of teaching. *Peabody Journal of Education, 73*(1), 6-14.

O'Hair, M. J., McLaughlin, J., & Reitzug, U. C. (2000). *Foundations of democratic education.* Belmont, CA: Wadsworth.

Osterman, K. (1990). Reflective practice: A new agenda for education. *Education and Urban Society, 22*(2), 133-152.

Parker, L., & Shapiro, J. P. (1992). Where is the discussion of diversity in educational administration programs? Graduate students' voices addressing an omission in their preparation. *Journal of School Leadership, 2*(1), 7-33.

Pounder, D. G. (1998). (Ed.). *Restructuring schools for collaboration: Promises and pitfalls*. Albany, NY: SUNY Press.

Pounder, D. G. (1999). Teacher teams: Exploring job characteristics and work-related outcomes of work group enhancement. *Educational Administration Quarterly, 35*, 317-348.

Reitzug, U. C. (1994). A case study of empowering principal behavior. *American Educational Research Journal, 31*(2), 283-307.

Reitzug, U. C. (1997). Images of principal instructional leadership: From super-vision to collaborative inquiry. *Journal of Curriculum & Supervision, 12*(4), 324-343.

Reitzug, U. C., & O'Hair, M. J. (in press). From conventional school to democratic school community: The dilemmas of teaching and leadership. In Gail Furman-Brown (Ed.), *School as community: From promise to practice*. New York: SUNY Press.

Resnick, L. B., & Klopfer, L. E. (1989). *Toward the thinking curriculum: Current cognitive research*. Alexandria, VA: Association for Supervision and Curriculum Development.

Restine, L. N. (1997). Learning and development in the context(s) of leadership preparation. *Peabody Journal of Education, 72*(2), 117-130.

Riehl, C. (2000). The principal's role in creating inclusive schools for diverse students: A review of normative, empirical, and critical literature on the practice of educational administration. *Review of Educational Research, 70*(1), 55-82.

Rosenholtz, S. (1989). *Teachers workplace*. New York: Longman.

Scheurich, J. J., & Young, M. D. (1997). Coloring epistemologies: Are our research epistemologies racially biased? *Educational Researcher, 26*(4), 4-18.

Sergiovanni, T. J. (1992). *Moral leadership: Getting to the heart of school improvement*. San Francisco: Jossey-Bass.

Sergiovanni, T. J. (1996). *Leadership for the schoolhouse: How is it different? Why is it important?* San Francisco: Jossey-Bass.

Sizer, T. R. (1984). *Horace's compromise: The dilemma of the American high school*. Boston: Houghton-Mifflin.

Smylie, M. A., Lazarus, V., & Brownlee-Conyers, J. (1996). Instructional outcomes of school based participative decision-making. *Educational Evaluation and Policy Analysis, 18*, 181-198.

Sousa, D. (2000). *How the brain learns*. Thousand Oaks, CA: Corwin Press.

Spencer, D. A. (1986). *Contemporary women teachers: Balancing school and home*. New York: Longman.

Starratt, R. J. (1991). Building an ethical school: A theory for practice in educational leadership. *Educational Administration Quarterly, 27*(2), 185-202.

Stefanich, G. P., Wills, F. A., & Buss, R. R. (1991). The use of interdisciplinary teaming and its influence on student self-concept in the middle school. *Journal of Early Adolescence, 11*, 404-419.

Strike, K. A. (1993). Professionalism, democracy, and discursive communities. *American Educational Research Journal, 30*(2), 255-275.

Tirozzi, G. (2001). The artistry of leadership: The evolving role of the secondary school principal. *Phi Delta Kappan, 82*(6), 434-439.

Walker, D., & Lambert, L. (1995). Learning and leading theory: A century in the making. In L. Lambert, D. Walker, D. P. Zimmerman, J. E. Cooper, M. D. Lambert, M. E. Gardner, & P. J. Ford Slack (Eds.), *The constructivist leader* (pp. 1-27). New York: Teachers College Press.

Young, M. D. (1999, October). *Preparing leaders for social justice*. Paper presented at the University Council for Educational Administration Conference, Minneapolis, MN.

Young, M. D., & Laible, J. (2000). White racism, anti-racism, and school leadership preparation. *Journal of School Leadership, 10*(5), 374-415.

CHAPTER 13

Rethinking the Professional Development of School Leaders

FRANCES K. KOCHAN, PAUL BREDESON, AND CAROLYN RIEHL

By almost any yardstick the work of school leaders has become more complex in recent years (Kochan, Jackson, & Duke, 1999). Principals of the 21st century must help create appropriate school and classroom environments, develop supportive school cultures, ensure the productive use of human and other resources, and become involved in new forms of policy development and implementation. The principal's job responsibilities have been further complicated by expanded demands from external constituencies, rapid growth in research on teaching and learning, changing demographics of our population, and burgeoning access to information resulting from an explosion of new technologies.

The myriad changes and demands related to the job of the school leader make it imperative that principals engage in a continuous cycle of learning (King, 1999). Not only is the professional growth of principals vital to their job performance, but there are also indicators suggesting that principal learning has positive effects on teacher development, school culture, systemic educational reform, and student learning (Bredeson & Scribner, 2000; NSDC, 1995). The importance of the principal as learner led one educator to conclude that the litmus test for the selection of a school leader should be to "find the one man or woman most genuinely committed to their professional development and (that of) their colleagues" (quoted in Pohland and Bova, 2000, p. 137).

In the educational realm, the phrase "professional development" often conjures up a vision of people sitting in small groups or "lecture style" rows, listening intently as an "expert" explains the secret of how things should or must be done. Often these professional development

Paul Bredeson is Professor of Educational Administration at the University of Wisconsin–Madison. Frances K. Kochan is Professor of Educational Leadership and Associate Dean for Administration and Research at Auburn University. Carolyn Riehl is Assistant Professor in the Department of Educational Leadership and Cultural Foundations at the University of North Carolina at Greensboro.

activities are organized into one-day to one-week seminars conducted in a residential setting that is separated from the context of the job. These types of activities, which are supposed to enhance principals' abilities and performance, are seldom related to the realities of the job and rarely result in changes in participant behavior or in improving either the school or student learning (Sparks & Hirsch, 1997). Nonetheless, this traditional model presents a formidable challenge to newer models of professional development that require considerable time, commitment, and effort from administrators and those who plan and deliver instructional activities for them.

This chapter discusses the professional development of principals as it exists and as it might be. We begin by examining the problems and paradoxes traditionally associated with the professional development of principals. Next, we propose a new conceptual framework to enhance the continuous learning of school leaders. Our framework includes a definition of professional development as well as strategies to design and deliver learning experiences that complement it. It also recommends that principals take a leadership role in their own development and the development of others by assuming three interrelated roles: model learner, steward of learning, and community builder.

Problems and Paradoxes in the Professional Development of Principals

The call for school leaders to engage in continuous professional growth is replete with problems and paradoxes, making what seems a simple concept an idea fraught with complexity (Murphy & Hallinger, 1987). One of these problems arises out of the nature of the job of the school leader. Principals' work is marked by variety, fragmentation, and brevity of activity. Rarely do principals spend more than ten minutes at a time on a single task, and much of their day is spent reacting to problems that others bring to them (Kochan & Spencer, 1999). The resulting pressure to address immediate and concrete problems tends to bias principals toward solution-oriented learning that fits into their hectic schedules. Thus, quick fixes and nuggets of knowledge that can be immediately applied are preferred over solutions requiring reflection and long-term study, which are more likely to result in a change in practice.

A second barrier to principal professional development is that there is little general acknowledgment that principals need to engage in learning as part of their daily professional work (Bredeson, 2000). In the educational realm, there exists a public mindset that professional development, which tends to occur during "in-service" or "teacher days," constitutes "days off" rather than an integral and essential part of the work life of educators. When professional development is not viewed as legitimate and essential work, schools and communities hesitate to invest time, money, and institutional support to sustain ongoing learning for principals (or teachers).

A paradox that may limit principals' professional growth stems from external accountability requirements that are imposed upon schools. Mandates that dictate curriculum standards, performance assessments, and in some cases even teaching materials and instructional strategies can cause principals to focus on compliance with external demands rather than on the creative development of new ideas and approaches. Thus, while accountability measures are often coupled with calls for school reform and change, the mandates that come with these measures make it unlikely that administrators will choose to engage in professional development opportunities that involve reflection, innovation, and risk-taking actions. Rather, they may tend to select those that deal with efficient ways to respond to legislative requirements (Bruckerhoff, 1995).

In order for school leaders to engage in meaningful professional development experiences that overcome these problems and paradoxes, we must alter the definition and focus of professional development, restructure the way professional development is designed and delivered, and reframe the role of school leaders in the professional development process. In this chapter, we present our perspective on reshaping the professional development process for school leaders by addressing each of these requirements.

A Framework for Redefining and Reculturing the Professional Development of School Leaders

REDEFINING PROFESSIONAL DEVELOPMENT

Bredeson (1999) defines professional development for school leaders as "learning opportunities that engage educators' creative capacities in ways that strengthen their own practice and the practice of other educators." We have adapted this definition by adding the words "critical and reflective" to modify the capacities that are engaged. This definition acknowledges the importance of leaders' capabilities to anticipate challenges and to develop innovative strategies to deal with them. It also recognizes the necessity for leaders to continually examine and critique their values when considering the ways in which they use power and their willingness to share power with others. Our definition incorporates the notions proposed by Schön (1983, 1984) that individuals must engage in reflective learning and inquiry to be successful leaders. Finally, our definition stresses the notion that the leader's learning is integrally connected to the work and learning of other educators and thus must be designed to enhance the learning of all.

DESIGNING AND DELIVERING EFFECTIVE PROFESSIONAL DEVELOPMENT

Professional development built upon our definition requires that adult learning principles and high quality standards be incorporated into the process. We will deal briefly with each of these elements and then propose four areas that should be included when designing and delivering professional development for principals.

One reason traditional approaches to professional development have been unsuccessful is that they have not considered the needs of adults in the learning situation. Those who lead professional development activities often simply adapt the teaching and learning techniques used with children to adult learning settings. An early leader in adult education, Malcolm Knowles (1973; Knowles, Holton, & Swanson, 1998) suggested that this approach was inappropriate and proposed that adult education activities be built around the theory of andragogy. Although recent scholars (e.g., Brookfield, 1986, 1987; Merriam & Caffarella, 1999) have explored new dimensions of adult learning, such as the notion of "critically reflective practice" and the relationships between learning and power, the basic principles espoused by Knowles appear to be well accepted as a foundation upon which to construct learning experiences for adults. The theory of andragogy proposes that adult learners are self-directed, have life experiences that are a learning resource, seek learning based on their experiences and needs, focus their learning on solving problems, and want their learning experiences to be experiential in nature and have immediate application to their needs.

The theory of andragogy is closely aligned with the high quality standards for professional development proposed by the National Staff Development Council (1995). The NSDC standards, which include criteria for the context, process, and content of professional development activities, point to the need to engage people in understanding the processes of teaching and learning, aligning professional development with the goals of the individual and the institution, and providing follow-up and support. They stress the need to make adult learning activities meaningful and related to the context in which participants must operate.

Using adult learning principles and effective professional development standards as a foundation, we propose four areas that should be addressed when designing and delivering professional development for school leaders. First, the learner's motivation must be considered, and learners must have a role in directing their professional development. Second, there should be a rich combination of learning opportunities in diverse settings to meet learner needs. Third, the process should include support personnel who are prepared, willing, and available to assist the learner. Finally, learning must be related to the practice and role of the educational leader.

CONSIDERING LEARNER MOTIVATION

Continuous professional development for its own sake is something we would hope all educators seek. However, professional growth is not necessarily easy or comfortable. Thus, a principal's disposition toward learning and growth is an important factor in his or her learning. Also of vital significance is the individual's capacity to deal with cognitive dissonance, abstraction, uncertainty, and role ambiguity. What principals bring to their learning experiences (personal biography, prior knowledge, experience, values, desire, habits of mind, and innate curiosity) greatly influences the quality and outcomes of their professional development.

Principals' motivations may emerge not only from their personal attributes but also from their personal and professional goals. Career advancement, evaluations, salary increases, and pay-for-performance contracts can be important elements in stimulating principals to seek additional knowledge and abilities.

While it can have both negative and positive consequences for the school and students, a powerful influence on principals' desire to develop higher levels of competency may be the accountability environment in which they now function. The emphasis on student test scores and other assessments, often publicly displayed in the media, can exert a strong force on principals' drive for further learning. Likewise, the adoption of national standards and tests for school leaders, as well as the push by state education agencies to assess professional competence, can motivate, encourage and, in some cases, support principals' desire to learn.

A good way to determine what motivates individuals to learn is to involve them in the design and delivery of their professional development. Providing opportunities for principals to examine and reflect on their values and beliefs, competencies and strengths, areas for improvement, and professional goals can help to foster such involvement (Day, 2000). Self-inventories, evaluation results, and examining data related to past performance can also provide rich resources to engage school leaders in creating a learning plan for their own development.

PROVIDING DIVERSE LEARNING OPPORTUNITIES

If the professional learning needs of school leaders are to be met, a variety of learning opportunities must be available to them. This requires a combination of appropriate materials, conditions, and resources. A range of activities and settings for professional development is now emerging that can provide such variety. While we do not offer a complete description of the array of possibilities, we discuss some of the more promising possibilities for fostering professional growth for school leaders, in the hope of facilitating a more extensive discussion on this topic within the field.

A principal's school provides the first context for that leader's learning (Louis, Kruse, & Associates, 1995; Scribner, 1999). Thus, all of the on-site opportunities generally available for the professional development of teachers, including collective reflection on instructional practice, review of data-based indicators of school effectiveness, and action research, should be available to the school leader as well. Principals who avail themselves of these opportunities not only benefit from learning that is tied closely to their actual work environment but also convey crucial messages about the importance of everyone's learning within the school context.

In addition to learning within the school, principals should seek experiences in other settings to examine the practices of their colleagues. Observing others through shadowing, engaging in peer visitations and job exchanges, and taking a sabbatical to learn in another context have all proven effective in principal growth. Such activities are particularly valuable in facilitating reflective and critical thinking about values and practice.

While some of the off-site activities such as peer visitation may be easier in urban settings than in rural school districts where many miles separate professional administrative colleagues, technology—especially the Internet—provides promising opportunities to enhance principals' collegiality, learning, and practice outside their accustomed environment. Email-based discussion groups can provide a wide network of colleagues to answer specific questions and/or discuss general issues facing school leaders. Chat rooms on the websites of professional associations provide another avenue for growth, as do the variety of materials and resources that are available through education-related websites and full-text journal services. For example, the National Association of Secondary School Administrators website offers bulletin boards, live chat sessions, and chat transcripts for administrators, in addition to online courses. The Association for Supervision and Curriculum Development offers online courses and tutorials as well as full-text availability of its professional publications.

Another form of learning that can enhance school leaders' professional development is participation in graduate programs that include a wide variety of relevant learning experiences. Cohort groups, case studies, field-based and applied research, and mentoring relationships are among the most successful strategies presently being used in graduate leadership programs. A growing number of online courses, along with electronic communication networks with professors and peer students, also offer promising new graduate school learning opportunities for principals, especially those located far from universities, and can make learning available to school leaders around the clock.

PROVIDING SUPPORT

One of the most efficient means of developing professional competence is through the support and counsel of other professionals. Principals often rely on other principals or school system administrators as a source of information. Using telephones or email, principals can easily consult trusted colleagues to obtain insights, ideas, solutions, and—perhaps most important—support, as they gain insights into their practice.

Although it may be a very practical and valuable approach to acquiring insights and expanding professional capacity, relying on supportive colleagues within one's own setting may be limiting in several ways. First, most school leaders who serve as consultants to others are themselves fully employed as administrators and thus have limited time and opportunity to orient and initiate the novice or re-engage the seasoned principal. A second limitation is that within one's own school system, a principal may feel obligated to adopt or adapt the advice given by a mentor rather than to challenge assumptions and reflect upon the positive and negative aspects of the mentor's work or ideas.

Using individuals from outside the school or system as support team members often eliminates these difficulties. For example, some new state regulations for licensing principals call for support teams that include representatives from higher education. Including someone from outside the system with expertise in leadership may give the principal a greater opportunity to question status quo thinking. However, many higher education programs do not have sufficient faculty to adequately serve on school support teams. A number of educational administration programs across the country are currently examining ways they can use technology to overcome such barriers and provide the support required by state licensing regulations. Another possibility for enhancing support teams is to involve retired principals who have been successful administrators, since they may have more time.

Another means of gaining personal insight is through mentoring relationships. Principals can use such relationships to reflect collaboratively on their work and find guidance in areas in which they feel they need to improve. Mentoring relationships can include individuals within or outside of the school system. These relationships can focus on a single skill for a short period of time or, over a longer term, delve into a complex series of issues that are related not only to the context of the principal's work, but to the essence of his or her professional life. School leaders can be assigned a mentor through their school system, or a mentoring relationship can emerge from the personal contact of two or more leaders.

Another powerful means of creating support is by linking individuals or schools in supportive learning relationships to solve common problems. School board members, parents and community leaders might all be a part of these groups. These arrangements, connected to but simultaneously removed from the day-to-day exigencies of school leadership, can provide opportunities for fostering collaborative work in researching problems and proposing solutions as well as in strengthening norms of collaborative learning and mutual support.

Another promising strategy for working with others is the notion of "critical friends," in which school leaders form dyads or groups to examine one another's practice and to offer challenging and constructive reflections on each other's work (Costa & Kallick, 1993). Critical friends partnerships and groups require the development of new norms of openness and critique. Although they may be time-consuming endeavors, they are based on a firm foundation of support and offer fresh opportunities for collegiality.

In some states, such groups are being recommended as a means of improving schools. In North Carolina, for example, the State Department of Public Instruction has recommended that principals ask their school districts to conduct regularly scheduled meetings to evaluate and critique school improvement plans. Principal study groups aimed at creating a support network have also been implemented in Boston, New York City, and other locations (National Institute, 1999).

LEARNING RELATED TO PRACTICE

Professional development activities, whether held on- or off-site, with school-based colleagues or with others, will be most successful in enhancing principals' leadership if these activities are related to the professional knowledge base of school administrators and to the role of the school leader in practice. Principal effectiveness is not measured merely by the possession of knowledge. Rather, it is based on the principal's ability to integrate knowledge, skills, and values into purposeful action working with and through other professionals.

The highly complex nature of principals' work and the expansive knowledge base that supports their practice suggest that leaders' learning activities must range over a wide spectrum of content and application. However, this very complexity means that creating meaningful professional development experiences can be daunting to everyone involved. Activities that enable principals to integrate and apply what they are learning must be rich in substantive content and clearly situated in a leadership context, provide for opportunities to practice, include time to reflect on the application, and provide opportunities to consult with others.

Although connections to practice are critical, a cautionary note is necessary. When professional development is sponsored by and tightly coupled to specific contexts, such as schools and school districts, there is a risk that it will be conceived in terms that are primarily instrumental and focused on explicit targets and measurable outcomes. Thus, while professional development focused on accountability certainly has its place, it is also vital for school leaders to have opportunities to apply a longer-term and potentially more transformational perspective when engaging in activities to enhance their professional growth. In this regard, we refer to Anderson's and Jones' (2000) and Kochan's (2000) discussions of Habermas' (1971) knowledge interests and their relationship to educational leadership practice.

School leaders pursuing technical knowledge through professional development will seek to acquire knowledge that helps them predict and control situations. Leaders pursuing practical knowledge through professional development will acquire knowledge that helps them understand and interpret situations. Leaders pursuing emancipatory knowledge will engage in critical examinations that enable them to be freed from tradition, coercion, or self-deception. It is this last form of knowledge that can foster a more deeply critical and reconstructive approach to school leadership. Yet it is the form of knowledge that is most often left out of the professional development process. Such knowledge may be most easily explored when it is removed from the specific leadership setting, but it cannot be divorced entirely from the realities of that setting.

An intriguing learning opportunity for school leaders that related theory to practice while fostering in-depth analysis and thoughtful reflection was described by Nelson and Sassi (2000). Twenty-four school administrators met voluntarily with teachers and educational consultants/researchers in a yearlong professional development seminar to reflect on teacher supervision in elementary mathematics. During each meeting of the seminar the administrators viewed a videotape of a mathematics lesson, practiced and discussed the mathematical content of the lesson, and discussed their views of the subject matter content and pedagogical strategies of the lesson. They explored different strategies for observing lessons and for making practical judgments about instructional performance. Over time, the administrators came to value the need to attend both to the intellectual demands of classroom lessons and to the teachers' pedagogical strategies for fostering student learning. This project demonstrates how administrators can develop their critical eye with regard to teaching and learning. It also underscores the need for supervisory leadership to be a distributed practice involving subject matter experts, teachers, and administrators.

Another approach to fostering continuous professional growth is maintaining a portfolio that documents work and facilitates reflective thinking about it. Dutschl and Gitomer (1991) suggest that principals establish a "portfolio culture" within their schools as part of their own growth and the growth of others. The term "portfolio culture" connotes taking responsibility for one's own learning and practice and helping others do the same. In this model the principal and teachers in a school create an individual or a joint portfolio to compile information about activities, goals, or operations of the school and use the portfolio as a tool to foster reflection, performance, and improvement. The portfolio presents evidence of learning and relates to the performance of everyone in the school. It includes artifacts and reproductions demonstrating knowledge, skills, and competencies and how they have been applied in practice. Portfolios provide a valuable tool to document the continuum of competence and learning from beginning to advanced stages. They enable leaders and school personnel to embed their learning within the context of the school while documenting their progress as individuals and as an organization (Guaglianone & Yerkes, 1998). This information is used to foster individual and organizational growth and development and promote reflection and critical analysis.

The Principal's Role in Fostering Individual and Organizational Learning

Individual learning is an important aspect of professional development for school principals. But in a professional community such as a school, professional development should not occur apart from the development of others. One of the most important elements in a school leader's professional development is forging connections between the principal's learning and the work of others in the school.

In a recent study, Bredeson and Johansson (2000) found that school principals have a significant influence on teacher professional development in four ways. First, what principals believe and espouse and what they do greatly affects teacher work and professional learning. Second, principals have an impact on creating and maintaining healthy and productive learning environments in schools. Third, using resources and expertise, principals directly influence the design, delivery, and content of professional learning opportunities in their schools. Finally, principals, in collaboration with others, evaluate professional needs and outcomes.

We agree that the role of the principal in professional development should include these tasks, but we believe that it should be even more encompassing. We propose that the principal must become a transformative leader who reflects upon and engages in personal growth and development and facilitates the professional development of the faculty and staff. The ultimate goal of such professional development should be to improve teaching and learning in the school (Interstate School Leaders Licensure Consortium, 2000). To that end, we recommend that principals assume three key roles: model learners, stewards of learning, and (Bredeson & Johansson, 2000) community builders.

MODEL LEARNERS

There are indications that principals' beliefs about their own learning and the learning of others have an impact on the school culture, teacher development, and student learning (Bredeson & Johansson, 2000; NSDC, 1995). The school leader sets the tone, direction, and climate for learning. It is therefore imperative that the principal serve as a "model learner" in the school.

To be model learners, principals must share their beliefs about the importance of continuous learning with their faculty. It is vital that their espoused beliefs about the need for professional renewal are reflected by their actions. Being a "model learner" requires that principals demonstrate curiosity and become engaged, enthusiastic learners. They must also develop a plan for regularly updating their knowledge and skills in ways that strengthen their practice and improve the quality of learning and life experiences for everyone in their schools. The plan should include learning goals and methods that demonstrate a willingness to be accountable for their professional growth (King, 1999).

School leaders should participate in school-based professional development and should also be involved in local, state, and national professional associations focused on leadership, management, teaching, and learning. Principals should attend professional conferences and make presentations at these conferences. They should also make presentations to their faculty describing what they learned at these meetings. School leaders should create opportunities for sharing their own learning and use these occasions for stimulating discussion and dialogue among faculty and other administrators in the school and school system.

As model learners, principals should be actively engaged in reading professional journals and books, have them prominently displayed in their offices, and make faculty aware of what they are reading and why. School leaders should stress that their learning is an ongoing, continuous process and that they view this learning as part of the professional responsibility of everyone in the school. Such an attitude can influence not only teachers, but also students—indeed, the entire school community.

An important dimension of being a "model learner" involves assuming the role of active researcher. Having people actively engaged in knowledge generation inside the school has great potential for the field and for the setting in which the research occurs (Anderson & Jones, 2000). Although the concept of teacher as researcher is often discussed in the literature, the notion of school leader as researcher is not as prevalent. We believe that the principal should be continuously engaged in collecting, analyzing, and sharing data and findings so that research activities are a vital part of his or her development and the life of the school.

STEWARDS OF LEARNING

Closely aligned with the idea of the principal as a model learner is the concept of the school leader as the steward of learning. Social, political, and economic forces that sometimes veer sharply away from the core purposes of schooling constantly buffet the educational system.

While adjusting to new realities and imperatives stemming from these forces, principals must become stewards of learning who strive to keep the focus of the school on learning for students, teachers, and themselves. Just as McNeil (1986) found that ideologies of control filter from administrators through teachers to classrooms, principals' norms about learning likewise extend from leaders to teachers to students. Thus, it is vital that principals, as stewards of learning in the school, commit themselves to the fair and ethical treatment of all learners. Principals must recognize and stress that educational equity and justice call for both understanding of and responsiveness to diverse needs and learning styles.

As stewards, school leaders must continually identify and articulate the connections between and among leader professional development, teacher professional development, student learning, and school quality. They must use these connections to stimulate collaboration and learning across varied dimensions and levels. School principals can also influence the learning of others by sharing professional expertise in teaching, learning, and leading.

Principals who are stewards of learning communicate the message that learning is central to the life of the school and everyone in it. Among many other responsibilities, school principals should assume the roles of mentor, coach, and collaborator to work with others to create, support, and maintain a healthy, accepting, and successful learning environment for everyone.

As stewards of learning, school leaders should work with faculty, students, parents, and the community to help frame and measure what they collectively believe really counts in making their school successful. Today's environment of mandated, narrowly based accountability measures makes it imperative that principals enable those who work and learn in the school to become a force in deciding how they will be judged (Reed & Kochan, 2001). Addressing what type of learning matters and how it will be measured and judged should become a part of the total professional development process of all those responsible for school success. The principal should be the leader in this initiative.

The final role of principals as stewards of learning is to ensure that adequate resources are available to support their own learning and that of their entire staff. School leaders must be innovative in structuring adequate time for staff to learn together, to share their knowledge with one another, and to develop necessary competencies and skills. Creative methods for ensuring that such time can be provided without the loss of instructional time for students is particularly important. Some principals have incorporated "community learning times" when community members or outside groups come into classrooms to teach special skills, read to children, or offer theatrical or musical presentations so that faculty can engage in their own learning activities. "Learning lunches," where teachers gather in a quiet room to eat together and share ideas, readings, and teaching strategies, are another approach that provides professional development time. Principals should work with their staffs to develop methods for guaranteeing that the learning of students and adults in their school is nurtured and supported.

COMMUNITY BUILDERS

The third role of the school leader as an instrumental part of the professional development of the entire school is that of community builder. Since principals' professional development activities are anchored in the learning and success of others in their schools, they must become involved in forming a community of learners within their school environment and beyond. As community builders, school principals must work daily to infuse learning into the everyday lives of students, faculty, and staff. Principals should use symbols, rituals, traditions, and ceremonies to encourage and celebrate learning and to place it front and center in the school community. They must work to make learning a community value and capacity, not an individual activity.

A number of theoretical constructs support the importance of building learning communities in schools. First, theories of human cognition suggest that individual learning is primarily a social process that occurs most successfully when situated within authentic activity within a community of practice (Brown, Collins, & Duguid, 1989; Wenger, 1998). People learn more when nestled in a community in which others pursue similar activity and talk about it in similar ways.

Similarly, theories of organizational behavior suggest that the "learning organization" is an important context for individual learning. Learning organizations are characterized by strong cultural norms that support learning that is clearly embedded in their routine structures and practices (Weick & Westley, 1996). Learning organizations are flexible entities that support innovation and risk. Educators who wish to foster ongoing learning and continuous improvement anticipate that this will be most probable within schools that are deliberate learning organizations.

Finally, educational research suggests that both teacher and student engagement and accomplishment are higher in schools where a value-centered community with strong and positive norms for learning flourishes (Louis, Kruse, & Associates, 1995). Schools with strong learning communities are those in which experimentation, collaboration, and reflective practice are common approaches among teachers, and where students benefit from an enthusiastic and thoughtful faculty.

Traditional cultural norms and existing structures tend to counteract the development of powerful learning communities in schools. Therefore, school leaders must focus on helping people inside and outside the school to reevaluate current norms, expectations, structures, and cultures so that new ways of thinking about teaching, learning, and schooling can emerge. Such reevaluation is being incorporated into the structure of schooling through innovations like collaborative planning time; increased noninstructional days in the school calendar for professional learning; teacher and administrator practical research efforts; and more school-based, collective forms of professional development. The school leader should be a vital force in developing and implementing such strategies.

Principals can link the school learning community with external entities and stakeholders to form broader communities of practice. At present, much of this activity is relatively unorganized, but it has the potential to create useful alliances between schools and other institutions, such as religious organizations and social service agencies. Learning opportunities that currently are shared between parents and educators, for example within the context of parent-teacher organizations, could be redesigned as more powerful opportunities for learning for all parties. In addition, school leaders can promote seamless learning connections among initial preparation, early socialization, and ongoing professional development experiences. Graduate programs in educational leadership can provide linkages to connect prospective and current students with alumni. These linkages could include technology-based communication forums, internship experiences that connect prospective principals with experienced leaders, and collaborative research opportunities that connect universities and schools.

Conclusion

In this chapter we have offered ideas that we believe will facilitate a reconsideration of professional development for school leaders. We have redefined the concept of professional development for school leaders, proposed a framework for its design and delivery, and reconceptualized the role of the school leader in the wider context of school-based professional learning. Our proposals have stressed the need to connect the learning of the principal with the learning of the faculty and staff and showed how this will ultimately improve student learning.

School leaders are pivotal agents in assuring their own development and the development of others in the school environment. Creating environments where everyone is engaged in self-development and organizational learning does not happen by accident. Leaders must devote sustained attention to creating structures and cultures of learning if they wish to become continuous learners and stimulate others to learn along with them. To accomplish this, school leaders' efforts must be valued and supported by superintendents, parents, teachers, and others. We hope that our proposals will assist in making such support a reality.

REFERENCES

Anderson, G. L., & Jones, F. (2000). Knowledge generation in educational administration from the inside out: The promise and perils of site-based administrator research. *Educational Administration Quarterly, 36*(3), 391–427.

Bredeson, P. V. (1999, April). *Negotiated learning: Union contracts and teacher professional development.* Paper presented at the annual meeting of the American Educational Research Association, Montreal, Canada.

Bredeson, P. V. (2000). Teacher learning as work and at work: Exploring the content and context of teacher professional development. *Journal of Inservice Education, 26*(1), 63–72.

Bredeson, P. V., & Johansson, O. (2000). The school principal's role in teacher professional development. *Journal of Inservice Education, 26*(2), 385–401.

Bredeson, P. V., & Scribner, J. (2000). A statewide professional development conference: Useful strategy for learning or inefficient use of resources? *Education Policy Analysis Archives, 18*(13). Retrieved from http://epaa.asu.edu/epaa/v8n13.html

Brookfield, S. D. (1986). *Understanding and facilitating adult learning: A comprehensive analysis of principles and effective practices.* San Francisco: Jossey-Bass.

Brookfield, S. D. (1987). *Developing critical thinkers: Challenging adults to explore alternative ways of thinking and acting.* San Francisco: Jossey-Bass.

Brown, J. S., Collins, A., & Duguid, P. (1989). Situated cognition and the culture of learning. *Educational Researcher, 18*(1), 32-42.

Bruckerhoff, C. (1995). *School routines and the failure of school reform.* Paper presented at the Annual Meeting of the American Educational Research Association, San Francisco, CA.

Costa, A. L., & Kallick, B. (1993). Through the lens of a critical friend. *Educational Leadership, 51*(2), 49–51.

Day, C. (2000). Beyond transformational leadership. *Educational Leadership, 57*(7), 56–59.

Dutschl, G. A., & Gitomer, H. (1991). Epistemological perspectives on conceptual change: Implications of educational practice. *Journal of Research in Science Teaching, 28*, 839–858.

Guaglianone, C. L., & Yerkes, D. M. (1998). *Administrative portfolios: Current uses and development by prospective and practicing administrators.* Paper presented at the annual meeting of the American Educational Research Association, San Diego, CA.

Habermas, J. (1971). *Knowledge and human interests.* Boston: Beacon Press.

Interstate School Leaders Licensure Consortium. (2000). *Proposition for quality professional development of school leaders.* Washington, DC: Council of Chief State School Officers.

King, S. P. (1999). Leadership in the 21st century: Using feedback to maintain focus and direction. In D. D. Marsh (Ed.), *ASCD 1999 yearbook* (pp. 165–183). Alexandria, VA: Association for Supervision and Curriculum Development.

Knowles, M. (1973). *The adult learner: A neglected species.* Houston, TX: Gulf Publishing Company.

Knowles, M. S., Holton, E. F., III, & Swanson, R. A. (1998). *The adult learner: The definitive classic in adult education and human resource development* (5th ed.). Houston, TX: Gulf Publishing Company.

Kochan, F., & Spencer, W. (1999). The principalship: The practitioner's perspective. *Mid-South Educational Research Journal, 6*(1), 9–16.

Kochan, F. (2001). Hope and possibility: Advancing an argument for a Habermasian perspective in educational administration. *Studies in Philosophy and Education 1*(2), 1-20.

Kochan, F., Jackson, B., & Duke, D. (1999). *Voices from the firing line: A study of educational leaders' perceptions of their job, the challenges they face, and their preparation.* Columbia, MO: UCEA Press.

Louis, K. S., Kruse, S. D., & Associates. (1995). *Professionalism and community: Perspectives on reforming urban schools.* Thousand Oaks, CA: Corwin Press.

McNeil, L. M. (1986). *Contradictions of control: School structure and school knowledge*. New York: Routledge.

Merriam, S. B., & Caffarella, R. S. (1999). *Learning in adulthood: A comprehensive guide* (2nd ed.). San Francisco: Jossey-Bass.

Murphy, J., & Hallinger, P. (1987). New directions in the professional development of school administrators: A synthesis of suggestions and improvements. In J. Murphy & P. Hallinger (Eds.), *Approaches to administrative training in education* (pp. 245–282). Albany, NY: SUNY Press.

National Institute on Educational Governance, Finance, Policymaking, and Management. (1999). *Effective leaders for today's schools: Synthesis of a policy forum on educational leadership*. Washington, DC: U.S. Department of Education, Office of Educational Research and Improvement.

National Staff Development Council. (1995). *Standards for staff development*. Oxford, OH: Author.

Nelson, B. S., & Sassi, A. (2000). Shifting approaches to supervision: The case of mathematics supervision. *Educational Administration Quarterly, 36*(4), 553–584.

Pohland, P., & Bova, B. (2000). Professional development and transformative learning. *International Journal of Leadership in Education, 3*(2), 121-136.

Reed, C., & Kochan, F. K. (in press). Facilitating proactive engagement of educational leaders in the policy development process. *Journal of Educational Leadership*.

Schön, D. A. (1984). Leadership as reflection-in-action. In T. J. Sergiovanni & J. E. Corbally (Eds.), *Leadership and organizational culture: New perspectives on administrative theory and practice* (pp. 36–63). Urbana, IL: University of Illinois Press.

Schön, D. A. (1983). *The reflective practitioner: How professionals think in action*. New York: Basic Books.

Scribner, J. P. (1999). Professional development: Untangling the influence of work context on teacher learning. *Educational Administration Quarterly, 35*(2) 238-266.

Sparks, D., & Hirsch, S. (1997). *A vision for staff development*. Alexandria, VA: Association for Supervision and Curriculum Development.

Weick, K. E., & Westley, F. (1996). Organizational learning: Affirming an oxymoron. In S. R. Clegg, C. Hardy, & W. R. Nord (Eds.), *Handbook of organization studies* (pp. 440–458). Thousand Oaks, CA: Sage Publications.

Wenger, E. (1998). *Communities of practice: Learning, meaning, and identity*. New York: Cambridge University Press.

Name Index

Note: This index includes names associated with a theory, concept, program, experiment or other work with a substantive description. It does not include names given in examples or passing references.

Anderson, G. L., 148
Apple, M. W., 106, 117-18, 121, 122, 127, 269, 270

Ball, Deborah, 84-85
Beane, J. A., 106, 117-18, 121, 122, 127, 269, 270
Beck, L., 48, 76, 140, 142, 231, 263
Bellah, R. N., 149, 150
Björk, L., 223-24, 229
Blumberg, A., 222-23
Bossert, S. T., 172, 173, 201
Bredeson, P. V., 202, 291, 299
Brunner, C., 229, 231
Bryk, A., 94, 197

Callahan, R. E., 218
Camburn, E., 94
Capper, C., 145, 270-71
Carter, G., 220, 221-22, 225
Clift, R. T. 170
Cochran-Smith, M., 91, 168-69, 272-73, 275
Cohen, David, 84-85
Cohen, S. G., 192, 194
Coleman, J. S., 245-46
Coons, J. E., 244
Crow, G. M., 112, 113-14, 178-79, 199
Cuban, L., 12
Cubberly, Ellwood P., 219
Cunningham, W., 220, 221-22, 225

Deasy, John E., 226-27
Dewey, John, 3, 105-7, 149, 163-64, 251-52, 269
Donaldson, G. A., 183
Drake, S. M., 169-70
Duke, D. L., 125-26
Dutschl, G. A., 298
Dwyer, D. C., 263-64

Elmore, R. F., 76, 226, 227, 230
Erb, T. O., 179-80

Firestone, W., 29, 172-73
Foster, W., 140, 231

Freire, Paulo, 143, 146, 147, 152
Friedman, Thomas, 189-90
Furman, G. C., 109, 110, 128

Gilland, T. M., 216
Gitomer, H., 298
Greenfield, Thomas, 137
Greenfield, W., 76
Grinberg, J., 145, 148
Grogan, M., 229, 230-31, 233

Hackman, J. R., 178, 195, 279
Hage, Jerald, 191, 193-94, 195, 204
Hallinger, P., 204-5
Hansot, E., 213, 214-15
Harris, B., 169-70
Hausman, C., 204-5
hooks, bell, 143
Houston, Paul, 227, 230, 232, 284

Jackson, B., 141
Jantzi, D., 99, 165, 174-75
Johansson, O., 202, 299

Kahne, J., 105-6, 109
Kelleher, P., 230, 231, 232
Kliebard, H., 72-73
Knowles, Malcolm, 292
Krug, S., 263, 264

Lambert, L., 126
Larson, C., 146, 148-49, 211, 233
Lather, P., 274, 275
Leithwood, K., 99, 125-26, 165, 174-75
Louis, K. S., 93, 94, 99, 180
Lytle, S. L., 91, 168-69

Mann, Horace, 215
Marks, H., 93, 94, 99
Maxcy, S. J., 107, 112, 113, 118, 125, 127
McLaughlin, M. W., 51
McNeil, Linda, 151-52
Meier, D., 117
Mitchell, K., 106-7
Mohrman, S. A., 192, 194

Murphy, J., 48, 76, 105, 163, 164, 211, 228-29, 263
Murtadha, K., 143

Nelson, B. S., 298
Neuman, M., 227
Newmann, F. M., 197, 198, 267
Noddings, Nel, 140
Norton, M. S., 217
Nussbaum, Martha, 154-56

Ogawa, R. T., 172, 173, 174, 201
Oldham, G. R., 279
Ovando, C., 211, 227, 233
Owens, J., 227

Piaget, J., 87
Pounder, D. G., 173-74, 178-79, 195
Powers, Charles, 191, 193-94, 195, 204
Purpel, D., 150, 151

Rau, W. C., 52
Reich, R. B., 26
Reitzug, U. C., 268
Rice, Joseph Mayer, 216
Rusch, E. A., 122-23

Sarason, S. B., 242, 244
Sassi, A., 298
Scheurich, J. J., 144
Schön, D. A., 292
Schultz, T. W., 24
Schwarz, P., 117
Sen, Amartya, 152-54

Senge, P. M., 95, 96
Sergiovanni, T. J., 77-78
Sewall, A., 228
Shakeshaft, C., 138
Shapiro, J., 140-41
Sherr, M., 142
Shulman, L. S., 86
Sidorkin, A. M., 119
Simmons, W., 227
Slater, R. O., 112, 113-14
Smith, Adam, 24
Smith, S., 119
Smylie, M. A., 166
Spencer, D. A., 273
Spillane, J., 97-98, 175, 176
Starratt, R. J., 115, 140, 200
Stefkovich, J., 140-41
Strike, K. A., 113, 120, 251
Sugarman, S. D., 244

Taylor, F. W., 191, 218
Tirozzi, G., 284
Toffler, A., 25-26
Toffler, H., 25-26
Tönnies, F., 108, 246
Tyack, D., 213, 214-15, 243

Wehlage, G. G., 197, 198, 267
Weick, K., 195

Young, M. D., 270-71

Zerchykov, R., 249

Subject Index

Accountability: "bundled" approaches to, 49-50; and contextual terrain, 29-32; decentralization approaches to, 45-46; frameworks for, 9-10; management approaches to, 46-47; market approaches to, 29-30, 43-45; principal's role in, 202-3; professional approaches to, 47-49; state, 27-29. *See also* under Superintendency

Achieve, 10

Administrator preparation: field and clinical experiences, 282-84; program structure, 281-82; student and faculty selection, 284-85

Annenberg Challenge, 170

Authentic pedagogy, 267

Bay Area School Reform Collaborative (BASRC), 170-71; Cycle of Inquiry, 170-71

Brown vs. Board of Education, 220, 242

Capacity, civic, 206-7

Capital: cultural, 110; social, 110, 245-46

Community, collaboration with, 206-7, 233; problematizing, 108-11

Constructivist learning, 266-67

Control of schools: community vs. bureaucracy, 244-46; history of, 240-1; professional vs. lay leadership, 243-44; state vs. local, 241-43

Democracy: and minimalism in schools, 112-13; "modern" liberal view of, 113-14; problematizing, 111-12; reconceptualizing, 114-15; thin and thick, 113

"Democratic community," 105-7; curriculum and instruction for, 120-22; leadership for, 122, 276-77; leadership practices, 122; leadership theory, 125-27; morality of, 120; participation processes for, 117-20; "Realpolitik" of enacting, 127-129; rethinking of, 115-17; in schools, 269-70

Democratic deliberation, 118, 250-55

Demographics, changing within schools, 8; contextual terrain, 32-34

Dialogue theory, 119

Distributed (distributive) leadership, 98-99, 172-77, 226-27

District leadership: Fairview case study, 51-61; role in standards based reform,

58-61; Standards, Assessment, Instruction (SAI) model, 54-61

Economic contextual terrain, 23-27

Educational knowledge: content, 86; content-specific pedagogical, 86; curricular, 86; general pedagogical, 86; of learners, 86

Educational leadership: core activities of, 5-6; dilemmas of, 11-15; moral dimensions of, 3-4; and participatory decision making, 14-15; and people-intensive activities, 6-7; and "principle of correspondence," 72-74; stewardship role of, 4-5; traditional approaches to, 66-68; traditional approaches to, problems with, 68-72

Educational leadership roles, 75-78: moral steward, 75-76; educator, 76-77; community builder, 77-78

Elementary and Secondary Education Act (ESEA), 22, 38

Families: coordination of services for, 278-79; multiple needs of, 277-78

Gemeinschaft/Gesellschaft, 108

Goals 2000: Educate America Act, 225, 244

Governance of schools: hybrid structures, 8-9

High stakes testing, 151-52, 265

Human capital theory, 24

Illinois State Board of Education (ISBE), 51-52

Illinois Standards Achievement Test (ISAT), 52-54, 56, 57, 61

Inequality Reexamined, 152-54

Institute of Educational Leadership, 249

Instruction: improvement of, 84-89; "instructional unit," 84-89; instructional capacity, 84-85; educational knowledge, 86-87; students as learners, 87-88; teacher beliefs and expectations, 88-89

Interstate School Leaders Licensure Consortium (ISLLC), 26

Is There a Public for Public Schools, 251

Lay leadership: ambiguity of purpose, 247; challenge for, 239; and community representation, 249-50; and democratic community, 251-55; meetings as ritual, 250-51; problems with, 246-51; professional leadership challenges with, 255-57; rationale for, 244-46; reactive stance of, 248-49; realities of, 246-51; (lack of) vision, 248

Leadership for social justice: and human capacity, 151-56; and multicultural communities, 148-51; for poor and marginalized communities, 145-147; theories, systems, and processes of, 144-56

Leadership Schools, 171

Leadership theory and practice: alternative images of, 139-44; alternative images of, African American, 141-42; alternative images of, feminist, 139-41; alternative images of, related to spirituality, love and leadership, 142-44; deconstructing, 137-39

Leadership: challenges for lay and professional, 239; changing activities of, 201-2; changing orientations to, 198-200; collaborative, 199; democratic, 200; distributive models of, 172-77; interactional, 199; organizational quality of, 201-2; through teams, 177-81

Lexus and the Olive Tree, The, 189-90

Market theory of schooling, 204-6 (*See also* Accountability)

Nation at Risk, A, 21, 23, 223

National Association of Elementary School Principals (NAESP), 34

National Association of Secondary School Principals (NASSP), 34

National Council of Teachers of Mathematics (NCTM) Standards, 31

National Center for Education Statistics, 34

National Defense Education Act (NDEA), 220-21

"New professionalism," 11

No Child Left Behind, 10

"Old Deluder" Law of 1647, 240

Organizational learning, principal's role in: 95-6; *See also* Principal's role

Organizations, primordial vs. constructed, 245-46

Pedagogy of the Oppressed, 146-47

"Portfolio culture," 298

Principal's role: community builder, 302-3; model learner, 299-300; steward of learning, 300-2

Principals' professional development: barriers to, 290-91; collegial support of, 295-98; covenants, 264-65; designing and delivering, 281-85, 292-93; disposition towards, 293-94; opportunities for, 294-95; in relation to practice, 297-98; redefining, 291-92

Professional community: assessing effectiveness of, 279-80; balancing continuity and change in, 196-98; and deprofessionalization, 11; developing, 10-11; organizational supports for, 92-95, 279

School improvement, 89-95: challenges to, 96-99; democratic purpose of, 269-70; factors contributing to, 89-90; and high stakes testing and authentic pedagogy, 265-68; and instructional leadership and administrative work, 263-65; and teacher learning in the classroom, 90-92; and teachers' professional community, 92-93; and schools as centers of inquiry and renewal, 268-69; and social justice, 270-74; and social trust, 12, 98

School reform: and statewide assessments, 22-23; centralization/decentralization of, 21-23

Site-based management (SBM), 45, 47-48

Social capital, 110, 245-46

Social justice: capabilities approach to, 154-56; importance of, 271-72; integration of, 274; pedagogical approaches to, 275-76; preparation for, 272-74; promoting, 270-71

Staffing: contextual terrain of, 35-37; and recruiting, 35-37; shortages, 35-37

Standards, Assessment and Instruction (SAI) model, 54-60

Superintendency: challenges for, 255-56; changing approaches to, 230-33; history of, 212-22. *See also* Superintendent's roles

Superintendent's role: as clerk, 212-14; as collaborator, 225-29; as communicator, 220-21; as conflict manager, 221-22; as expert manager, 217-20; as instructional leader, 214-17; as political strategist, 222-25

Teacher beliefs, 88

Teacher leadership: definitions of, 167-68; through distributive leadership, 172; in historical perspective, 163-67; through

leadership teams, 177-81; through teacher research, 168-72
Teacher learning, 90-92

"Understanding by Design," 54, 60
Unions, 11

Work: in industrial society, 191-92; in post-industrial society, 192-95

RECENT PUBLICATIONS OF THE SOCIETY

1. The Yearbooks

101:1 (2002) *The Educational Leadership Challenge: Redefining Leadership for the 21st Century.* Joseph Murphy, editor. Cloth.

101:2 (2002) *Educating At-Risk Students.* Sam Stringfield and Deborah Land, editors. Cloth.

100:1 (2001) *Education Across a Century: The Centennial Volume.* Lyn Corno, editor. Cloth.

100:2 (2001) *From Capitol to the Cloakroom: Standards-based Reform in the States.* Susan H. Fuhrman, editor. Cloth.

99:1 (2000) *Constructivism in Education.* D. C. Phillips, editor. Cloth.

99:2 (2000) *American Education: Yesterday, Today, and Tomorrow.* Thomas L. Good, editor. Cloth.

98:1 (1999) *The Education of Teachers*, Gary A. Griffin, editor. Cloth.

98:2 (1999) *Issues in Curriculum*, Margaret J. Early and Kenneth J. Rehage, editors. Cloth.

97:1 (1998) *The Adolescent Years: Social Influences and Educational Challenges.* Kathryn Borman and Barbara Schneider, editors. Cloth.

97:2 (1998) *The Reading-Writing Connection.* Nancy Nelson and Robert C. Calfee, editors. Cloth.

96:1 (1997) *Service Learning.* Joan Schine, editor. Cloth.

96:2 (1997) *The Construction of Children's Character.* Alex Molnar, editor. Cloth.

95:1 (1996) *Performance-Based Student Assessment: Challenges and Possibilities.* Joan B. Baron and Dennie P. Wolf, editors. Cloth.

95:2 (1996) *Technology and the Future of Schooling.* Stephen T. Kerr, editor. Cloth.

94:1 (1995) *Creating New Educational Communities.* Jeannie Oakes and Karen Hunter Quartz, editors. Cloth.

94:2 (1995) *Changing Populations/Changing Schools.* Erwin Flaxman and A. Harry Passow, editors. Cloth.

93:1 (1994) *Teacher Research and Educational Reform.* Sandra Hollingsworth and Hugh Sockett, editors. Cloth.

93:2 (1994) *Bloom's Taxonomy: A Forty-year Retrospective.* Lorin W. Anderson and Lauren A. Sosniak, editors. Cloth.

92:1 (1993) *Gender and Education.* Sari Knopp Biklen and Diane Pollard, editors. Cloth.

92:2 (1993) *Bilingual Education: Politics, Practice, and Research.* M. Beatriz Arias and Ursula Casanova, editors. Cloth.

91:1 (1992) *The Changing Contexts of Teaching.* Ann Lieberman, editor. Cloth.

91:2 (1992) *The Arts, Education, and Aesthetic Knowing.* Bennett Reimer and Ralph A. Smith, editors. Cloth.

Order the above titles from the University of Chicago Press, 11030 S. Langley Ave., Chicago, IL 60628. For a list of earlier Yearbooks still available, write to the Secretary, NSSE, University of Illinois at Chicago, College of Education, MC 147, 1040 W. Harrison, Chicago, IL 60607, or consult the University of Chicago Press website: www.press.uchicago.edu

2. The Series on Contemporary Educational Issues

This series has been discontinued.

The following volumes in the series may be ordered from the McCutchan Publishing Corporation, 3220 Blume Drive, Suite 197, Richmond, CA 94806. Local phone: (510)758-5510, Toll free: 1-800-227-1540, Fax: (510)758-6078, e-mail: mccutchanpublish@aol

Academic Work and Educational Excellence: Raising Student Productivity (1986). Edited by Tommy M. Tomlinson and Herbert J. Walberg.

Adapting Instruction to Student Differences (1985). Edited by Margaret C. Wang and Herbert J. Walberg.

Choice in Education (1990). Edited by William Lowe Boyd and Herbert J. Walberg.

Colleges of Education: Perspectives on Their Future (1985). Edited by Charles W. Case and William A. Matthes.

Contributing to Educational Change: Perspectives on Research and Practice (1988). Edited by Philip W. Jackson.

Effective Teaching: Current Research (1991). Edited by Hersholt C. Waxman and Herbert J. Walberg.

Moral Development and Character Education (1989). Edited by Larry P. Nucci.

Motivating Students to Learn: Overcoming Barriers to High Achievement (1993). Edited by Tommy M. Tomlinson.

Radical Proposals for Educational Change (1994). Edited by Chester E. Finn, Jr. and Herbert J. Walberg.

Reaching Marginal Students: A Prime Concern for School Renewal (1987). Edited by Robert L. Sinclair and Ward Ghory.

Restructuring the Schools: Problems and Prospects (1992). Edited by John J. Lane and Edgar G. Epps.

Rethinking Policy for At-risk Students (1994). Edited by Kenneth K. Wong and Margaret C. Wang.

School Boards: Changing Local Control (1992). Edited by Patricia F. First and Herbert J. Walberg.

The two final volumes in this series were:

Improving Science Education (1995). Edited by Barry J. Fraser and Herbert J. Walberg.

Ferment in Education: A Look Abroad (1995). Edited by John J. Lane.

These two volumes may be ordered from the Book Order Department, University of Chicago Press, 11030 S. Langley Ave., Chicago, IL 60628. Phone: 1-800-621-2736; Fax: 1-800-621-8476.

The educational leadership
challenge : redefining
leadership for the 21st
century